CANTO I   STANZAS
CANTO II   17.
CANTO III   1 - 111

George Gordon, Lord Byron

GEORGE GORDON, LORD BYRON

Selected Poetry and Letters

EDITED WITH AN INTRODUCTION AND NOTES

BY EDWARD E. BOSTETTER

HOLT, RINEHART AND WINSTON
NEW YORK

Ninth Printing, April 1961

Introduction and notes copyright, 1951, by Edward E. Bostetter
Typography Design by Stefan Salter
Printed in the United States of America
21031-0111

INTRODUCTION

On October 15, 1821, Byron jotted down in his "Detached Thoughts" a list of some forty persons or things to which he had seen himself compared "personally or poetically" in English and European journals. The list included Rousseau, Goethe, Shakespeare, Milton, and Pope; Napoleon and Henry VIII; Harlequin, Timon of Athens, and Satan. "The object of so many contradictory comparisons," he decided, "must probably be like something different from them all; but what *that* is, is more than *I* know, or anybody else." And in one of the famous conversations with Lady Blessington in the spring of 1823 when he was speculating complacently on the difficulties of his future biographers, he said, "Now, if I know myself, I should say, that I have no character at all . . . what I think of myself is, that I am so changeable, being everything by turns and nothing long—I am such a strange *mélange* of good and evil, that it would be difficult to describe me."

This fascinated bewilderment of Byron confronted by his own personality has been shared by all who have been swept into his orbit. That he is "something different" is plain enough from the fact that the word "Byronic" has become part of the language and Byron himself a kind of mythical hero like Oedipus or Prometheus. But to say what is "different" has been as difficult as Byron hoped it would be. The best thing we can do is to spread the paradoxical elements of his character before us and see if by describing them we can find the clue to understanding the man.

Perhaps the most important and familiar of the paradoxes is the juxtaposition of romantic and classical characteristics in his life and art. On the one hand, Byron was the incarnation of the Romantic Ego. "The wandering outlaw of his own dark mind," cursed by a wild half-mad ancestry, his ancestral home a mouldering Gothic abbey, driven to every excess, haunted by remorse for the "unmentionable" sin, he defied the authority of God, man, and devil, sought to identify with the elemental forces of nature, and died miserably in Greece in one final, frustrated gesture of revolt. John Galt's startling memory of him, sitting in the moonlight "amidst the shrouds and railings" of the boat carrying him to Malta in 1810, is the perfect evocation of the Romantic Byron. "He was," said Galt, "as a mystery in a winding sheet, crowned with a halo."

On the other hand, Byron was the complete Regency gentleman and man of letters. For his romantic contemporaries, with the exception of Shelley and Scott whom he admired as his peers, he had little but contempt. His allegiance was to the followers of neoclassic tradition: Moore, Campbell, Rogers, and Gifford. In his admiration for Pope, he was almost idolatrous. He pretended to look upon writing as the avocation of a gentleman; his naïvely arrogant statement of this attitude in the Preface to *Hours of Idleness* led to the attack upon him in the *Edinburgh Review* which in turn provoked his first major poem, the Popean satire, *English Bards and Scotch Reviewers*. In this he accepted the neoclassic theory that one of the chief functions of poetry is to expose and ridicule social cant and hypocrisy, a theory which he defended to the end of his life. In fact, it became the principal motivation of *Don Juan*. It was as social satirist that Byron took most seriously his responsibilities as an artist; and, as we shall see, it was as satirist in *Don Juan* that he finally effected a reconciliation of the romantic and neoclassic elements in his art.

Within this paradox was contained, as within a Pandora's box, an infinite number of other paradoxes. As a romantic, Byron was a revolutionist. He ardently espoused the cause of the French Revolution and proclaimed in ringing rhetoric the ultimate triumph of freedom throughout the world. Freedom was the big Byronic word and by it he meant ambiguously many things. For nations he meant freedom from subjugation to other nations, and for this end he intrigued in Italy and fought in Greece. For the citizens of each nation, he meant freedom from tyranny, particularly the tyranny of monarchy. His most spectacular eruptions of invective flowed down upon kings and those he considered their tools—the Castlereaghs, Wellingtons, and Southeys. For the poor and oppressed he had genuine sympathy; two of his three speeches in Parliament were on behalf of Catholic emancipation and the Luddites, the weavers of Nottingham who had tried desperately to break the machines they thought were depriving them of livelihoods. For himself and his heroes he meant by freedom complete anarchy and independence of all law and authority outside the individual mind which "is its own origin of ill and end/ And its own place and time."

And yet Byron never forgot that he was an aristocrat whose noble lineage could be traced back to the days of William the Conqueror. Partly because he had inherited the title unexpectedly after a childhood of poverty and neglect, he never felt at ease in his rank and he paraded it with insolent and sometimes ludicrous ostentation. His behavior toward those who failed to show proper deference was childishly rude. Many of his most romantic and anarchistic actions were simply dramatizations of the privileges and customs of the Regency nobleman. Though he admired the United States, he hated democracy, which he called the worst of governments, "an aristocracy of Blackguards." Undoubtedly he would have been greatly tempted by the rumored suggestion that he be the first king of Greece following liberation. We must remember, however, that the paradox of the revolutionary aristocrat is much more apparent today than in Byron's day. Many of the great revolutionaries in England and France were aristocrats. What they sought was a republic in which each would be free within his class, and the benevolent aristocrat would be the freely chosen leader. Though he was aware of and amused by his own vanity as a lord of the realm, Byron would have seen no inconsistency in this attitude.

To most people in his own age and now, Byron was above all notorious as "the great lover." Far too many critics have peevishly disparaged or dismissed him as a poet because they disapproved of his conduct and were unable to see his art for his life. In fact, Byron serves as an excellent touchstone of critical objectivity, for if there is any of the Puritan in the critic, he is certain to draw it out. This is not to say that we should try to read and evaluate

Byron's poetry without reference to his life. On the contrary, there is, as I hope to show, a vital relationship between them unequalled in literature. The danger is that we are likely to be so goggle-eyed with the details of his life, particularly with his numerous affairs, that we are blinded to everything else. Even as lover, Byron was much more than the sum of his affairs. He was rake, Puritan, and romantic idealist. Physically he was extraordinarily beautiful, with a mysterious lameness or deformity that, in marring, enhanced his beauty. He possessed, said Trelawney extravagantly, "the form and features of an Apollo with the feet and legs of a sylvan satyr." In addition, his beauty was precariously held through bouts of excessive dieting and strong purgatives against the pressing threats of obesity. It was the dieting which probably gave to his face the pallor which made it look, according to Scott, "like an alabaster vase lighted up from within." Abnormally sensitive of his lameness and tendency to fatness, Byron was also shy and the pose of the "marble heart" he developed both as protection and compensation. He was, in fact, strangely passive in his role as lover, rarely seeking an affair, but rather fatalistically accepting those which were thrust upon him. "I have been more ravished myself than anybody since the Trojan War," he wrote indignantly in 1819 in denying a rumor that he had carried a girl off from a convent.

Allied to his passivity and partly explaining it was a strong Puritan strain. He was contemptuous of the women who fell so easily, and for his own conduct he suffered constant remorse. Puritanic sadism helps account for the ruthless cruelty of his behavior toward Caroline Lamb and Claire Clairmont; and the self-righteous, humorless tolerance of his wife, aggravating his sense of guilt, drove him to the hysterical brutality which led to the separation. Peter Quennell, in *Byron: the Years of Fame*, sums up the conflict well. "Byron was an immoralist, a man who sins with a consciousness of wrong-doing and sins again because the sense of guilt demands always fresh fuel." Above all, Byron was the true narcissistic romantic, dreaming of the perfect woman who would complement his own ego. He portrayed her in the heroines of his tales and dramas, in the sentimental idealization of Mary Cha-worth in the *Dream*, and, most movingly, in Haidée in *Don Juan*. The search for her, combined with what Du Bos called the "need of fatality", led to the affair with his half-sister Augusta in which, if we can put aside our prejudices, we see most clearly the whole nature of Byron as lover.

It is perhaps through an understanding of this "need of fatality" that we can best come at the paradoxes in Byron's religious and philosophical beliefs. To the end of his life, Byron could not shake off the baleful influence of the Calvinistic training with its empha-sis upon predestination, sin, and damnation which he received as a child from his mother and nurse. It fused in his mind with the superstitious awe with which he brooded over the fates of his an-cestors and underlay the conviction that he had been doomed from birth. Against it he revolted violently, both emotionally and intellectually. Emotionally he asserted the independence of his own will against the tyranny of destiny; intellectually he became a free thinker and sceptic, unable to accept the doctrine of Chris-tianity or put another in its place. He could only insist that the meaning of existence must be found in terms of the human mind. "Matter is eternal", he wrote in his "Detached Thoughts", "and why not Mind? Why should not the Mind act with and upon the Universe? As portions of it act upon and with the congregated dust called Mankind?" Yet, at the same time, he was fitfully at-tracted by Catholicism. He insisted that Allegra be raised a Catho-lic, and he wrote Moore, "I incline, myself, very much to the Cath-olic doctrines." Nor did he ever overcome his sense of fatal-ity, which took the form increasingly of morbid superstition. In 1801 a fortuneteller had warned his mother that he should beware of his thirty-seventh year. He set sail for Greece convinced that he would die there. And, as Mr. Nicolson points out, "It was with the reckless fatalism thus engendered that he chose as the defiant date of his embarcation a Sunday and the 13th of the month."

Byron's failure, indeed his refusal, to resolve his intellectual and emotional conflicts should not be shrugged away as evidence of superficiality or irresponsibility. On the contrary, Byron reflected more honestly and expressed more dramatically than most of his contemporaries the basic philosophic conflicts of an age of transition. He faced squarely, particularly in *Don Juan*, the implications of new scientific and social theory, and if he was unable to rationalize his doubts into an optimistic philosophy such as Wordsworth's, it is a sign of his intellectual honesty.

These are perhaps the most fascinating and important of the Byronic paradoxes, but there are many more. Byron was the generous, warm-hearted friend, craving affection and lavishing it in return; but he was also the misanthrope, cynical and vindictive, believing the worst of his friends, capable of savage cruelty and petty malice. Though he was notorious as the lover of women, it was in his friendships with men that he was most constant, most natural, and most at ease; in his letters to Hobhouse, Moore, and Murray his personality unfolded to its fullest extent. He was a profligate, recklessly squandering his income, quixotically displaying his rank and wealth, as when he lumbered through Italy with "seven servants, five carriages, nine horses, a monkey, a bull-dog and a mastiff, two cats, three pet fowls and some hens." Yet he was eminently sensible and practical in the conduct of his affairs, as in his handling of the situation in Greece. And in his last years he even took up the "good old gentlemanly vice" of avarice and became a "damned close calculating fellow," to the great disgust of such borrowers as Leigh Hunt. In Byron the antithetical characteristics of human nature existed unrepressed, unresolved, each expressed dramatically and unpredictably with equal power and sincerity. When he said to Lady Blessington, "If I know myself, I have no character at all," he was in a sense right; he had the character of Everyman.

II

But in another sense he was talking nonsense. He had molded the romantic elements of the paradox into a character which set him apart from Everyman and which has ever since borne his name—the character of the Byronic hero. It was an inseparable interweaving of life and art, bearing a startling resemblance to the hero of myth and tragic drama. His life had from the beginning, as Mr. Quennell points out, "something in common with that of Oedipus, a descendant of kings, reared amid humble surroundings . . . Oedipus the lame-footed who returned to his birthright only to involve those who were nearest him in death and disaster. If Oedipus was a predestined being, so was Byron." Or, what is as important, Byron thought that he was and tried to give his life the inevitability of myth. Consequently his development as an artist can best be understood by tracing the relation of the poet to the hero.

The chief characteristics of the Byronic hero were melancholy and ennui; misanthropy, defiant pride, and remorse. These were fashionable characteristics of the age found in varying degrees in the heroes and villains of Gothic romances and in such men of feeling as Goethe's Werther and Chateaubriand's René. They had been widely affected, particularly the melancholy and ennui, by young sentimentalists. That even in adolescence Byron dramatized himself in these terms is evident from the poem "Childish Recollections":

> Weary of love, of life, devour'd with spleen,
> I rest, a perfect Timon, not nineteen;
> World! I renounce thee! All my hope's o'ercast!
> One sigh I give thee, but that sigh's the last.

To his humorless friend Dallas who believed all he was told, Byron wrote grandly at the age of twenty, "The events of my short life have been of so singular a nature that . . . I have been already held up as the votary of licentiousness, and the disciple of infidelity. . . . My hand is almost as bad as my character." Such words and the deeds that accompanied them—such as the revels of the Merry Monks of Newstead and the drinking from a skull—were pretty much playacting, although there was undoubtedly a hard substratum of belief. It is probable that up to the morning of the publication of *Childe Harold* when he awoke to find himself famous, Byron's conduct differed little from that of his peers: the difference lay in his flair for self-dramatization, a morbid sensitivity of conscience, an "inverted hypocrisy" which led him to brood over, boast about, or even invent misdeeds which his more calloused and hypocritical contemporaries perpetrated without thought.

This difference helps us understand why during the two years of his travels he could have a wonderful time, indeed look back upon them as perhaps the happiest years of his life, and at the same time, interpret them through the gloomy eyes of Childe Harold. Childe Harold was, in part, a dramatic pose, a dream figure, and Byron was probably sincere in disavowing any connection between himself and this "child of the imagination." On the other hand, by the very fact that he was a dream figure, Childe Harold represented the poet's deepest convictions and emotions, his unconscious drives. Perhaps when Byron projected such a dream picture of himself and then lived it out to the last nightmarish detail, he was really "acting out his need of fatality" as the modern psychiatrist would put it. Ten years afterward, in 1821, Byron gives a brief but fascinating glimpse into his attitude toward the poem: "My passions were developed very early—so early, that few would believe me, if I were to state the period and the facts which accompanied it. Perhaps this was one of the reasons which caused the anticipated melancholy of my thoughts—having anticipated life. . . . The two first Cantos of C^e. H^d. were completed at twenty two, and they are written as if by a man older than I shall probably ever be." We may doubt that at the time he wrote the first two cantos, Byron had anticipated life in experience: we may raise our eyebrows at his extravagant opinion of, to us, so obviously youthful a poem, but there can be no doubt that he had anticipated his own life both emotionally and symbolically.

The modern reader may find it difficult to understand the immediate and sensational success of the first two cantos of *Childe Harold*. To him the poem may seem tawdry, trite, and even dull. But for Byron's contemporaries there had been nothing like it. It came at a moment when they were most ready for it and perhaps most needed it. Here was a hero who, unlike the heroes of Scott or the Gothic novels, lived in the contemporary world. His affectation of an archaic name and style nostalgically and quaintly brought the past into the present. He was presented in shockingly memorable phrases and with contagious conviction. To a people isolated and sick of a war which had lasted nearly twenty years, he was the roving columnist, commenting on lands they had known through the war like Portugal and Spain and exotic lands beyond the war like Albania and Greece. His disillusion, his terrible remorse, his unmentionable guilt was theirs, particularly those who felt uneasily that they had betrayed the principles of the French Revolution. As the astonishing letters in Quennell's *Byron: The Years of Fame* testify, Childe Harold made an appeal to all classes. To the lives of the jaded, bored aristocracy, he gave meaning and glamour; through him they could see themselves in a new perspective. To the mass of people he was an exciting escape from humdrum existence; he was for them like the sensational movie hero of our day who springs to stardom in one Class B picture. For the Puritans—and there were many—he was mysterious evil to be vicariously enjoyed and vigorously reformed, an exhilarating challenge. Every reader immediately identified the hero with the author and directly or indirectly with himself. Byron became overnight the expression of the English libido, so long repressed by religion, government, and war.

He was not slow to exploit his fame. Between 1812 and 1816 he wrote at breakneck speed a series of melodramatic oriental verse narratives in which against the background of dark and violent deeds he filled out in lurid detail the portrait of his hero. The most elaborate attempts to probe the psychology of the hero are found in the *Corsair* and *Lara*; even today there is power in the faded rhetoric of such a passage as the following from *Lara*:

> There was in him a vital scorn of all:
> As if the worst had fall'n which could befall,
> He stood a stranger in this breathing world,
> An erring spirit from another hurl'd;
> A thing of dark imaginings, that shaped
> By choice the perils he by chance escaped:
> But 'scaped in vain, for in their memory yet

His mind would half exult and half regret.

. . . . .

But haughty still and loth himself to blame,
He call'd on Nature's self to share the shame,
And charged all faults upon the fleshly form
She gave to clog the soul and feast the worm;
Till he at last confounded good and ill,
And half mistook for fate the acts of will.

The last two lines might be taken as Byron's epigram upon his own life during this period. It was easy for him to look and act the part of his hero; he wanted to and society was determined that he should. Soon there was no chance of escape. From acting the role, he turned to living it and that which suited a part became the habit of his mind. With the rapidity of one of his own narratives, he was driven to those acts that led to his disgrace and exile. That his life had taken on the characteristics of art was evident to his contemporaries. Goethe is reported as saying of the separation from Lady Byron, "that in its circumstances and the mystery in which it is involved it is so poetical that if Lord Byron had invented it he could hardly have had a more fortunate subject for his genius." His exile, though voluntary, had the inevitability and cathartic effect of drama. Both Byron and society demanded it: it was necessary to complete the pattern of his life. Macaulay points out that Byron had become for the British public a kind of ritual scapegoat or expiatory sacrifice "by whose vicarious agonies all the other transgressors of the same class are, it is supposed, sufficiently chastised," and, he might have added, the superiority of conventional morality is triumphantly reasserted.

The moment of exile is in Byron's life and art the moment, to use Kenneth Burke's phrase, of "symbolic action." It is the moment toward which the first cantos of *Childe Harold* and the Oriental tales have led and from which the later poems take their rise. But it is also the moment which makes possible his emancipation from the hero. For now that the identification is complete, he is set free imaginatively. He is forced into a self-searching analysis which enables him to see himself and his hero in proper perspective and to obtain the aesthetic distance and artistic control without which *Don Juan* could not have been written. In short, it is the moment which makes Byron a great poet.

In the summer of 1816 Byron wrote his first great poems, the *Epistle to Augusta* and the third canto of *Childe Harold*. If in the earlier *Childe Harold* he had anticipated life, he was now reflecting it. He had "outlived himself by many a day," had suffered the experiences which might have filled a century. Where he had posed as the jaded profligate or the Satanic outlaw, he was now defiantly himself, Byron broken by society, frustrated in the "nobler aim" he had once beheld, "one the more/ To baffled millions which had gone before." Standing "as a ruin amidst ruins," he boldly made his experiences symbolize the experiences of an era. By his analysis of the characteristics of Napoleon and Rousseau in terms of his own, he set himself up as the typical man of his age. By his contemplation of Waterloo and the defeat of the hopes of the French Revolution, he identified his failure with the failure of his generation. His mood, however, was not simply one of hopeless defeat. He found a "very life," a "vitality of poison" in despair which sustained and strengthened him and became the source of his artistic power. He discovered the purpose of art: "to create, and in creating live a being more intense" than the life he had "outlived." Through his poetry, through this "soul of his thought" he could triumph in defeat. He could assert that his mind was an indestructible force like the nature of which it was a part; that he had a force within him "which shall tire/ Torture and Time, and breathe when I expire;" that this power which found expression in his poetry was the same as the revolutionary force in society which, though temporarily eclipsed, would ultimately prevail. In this way, he made the Byronic hero not only the symbol of a lost generation but also the prophetic voice of a revolutionary future; and, above all, he made him the expression of the eternally defiant mind of man, unconquerable in its will to freedom.

The one step necessary to give his life truly universal significance Byron took in *Manfred*. This was to detach the hero from himself and from time and place and set him in conflict with cosmic forces. As Manfred, he aspired more or less successfully to the knowledge which would give him control over nature. But he aspired also to an ideal happiness, a union with one like himself which resulted in the destruction of the loved one. It is the unappeasable remorse which followed and Manfred's hysterical efforts to use his knowledge and power to obtain oblivion that Byron made the subject of his drama. But this subject became subordinate to Manfred's refusal to make any pact with or submit in any way to forces external to him, even in the moment of death that is fore-ordained by these very forces. It is obvious that Byron had translated his relationship with Augusta, his remorse and despair, his isolation and defiance into a dramatic myth of the superman. The superior individual's struggle for self-realization and fulfillment—his desire to be more than man—inevitably entails, he seems to say, a fatal violation of conventional morality. Yet somehow only in this way can the mind of man establish its identity, its independence, the responsibility for its own acts; only in this way may human existence become meaningful.

In finding in *Manfred* the perfect artistic expression for his experiences, Byron achieved an emotional release, a separation from his hero which freed him to develop the larger view of himself and the world in which the hero became increasingly unnecessary, even a little silly. To be sure, Byron used him as protagonist in *Cain* and the classical dramas, but these were simply interludes within the greater drama of *Don Juan*. One noticeable characteristic of the hero had been his lack of humor, his tendency to take himself very seriously indeed. In *Don Juan*, Byron at last could laugh at him. Don Juan is a mild, cheerful fellow, a far cry from Manfred or even from the legendary hero whose name he bears. True, he is a wanderer and has numerous affairs, but in both cases he acts only when Byron acts upon him. He is very brave, a man of quick and intelligent action, kind and generous, in fact—highminded. He commits no crime, suffers no remorse, and, far from revolting against society, adjusts quickly and beautifully to every environment whether it be the Turkish harem, the Russian army, or an English house party. In England, he is the polished diplomat, tactful, modest, a good listener, respected by men as much as he is pursued by women. He is the hero as he might be after successful psychoanalytic treatment, and you feel that Byron is really quite fond of him and would like to think that this is what he would or could have been if fate had permitted. Juan becomes the perfect straight man for Byron's own role in the poem which, in a sense, is that of the retired hero who somehow has been denied the oblivion he so defiantly sought and is now anticlimactically living on as the aging lover of the young countess. In relating Juan's life, he looks back with wry amusement on his own, and in a casual conversational way applies the wisdom he has acquired to any subject that comes to hand. He is cynical, mocking, sentimental, realistic by turns in pointing out the incongruities between man's aspirations and his achievements, between his real and pretended motives, between the grandiose picture he draws of himself and the ridiculous figure he really is. In general, he delights in emphasizing the insignificance of man in the universe and showing that life is not worth a potato. He turns upon the society which had hounded him and exposes with pitiless satire its pretensions and hypocrisies. From time to time, he forgets himself and strikes the old pose, but just as rapidly perceives the absurdity and by the twist of a rime turns the pose to burlesque. Over all there is a gusto, an enjoyment of himself and all that he observes that gives him the superiority to his environment he had always sought. Through laughter he found the freedom he could never obtain through defiance.

The appeal of the Byronic hero is not hard to understand. He is, in Herbert Read's delightful phrase, the "super-realist personality" who by the absolute courage of his defiance of moral and social taboos becomes "the unconfessed hero of humanity." He exists in one form or another in the dream life of all of us, whether we like it or not, as the embodiment of those impulses cramped or inhibited by society. He is the expression of our social insecurity, our distrust of our fellows, our dissatisfaction with authority, our disillusionment with social achievement. He is the symbol of our defiant refusal to accept the insignificant role of the individual ego in society or the universe which modern knowledge forces upon us. In short, he represents the ego in conflict with the forces battering to subdue or destroy it—the ego which triumphs even in the moment of defeat.

Each generation, of course, creates the hero anew in its own image. In our own generation he appears most clearly in the novels and stories of Ernest Hemingway. Between the Byronic and Hemingway heroes are striking similarities. The Hemingway hero is the product of a lost generation, disillusioned by the results of war and the hypocrisy of a materialist society. Like Byron, he is a wanderer and expatriate, lamenting the futility of existence and dramatizing it through self-indulgence and the violation of conventions. Like Byron, he aspires to an ideal love, and loses it through fate. He fears death, but both seeks and defies it. He is sometimes the revolutionist, sometimes the outlaw, always a law unto himself. He suffers from guilt and remorse more mysterious than Byron's. Perhaps the most important difference between them is the way in which each expresses his defiance. In Byron the conflict is at bottom intellectual, and the hero's ego is asserted through the independence and superiority of mind, but in Hemingway the conflict is physical and the hero establishes his identity through violence, through physical strength and courage. The difference is brought out in the styles of the two writers: Byron's rhetorical, discursive, reflective; Hemingway's terse, concrete, objective. It is interesting to speculate on the differences between nineteenth and twentieth century cultures implied by the differences between the two heroes. Whatever his opinion in this respect, however, the modern reader turning back to Byron will discover, to use Hemingway's favorite metaphor, that, as hero, he is still "the champ."

III

As an artist, Byron has rarely been taken as seriously as he deserves. For one thing, to separate his work from his life and per-

sonality is, as we have seen, almost impossible; too often, therefore, we are tempted to discuss the poetry simply as illustration of
the life. For another, it is easier to point out the faults than to ana-
lyze the merits; and many critics no doubt have found in this way
sweet revenge for the inferiority they have felt in the presence of
his personality or the response they could not help making at one
time or another to *Childe Harold* or *Manfred*. In one sense, Byron
asked for this cavalier condescension toward himself as an artist.
Not only did he assert loudly and aggressively at frequent intervals throughout his life that poetry was simply an avocation or
diversion, thereby attempting to excuse his faults, but, to add insult to injury, he boasted of the ease and rapidity with which he
wrote. He could compose "in the bath, in the study, or on horseback": the *Bride of Abydos,* 732 lines, was written in "four
nights to distract my dreams," and another favorite time for composition was at two or three in the morning after a party.

He hated to revise or correct: "I am like the Tiger: if I miss the
first spring, I go growling back to my Jungle again, but if I *do*
hit, it is crushing." Actually he reworked much more than
he liked to confess; in fact, he became quite painstaking and con-
scientious in the composition of the later poems. It is obvious that
he was proud of being a poet, and we have seen that after 1816
poetry became in a very real sense his life. Yet he could never bring
himself to admit it without hedging; and it is not surprising that
more often than not he has been taken at his word.

Furthermore, from the point of view of the twentieth century,
Byron along with his fellow romantics was guilty of the most hei-
nous of artistic crimes; he wrote too much. T. S. Eliot puts the
criticism bluntly: "The bulk of Byron's poetry is distressing in
proportion to its quality." Byron would have readily agreed. "I
have had a devilish deal of wear and tear of mind and body
in my time, besides having published too often and much already," he wrote Murray in 1817 upon the completion of *Childe
Harold* IV, one of the many occasions when he threatened to
write no more. Undoubtedly the body of his poetry has suffered a
devilish deal of wear and tear during the last century. The pres-

ent selection indicates fairly, I think, what has survived—in general, what was written after his exile in 1816. This is the poetry
upon which an evaluation of Byron as an artist must be based.
And immediately we see that bulk remains an essential characteristic of this poetry inseparable from the qualities which make it
great. The full appreciation of Byron as an artist comes only
through the accumulative impact of reading a lot of him. For it is
by repetition and digression, by accumulation and expansion that
Byron achieves the intensity a modern poet might achieve
though compression. His method is the statement of a theme and
the development of variations upon it as in *Childe Harold* or the
contrapuntal interweaving of many themes as in *Don Juan*. The
themes are large, so must be the forms through which they realize
themselves. The abundance and exuberance of his imagination
can find expression in no other way. And in the rush of words to
fill the forms there is created for the reader an effect of inexhaustible vitality unsurpassed in poetry. "Exuberance is beauty," cried
Blake in one of the Proverbs of Hell; and it could serve as Byron's artistic credo.

But in our intoxication with the rush of words, we are apt to
pay little attention to the details of diction and imagery sweeping
by. Critics like Eliot would say sourly that it is just as well. They
point to an artificiality of diction, to a falsity of tone, an incongruity between language and emotion; to a grammatical careless-
ness, to a commonplaceness of imagery and idea. Finally, Eliot
makes the sweeping charge that "of Byron one can say as of no
other English poet of his eminence that he added nothing to the
language, that he discovered nothing in the sounds and developed
nothing in the meaning of individual words." Now this is the
kind of negative statement that, apparently devastating, turns out to
be at best a half-truth, and its principal value is in the opportunity
for getting at what is the distinctive contribution of Byron to the
language of poetry.

It is true that Byron wrote primarily within the neoclassical tradition; he never consciously broke with it. In *Childe Harold*, for
example, he stayed happily within the limits of the Spenserian

stanza, taking no particular liberties with it; each canto can be seen as a pattern of stanzaic blocks. He delighted in the use of the balanced structure, antithesis, paradox, the rhetorical question. His vocabulary was conventionally literary with a high concentration of "poetic diction," except in such poems as *Don Juan*. Into this conventional mold he poured his personality. The tension between language and emotion so created was the artistic manifestation of the fundamental conflict in Byron's character: that of the Regency gentleman who was also the wandering outlaw of his own dark mind. The latter could express himself only in the language of the former. Just as the man struggled for freedom within the social convention, so the poet's imagination struggled for expression within the literary convention. The result was a conventional language highly personalized, charged with meaning drawn from himself, tightened to epigrammatic incisiveness. "If I *do hit*," he said, "it is crushing." He hit crushingly his own character and moods:

> But there is that within me what shall tire
> Torture and Time, and breathe when I expire . . .

> I have been cunning in mine overthrow,
> The careful pilot of my proper woe . . .

> Could I embody and unbosom now
> That which is most within me. . . .
> > into *one* word
> And that one word were Lightning, I would speak;
> But as it is, I live and die unheard
> With a most voiceless thought, sheathing it as a sword.

> I have not loved the world, nor the world me;
> I have not flatter'd its rank breath, nor bow'd
> To its idolatries a patient knee. . . .

He caught in a phrase the places he saw, like Venice, "fairy city of the heart,"

> Rising with her tiara of proud towers
> At airy distance, with majestic motion . . .

or Rome "mother of dead empires," the "Niobe of nations,"

> An empty urn within her wither'd hands,
> Whose holy dust was scatter'd long ago . . .

And in an epigram he epitomized the great men of his age, like Napoleon "conqueror and captive of the earth," or Rousseau "self-torturing sophist,"

> . . . phrensied by disease or war
> To that worst pitch of all, which wears a reasoning show,

or Gibbon "sapping a solemn creed with solemn sneer." Wherever he touched the language, it sprang to life.

Byron's poetry, said Hazlett, "consists mostly of a tissue of superb commonplaces." And I suppose it depends upon the way we like our commonplaces served up whether we find this a fault or a virtue. The large fundamental relationships of life and death, growth and decay, man and nature are the subjects of all poetry, but Byron never bothered to transform or conceal them in intricacies of language or symbol, or to explore them in subtleties of emotion so that we come upon the basic paradox with surprise, finding it something different or new and therefore more meaningful. On the contrary, he was constantly rediscovering the larger relationships with wonder in all that he saw and did, and his poetry is the translation of his experience into them:

> I live not in myself, but I become
> Portion of that around me . . .

> There is the moral of all human tales;
> 'Tis but the same rehearsal of the past,
> First Freedom and then Glory—when that fails,
> Wealth, vice, corruption,—barbarism at last.
> And History, with all her volumes vast,
> Hath but *one* page . . .

> Yet Freedom! yet thy banner, torn but flying,
> Streams like the thunderstorm *against* the wind . . .

There is a very life in our despair,
Vitality of poison,—a quick root
Which feeds these deadly branches . . .

Similar examples could be found in nearly every stanza of *Childe Harold* III and IV. In this way, Byron revitalized the conventional idiom into the "thoughts that breathe and words that burn."

Perhaps the reason why the poetry of Byron makes its most immediate appeal when we are young is that we are "feeling upon our pulses" and making, in terms of our own experience, the same discoveries that Byron is expressing, and his poetry has consequently the freshness and force of revelation. But if at any age we are not exhilarated by Byron's apotheosis of the commonplace, the loss is ours, for this is one of his great contributions to the language of poetry.

Most of the objections to Byron's poetry fade away before *Don Juan* and its small companion masterpiece, *The Vision of Judgment*. Perhaps the best introduction to these poems are his letters, because it is the characteristics of the letters carried over into the poetry that make the poems unique. The letters themselves are among the most wonderful ever written. Freed of the inhibitions and cramping restrictions of literary convention, Byron developed in them an easy flexible style which became a magic mirror reflecting day by day his ever-changing personality. In his casual reading of Pulci and a contemporary English imitation of Pulci by "the brothers Whistlecraft" (pseudonym of John Hookham Frere), he found the equivalent verse style. He discovered delightedly that in the *ottava rima* "without straining hard to versify," he could "rattle on exactly as I talk/ With anybody in a ride or walk."

When he began *Don Juan*, Byron seemed to have no purpose except "to giggle and make giggle" through a playful burlesque of the epic manner. But almost haphazardly through the process of writing a more definite purpose evolved; it was to write an "epic satire" which by carrying his hero through the situations of the heroic epic would reveal "things as they really are," the essentially unheroic motivations and actions of modern man. The loud-

mouthed and self-righteous outcry against the immorality of the
first five cantos set Byron in a rage, and he settled down in deadly
earnest to expose the cant and hypocrisy of society. "*Don Juan*
will be known by and bye, for what it is intended," he wrote Murray in December, 1822, "a *Satire* on *abuses* of the present states of
Society, and not an eulogy of vice." The change of purpose is
shown in the change of narrative structure of the poem. The first
eight cantos contain well-developed episodes "of love, tempest,
travel, war. All very accurate . . . and *epic*"; but beginning with
Canto IX, plot elements almost disappear and the narrative
becomes a thin thread on which to hang satiric comments and
character sketches. How the poem would have ended, to
how many cantos it would have run, Byron did not know. In
1821 he told Murray that he intended Juan "to be a cause for a
divorce in England, and a Sentimental 'Werther-faced man' in
Germany . . . and to have displayed him gradually *gâté* and *blasé*
as he grew older, as is natural. But I had not quite fixed whether
to make him end in Hell, or in an unhappy marriage, not knowing which would be the severest." It really doesn't matter, for
Don Juan by its very nature could not have a conventional end-
ing; like Byron's letters and conversation, it could end only with
the death of its author.

Although the narrative becomes of secondary importance, Byron's narrative skill and versatility have been surpassed in English
poetry perhaps only by Chaucer. The Rabelaisian gusto of the first
canto and of the night in the harem; the brutal realism of the
shipwreck and the Siege of Ismail; the lyric loveliness of the Don
Juan-Haidée romance; and the acid satire of the "monstrous"
house-party—these indicate his extraordinary range and power.
But the unique greatness of *Don Juan* lies finally in the omnipres-
ence of the author's comments. "Why, Man," he cried to Murray,
"the Soul of such writing is its license; at least the *liberty* of that
license." He never abused the license: the clarity and sanity of his
comic sense prevented that. But he used it to add to the language
of poetry the colloquial richness and informality of prose and conversation. He developed as no other poet ever had the language's

apparently inexhaustible potentialities for multiple rime. He made the *ottava rima* the most flexible of verse forms by molding it with equal skill for lyric, dramatic or satiric purposes. In particular, he used his license to develop the device of incongruity, the lightning shift from one state of mind to its opposite, usually from the sublime to the ridiculous. In its simplest form, the device takes on something of the characteristics of the practical joke. Byron leads us to make all the proper psychological responses to a stock situation; then by a phrase or rime—his favorite weapon is the end couplet of the stanza—he whips the situation, like a chair, out from under us. As a satiric device, it takes the form of debunking, of stripping the mask from our pretenses, and showing us our true motivations. In its most subtle and complicated form, it becomes romantic irony—the half-sad, half-comic juxtaposition of the illusion and the reality, of the ideal and the actual, of what we should be and what we are. In this form it establishes the dominant mood of the poem.

The most frequent criticism of *Don Juan* has been that it is superficially and cheaply cynical, that its destructive satire is not balanced by any constructive philosophy, that, in De Selincourt's phrase, it lacks *vision*. Such criticism was more understandable in the days of Victorian illusion than now, but I cannot see that it ever had much validity. In replying to the charge of immorality, Byron said, "No Girl will ever be seduced by reading D. J.—no, no," and we could add that no man will ever put a bullet through his head either. On the contrary, the sustained intellectual shock, by which we are forced continually to re-examine the illusions by which we live, is one of the most salutary and exhilarating experiences we can receive in literature. For it is a shock that shakes us out of our apathy and into action as no doctrine of optimism could ever do. There is a brief statement in the "Detached Thoughts" which sums up the final Byronic view of life: "**Man is** born *passionate* of body, but with an innate though secret tendency to the love of Good in his Mainspring of Mind. But God help us all! It is at present a sad jar of atoms." When we read *Don Juan* we want, like Byron, to do something about it.

CHRONOLOGY

1788 January 22. Born in London.

1790 Taken by mother to Aberdeen, Scotland.

1791 Father, Captain ("Mad Jack") Byron, dies in France.

1792 Attends day school in Aberdeen. Later privately tutored.

1794 Becomes heir to the title of his grand-uncle, the "wicked" Lord Byron.

1798 Inherits title and Newstead Abbey upon death of grand-uncle. Moves to Newstead.

1799 Attends Dr. Glennie's Academy at Dulwich.

1801–1805 Attends Harrow. Falls in love with Mary Chaworth, grand-niece of Lord Chaworth, killed by "wicked" Lord Byron in a duel. She laughs at him and in 1805 marries John Muster (Cf. *The Dream*).

1805 Enters Trinity College, Cambridge.

1806 *Fugitive Pieces*, first volume of poems, privately printed and then destroyed upon the Rev. John Becher's protests against certain of the poems.

1807 *Poems on Various Occasions*, an expurgated edition, again privately printed. In June publicly printed as *Hours of Idleness*.

1808 Attack on *Hours of Idleness* by Henry Brougham in *Edinburgh Review*. Receives M.A. degree at Cambridge, July 4th.

1809 Attains majority; takes seat in House of Lords. *English Bards and Scotch Reviewers* published in March. With Hobhouse sails from England, July 2, for Lisbon. Journeys through Portugal and Spain, sails to Albania by way of Malta, visits the Albanian leader, Ali Pasha, and reaches Athens by the end of the year. Completes first canto of *Childe Harold*, Dec. 30th.

1810 Travels through Greece and Turkey; swims Hellespont. May 3. Completes second canto of *Childe Harold* in Athens, March 28.

1811 Returns to England in July. Mother dies in August.

1812   Gives three speeches in House of Lords. *Childe Harold* pub-
       lished in March by John Murray who remains Byron's pub-
       lisher until 1822. Immediate fame. Affair with Lady Caroline
       Lamb.

1813   In June begins affair with Augusta. First Oriental tales, *The
       Giaour* and *The Bride of Abydos*, published.

1814   Daughter, Medora, born to Augusta in April. Engaged to
       Annabella Milbanke in September. *Corsair* and *Lara* pub-
       lished.

1815   Married to Annabella, Jan. 2. Daughter, Augusta Ada, born
       Dec. 10. *Hebrew Melodies* published.

1816   Lady Byron leaves Byron in January. Formal separation
       agreed upon and signed in April. Ostracized by society.
       Byron leaves England for good, April 25. Journeys through
       Belgium and up the Rhine to Geneva. Spends summer in com-
       pany of Shelley, Mary Godwin, and Claire Clairmont. Travels
       to Venice with Hobhouse. *The Siege of Corinth, Parisina*
       published in February; *Childe Harold* III in November; *The
       Prisoner of Chillon* in December.

1817   Allegra, daughter of Byron and Claire Clairmont, born Jan.
       12. Byron makes Venice his home. Takes trip to Florence
       and Rome. Sells Newstead Abbey. *Manfred* published in
       June.

1818   The Shelleys come to Italy in March. Byron and Shelley
       frequently together until November when Shelleys go to
       Rome. Byron begins *Don Juan* in July. *Beppo* (first experi-
       ment in style of *Don Juan*) published in February; *Childe
       Harold* IV in April.

1819   Meets Teresa, Countess Guiccioli, in Venice in April. At
       end of year moves to Ravenna to be with her. *Mazeppa* pub-
       lished in June; *Don Juan* I and II in July.

1820   Becomes involved through the Gambas, Teresa's father and
       brothers, in the revolutionary Carbonari movement to free
       Italy from Austrian rule. Byron lives in the Guiccioli palace
       with his daughter Allegra.

1821   Carbonari movement defeated; Gambas banished to Pisa

where Byron joins them. *Don Juan* III, IV, V, published in
August. Byron promises Countess to write no more of *Don
Juan.* In the meantime has turned to classical dramas: *Marino
Faliero* published in April; *Cain, Two Foscari,* and *Sarda-
napalus* in December.

1822 Byron meets Trelawney. In April Allegra dies in convent
where Byron had placed her. Leigh Hunt moves to Byron's
house in June. Byron returns to *Don Juan.* Shelley drowned
in July. Byron moves to Genoa. Supports Leigh Hunt in
publication of periodical, *The Liberal. Vision of Judgment*
published in October.

1823 In July Byron sails for Greece. Arrives in Missolonghi, after
many delays and misadventures, on Dec. 30. Cantos VI to
XIV of *Don Juan* published.

1824 Is taken ill, April 9, after horseback ride in heavy downpour.
Dies April 19. Buried July 16 in Hucknell Torkard Church
near Newstead. Cantos XV, XVI of *Don Juan* published in
March.

SELECTED BIBLIOGRAPHY

I. EDITIONS

Byron: A Self-Portrait. Letters and Diaries. Ed. by Peter Quennell.
London, 1950. 2 vols. Includes over fifty new letters.

Complete Poetical Works of Lord Byron. Ed. by Paul Elmer More.
Boston, 1905.

Letters of Lord Byron. Ed. by R. G. Howarth. London, 1933.
(Everyman Library) Excellent selection of letters.

Lord Byron's Correspondence. Ed. by John Murray. London, 1922.
2 vols. Supplement to the Prothero edition.

Poetical Works of Lord Byron. New York and London, 1904.
Oxford Standard Authors Series.

Works of Lord Byron, The. London, 1898–1903; reissue, 1922. 13
vols. *Poetical Works.* Ed. by E. H. Coleridge, 7 vols. *Letters and
Journals.* Ed. by R. E. Prothero, 6 vols.

II. BOOKS ABOUT BYRON
BY HIS CONTEMPORARIES

Blessington, The Countess of. *Conversations of Lord Byron*. London, 1834.

Galt, John. *The Life of Lord Byron*. London, 1830.

Guiccioli, Teresa, Countess. *My Recollections of Lord Byron*. London, 1869.

Hobhouse, John Cam (Lord Broughton). *Recollections of a Long Life*. Ed. by Lady Dorchester. London, 1909–1911. 4 vols.

Hunt, Leigh. *Lord Byron and Some of His Contemporaries*. London, 1828. 2 vols.

Medwin, Thomas. *Journal of the Conversations of Lord Byron . . . At Pisa*. London, 1824.

Moore, Thomas. *The Life of Lord Byron with His Letters and Journals*. London, 1830. 2 vols.

Trelawney, E. J. *Records of Shelley, Byron and the Author*. London, 1878. 2 vols.

III. BIOGRAPHY AND CRITICISM

Boyd, Elizabeth. *Byron's Don Juan*. New Brunswick, N. J., 1945.

Calvert, W. J. *Byron: Romantic Paradox*. Chapel Hill, N. C., 1935.

Chew, Samuel C. *Byron in England: His Fame and After-Fame*. London, 1924.

Drinkwater, John. *The Pilgrim of Eternity*. London, 1925.

Du Bos, Charles. *Byron and the Need of Fatality*. Trans. by E. C. Mayne. London, 1932.

Fox, Sir John C. *The Byron Mystery*. London, 1925.

Lovelace, Ralph, Earl of. *Astarte*. London, 1905; revised and enlarged, 1921.

Marjarum, E. W. *Byron as Skeptic and Believer*. Princeton, 1938.

Maurois, Andre. *Byron*. London, 1930.

Mayne, Ethel. *Byron*. London, 1912. 2 vols. Rev. ed., 1924.

——*The Life and Letters of Lady Byron*. London, 1929.

Nicolson, Harold. *Byron; the Last Journey, April 1823–April 1824*. London, 1924.

Origo, Iris. *The Last Attachment: the Story of Byron and Teresa Guiccioli*. New York and London, 1949.

Quennell, Peter. *The Years of Fame*. London, 1935.

————*Byron in Italy*. London, 1941.

Russell, Bertrand. "Byron" in *History of Western Philosophy*. New York, 1946.

Trueblood, Paul. *The Flowering of Byron's Genius: Studies in Byron's Don Juan*. Stanford University, 1945.

Vulliamy, C. E. *Byron*. London, 1948.

IV. BIBLIOGRAPHICAL GUIDES

Bernbaum, Ernest. *Guide through the Romantic Movement*, 2d ed. New York, 1949.

Raysor, Thomas M. (ed.) *The English Romantic Poets: A Review of Research*. New York, 1950.

TEXTUAL NOTE

The text of the poems is that of the 1832–1833 edition of the *Works of Lord Byron*, published by John Murray. It has been carefully compared with E. H. Coleridge's edition of the *Poetical Works* (London, 7 vols. 1898–1904) with the permission of John Murray, publisher. In general, the editor has followed in questions of punctuation, capitalization, italics and spelling the practice of the one volume edition of the poetry in the Oxford Standard Authors Series, as being the most clear and desirable.

The text of the letters is that of R. E. Prothero's edition of the *Letters and Journals* (London, 6 vols. 1898–1901) and this has been used through the kind permission of the publishers, John Murray, London, and Charles Scribner's Sons, New York.

[...], The [...] Accountant: the Story of Puffin and Spittler (Faber, New York and London, 1936.

Spiller, R. E. The [...] of Fenimore Cooper, Harrap and Co. of London, 1931.

[...] Journal, [...] No. [...] April 30 (Russel [...] 1896.

[...] James Fenimore Cooper, [...] [...]s, [...]; Scribner, [...] New York, [...].

[...], [...], New York, [...].

[...] Cooper, [...] [...] Fenimore Cooper, Russel and Russell, [...] New York, [...].

TEXTUAL NOTE

In setting [...] popular edition of [...]-[...]r's novels of the sea the text [...] (Cooper's own, published in London [...]) has been carefully compared with [...] The textual changes, chiefly those of [...], have [...] corrected, [...] through the printer's errors [...] [...] in general, the [...] [...] punctuation of the [...] has [...] retained, [...] where [...] so grossly misleading as to obscure the [...] [...]

A number of the changes [...] that in all [...] editions of the [...] text (several volumes) [...] and ha[...] [...] complete and permanent [...] the publishers [...] Mohawk [...] Leatherstocking [...] ([...] Scribner's Sons, New York.

CONTENTS

INTRODUCTION	v
CHRONOLOGY	xxvii
SELECTED BIBLIOGRAPHY	xxxi
TEXTUAL NOTE	xxxi

EARLY LYRICS

When We Two Parted	1
Lines Inscribed Upon a Cup Formed From a Skull	2
Inscription on the Monument of a Newfoundland Dog	3
Written After Swimming From Sestos to Abydos	4
Maid of Athens, Ere We Part	5
Remember Thee!	6
Stanzas For Music (I speak not)	6
She Walks in Beauty	7
The Destruction of Sennacherib	8
Stanzas For Music (There be none of Beauty's daughters)	9
Stanzas For Music (There's not a joy)	9

From English Bards and Scotch Reviewers

Lines 103–264	11

POEMS OF THE SEPARATION

Fare Thee Well	16
Stanzas to Augusta (Though the day)	18
Epistle to Augusta	20
The Dream	24
Lines on Hearing that Lady Byron Was Ill	30
Darkness	33
Prometheus	36
Sonnet on Chillon	38
Prisoner of Chillon	38
From Childe Harold's Pilgrimage	50
Canto the Third	50
Canto the Fourth,	
Stanzas 1–10; 18–29; 78–82; 93–98; 107–109; 120–145; 153–163; 177–186	87

Manfred   113

Vision of Judgment   157

From Don Juan   187

  Dedication   187

  Canto the First   192
  Canto the Second   253
  Canto the Third   312
  Canto the Fourth,
      Stanzas 1–73   346
  Canto the Seventh,
      Stanzaas 80–84   366
  Canto the Eighth,
      Stanzas 6–18; 82–95; 120–127   367
  Canto the Tenth,
      Stanzas 66–83   377
  Canto the Eleventh,
      Stanzas 1–20; 45–90   382
  Canto the Fourteenth,
      Stanzas 8–20   401
  Canto the Fifteenth,
      Stanzas 40–58   405

LETTERS

  To Thomas Moore, Sept. 20, 1814   411
  To Lady Byron, April (14) 1816   412
  To Thomas Moore, Feb. 28, 1817   413
  To John Murray, April 9, 1817   414
  To John Murray, May 30, 1817   415
  To John Murray, April 6, 1819   416
  To Countess Guiccioli, August 25, 1819   418
  To Percy Bysshe Shelley, April 26, 1821   418
  To John Murray, July 30, 1821   420
  To Thomas Moore, August 27, 1822   420
  To [Mary Shelley] (December, 1822)   422
  To Thomas Moore, Dec. 27, 1823   423
  To Augusta Leigh, Feb. 23, 1824   424

On This Day I Complete My Thirty-sixth Year   426

NOTES   429

WHEN WE TWO PARTED

When we two parted
   In silence and tears,
Half broken-hearted
   To sever for years,
Pale grew thy cheek and cold,
   Colder thy kiss;
Truly that hour foretold
   Sorrow to this.

The dew of the morning
   Sunk chill on my brow—
It felt like the warning
   Of what I feel now.
Thy vows are all broken,
   And light is thy fame:
I hear thy name spoken,
   And share in its shame.

They name thee before me,
   A knell to mine ear;
A shudder comes o'er me—
   Why wert thou so dear?
They know not I knew thee,
   Who knew thee too well:—
Long, long shall I rue thee,
   Too deeply to tell.

In secret we met—
   In silence I grieve,

That thy heart could forget,
    Thy spirit deceive.
If I should meet thee
    After long years,
How should I greet thee?
    With silence and tears.

1808   1816

LINES INSCRIBED UPON A CUP
FORMED FROM A SKULL

Start not—nor deem my spirit fled;
    In me behold the only skull,
From which, unlike a living head,
    Whatever flows is never dull.

I lived, I loved, I quaff'd, like thee:
    I died: let earth my bones resign;
Fill up—thou canst not injure me;
    The worm hath fouler lips than thine.

Better to hold the sparkling grape,
    Than nurse the earth-worm's slimy brood;
And circle in the goblet's shape
    The drink of gods, than reptile's food.

Where once my wit, perchance, hath shone,
    In aid of others' let me shine;
And when, alas! our brains are gone,
    What nobler substitute than wine?

Quaff while thou canst: another race,
    When thou and thine, like me, are sped,
May rescue thee from earth's embrace,
    And rhyme and revel with the dead.

Why not? since through life's little day
   Our heads such sad effects produce;
Redeem'd from worms and wasting clay,
   This chance is theirs, to be of use.

1808   1814

INSCRIPTION ON THE MONUMENT
OF A NEWFOUNDLAND DOG

When some proud son of man returns to earth,
Unknown to glory, but upheld by birth,
The sculptor's art exhausts the pomp of woe,
And storied urns record who rest below:
When all is done, upon the tomb is seen,
Not what he was, but what he should have been:
But the poor dog, in life the firmest friend,
The first to welcome, foremost to defend,
Whose honest heart is still his master's own,
Who labours, fights, lives, breathes for him alone,
Unhonour'd falls, unnoticed all his worth,
Denied in heaven the soul he held on earth,
While man, vain insect! hopes to be forgiven,
And claims himself a sole exclusive heaven.
Oh man! thou feeble tenant of an hour,
Debased by slavery, or corrupt by power,
Who knows thee well must quit thee with disgust,
Degraded mass of animated dust!
Thy love is lust, thy friendship all a cheat,
Thy smiles hypocrisy, thy words deceit!
By nature vile, ennobled but by name,
Each kindred brute might bid thee blush for shame.
Ye! who perchance behold this simple urn,
Pass on—it honours none you wish to mourn:

To mark a friend's remains these stones arise;
I never knew but one,—and here he lies.

1808   1809

WRITTEN AFTER SWIMMING
FROM SESTOS TO ABYDOS

If, in the month of dark December,
  Leander, who was nightly wont
(What maid will not the tale remember?)
  To cross thy stream, broad Hellespont!

If, when the wintry tempest roar'd,
  He sped to Hero, nothing loth,
And thus of old thy current pour'd,
  Fair Venus! how I pity both!

For *me*, degenerate modern wretch,
  Though in the genial month of May,
My dripping limbs I faintly stretch,
  And think I've done a feat to-day.

But since he cross'd the rapid tide,
  According to the doubtful story,
To woo,—and—Lord knows what beside,
  And swam for Love, as I for Glory;

'Twere hard to say who fared the best:
  Sad mortals! thus the gods still plague you!
He lost his labour, I my jest;
  For he was drown'd, and I've the ague.

1810   1812

MAID OF ATHENS, ERE WE PART

Ζώη μοῦ, σὰς αγάπῶ.

Maid of Athens, ere we part,
Give, oh give me back my heart!
Or, since that has left my breast,
Keep it now, and take the rest!
Hear my vow before I go,
Ζώη μοῦ, σάς ἀγαπῶ.

By those tresses unconfined,
Woo'd by each Aegean wind;
By those lids whose jetty fringe
Kiss thy soft cheeks' blooming tinge;
By those wild eyes like the roe,
Ζώη μοῦ, σάς ἀγαπῶ.

By that lip I long to taste;
By that zone-encircled waist;
By all the token-flowers that tell
What words can never speak so well;
By love's alternate joy and woe,
Ζώη μοῦ, σάς ἀγαπῶ.

Maid of Athens! I am gone:
Think of me, sweet! when alone.
Though I fly to Istambol,
Athens holds my heart and soul:
Can I cease to love thee? No!
Ζώη μοῦ, σάς ἀγαπῶ.

1810   1812

REMEMBER THEE! REMEMBER
THEE!

Remember thee! remember thee!
  Till Lethe quench life's burning stream
Remorse and shame shall cling to thee,
  And haunt thee like a feverish dream!

Remember thee! Ay, doubt it not.
  Thy husband too shall think of thee!
By neither shalt thou be forgot,
  Thou *false* to him, thou *fiend* to me!

1813   1824

STANZAS FOR MUSIC

I speak not, I trace not, I breathe not thy name,
There is grief in the sound, there is guilt in the fame:
But the tear which now burns on my cheek may impart
The deep thoughts that dwell in that silence of heart.

Too brief for our passion, too long for our peace,
Were those hours—can their joy or their bitterness cease?
We repent, we abjure, we will break from our chain,—
We will part, we will fly to—unite it again!

Oh! thine be the gladness, and mine be the guilt!
Forgive me, adored one!—forsake, if thou wilt;—
But the heart which is thine shall expire undebased,
And *man* shall not break it—whatever *thou* mayst.

And stern to the haughty, but humble to thee,
This soul, in its bitterest blackness, shall be;
And our days seem as swift, and our moments more sweet,
With thee by my side, than with worlds at our feet,

One sigh of thy sorrow, one look of thy love,
Shall turn me or fix, shall reward or reprove;
And the heartless may wonder at all I resign—
Thy lip shall reply, not to them, but to *mine*.

1814   1829

SHE WALKS IN BEAUTY

1

She walks in beauty, like the night
  Of cloudless climes and starry skies;
And all that's best of dark and bright
  Meet in her aspect and her eyes:
Thus mellow'd to that tender light
  Which heaven to gaudy day denies.

2

One shade the more, one ray the less,
  Had half impair'd the nameless grace
Which waves in every raven tress,
  Or softly lightens o'er her face;
Where thoughts serenely sweet express
  How pure, how dear their dwelling-place.

3

And on that cheek, and o'er that brow,
  So soft, so calm, yet eloquent,
The smiles that win, the tints that glow,
  But tell of days in goodness spent,
A mind at peace with all below,
  A heart whose love is innocent!

1814   1815

THE DESTRUCTION OF SENNACHERIB

1

The Assyrian came down like the wolf on the fold,
And his cohorts were gleaming in purple and gold;
And the sheen of their spears was like stars on the sea,
When the blue wave rolls nightly on deep Galilee.

2

Like the leaves of the forest when Summer is green,
That host with their banners at sunset were seen:
Like the leaves of the forest when Autumn hath blown,
That host on the morrow lay wither'd and strown.

3

For the Angel of Death spread his wings on the blast,
And breathed in the face of the foe as he pass'd;
And the eyes of the sleepers wax'd deadly and chill,
And their hearts but once heaved, and for ever grew still!

4

And there lay the steed with his nostril all wide,
But through it there roll'd not the breath of his pride;
And the foam of his gasping lay white on the turf,
And cold as the spray of the rock-bearing surf.

5

And there lay the rider distorted and pale,
With the dew on his brow, and the rust on his mail:
And the tents were all silent, the banners alone,
The lances unlifted, the trumpet unblown.

6

And the widows of Ashur are loud in their wail,
And the idols are broke in the temple of Baal;
And the might of the Gentile, unsmote by the sword,
Hath melted like snow in the glance of the Lord!

1815   1815

STANZAS FOR MUSIC

There be none of Beauty's daughters
 With a magic like thee;
And like music on the waters
 Is thy sweet voice to me:
When, as if its sound were causing
The charmed ocean's pausing,
The waves lie still and gleaming
And the lull'd winds seem dreaming:

And the midnight moon is weaving
 Her bright chain o'er the deep;
Whose breast is gently heaving,
 As an infant's asleep:
So the spirit bows before thee,
To listen and adore thee;
With a full but soft emotion,
Like the swell of Summer's ocean.

1816

STANZAS FOR MUSIC

There's not a joy the world can give like that it takes away,
When the glow of early thought declines in feeling's dull decay;
'Tis not on youth's smooth cheek the blush alone, which fades so
        fast,
But the tender bloom of heart is gone, ere youth itself be past.

Then the few whose spirits float above the wreck of happiness
Are driven o'er the shoals of guilt or ocean of excess:
The magnet of their course is gone, or only points in vain
The shore to which their shiver'd sail shall never stretch again.

Then the mortal coldness of the soul like death itself comes down;
It cannot feel for others' woes, it dare not dream its own;
That heavy chill has frozen o'er the fountain of our tears,
And though the eye may sparkle still, 'tis where the ice appears.

Though wit may flash from fluent lips, and mirth distract the
        breast,
Through midnight hours that yield no more their former hope of
        rest;
'Tis but as ivy-leaves around the ruin'd turret wreath,
All green and wildly fresh without, but worn and grey beneath.

Oh could I feel as I have felt,—or be what I have been,
Or weep as I could once have wept o'er many a vanish'd scene;
As springs in deserts found seem sweet, all brackish though they
        be,
So, midst the wither'd waste of life, those tears would flow to me.

1815   1816

From ENGLISH BARDS
AND
SCOTCH REVIEWERS

Time was, ere yet in these degenerate days
Ignoble themes obtain'd mistaken praise,
When sense and wit with poesy allied,
No fabled graces, flourish'd side by side;
From the same fount their inspiration drew,
And, rear'd by taste, bloom'd fairer as they grew.
Then, in this happy isle, a Pope's pure strain
Sought the rapt soul to charm, nor sought in vain;   110
A polish'd nation's praise aspired to claim,
And raised the people's, as the poet's fame.
Like him great Dryden pour'd the tide of song,
In stream less smooth, indeed, yet doubly strong.
Then Congreve's scenes could cheer, or Otway's melt —
For nature then an English audience felt.
But why these names, or greater still, retrace,
When all to feebler bards resign their place?
Yet to such times our lingering looks are cast,
When taste and reason with those times are past.   120
Now look around, and turn each trifling page,
Survey the precious works that please the age;
This truth at least let satire's self allow,
No dearth of bards can be complain'd of now.
The loaded press beneath her labour groans,
And printers' devils shake their weary bones;
While Southey's epics cram the creaking shelves,
And Little's lyrics shine in hot-press'd twelves.
Thus saith the Preacher: "Nought beneath the sun

Is new," yet still from change to change we run: 130
What varied wonders tempt us as they pass!
The cow-pox, tractors, galvanism, and gas,
In turns appear, to make the vulgar stare,
Till the swoln bubble bursts—and all is air!
Nor less new schools of Poetry arise,
Where dull pretenders grapple for the prize:
O'er taste awhile these pseudo-bards prevail;
Each country book-club bows the knee to Baal,
And, hurling lawful genius from the throne,
Erects a shrine and idol of its own;   140
Some leaden calf—but whom it matters not,
From soaring Southey down to grovelling Stott.

Behold! in various throngs the scribbling crew,
For notice eager, pass in long review:
Each spurs his jaded Pegasus apace,
And rhyme and blank maintain an equal race;
Sonnets on sonnets crowd, and ode on ode;
And tales of terror jostle on the road;
Immeasurable measures move along;
For simpering folly loves a varied song,   150
To strange mysterious dulness still the friend,
Admires the strain she cannot comprehend.
Thus Lays of Minstrels—may they be the last!—
On half-strung harps whine mournful to the blast.
While mountain spirits prate to river sprites,
That dames may listen to the sound at nights;
And goblin brats, of Gilpin Horner's brood,
Decoy young border-nobles through the wood,
And skip at every step, Lord knows how high,
And frighten foolish babes, the Lord knows why;   160
While high-born ladies in their magic cell,
Forbidding knights to read who cannot spell,
Despatch a courier to a wizard's grave,
And fight with honest men to shield a knave.

Next view in state, proud prancing on his roan,
The golden-crested haughty Marmion,
Now forging scrolls, now foremost in the fight,
Not quite a felon, yet but half a knight,
The gibbet or the field prepared to grace;
A mighty mixture of the great and base.   170
And think'st thou, Scott! by vain conceit perchance,
On public taste to foist thy stale romance,
Though Murray with his Miller may combine
To yield thy muse just half-a-crown per line?
No! when the sons of song descend to trade,
Their bays are sear, their former laurels fade.
Let such forego the poet's sacred name,
Who rack their brains for lucre, not for fame:
Still for stern Mammon may they toil in vain!
And sadly gaze on gold they cannot gain!   180
Such be their meed, such still the just reward
Of prostituted muse and hireling bard!
For this we spurn Apollo's venal son,
And bid a long "good night to Marmion."

These are the themes that claim our plaudits now;
These are the bards to whom the muse must bow;
While Milton, Dryden, Pope, alike forgot,
Resign their hallow'd bays to Walter Scott.

The time has been, when yet the muse was young,
When Homer swept the lyre, and Maro sung,   190
An epic scarce ten centuries could claim,
While awe-struck nations hail'd the magic name;
The work of each immortal bard appears
The single wonder of a thousand years.
Empires have moulder'd from the face of earth,
Tongues have expired with those who gave them birth,
Without the glory such a strain can give,
As even in ruin bids the language live.

Not so with us, though minor bards, content
On one great work a life of labour spent: 200
With eagle pinion soaring to the skies,
Behold the ballad-monger Southey rise!
To him let Camoëns, Milton, Tasso yield,
Whose annual strains, like armies, take the field.
First in the ranks see Joan of Arc advance,
The scourge of England and the boast of France!
Though burnt by wicked Bedford for a witch,
Behold her statue placed in glory's niche;
Her fetters burst, and just released from prison,
A virgin phoenix from her ashes risen.   210
Next see tremendous Thalaba come on,
Arabia's monstrous, wild, and wondrous son:
Domdaniel's dread destroyer, who o'erthrew
More mad magicians than the world e'er knew.
Immortal hero! all thy foes o'ercome,
For ever reign—the rival of Tom Thumb!
Since startled metre fled before thy face,
Well wert thou doom'd the last of all thy race!
Well might triumphant genii bear thee hence,
Illustrious conqueror of common sense!   220
Now, last and greatest, Madoc spreads his sails,
Cacique in Mexico, and prince in Wales;
Tells us strange tales, as other travellers do,
More old than Mandeville's, and not so true.
Oh! Southey! Southey! cease thy varied song!
A bard may chant too often and too long:
As thou art strong in verse, in mercy, spare!
A fourth, alas! were more than we could bear.
But if, in spite of all the world can say,
Thou still wilt verseward plod thy weary way;   230
If still in Berkley ballads most uncivil,
Thou wilt devote old women to the devil,
The babe unborn thy dread intent may rue:
"God help thee," Southey, and thy readers too.

Next comes the dull disciple of thy school,
That mild apostate from poetic rule,
The simple Wordsworth, framer of a lay
As soft as evening in his favourite May,
Who warns his friend "to shake off toil and trouble,
And quit his books, for fear of growing double;"   240
Who, both by precept and example, shows
That prose is verse, and verse is merely prose;
Convincing all, by demonstration plain,
Poetic souls delight in prose insane;
And Christmas stories tortured into rhyme
Contain the essence of the true sublime.
Thus, when he tells the tale of Betty Foy,
The idiot mother of "an idiot boy";
A moon-struck, silly lad, who lost his way,
And, like his bard, confounded night with day;   250
So close on each pathetic part he dwells,
And each adventure so sublimely tells,
That all who view the "idiot in his glory"
Conceive the bard the hero of the story.

Shall gentle Coleridge pass unnoticed here,
To turgid ode and tumid stanza dear?
Though themes of innocence amuse him best,
Yet still obscurity's a welcome guest.
If Inspiration should her aid refuse
To him who takes a pixy for a muse,   260
Yet none in lofty numbers can surpass
The bard who soars to elegise an ass.
So well the subject suits his noble mind,
He brays the laureat of the long-ear'd kind.

1809

FARE THEE WELL

Alas! they had been friends in youth;
But whispering tongues can poison truth;
And constancy lives in realms above;
And life is thorny; and youth is vain;
And to be wroth with one we love,
Doth work like madness in the brain;

    .   .   .   .   .

But never either found another
To free the hollow heart from paining—
They stood aloof, the scars remaining,
Like cliffs which had been rent asunder;
A dreary sea now flows between,
But neither heat, nor frost, nor thunder,
Shall wholly do away, I ween,
The marks of that which once hath been.
COLERIDGE'S Christabel.

Fare thee well! and if for ever,
  Still for ever, fare thee well:
Even though unforgiving, never
  'Gainst thee shall my heart rebel.
Would that breast were bared before thee
  Where thy head so oft harh lain,
While that placid sleep came o'er thee
  Which thou ne'er canst know again:
Would that breast, by thee glanced over,
  Every inmost thought could show!   10
Then thou wouldst at last discover
  'Twas not well to spurn it so.
Though the world for this commend thee—
  Though it smile upon the blow,
Even its praises must offend thee,
  Founded on another's woe:
Though my many faults defaced me,

Could no other arm be found,
Than the one which once embraced me,
    To inflict a cureless wound?   20
Yet, oh yet, thyself deceive not;
    Love may sink by slow decay,
But by sudden wrench, believe not
    Hearts can thus be torn away:
Still thine own its life retaineth,
    Still must mine, though bleeding, beat;
And the undying thought which paineth
    Is—that we no more may meet.
These are words of deeper sorrow
    Than the wail above the dead;   30
Both shall live, but every morrow
    Wake us from a widow'd bed.
And when thou wouldst solace gather,
    When our child's first accents flow,
Wilt thou teach her to say "Father!"
    Though his care she must forego?
When her little hands shall press thee,
    When her lip to thine is press'd,
Think of him whose prayer shall bless thee,
    Think of him thy love had bless'd!   40
Should her lineaments resemble
    Those thou never more may'st see,
Then thy heart will softly tremble
    With a pulse yet true to me.
All my faults perchance thou knowest,
    All my madness none can know;
All my hopes, where'er thou goest,
    Wither, yet with *thee* they go.
Every feeling hath been shaken;
    Pride, which not a world could bow,   50
Bows to thee—by thee forsaken,
    Even my soul forsakes me now:
But 'tis done—all words are idle—
    Words from me are vainer still;

But the thoughts we cannot bridle
   Force their way without the will.
Fare thee well! thus disunited,
   Torn from every nearer tie,
Sear'd in heart, and lone, and blighted,
   More than this I scarce can die.   60

March 18, 1816   1816

STANZAS TO AUGUSTA

1

Though the day of my destiny's over,
   And the star of my fate hath declined,
Thy soft heart refused to discover
   The faults which so many could find;
Though thy soul with my grief was acquainted,
   It shrunk not to share it with me,
And the love which my spirit hath painted
   It never hath found but in *thee*.

2

Then when nature around me is smiling,
   The last smile which answers to mine,
I do not believe it beguiling,
   Because it reminds me of thine;
And when winds are at war with the ocean,
   As the breasts I believed in with me,
If their billows excite an emotion,
   It is that they bear me from *thee*.

3

Though the rock of my last hope is shiver'd,
   And its fragments are sunk in the wave,
Though I feel that my soul is deliver'd
   To pain—it shall not be its slave.

There is many a pang to pursue me:
    They may crush, but they shall not contemn;
They may torture, but shall not subdue me;
    'Tis of *thee* that I think—not of them.

4

Though human, thou didst not deceive me,
    Though woman, thou didst not forsake,
Though loved, thou forborest to grieve me,
    Though slander'd, thou never couldst shake;
Though trusted, thou didst not disclaim me,
    Though parted, it was not to fly,
Though watchful, 'twas not to defame me,
    Nor, mute, that the world might belie.

5

Yet I blame not the world, nor despise it,
    Nor the war of the many with one;
If my soul was not fitted to prize it,
    'Twas folly not sooner to shun:
And if dearly that error hath cost me,
    And more than I once could foresee,
I have found that, whatever it lost me,
    It could not deprive me of *thee*.

6

From the wreck of the past, which hath perish'd,
    Thus much I at least may recall,
It hath taught me that what I most cherish'd
    Deserved to be dearest of all:
In the desert a fountain is springing,
    In the wide waste there still is a tree,
And a bird in the solitude singing,
    Which speaks to my spirit of *thee*.

July 24, 1816   1816

EPISTLE TO AUGUSTA

1

My sister! my sweet sister! if a name
Dearer and purer were, it should be thine;
Mountains and seas divide us, but I claim
No tears, but tenderness to answer mine:
Go where I will, to me thou art the same—
A loved regret which I would not resign.
There yet are two things in my destiny,—
A world to roam through, and a home with thee.

2

The first were nothing—had I still the last,
It were the haven of my happiness;
But other claims and other ties thou hast,
And mine is not the wish to make them less.
A strange doom is thy father's son's, and past
Recalling, as it lies beyond redress;
Reversed for him our grandsire's fate of yore,—
He had no rest at sea, nor I on shore.

3

If my inheritance of storms hath been
In other elements, and on the rocks
Of perils, overlook'd or unforeseen,
I have sustain'd my share of worldly shocks,
The fault was mine; nor do I seek to screen
My errors with defensive paradox;
I have been cunning in mine overthrow,
The careful pilot of my proper woe.

4

Mine were my faults, and mine be their reward.
My whole life was a contest, since the day

That gave me being, gave me that which marr'd
The gift,—a fate, or will, that walk'd astray;
And I at times have found the struggle hard,
And thought of shaking off my bonds of clay:
But now I fain would for a time survive,
If but to see what next can well arrive.

5

Kingdoms and empires in my little day
I have outlived, and yet I am not old;
And when I look on this, the petty spray
Of my own years of trouble, which have roll'd
Like a wild bay of breakers, melts away:
Something—I know not what—does still uphold
A spirit of slight patience;—not in vain,
Even for its own sake, do we purchase pain.

6

Perhaps the workings of defiance stir
Within me—or perhaps a cold despair,
Brought on when ills habitually recur,—
Perhaps a kinder clime, or purer air,
(For even to this may change of soul refer,
And with light armour we may learn to bear,)
Have taught me a strange quiet, which was not
The chief companion of a calmer lot.

7

I feel almost at times as I have felt
In happy childhood; trees, and flowers, and brooks,
Which do remember me of where I dwelt
Ere my young mind was sacrificed to books,
Come as of yore upon me, and can melt
My heart with recognition of their looks;
And even at moments I could think I see
Some living thing to love—but none like thee.

8

Here are the Alpine landscapes which create
A fund for contemplation;—to admire
Is a brief feeling of a trivial date;
But something worthier do such scenes inspire:
Here to be lonely is not desolate,
For much I view which I could most desire,
And, above all, a lake I can behold
Lovelier, not dearer, than our own of old.

9

Oh that thou wert but with me!—but I grow
The fool of my own wishes, and forget
The solitude which I have vaunted so
Has lost its praise in this but one regret;
There may be others which I less may show;—
I am not of the plaintive mood, and yet
I feel an ebb in my philosophy,
And the tide rising in my alter'd eye.

10

I did remind thee of our own dear Lake,
By the old Hall which may be mine no more.
Leman's is fair; but think not I forsake
The sweet remembrance of a dearer shore:
Sad havoc Time must with my memory make,
Ere *that* or *thou* can fade these eyes before;
Though, like all things which I have loved, they are
Resign'd for ever, or divided far.

11

The world is all before me; I but ask
Of Nature that with which she will comply—
It is but in her summer's sun to bask,
To mingle with the quiet of her sky,
To see her gentle face without a mask,

And never gaze on it with apathy.
She was my early friend, and now shall be
My sister—till I look again on thee.

12

I can reduce all feelings but this one;
And that I would not;—for at length I see
Such scenes as those wherein my life begun,
The earliest—even the only paths for me—
Had I but sooner learnt the crowd to shun,
I had been better than I now can be;
The passions which have torn me would have slept;
I had not suffer'd, and *thou* hadst not wept.

13

With false Ambition what had I to do?
Little with Love, and least of all with Fame;
And yet they came unsought, and with me grew,
And made me all which they can make—a name.
Yet this was not the end I did pursue;
Surely I once beheld a nobler aim.
But all is over—I am one the more
To baffled millions which have gone before.

14

And for the future, this world's future may
From me demand but little of my care;
I have outlived myself by many a day,
Having survived so many things that were;
My years have been no slumber, but the prey
Of ceaseless vigils; for I had the share
Of life which might have fill'd a century,
Before its fourth in time had pass'd me by.

15

And for the remnant which may be to come
I am content; and for the past I feel

Not thankless,—for within the crowded sum
Of struggles, happiness at times would steal,
And for the present, I would not benumb
My feelings further.—Nor shall I conceal
That with all this I still can look around,
And worship Nature with a thought profound.

16

For thee, my own sweet sister, in thy heart
I know myself secure, as thou in mine;
We were and are—I am, even as thou art—
Beings who ne'er each other can resign;
It is the same, together or apart,
From life's commencement to its slow decline
We are entwined—let death come slow or fast,
The tie which bound the first endures the last!

1816   1830

THE DREAM

1

Our life is two-fold: Sleep hath its own world,
A boundary between the things misnamed
Death and existence: Sleep hath its own world,
And a wide realm of wild reality.
And dreams in their development have breath,
And tears, and tortures, and the touch of joy;
They leave a weight upon our waking thoughts,
They take a weight from off our waking toils,
They do divide our being; they become
A portion of ourselves as of our time,   19
And look like heralds of eternity;
They pass like spirits of the past,—they speak
Like Sibyls of the future: they have power—
The tyranny of pleasure and of pain;

They make us what we were not—what they will,
And shake us with the vision that's gone by,
The dread of vanish'd shadows—Are they so?
Is not the past all shadow?—What are they?
Creations of the mind?—The mind can make
Substance, and people planets of its own   20
With beings brighter than have been, and give
A breath to forms which can outlive all flesh.
I would recall a vision which I dream'd
Perchance in sleep—for in itself a thought,
A slumbering thought, is capable of years,
And curdles a long life into one hour.

2

I saw two beings in the hues of youth
Standing upon a hill, a gentle hill,
Green and of mild declivity, the last
As 'twere the cape of a long ridge of such,   30
Save that there was no sea to lave its base,
But a most living landscape, and the wave
Of woods and corn-fields, and the abodes of men
Scatter'd at intervals, and wreathing smoke
Arising from such rustic roofs;—the hill
Was crown'd with a peculiar diadem
Of trees, in circular array, so fix'd,
Not by the sport of nature, but of man:
These two, a maiden and a youth, were there
Gazing—the one on all that was beneath   40
Fair as herself—but the boy gazed on her;
And both were young, and one was beautiful:
And both were young—yet not alike in youth.
As the sweet moon on the horizon's verge,
The maid was on the eve of womanhood;
The boy had fewer summers, but his heart
Had far outgrown his years, and to his eye
There was but one beloved face on earth,
And that was shining on him: he had look'd

Upon it till it could not pass away;   50
He had no breath, no being, but in hers;
She was his voice; he did not speak to her,
But trembled on her words; she was his sight,
For his eye follow'd hers, and saw with hers,
Which colour'd all his objects:—he had ceased
To live within himself; she was his life,
The ocean to the river of his thoughts,
Which terminated all: upon a tone,
A touch of hers, his blood would ebb and flow,
And his cheek change tempestuously—his heart   60
Unknowing of its cause of agony.
But she in these fond feelings had no share:
Her sighs were not for him; to her he was
Even as a brother—but no more; 'twas much,
For brotherless she was, save in the name
Her infant friendship had bestow'd on him;
Herself the solitary scion left
Of a time-honour'd race.—It was a name
Which pleased him, and yet pleased him not—and why?
Time taught him a deep answer—when she loved   70
Another; even *now* she loved another,
And on the summit of that hill she stood
Looking afar if yet her lover's steed
Kept pace with her expectancy, and flew.

3

A change came o'er the spirit of my dream.
There was an ancient mansion, and before
Its walls there was a steed caparison'd;
Within an antique Oratory stood
The Boy of whom I spake;—he was alone,
And pale, and pacing to and fro: anon   80
He sate him down, and seized a pen, and traced
Words which I could not guess of; then he lean'd
His bow'd head on his hands, and shook as 'twere
With a convulsion—then arose again,

And with his teeth and quivering hands did tear
What he had written, but he shed no tears,
And he did calm himself, and fix his brow
Into a kind of quiet: as he paused,
The Lady of his love re-entered there;
She was serene and smiling then, and yet   90
She knew she was by him beloved,—she knew,
For quickly comes such knowledge, that his heart
Was darken'd with her shadow, and she saw
That he was wretched, but she saw not all.
He rose, and with a cold and gentle grasp
He took her hand; a moment o'er his face
A tablet of unutterable thoughts
Was traced, and then it faded, as it came;
He dropp'd the hand he held, and with slow steps
Retired, but not as bidding her adieu,   100
For they did part with mutual smiles; he pass'd
From out the massy gate of that old Hall,
And mounting on his steed he went his way;
And ne'er repass'd that hoary threshold more.

4

A change came o'er the spirit of my dream.
The Boy was sprung to manhood: in the wilds
Of fiery climes he made himself a home,
And his soul drank their sunbeams: he was girt
With strange and dusky aspects; he was not
Himself like what he had been; on the sea   110
And on the shore he was a wanderer.
There was a mass of many images
Crowded like waves upon me, but he was
A part of all; and in the last he lay
Reposing from the noontide sultriness,
Couch'd among fallen columns, in the shade
Of ruin'd walls that had survived the names
Of those who rear'd them; by his sleeping side
Stood camels grazing, and some goodly steeds

Were fasten'd near a fountain; and a man   120
Clad in a flowing garb did watch the while,
While many of his tribe slumber'd around:
And they were canopied by the blue sky,
So cloudless, clear, and purely beautiful,
That God alone was to be seen in heaven.

5

A change came o'er the spirit of my dream.
The Lady of his love was wed with One
Who did not love her better:—in her home,
A thousand leagues from his,—her native home,
She dwelt, begirt with growing Infancy,   130
Daughters and sons of Beauty,—but behold!
Upon her face there was the tint of grief,
The settled shadow of an inward strife,
And an unquiet drooping of the eye,
As if its lid were charged with unshed tears.
What could her grief be?—she had all she loved,
And he who had so loved her was not there
To trouble with bad hopes, or evil wish,
Or ill-repress'd affliction, her pure thoughts.
What could her grief be?—she had loved him not,   140
Nor given him cause to deem himself beloved,
Nor could he be a part of that which prey'd
Upon her mind—a spectre of the past.

6

A change came o'er the spirit of my dream.
The Wanderer was return'd.—I saw him stand
Before an Altar—with a gentle bride;
Her face was fair, but was not that which made
The Starlight of his Boyhood;—as he stood
Even at the altar, o'er his brow there came
The self-same aspect, and the quivering shock   150
That in the antique Oratory shook
His bosom in its solitude; and then—
As in that hour—a moment o'er his face

The tablet of unutterable thoughts
Was traced,—and then it faded as it came,
And he stood calm and quiet, and he spoke
The fitting vows, but heard not his own words,
And all things reel'd around him; he could see
Not that which was, nor that which should have been—
But the old mansion, and the accustom'd hall,   160
And the remember'd chambers, and the place,
The day, the hour, the sunshine, and the shade,
All things pertaining to that place and hour,
And her who was his destiny,—came back
And thrust themselves between him and the light:
What business had they there at such a time?

7

A change came o'er the spirit of my dream.
The Lady of his love:—Oh! she was changed
As by the sickness of the soul; her mind
Had wander'd from its dwelling, and her eyes   170
They had not their own lustre, but the look
Which is not of the earth; she was become
The queen of a fantastic realm; her thoughts
Were combinations of disjointed things;
And forms impalpable and unperceived
Of others' sight familiar were to hers.
And this the world calls frenzy; but the wise
Have a far deeper madness, and the glance
Of melancholy is a fearful gift;
What is it but the telescope of truth?   180
Which strips the distance of its fantasies,
And brings life near in utter nakedness,
Making the cold reality too real!

8

A change came o'er the spirit of my dream.
The Wanderer was alone as heretofore,
The beings which surrounded him were gone,

Or were at war with him; he was a mark
For blight and desolation, compass'd round
With Hatred and Contention; Pain was mix'd
In all which was served up to him, until,   190
Like to the Pontic monarch of old days,
He fed on poisons, and they had no power,
But were a kind of nutriment; he lived
Through that which had been death to many men,
And made him friends of mountains: with the stars
And the quick Spirit of the Universe
He held his dialogues; and they did teach
To him the magic of their mysteries;
To him the book of Night was open'd wide,
And voices from the deep abyss reveal'd   200
A marvel and a secret—Be it so.

9

My dream was past; it had no further change.
It was of a strange order, that the doom
Of these two creatures should be thus traced out
Almost like a reality—the one
To end in madness—both in misery.

July, 1816   1816

LINES ON HEARING THAT LADY BYRON WAS ILL

And thou wert sad—yet I was not with thee;
    And thou wert sick, and yet I was not near;
Methought that joy and health alone could be
    Where I was *not*—and pain and sorrow here!
And is it thus?—it is as I foretold,
    And shall be more so; for the mind recoils
Upon itself, and the wreck'd heart lies cold,
    While heaviness collects the shatter'd spoils.
It is not in the storm nor in the strife

We feel benumb'd, and wish to be no more,   10
    But in the after-silence on the shore,
When all is lost, except a little life.

I am too well avenged!—but 'twas my right;
    Whate'er my sins might be, *thou* wert not sent
To be the Nemesis who should requite—
    Nor did Heaven choose so near an instrument.
Mercy is for the merciful!—if thou
Hast been of such, 'twill be accorded now.
Thy nights are banish'd from the realms of sleep!—
    Yes! they may flatter thee, but thou shalt feel   20
    A hollow agony which will not heal,
For thou art pillow'd on a curse too deep;
Thou hast sown in my sorrow, and must reap
    The bitter harvest in a woe as real!
I have had many foes, but none like thee;
    For 'gainst the rest myself I could defend,
    And be avenged, or turn them into friend;
But thou in safe implacability
Hadst nought to dread—in thy own weakness shielded,
And in my love, which hath but too much yielded,   30
    And spared, for thy sake, some I should not spare;
And thus upon the world—trust in thy truth,
And the wild fame of my ungovern'd youth—
    On things that were not, and on things that are—
Even upon such a basis hast thou built
A monument, whose cement hath been guilt!
    The moral Clytemnestra of thy lord,
    And hew'd down, with an unsuspected sword,
Fame, peace, and hope—and all the better life,
    Which, but for this cold treason of thy heart,   40
Might still have risen from out the grave of strife,
    And found a nobler duty than to part.
But of thy virtues didst thou make a vice,
    Trafficking with them in a purpose cold,
    For present anger, and for future gold—

And buying other's grief at any price.
And thus once enter'd into crooked ways,
The early truth, which was thy proper praise,
Did not still walk beside thee—but at times,
And with a breast unknowing its own crimes,   50
Deceit, averments incompatible,
Equivocations, and the thoughts which dwell
    In Janus-spirits—the significant eye
Which learns to lie with silence—the pretext
Of prudence, with advantages annex'd—
The acquiescence in all things which tend,
No matter how, to the desired end—
    All found a place in thy philosophy.
The means were worthy, and the end is won—
I would not do by thee as thou hast done!   60

1816   1832

DARKNESS

I had a dream, which was not all a dream.
The bright sun was extinguish'd, and the stars
Did wander darkling in the eternal space,
Rayless, and pathless, and the icy earth
Swung blind and blackening in the moonless air;
Morn came and went—and came, and brought no day,
And men forgot their passions in the dread
Of this their desolation; and all hearts
Were chill'd into a selfish prayer for light:
And they did live by watchfires—and the thrones,   o
The palaces of crowned kings—the huts,
The habitations of all things which dwell,
Were burnt for beacons; cities were consumed,
And men were gather'd round their blazing homes
To look once more into each other's face;
Happy were those who dwelt within the eye
Of the volcanos, and their mountain-torch:
A fearful hope was all the world contain'd;
Forests were set on fire—but hour by hour
They fell and faded—and the crackling trunks   20
Extinguish'd with a crash—and all was black.
The brows of men by the despairing light
Wore an unearthly aspect, as by fits
The flashes fell upon them; some lay down
And hid their eyes and wept; and some did rest
Their chins upon their clenched hands, and smiled;
And others hurried to and fro, and fed
Their funeral piles with fuel, and look'd up
With mad disquietude on the dull sky,
The pall of a past world; and then again   30
With curses cast them down upon the dust,
And gnash'd their teeth and howl'd: the wild birds shriek'd

33

And, terrified, did flutter on the ground,
And flap their useless wings; the wildest brutes
Came tame and tremulous; and vipers crawl'd
And twined themselves among the multitude,
Hissing, but stingless—they were slain for food.
And War, which for a moment was no more,
Did glut himself again:—a meal was bought
With blood, and each sate sullenly apart   40
Gorging himself in gloom: no love was left;
All earth was but one thought—and that was death
Immediate and inglorious; and the pang
Of famine fed upon all entrails—men
Died, and their bones were tombless as their flesh;
The meagre by the meagre were devour'd,
Even dogs assail'd their masters, all save one,
And he was faithful to a corse, and kept
The birds and beasts and famish'd men at bay,
Till hunger clung them, or the dropping dead   50
Lured their lank jaws; himself sought out no food,
But with a piteous and perpetual moan,
And a quick desolate cry, licking the hand
Which answer'd not with a caress—he died.
The crowd was famish'd by degrees; but two
Of an enormous city did survive,
And they were enemies: they met beside
The dying embers of an altar-place
Where had been heap'd a mass of holy things
For an unholy usage; they raked up,   60
And shivering scraped with their cold skeleton hands
The feeble ashes, and their feeble breath
Blew for a little life, and made a flame
Which was a mockery; then they lifted up
Their eyes as it grew lighter, and beheld
Each other's aspects—saw, and shriek'd, and died—
Even of their mutual hideousness they died,
Unknowing who he was upon whose brow
Famine had written Fiend. The world was void,

The populous and the powerful was a lump,   70
Seasonless, herbless, treeless, manless, lifeless,
A lump of death—a chaos of hard clay.
The rivers, lakes, and ocean all stood still,
And nothing stirr'd within their silent depths;
Ships sailorless lay rotting on the sea,
And their masts fell down piecemeal: as they dropp'd
They slept on the abyss without a surge—
The waves were dead; the tides were in their grave,
The moon, their mistress, had expired before;
The winds were wither'd in the stagnant air,   80
And the clouds perish'd; Darkness had no need
Of aid from them—She was the Universe.

1816   1816

PROMETHEUS

1

Titan! to whose immortal eyes
  The sufferings of mortality,
  Seen in their sad reality,
Were not as things that gods despise;
What was thy pity's recompense?
A silent suffering, and intense;
The rock, the vulture, and the chain,
All that the proud can feel of pain,
The agony they do not show,
The suffocating sense of woe,   10
  Which speaks but in its loneliness,
And then is jealous lest the sky
Should have a listener, nor will sigh
  Until its voice is echoless.

2

Titan! to thee the strife was given
  Between the suffering and the will,
  Which torture where they cannot kill;
And the inexorable Heaven,
And the deaf tyranny of Fate,
The ruling principle of Hate,   20
Which for its pleasure doth create
The things it may annihilate,
Refused thee even the boon to die:
The wretched gift eternity
Was thine—and thou hast borne it well.
All that the Thunderer wrung from thee
Was but the menace which flung back
On him the torments of thy rack;

The fate thou didst so well foresee,
But would not to appease him tell;   30
And in thy Silence was his Sentence,
And in his Soul a vain repentance,
And evil dread so ill dissembled,
That in his hand the lightnings trembled.

3

Thy Godlike crime was to be kind,
    To render with thy precepts less
    The sum of human wretchedness,
And strengthen Man with his own mind;
But baffled as thou wert from high,
Still in thy patient energy,   40
In the endurance, and repulse
    Of thine impenetrable Spirit,
Which Earth and Heaven could not convulse,
    A mighty lesson we inherit:
Thou art a symbol and a sign
    To Mortals of their fate and force;
Like thee, Man is in part divine,
    A troubled stream from a pure source;
And Man in portions can foresee
His own funereal destiny;
His wretchedness, and his resistance,
And his sad unallied existence:
To which his Spirit may oppose
Itself—an equal to all woes,
    And a firm will, and a deep sense,
Which even in torture can descry
    Its own concenter'd recompense,
Triumphant where it dares defy,
And making Death a Victory.

1816   1816

THE PRISONER OF CHILLON

SONNET ON CHILLON

Eternal Spirit of the chainless Mind!
  Brightest in dungeons, Liberty! thou art,
  For there thy habitation is the heart—
The heart which love of thee alone can bind;
And when thy sons to fetters are consign'd—
  To fetters, and the damp vault's dayless gloom,
  Their country conquers with their martyrdom,
And Freedom's fame finds wings on every wind.
Chillon! thy prison is a holy place,
  And thy sad floor an altar—for 'twas trod,
Until his very steps have left a trace
  Worn, as if thy cold pavement were a sod,
By Bonnivard! May none those marks efface!
  For they appeal from tyranny to God.

I

My hair is grey, but not with years,
    Nor grew it white
    In a single night,
As men's have grown from sudden fears:
My limbs are bow'd, though not with toil,
  But rusted with a vile repose,
For they have been a dungeon's spoil,
  And mine has been the fate of those
To whom the goodly earth and air
Are bann'd, and barr'd—forbidden fare: 10
But this was for my father's faith
I suffer'd chains and courted death;

That father perish'd at the stake
For tenets he would not forsake;
And for the same his lineal race
In darkness found a dwelling-place;
We were seven—who now are one,
    Six in youth, and one in age,
Finish'd as they had begun,
    Proud of Persecution's rage;   20
One in fire, and two in field,
Their belief with blood have seal'd,
Dying as their father died,
For the God their foes denied;
Three were in a dungeon cast,
Of whom this wreck is left the last.

2

There are seven pillars of Gothic mould,
In Chillon's dungeons deep and old,
There are seven columns, massy and grey,
Dim with a dull imprison'd ray,   30
A sunbeam which hath lost its way,
And through the crevice and the cleft
Of the thick wall is fallen and left;
Creeping o'er the floor so damp,
Like a marsh's meteor lamp:
And in each pillar there is a ring,
    And in each ring there is a chain;
That iron is a cankering thing,
    For in these limbs its teeth remain,
With marks that will not wear away,   40
Till I have done with this new day,
Which now is painful to these eyes,
Which have not seen the sun so rise
For years—I cannot count them o'er,
I lost their long and heavy score,
When my last brother droop'd and died,
And I lay living by his side.

3

They chain'd us each to a column stone,
And we were three—yet, each alone;
We could not move a single pace,   50
We could not see each other's face,
But with that pale and livid light
That made us strangers in our sight:
And thus together—yet apart,
Fetter'd in hand, but join'd in heart,
'Twas still some solace, in the dearth
Of the pure elements of earth,
To hearken to each other's speech,
And each turn comforter to each
With some new hope, or legend old,   60
Or song heroically bold;
But even these at length grew cold.
Our voices took a dreary tone,
An echo of the dungeon stone,
    A grating sound, not full and free,
    As they of yore were wont to be:
    It might be fancy, but to me
They never sounded like our own.

4

I was the eldest of the three,
    And to uphold and cheer the rest   70
    I ought to do—and did my best—
And each did well in his degree.
    The youngest, whom my father loved,
Because our mother's brow was given
To him, with eyes as blue as heaven—
    For him my soul was sorely moved;
And truly might it be distress'd
To see such bird in such a nest;
For he was beautiful as day—
    (When day was beautiful to me   80
    As to young eagles, being free)—

A polar day, which will not see
A sunset till its summer's gone,
  Its sleepless summer of long light,
The snow-clad offspring of the sun:
  And thus he was as pure and bright,
And in his natural spirit gay,
With tears for nought but others' ills,
And then they flow'd like mountain rills,
Unless he could assuage the woe   90
Which he abhorr'd to view below.

5

The other was as pure of mind,
But form'd to combat with his kind;
Strong in his frame, and of a mood
Which 'gainst the world in war had stood,
And perish'd in the foremost rank
  With joy:—but not in chains to pine:
His spirit wither'd with their clank,
  I saw it silently decline—
  And so perchance in sooth did mine: 100
But yet I forced it on to cheer
Those relics of a home so dear.
He was a hunter of the hills,
  Had follow'd there the deer and wolf;
  To him his dungeon was a gulf,
And fetter'd feet the worst of ills.

6

Lake Leman lies by Chillon's walls:
A thousand feet in depth below
Its massy waters meet and flow;
Thus much the fathom-line was sent   110
From Chillon's snow-white battlement,
  Which round about the wave inthrals:
A double dungeon wall and wave
Have made—and like a living grave

Below the surface of the lake
The dark vault lies wherein we lay,
We heard it ripple night and day;
　Sounding o'er our heads it knock'd;
And I have felt the winter's spray
Wash through the bars when winds were high　　120
And wanton in the happy sky;
　And then the very rock hath rock'd,
　And I have felt it shake, unshock'd,
Because I could have smiled to see
The death that would have set me free.

7

I said my nearer brother pined,
I said his mighty heart declined,
He loathed and put away his food;
It was not that 'twas coarse and rude,
For we were used to hunter's fare,　　130
And for the like had little care:
The milk drawn from the mountain goat
Was changed for water from the moat,
Our bread was such as captives' tears
Have moisten'd many a thousand years,
Since man first pent his fellow men
Like brutes within an iron den;
But what were these to us or him?
These wasted not his heart or limb;
My brother's soul was of that mould　　140
Which in a palace had grown cold,
Had his free breathing been denied
The range of the steep mountain's side;
But why delay the truth?—he died.
I saw, and could not hold his head,
Nor reach his dying hand—nor dead,—
Though hard I strove, but strove in vain,
To rend and gnash my bonds in twain.
He died, and they unlock'd his chain,

And scoop'd for him a shallow grave   150
Even from the cold earth of our cave.
I begg'd them as a boon to lay
His corse in dust whereon the day
Might shine—it was a foolish thought,
But then within my brain it wrought,
That even in death his freeborn breast
In such a dungeon could not rest.
I might have spared my idle prayer—
They coldly laugh'd, and laid him there:
The flat and turfless earth above   160
The being we so much did love;
His empty chain above it leant,
Such murder's fitting monument!

8

But he, the favourite and the flower,
Most cherish'd since his natal hour,
His mother's image in fair face,
The infant love of all his race,
His martyr'd father's dearest thought,
My latest care, for whom I sought
To hoard my life, that his might be   170
Less wretched now, and one day free;
He, too, who yet had held untired
A spirit natural or inspired—
He, too, was struck, and day by day
Was wither'd on the stalk away.
Oh, God! it is a fearful thing
To see the human soul take wing
In any shape, in any mood:
I've seen it rushing forth in blood,
I've seen it on the breaking ocean   180
Strive with a swoln convulsive motion,
I've seen the sick and ghastly bed
Of Sin delirious with its dread;
But these were horrors—this was woe

Unmix'd with such—but sure and slow:
He faded, and so calm and meek,
So softly worn, so sweetly weak,
So tearless, yet so tender, kind,
And grieved for those he left behind;
With all the while a cheek whose bloom　　190
Was as a mockery of the tomb,
Whose tints as gently sunk away
As a departing rainbow's ray;
An eye of most transparent light,
That almost made the dungeon bright,
And not a word of murmur, not
A groan o'er his untimely lot,—
A little talk of better days,
A little hope my own to raise,
For I was sunk in silence—lost　　200
In this last loss, of all the most;
And then the sighs he would suppress
Of fainting nature's feebleness,
More slowly drawn, grew less and less:
I listen'd, but I could not hear;
I call'd, for I was wild with fear;
I knew 'twas hopeless, but my dread
Would not be thus admonished;
I call'd, and thought I heard a sound—
I burst my chain with one strong bound,　　210
And rush'd to him:—I found him not,
I only stirr'd in this black spot,
I only lived, *I* only drew
The accursed breath of dungeon-dew;
The last, the sole, the dearest link
Between me and the eternal brink,
Which bound me to my failing race,
Was broken in this fatal place.
One on the earth, and one beneath—
My brothers—both had ceased to breathe:　　220
I took that hand which lay so still,

Alas! my own was full as chill;
I had not strength to stir, or strive,
But felt that I was still alive—
A frantic feeling, when we know
That what we love shall ne'er be so.
    I know not why
    I could not die,
I had no earthly hope but faith,
And that forbade a selfish death. 230

9

What next befell me then and there
    I know not well—I never knew—
First came the loss of light, and air,
    And then of darkness too:
I had no thought, no feeling—none—
Among the stones I stood a stone,
And was, scarce conscious what I wist,
As shrubless crags within the mist;
For all was blank, and bleak, and grey;
It was not night, it was not day; 240
It was not even the dungeon-light,
So hateful to my heavy sight,
But vacancy absorbing space,
And fixedness without a place;
There were no stars, no earth, no time,
No check, no change, no good, no crime,
But silence, and a stirless breath
Which neither was of life nor death;
A sea of stagnant idleness,
Blind, boundless, mute, and motionless! 250

10

A light broke in upon my brain,—
    It was the carol of a bird;
It ceased, and then it came again,
    The sweetest song ear ever heard,

And mine was thankful till my eyes
Ran over with the glad surprise,
And they that moment could not see
I was the mate of misery;
But then by dull degrees came back
My senses to their wonted track;   260
I saw the dungeon walls and floor
Close slowly round me as before,
I saw the glimmer of the sun
Creeping as it before had done,
But through the crevice where it came
That bird was perch'd, as fond and tame,
    And tamer than upon the tree;
A lovely bird, with azure wings,
And song that said a thousand things,
    And seem'd to say them all for me!   270
I never saw its like before,
I ne'er shall see its likeness more:
It seem'd like me to want a mate,
But was not half so desolate,
And it was come to love me when
None lived to love me so again,
And cheering from my dungeon's brink,
Had brought me back to feel and think.
I know not if it late were free,
    Or broke its cage to perch on mine,   280
But knowing well captivity,
    Sweet bird! I could not wish for thine!
Or if it were, in winged guise,
A visitant from Paradise;
For—Heaven forgive that thought! the while
Which made me both to weep and smile—
I sometimes deem'd that it might be
My brother's soul come down to me;
But then at last away it flew,
And then 'twas mortal well I knew,   290
For he would never thus have flown,

And left me twice so doubly lone,
Lone as the corse within its shroud,
Lone as a solitary cloud,—
   A single cloud on a sunny day,
While all the rest of heaven is clear,
A frown upon the atmosphere,
That hath no business to appear
   When skies are blue, and earth is gay.

11

A kind of change came in my fate,   300
My keepers grew compassionate;
I know not what had made them so,
They were inured to sights of woe,
But so it was:—my broken chain
With links unfasten'd did remain,
And it was liberty to stride
Along my cell from side to side,
And up and down, and then athwart,
And tread it over every part;
And round the pillars one by one,   310
Returning where my walk begun,
Avoiding only, as I trod,
My brothers' graves without a sod;
For if I thought with heedless tread
My step profaned their lowly bed,
My breath came gaspingly and thick,
And my crush'd heart felt blind and sick.

12

I made a footing in the wall,
   It was not therefrom to escape,
For I had buried one and all   320
   Who loved me in a human shape;
And the whole earth would henceforth be
A wider prison unto me:
No child. no sire, no kin had I,

No partner in my misery;
I thought of this, and I was glad,
For thought of them had made me mad;
But I was curious to ascend
To my barr'd windows, and to bend
Once more, upon the mountains high,   330
The quiet of a loving eye.

13

I saw them, and they were the same,
They were not changed like me in frame;
I saw their thousand years of snow
On high—their wide long lake below,
And the blue Rhone in fullest flow;
I heard the torrents leap and gush
O'er channell'd rock and broken bush;
I saw the white-wall'd distant town,
And whiter sails go skimming down;   340
And then there was a little isle,
Which in my very face did smile,
    The only one in view;
A small green isle, it seem'd no more,
Scarce broader than my dungeon floor,
But in it there were three tall trees,
And o'er it blew the mountain breeze,
And by it there were waters flowing,
And on it there were young flowers growing,
    Of gentle breath and hue.   350
The fish swam by the castle wall,
And they seem'd joyous each and all;
The eagle rode the rising blast,
Methought he never flew so fast
As then to me he seem'd to fly;
And then new tears came in my eye,
And I felt troubled—and would fain
I had not left my recent chain;
And when I did descend again,

The darkness of my dim abode 360
Fell on me as a heavy load;
It was as is a new-dug grave,
Closing o'er one we sought to save,—
And yet my glance, too much opprest,
Had almost need of such a rest.

14

It might be months, or years, or days,
   I kept no count, I took no note,
I had no hope my eyes to raise,
   And clear them of their dreary mote;
At last men came to set me free; 370
   I ask'd not why, and reck'd not where;
It was at length the same to me,
Fetter'd or fetterless to be,
   I learn'd to love despair.
And thus when they appear'd at last,
And all my bonds aside were cast,
These heavy walls to me had grown
A hermitage—and all my own!
And half I felt as they were come
To tear me from a second home: 380
With spiders I had friendship made,
And watch'd them in their sullen trade,
Had seen the mice by moonlight play,
And why should I feel less than they?
We were all inmates of one place,
And I, the monarch of each race,
Had power to kill—yet, strange to tell!
In quiet we had learn'd to dwell;
My very chains and I grew friends,
So much a long communion tends 390
To make us what we are:—even I
Regain'd my freedom with a sigh.

CHILDE HAROLD'S PILGRIMAGE

CANTO THE THIRD

Afin que cette application vous forçât de penser à
autre chose; il n'y a en vérité de remède que celui-là
et le temps.—*Lettre du Roi de Prusse à D'Alembert*,
Sept. 7, 1776.

I

Is thy face like thy mother's, my fair child!
Ada! sole daughter of my house and heart?
When last I saw thy young blue eyes they smiled,
And then we parted,—not as now we part,
But with a hope.—
        Awaking with a start,
The waters heave around me; and on high
The winds lift up their voices: I depart,
Whither I know not; but the hour's gone by,
When Albion's lessening shores could grieve or glad mine eye.

2

Once more upon the waters! yet once more!
And the waves bound beneath me as a steed
That knows his rider. Welcome to their roar!
Swift be their guidance, wheresoe'er it lead!
Though the strain'd mast should quiver as a reed,
And the rent canvas fluttering strew the gale,
Still must I on; for I am as a weed,
Flung from the rock, on Ocean's foam to sail
Where'er the surge may sweep, the tempest's breath prevail.

3

In my youth's summer I did sing of One,
The wandering outlaw of his own dark mind;

Again I seize the theme, then but begun,
And bear it with me, as the rushing wind
Bears the cloud onwards: in that Tale I find
The furrows of long thought, and dried-up tears,
Which, ebbing, leave a sterile track behind,
O'er which all heavily the journeying years
Plod the last sands of life,—where not a flower appears.

4

Since my young days of passion—joy, or pain,
Perchance my heart and harp have lost a string,
And both may jar: it may be, that in vain
I would essay as I have sung to sing.
Yet, though a dreary strain, to this I cling;
So that it wean me from the weary dream
Of selfish grief or gladness—so it fling
Forgetfulness around me—it shall seem
To me, though to none else, a not ungrateful theme.

5

He, who grown aged in this world of woe,
In deeds, not years, piercing the depths of life,
So that no wonder waits him; nor below
Can love or sorrow, fame, ambition, strife,
Cut to his heart again with the keen knife
Of silent, sharp endurance: he can tell
Why thought seeks refuge in lone caves, yet rife
With airy images, and shapes which dwell
Still unimpair'd, though old, in the soul's haunted cell.

6

'Tis to create, and in creating live
A being more intense, that we endow
With form our fancy, gaining as we give
The life we image, even as I do now.
What am I? Nothing: but not so art thou,
Soul of my thought! with whom I traverse earth,

Invisible but gazing, as I glow
Mix'd with thy spirit, blended with thy birth,
And feeling still with thee in my crush'd feelings' dearth.

7

Yet must I think less wildly:—I *have* thought
Too long and darkly, till my brain became,
In its own eddy boiling and o'er-wrought,
A whirling gulf of phantasy and flame:
And thus, untaught in youth my heart to tame,
My springs of life were poison'd. 'Tis too late!
Yet am I changed; though still enough the same
In strength to bear what time cannot abate,
And feed on bitter fruits without accusing Fate.

8

Something too much of this:—but now 'tis past,
And the spell closes with its silent seal.
Long absent HAROLD re-appears at last;
He of the breast which fain no more would feel,
Wrung with the wounds which kill not, but ne'er heal,
Yet Time, who changes all, had alter'd him
In soul and aspect as in age: years steal
Fire from the mind as vigour from the limb;
And life's enchanted cup but sparkles near the brim.

9

His had been quaff'd too quickly, and he found
The dregs were wormwood; but he fill'd again,
And from a purer fount, on holier ground,
And deem'd its spring perpetual; but in vain!
Still round him clung invisibly a chain
Which gall'd for ever, fettering though unseen,
And heavy though it clank'd not; worn with pain,
Which pined although it spoke not, and grew keen,
Entering with every step he took through many a scene.

10

Secure in guarded coldness, he had mix'd
Again in fancied safety with his kind,
And deem'd his spirit now so firmly fix'd
And sheath'd with an invulnerable mind,
That, if no joy, no sorrow lurk'd behind;
And he, as one, might 'midst the many stand
Unheeded, searching through the crowd to find
Fit speculation; such as in strange land
He found in wonder-works of God and Nature's hand.

11

But who can view the ripen'd rose, nor seek
To wear it? who can curiously behold
The smoothness and the sheen of beauty's cheek,
Nor feel the heart can never all grow old?
Who can contemplate Fame through clouds unfold
The star which rises o'er her steep, nor climb?
Harold, once more within the vortex, roll'd
On with the giddy circle, chasing Time,
Yet with a nobler aim than in his youth's fond prime.

12

But soon he knew himself the most unfit
Of men to herd with Man; with whom he held
Little in common; untaught to submit
His thoughts to others, though his soul was quell'd
In youth by his own thoughts; still uncompell'd,
He would not yield dominion of his mind
To spirits against whom his own rebell'd;
Proud though in desolation; which could find
A life within itself, to breathe without mankind.

13

Where rose the mountains, there to him were friends;
Where roll'd the ocean, thereon was his home;

Where a blue sky, and glowing clime, extends,
He had the passion and the power to roam;
The desert, forest, cavern, breaker's foam,
Were unto him companionship; they spake
A mutual language, clearer than the tome
Of his land's tongue, which he would oft forsake
For Nature's pages glass'd by sunbeams on the lake.

14

Like the Chaldean, he could watch the stars,
Till he had peopled them with beings bright
As their own beams; and earth, and earthborn jars,
And human frailties, were forgotten quite:
Could he have kept his spirit to that flight
He had been happy; but this clay will sink
Its spark immortal, envying it the light
To which it mounts, as if to break the link
That keeps us from yon heaven which woos us to its brink.

15

But in Man's dwellings he became a thing
Restless and worn, and stern and wearisome,
Droop'd as a wild-born falcon with clipt wing,
To whom the boundless air alone were home:
Then came his fit again, which to o'er-come,
As eagerly the barr'd-up bird will beat
His breast and beak against his wiry dome
Till the blood tinge his plumage, so the heat
Of his impeded soul would through his bosom eat.

16

Self-exiled Harold wanders forth again,
With nought of hope left, but with less of gloom;
The very knowledge that he lived in vain,
That all was over on this side the tomb,
Had made Despair a smilingness assume,
Which, though 'twere wild,—as on the plunder'd wreck

When mariners would madly meet their doom
With draughts intemperate on the sinking deck,—
Did yet inspire a cheer, which he forbore to check.

17

Stop!—for thy tread is on an Empire's dust!
An Earthquake's spoil is sepulchred below!
Is the spot mark'd with no colossal bust?
Nor column trophied for triumphal show?
None; but the moral's truth tells simpler so,
As the ground was before, thus let it be;—
How that red rain hath made the harvest grow!
And is this all the world has gain'd by thee,
Thou first and last of fields! king-making Victory?

18

And Harold stands upon this place of skulls,
The grave of France, the deadly Waterloo!
How in an hour the power which gave annuls
Its gifts, transferring fame as fleeting too!
In "pride of place" here last the eagle flew,
Then tore with bloody talon the rent plain,
Pierced by the shaft of banded nations through;
Ambition's life and labours all were vain;
He wears the shatter'd links of the world's broken chain.

19

Fit retribution! Gaul may champ the bit
And foam in fetters;—but is Earth more free?
Did nations combat to make *One* submit;
Or league to teach all kings true sovereignty?
What! shall reviving Thraldom again be
The patch'd-up idol of enlighten'd days?
Shall we, who struck the Lion down, shall we
Pay the Wolf homage? proffering lowly gaze
And servile knees to thrones? No; *prove* before ye praise!

20

If not, o'er one fallen despot boast no more!
In vain fair cheeks were furrow'd with hot tears
For Europe's flowers long rooted up before
The trampler of her vineyards; in vain years
Of death, depopulation, bondage, fears,
Have all been borne, and broken by the accord
Of roused-up millions; all that most endears
Glory, is when the myrtle wreathes a sword
Such as Harmodius drew on Athens' tyrant lord.

21

There was a sound of revelry by night,
And Belgium's capital had gather'd then
Her Beauty and her Chivalry, and bright
The lamps shone o'er fair women and brave men;
A thousand hearts beat happily; and when
Music arose with its voluptuous swell,
Soft eyes look'd love to eyes which spake again,
And all went merry as a marriage bell;
But hush! hark! a deep sound strikes like a rising knell!

22

Did ye not hear it?—No; 'twas but the wind,
Or the car rattling o'er the stony street;
On with the dance! let joy be unconfined;
No sleep till morn, when Youth and Pleasure meet
To chase the glowing Hours with flying feet—
But hark!—that heavy sound breaks in once more,
As if the clouds its echo would repeat;
And nearer, clearer, deadlier than before!
Arm! Arm! it is—it is—the cannon's opening roar!

23

Within a window'd niche of that high hall
Sate Brunswick's fated chieftain; he did hear

That sound the first amidst the festival,
And caught its tone with Death's prophetic ear;
And when they smiled because he deem'd it near,
His heart more truly knew that peal too well
Which stretch'd his father on a bloody bier,
And roused the vengeance blood alone could quell;
He rush'd into the field, and, foremost fighting, fell.

24

Ah! then and there was hurrying to and fro,
And gathering tears, and tremblings of distress,
And cheeks all pale, which but an hour ago
Blush'd at the praise of their own loveliness;
And there were sudden partings, such as press
The life from out young hearts, and choking sighs
Which ne'er might be repeated; who could guess
If ever more should meet those mutual eyes,
Since upon night so sweet such awful morn could rise!

25

And there was mounting in hot haste: the steed,
The mustering squadron, and the clattering car,
Went pouring forward with impetuous speed,
And swiftly forming in the ranks of war;
And the deep thunder peal on peal afar;
And near, the beat of the alarming drum
Roused up the soldier ere the morning star;
While throng'd the citizens with terror dumb,
Or whispering, with white lips—"The foe! they come! they
        come!"

26

And wild and high the "Cameron's gathering" rose!
The war-note of Lochiel, which Albyn's hills
Have heard, and heard, too, have her Saxon foes:—
How in the noon of night that pibroch thrills,
Savage and shrill! But with the breath which fills

Their mountain-pipe, so fill the mountaineers
With the fierce native daring which instils
The stirring memory of a thousand years,
And Evan's, Donald's fame rings in each clansman's ears!

27

And Ardennes waves above them her green leaves,
Dewy with nature's tear-drops as they pass,
Grieving, if aught inanimate e'er grieves,
Over the unreturning brave,—alas!
Ere evening to be trodden like the grass
Which now beneath them, but above shall grow
In its next verdure, when this fiery mass
Of living valour, rolling on the foe
And burning with high hope shall moulder cold and low.

28

Last noon beheld them full of lusty life,
Last eve in Beauty's circle proudly gay,
The midnight brought the signal-sound of strife,
The morn the marshalling in arms,—the day
Battle's magnificently stern array!
The thunder-clouds close o'er it, which when rent
The earth is cover'd thick with other clay,
Which her own clay shall cover, heap'd and pent,
Rider and horse,—friend, foe,—in one red burial blent!

29

Their praise is hymn'd by loftier harps than mine:
Yet one I would select from that proud throng,
Partly because they blend me with his line,
And partly that I did his sire some wrong,
And partly that bright names will hallow song;
And his was of the bravest, and when shower'd
The death-bolts deadliest the thinn'd files along,
Even where the thickest of war's tempest lower'd,
They reach'd no nobler breast than thine, young gallant Howard!

30

There have been tears and breaking hearts for thee,
And mine were nothing had I such to give;
But when I stood beneath the fresh green tree,
Which living waves where thou didst cease to live,
And saw around me the wide field revive
With fruits and fertile promise, and the Spring
Came forth her work of gladness to contrive,
With all her reckless birds upon the wing,
I turn'd from all she brought to those she could not bring.

31

I turn'd to thee, to thousands, of whom each
And one as all a ghastly gap did make
In his own kind and kindred, whom to teach
Forgetfulness were mercy for their sake;
The Archangel's trump, not Glory's, must awake
Those whom they thirst for; though the sound of Fame
May for a moment soothe, it cannot slake
The fever of vain longing, and the name
So honour'd but assumes a stronger, bitterer claim.

32

They mourn, but smile at length; and, smiling, mourn;
The tree will wither long before it fall;
The hull drives on, though mast and sail be torn;
The roof-tree sinks, but moulders on the hall
In massy hoariness; the ruin'd wall
Stands when its wind-worn battlements are gone;
The bars survive the captive they enthral;
The day drags through, though storms keep out the sun;
And thus the heart will break, yet brokenly live on:

33

Even as a broken mirror, which the glass
In every fragment multiplies; and makes

A thousand images of one that was,
The same, and still the more, the more it breaks;
And thus the heart will do which not forsakes,
Living in shatter'd guise; and still, and cold,
And bloodless, with its sleepless sorrow aches,
Yet withers on till all without is old,
Showing no visible sign, for such things are untold.

34

There is a very life in our despair,
Vitality of poison,—a quick root
Which feeds these deadly branches; for it were
As nothing did we die; but Life will suit
Itself to Sorrow's most detested fruit,
Like to the apples on the Dead Sea's shore,
All ashes to the taste: Did man compute
Existence by enjoyment, and count o'er
Such hours 'gainst years of life,—say, would he name threescore?

35

The Psalmist number'd out the years of man:
They are enough; and if thy tale be *true*,
Thou, who didst grudge him even that fleeting span,
More than enough, thou fatal Waterloo!
Millions of tongues record thee, and anew
Their children's lips shall echo them, and say—
"Here, where the sword united nations drew,
Our countrymen were warring on that day!"
And this is much, and all which will not pass away.

36

There sunk the greatest, nor the worst of men,
Whose spirit, antithetically mixt,
One moment of the mightiest, and again
On little objects with like firmness fixt;
Extreme in all things! hadst thou been betwixt,
Thy throne had still been thine, or never been;

For daring made thy rise as fall: thou seek'st
Even now to re-assume the imperial mien,
And shake again the world, the Thunderer of the scene!

37

Conqueror and captive of the earth art thou!
She trembles at thee still, and thy wild name
Was ne'er more bruited in men's minds than now
That thou art nothing, save the jest of Fame,
Who woo'd thee once, thy vassal, and became
The flatterer of thy fierceness, till thou wert
A god unto thyself; nor less the same
To the astounded kingdoms all inert,
Who deem'd thee for a time whate'er thou didst assert.

38

Oh, more or less than man—in high or low,
Battling with nations, flying from the field;
Now making monarchs' necks thy footstool, now
More than thy meanest soldier taught to yield;
An empire thou couldst crush, command, rebuild,
But govern not thy pettiest passion, nor,
However deeply in men's spirits skill'd,
Look through thine own, nor curb the lust of war,
Nor learn that tempted Fate will leave the loftiest star.

39

Yet well thy soul hath brook'd the turning tide
With that untaught innate philosophy,
Which, be it wisdom, coldness, or deep pride,
Is gall and wormwood to an enemy.
When the whole host of hatred stood hard by,
To watch and mock thee shrinking, thou hast smiled
With a sedate and all-enduring eye;—
When Fortune fled her spoil'd and favourite child,
He stood unbow'd beneath the ills upon him piled.

40

Sager than in thy fortunes; for in them
Ambition steel'd thee on too far to show
That just habitual scorn, which could contemn
Men and their thoughts; 'twas wise to feel, not so
To wear it ever on thy lip and brow,
And spurn the instruments thou wert to use
Till they were turn'd unto thine overthrow;
'Tis but a worthless world to win or lose;
So hath it proved to thee, and all such lot who choose.

41

If, like a tower upon a headland rock,
Thou hadst been made to stand or fall alone,
Such scorn of man had help'd to brave the shock;
But men's thoughts were the steps which paved thy throne,
Their admiration thy best weapon shone;
The part of Philip's son was thine, not then
(Unless aside thy purple had been thrown)
Like stern Diogenes to mock at men;
For sceptred cynics earth were far too wide a den.

42

But quiet to quick bosoms is a hell,
And *there* hath been thy bane; there is a fire
And motion of the soul which will not dwell
In its own narrow being, but aspire
Beyond the fitting medium of desire;
And, but once kindled, quenchless evermore,
Preys upon high adventure, nor can tire
Of aught but rest; a fever at the core,
Fatal to him who bears, to all who ever bore.

43

This makes the madmen who have made men mad
By their contagion; Conquerors and Kings,

Founders of sects and systems, to whom add
Sophists, Bards, Statesmen, all unquiet things
Which stir too strongly the soul's secret springs,
And are themselves the fools to those they fool;
Envied, yet how unenviable! what stings
Are theirs! One breast laid open were a school
Which would unteach mankind the lust to shine or rule:

44

Their breath is agitation, and their life
A storm whereon they ride, to sink at last,
And yet so nursed and bigoted to strife,
That should their days, surviving perils past,
Melt to calm twilight, they feel overcast
With sorrow and supineness, and so die;
Even as a flame unfed, which runs to waste
With its own flickering, or a sword laid by,
Which eats into itself, and rusts ingloriously.

45

He who ascends to mountain-tops, shall find
The loftiest peaks most wrapt in clouds and snow;
He who surpasses or subdues mankind,
Must look down on the hate of those below.
Though high *above* the sun of glory glow,
And far *beneath* the earth and ocean spread,
Round him are icy rocks, and loudly blow
Contending tempests on his naked head,
And thus reward the toils which to those summits led.

46

Away with these! true Wisdom's world will be
Within its own creation, or in thine,
Maternal Nature! for who teems like thee,
Thus on the banks of thy majestic Rhine?
There Harold gazes on a work divine,
A blending of all beauties; streams and dells,

Fruit, foliage, crag, wood, cornfield, mountain, vine,
  And chiefless castles breathing stern farewells
From gray but leafy walls, where Ruin greenly dwells.

47

And there they stand, as stands a lofty mind,
  Worn, but unstooping to the baser crowd,
All tenantless, save to the crannying wind,
  Or holding dark communion with the crowd.
  There was a day when they were young and proud;
Banners on high, and battles pass'd below;
  But they who fought are in a bloody shroud,
  And those which waved are shredless dust ere now,
And the bleak battlements shall bear no future blow.

48

Beneath those battlements, within those walls,
  Power dwelt amidst her passions; in proud state
Each robber chief upheld his armed halls,
  Doing his evil will, nor less elate
  Than mightier heroes of a longer date.
What want these outlaws conquerors should have
  But history's purchased page to call them great?
  A wider space, an ornamented grave?
Their hopes were not less warm, their souls were full as brave.

49

In their baronial feuds and single fields,
  What deeds of prowess unrecorded died!
And Love, which lent a blazon to their shields,
  With emblems well devised by amorous pride,
  Through all the mail of iron hearts would glide;
But still their flame was fierceness, and drew on
  Keen contest and destruction near allied,
  And many a tower for some fair mischief won,
Saw the discolour'd Rhine beneath its ruin run.

50

But Thou, exulting and abounding river!
Making thy waves a blessing as they flow
Through banks whose beauty would endure for ever
Could man but leave thy bright creation so,
Nor its fair promise from the surface mow
With the sharp scythe of conflict,—then to see
Thy valley of sweet waters, were to know
Earth paved like Heaven; and to seem such to me,
Even now what wants thy stream?—that it should Lethe be.

51

A thousand battles have assail'd thy banks,
But these and half their fame have pass'd away,
And Slaughter heap'd on high his weltering ranks;
Their very graves are gone, and what are they?
Thy tide wash'd down the blood of yesterday,
And all was stainless, and on thy clear stream
Glass'd, with its dancing light, the sunny ray;
But o'er the blacken'd memory's blighting dream
Thy waves would vainly roll, all sweeping as they seem.

52

Thus Harold inly said, and pass'd along,
Yet not insensible to all which here
Awoke the jocund birds to early song
In glens which might have made even exile dear:
Though on his brow were graven lines austere,
And tranquil sternness, which had ta'en the place
Of feelings fierier far but less severe,
Joy was not always absent from his face,
But o'er it in such scenes would steal with transient trace.

53

Nor was all love shut from him, though his days
Of passion had consumed themselves to dust.

It is in vain that we would coldly gaze
On such as smile upon us; the heart must
Leap kindly back to kindness, though disgust
Hath wean'd it from all worldlings: thus he felt,
For there was soft remembrance, and sweet trust
In one fond breast, to which his own would melt,
And in its tenderer hour on that his bosom dwelt.

54

And he had learn'd to love,—I know not why,
For this in such as him seems strange of mood,—
The helpless looks of blooming infancy,
Even in its earliest nurture; what subdued,
To change like this, a mind so far imbued
With scorn of man, it little boots to know;
But thus it was; and though in solitude
Small power the nipp'd affections have to grow,
In him this glow'd when all beside had ceased to glow.

55

And there was one soft breast, as hath been said,
Which unto his was bound by stronger ties
Than the church links withal; and, though unwed,
That love was pure, and, far above disguise,
Had stood the test of mortal enmities
Still undivided, and cemented more
By peril, dreaded most in female eyes;
But this was firm, and from a foreign shore
Well to that heart might his these absent greetings pour!

I

The castled crag of Drachenfels
Frowns o'er the wide and winding Rhine,
Whose breast of waters broadly swells
Between the banks which bear the vine,
And hills all rich with blossom'd trees,
And fields which promise corn and wine,

And scatter'd cities crowning these,
Whose far white walls along them shine,
Have strew'd a scene, which I should see
With double joy wert *thou* with me.

II

And peasant girls, with deep blue eyes,
And hands which offer early flowers,
Walk smiling o'er this paradise;
Above, the frequent feudal towers
Through green leaves lift their walls of gray;
And many a rock which steeply lowers,
And noble arch in proud decay,
Look o'er this vale of vintage-bowers;
But one thing want these banks of Rhine,—
Thy gentle hand to clasp in mine!

III

I send the lilies given to me;
Though long before thy hand they touch,
I know that they must wither'd be,
But yet reject them not as such;
For I have cherish'd them as dear,
Because they yet may meet thine eye,
And guide thy soul to mine even here,
When thou behold'st them drooping nigh,
And know'st them gather'd by the Rhine,
And offer'd from my heart to thine!

IV

The river nobly foams and flows,
The charm of this enchanted ground,
And all its thousand turns disclose
Some fresher beauty varying round:
The haughtiest breast its wish might bound
Through life to dwell delighted here;
Nor could on earth a spot be found

To nature and to me so dear,
Could thy dear eyes in following mine
Still sweeten more these banks of Rhine!

56

By Coblenz, on a rise of gentle ground,
There is a small and simple pyramid,
Crowning the summit of the verdant mound;
Beneath its base are heroes' ashes hid,
Our enemy's—but let not that forbid
Honour to Marceau! o'er whose early tomb
Tears, big tears, gush'd from the rough soldier's lid,
Lamenting and yet envying such a doom,
Falling for France, whose rights he battled to resume.

57

Brief, brave, and glorious was his young career,—
His mourners were two hosts, his friends and foes;
And fitly may the stranger lingering here
Pray for his gallant spirit's bright repose;
For he was Freedam's champion, one of those,
The few in number, who had not o'er-stept
The charter to chastise which she bestows
On such as wield her weapons; he had kept
The whiteness of his soul, and thus men o'er him wept.

58

Here Ehrenbreitstein, with her shatter'd wall
Black with the miner's blast, upon her height
Yet shows of what she was, when shell and ball
Rebounding idly on her strength did light:
A tower of victory! from whence the flight
Of baffled foes was watch'd along the plain:
But Peace destroy'd what War could never blight,
And laid those proud roofs bare to Summer's rain—
On which the iron shower for years had pour'd in vain.

59

Adieu to thee, fair Rhine! How long delighted
The stranger fain would linger on his way!
Thine is a scene alike where souls united
Or lonely Contemplation thus might stray:
And could the ceaseless vultures cease to prey
On self-condemning bosoms, it were here,
Where Nature, nor too sombre nor too gay,
Wild but not rude, awful yet not austere,
Is to the mellow Earth as Autumn to the year.

60

Adieu to thee again! a vain adieu!
There can be no farewell to scene like thine;
The mind is colour'd by thy every hue;
And if reluctantly the eyes resign
Their cherish'd gaze upon thee, lovely Rhine!
'Tis with the thankful heart of parting praise;
More mighty spots may rise, more glaring shine,
But none unite in one attaching maze
The brilliant, fair, and soft,—the glories of old days.

61

The negligently grand, the fruitful bloom
Of coming ripeness, the white city's sheen,
The rolling stream, the precipice's gloom,
The forest's growth, and Gothic walls between,
The wild rocks shaped as they had turrets been,
In mockery of man's art; and these withal
A race of faces happy as the scene,
Whose fertile bounties here extend to all,
Still springing o'er thy banks, though Empires near them fall.

62

But these recede. Above me are the Alps,
The palaces of Nature, whose vast walls

Have pinnacled in clouds their snowy scalps,
And throned Eternity in icy halls
Of cold sublimity, where forms and falls
The avalanche—the thunderbolt of snow!
All that expands the spirit, yet appals,
Gather around these summits, as to show
How Earth may pierce to Heaven, yet leave vain man below.

63

But ere these matchless heights I dare to scan,
There is a spot should not be pass'd in vain,—
Morat! the proud, the patriot field! where man
May gaze on ghastly trophies of the slain,
Nor blush for those who conquer'd on that plain;
Here Burgundy bequeath'd his tombless host,
A bony heap, through ages to remain,
Themselves their monument;—the Stygian coast
Unsepulchred they roam'd, and shriek'd each wandering ghost.

64

While Waterloo with Cannae's carnage vies,
Morat and Marathon twin names shall stand;
They were true Glory's stainless victories,
Won by the unambitious heart and hand
Of a proud, brotherly, and civic band,
All unbought champions in no princely cause
Of vice-entail'd Corruption; they no land
Doom'd to bewail the blasphemy of laws
Making kings' rights divine, by some Draconic clause.

65

By a lone wall a lonelier column rears
A gray and grief-worn aspect of old days;
'Tis the last remnant of the wreck of years,
And looks as with the wild-bewilder'd gaze
Of one to stone converted by amaze,
Yet still with consciousness; and there it stands

Making a marvel that it not decays,
When the coeval pride of human hands,
Levell'd Adventicum, hath strew'd her subject lands.

66

And there—oh! sweet and sacred be the name!—
Julia—the daughter, the devoted—gave
Her youth to Heaven; her heart, beneath a claim
Nearest to Heaven's, broke o'er a father's grave.
Justice is sworn 'gainst tears, and hers would crave
The life she lived in; but the judge was just,
And then she died on him she could not save.
Their tomb was simple, and without a bust,
And held within their urn one mind, one heart, one dust.

67

But these are deeds which should not pass away,
And names that must not wither, though the earth
Forgets her empires with a just decay,
The enslavers and the enslaved, their death and birth;
The high, the mountain-majesty of worth
Should be, and shall, survivor of its woe,
And from its immortality look forth
In the sun's face, like yonder Alpine snow,
Imperishably pure beyond all things below.

68

Lake Leman woos me with its crystal face,
The mirror where the stars and mountains view
The stillness of their aspect in each trace
Its clear depth yields of their far height and hue:
There is too much of man here, to look through
With a fit mind the might which I behold;
But soon in me shall Loneliness renew
Thoughts hid, but not less cherish'd than of old,
Ere mingling with the herd had penn'd me in their fold.

69

To fly from, need not be to hate, mankind:
All are not fit with them to stir and toil,
Nor is it discontent to keep the mind
Deep in its fountain, lest it over boil
In the hot throng, where we become the spoil
Of our infection, till too late and long
We may deplore and struggle with the coil,
In wretched interchange of wrong for wrong
Midst a contentious world, striving where none are strong.

70

There, in a moment we may plunge our years
In fatal penitence, and in the blight
Of our own soul turn all our blood to tears,
And colour things to come with hues of Night;
The race of life becomes a hopeless flight
To those that walk in darkness: on the sea
The boldest steer but where their ports invite;
But there are wanderers o'er Eternity
Whose bark drives on and on, and anchor'd ne'er shall be.

71

Is it not better, then, to be alone,
And love Earth only for its earthly sake?
By the blue rushing of the arrowy Rhone,
Or the pure bosom of its nursing lake,
Which feeds it as a mother who doth make
A fair but froward infant her own care,
Kissing its cries away as these awake;—
Is it not better thus our lives to wear,
Than join the crushing crowd, doom'd to inflict or bear?

72

I live not in myself, but I become
Portion of that around me; and to me

High mountains are a feeling, but the hum
Of human cities torture: I can see
Nothing to loathe in nature, save to be
A link reluctant in a fleshly chain,
Class'd among creatures, when the soul can flee,
And with the sky, the peak, the heaving plain
Of ocean, or the stars, mingle, and not in vain.

73

And thus I am absorb'd, and this is life:
I look upon the peopled desert past,
As on a place of agony and strife,
Where, for some sin, to sorrow I was cast,
To act and suffer, but remount at last
With a fresh pinion; which I feel to spring,
Though young, yet waxing vigorous as the blast
Which it would cope with, on delighted wing,
Spurning the clay-cold bonds which round our being cling.

74

And when, at length, the mind shall be all free
From what it hates in this degraded form,
Reft of its carnal life, save what shall be
Existent happier in the fly and worm,—
When elements to elements conform,
And dust is as it should be, shall I not
Feel all I see, less dazzling, but more warm?
The bodiless thought? the Spirit of each spot?
Of which, even now, I share at times the immortal lot?

75

Are not the mountains, waves, and skies, a part
Of me and of my soul, as I of them?
Is not the love of these deep in my heart
With a pure passion? should I not contemn
All objects, if compared with these? and stem
A tide of suffering, rather than forego

Such feelings for the hard and worldly phlegm
Of those whose eyes are only turn'd below,
Gazing upon the ground, with thoughts which dare not glow?

76

But this is not my theme; and I return
To that which is immediate, and require
Those who find contemplation in the urn,
To look on One, whose dust was once all fire,
A native of the land where I respire
The clear air for a while—a passing guest,
Where he became a being,—whose desire
Was to be glorious; 'twas a foolish quest,
The which to gain and keep, he sacrificed all rest.

77

Here the self-torturing sophist, wild Rousseau,
The apostle of affliction, he who threw
Enchantment over passion, and from woe
Wrung overwhelming eloquence, first drew
The breath which made him wretched; yet he knew
How to make madness beautiful, and cast
O'er erring deeds and thoughts a heavenly hue
Of words, like sunbeams, dazzling as they past
The eyes, which o'er them shed tears feelingly and fast.

78

His love was passion's essence:—as a tree
On fire by lightning, with ethereal flame
Kindled he was, and blasted; for to be
Thus, and enamour'd, were in him the same.
But his was not the love of living dame,
Nor of the dead who rise upon our dreams,
But of ideal beauty, which became
In him existence, and o'erflowing teems
Along his burning page, distemper'd though it seems.

79

This breathed itself to life in Julie, *this*
Invested her with all that's wild and sweet;
This hallow'd, too, the memorable kiss
Which every morn his fever'd lip would greet,
From hers, who but with friendship his would meet;
But to that gentle touch through brain and breast
Flash'd the thrill'd spirit's love-devouring heat;
In that absorbing sigh perchance more blest
Than vulgar minds may be with all they seek possest.

80

His life was one long war with self-sought foes,
Or friends by him self-banish'd; for his mind
Had grown Suspicion's sanctuary, and chose,
For its own cruel sacrifice, the kind,
'Gainst whom he raged with fury strange and blind.
But he was phrensied,—wherefore, who may know?
Since cause might be which skill could never find;
But he was phrensied by disease or woe,
To that worst pitch of all, which wears a reasoning show.

81

For then he was inspired, and from him came,
As from the Pythian's mystic cave of yore,
Those oracles which set the world in flame,
Nor ceased to burn till kingdoms were no more:
Did he not this for France? which lay before
Bow'd to the inborn tyranny of years?
Broken and trembling to the yoke she bore,
Till by the voice of him and his compeers
Roused up to too much wrath, which follows o'ergrown fears?

82

They made themselves a fearful monument!
The wreck of old opinions—things which grew,

Breathed from the birth of time: the veil they rent,
And what behind it lay, all earth shall view.
But good with ill they also overthrew,
Leaving but ruins, wherewith to rebuild
Upon the same foundation, and renew
Dungeons and thrones, which the same hour refill'd
As heretofore, because ambition was self-will'd.

83

But this will not endure, nor be endured!
Mankind have felt their strength, and made it felt.
They might have used it better, but, allured
By their new vigour, sternly have they dealt
On one another; pity ceased to melt
With her once natural charities. But they,
Who in oppression's darkness caved had dwelt,
They were not eagles, nourish'd with the day;
What marvel then, at times, if they mistook their prey?

84

What deep wounds ever closed without a scar?
The heart's bleed longest, and but heal to wear
That which disfigures it; and they who war
With their own hopes, and have been vanquish'd, bear
Silence, but not submission: in his lair
Fix'd Passion holds his breath, until the hour
Which shall atone for years; none need despair:
It came, it cometh, and will come,—the power
To punish or forgive—in *one* we shall be slower.

85

Clear, placid Leman! thy contrasted lake,
With the wild world I dwelt in, is a thing
Which warns me, with its stillness, to forsake
Earth's troubled waters for a purer spring.
This quiet sail is as a noiseless wing
To waft me from distraction; once I loved

Torn ocean's roar, but thy soft murmuring
Sounds sweet as if a Sister's voice reproved,
That I with stern delights should e'er have been so moved.

86

It is the hush of night, and all between
Thy margin and the mountains, dusk, yet clear,
Mellow'd and mingling, yet distinctly seen,
Save darken'd Jura, whose capt heights appear
Precipitously steep; and drawing near,
There breathes a living fragrance from the shore,
Of flowers yet fresh with childhood; on the ear
Drops the light drip of the suspended oar,
Or chirps the grasshopper one good-night carol more;

87

He is an evening reveller, who makes
His life an infancy, and sings his fill;
At intervals, some bird from out the brakes
Starts into voice a moment, then is still.
There seems a floating whisper on the hill,
But that is fancy, for the starlight dews
All silently their tears of love instil,
Weeping themselves away, till they infuse
Deep into nature's breast the spirit of her hues.

88

Ye stars! which are the poetry of heaven!
If in your bright leaves we would read the fate
Of men and empires,—'tis to be forgiven,
That in our aspirations to be great,
Our destinies o'erleap their mortal state,
And claim a kindred with you; for ye are
A beauty and a mystery, and create
In us such love and reverence from afar,
That fortune, fame, power, life, have named themselves a star.

89

All heaven and earth are still—though not in sleep,
But breathless, as we grow when feeling most;
And silent, as we stand in thoughts too deep:—
All heaven and earth are still: From the high host
Of stars, to the lull'd lake and mountain-coast,
All is concenter'd in a life intense,
Where not a beam, nor air, nor leaf is lost,
But hath a part of being, and a sense
Of that which is of all Creator and defence.

90

Then stirs the feeling infinite, so felt
In solitude, where we are *least* alone;
A truth, which through our being then doth melt,
And purifies from self: it is a tone,
The soul and source of music, which makes known
Eternal harmony, and sheds a charm
Like to the fabled Cytherea's zone,
Binding all things with beauty;—'twould disarm
The spectre Death, had he substantial power to harm.

91

Not vainly did the early Persian make
His altar the high places, and the peak
Of earth-o'ergazing mountains, and thus take
A fit and unwall'd temple, there to seek
The Spirit, in whose honour shrines are weak,
Uprear'd of human hands. Come, and compare
Columns and idol-dwellings, Goth or Greek,
With Nature's realms of worship, earth and air,
Nor fix on fond abodes to circumscribe thy pray'r!

92

The sky is changed!—and such a change! Oh night,
And storm, and darkness, ye are wondrous strong,

Yet lovely in your strength, as is the light
Of a dark eye in woman! Far along,
From peak to peak, the rattling crags among
Leaps the live thunder! Not from one lone cloud,
But every mountain now hath found a tongue,
And Jura answers, through her misty shroud,
Back to the joyous Alps, who call to her aloud!

93

And this is in the night:—Most glorious night!
Thou wert not sent for slumber! let me be
A sharer in thy fierce and far delight,—
A portion of the tempest and of thee!
How the lit lake shines, a phosphoric sea,
And the big rain comes dancing to the earth!
And now again 'tis black,—and now, the glee
Of the loud hills shakes with its mountain-mirth,
As if they did rejoice o'er a young earthquake's birth.

94

Now, where the swift Rhone cleaves his way between
Heights which appear as lovers who have parted
In hate, whose mining depths so intervene,
That they can meet no more, though broken-hearted;
Though in their souls, which thus each other thwarted,
Love was the very root of the fond rage
Which blighted their life's bloom, and then departed:
Itself expired, but leaving them an age
Of years all winters,—war within themselves to wage.

95

Now, where the quick Rhone thus hath cleft his way,
The mightiest of the storms hath ta'en his stand:
For here, not one, but many, make their play,
And fling their thunder-bolts from hand to hand,
Flashing and cast around; of all the band,
The brightest through these parted hills hath fork'd

His lightnings,—as if he did understand,
That in such gaps as desolation work'd,
There the hot shaft should blast whatever therein lurk'd.

96

Sky, mountains, river, winds, lake, lightnings! ye!
With night, and clouds, and thunder, and a soul
To make these felt and feeling, well may be
Things that have made me watchful; the far roll
Of your departing voices, is the knoll
Of what in me is sleepless,—if I rest.
But where of ye, O tempests! is the goal?
Are ye like those within the human breast?
Or do ye find, at length, like eagles, some high nest?

97

Could I embody and unbosom now
That which is most within me,—could I wreak
My thoughts upon expression, and thus throw
Soul, heart, mind, passions, feelings, strong or weak,
All that I would have sought, and all I seek,
Bear, know, feel, and yet breathe—into *one* word,
And that one word were Lightning, I would speak;
But as it is, I live and die unheard,
With a most voiceless thought, sheathing it as a sword.

98

The morn is up again, the dewy morn,
With breath all incense, and with cheek all bloom,
Laughing the clouds away with playful scorn,
And living as if earth contain'd no tomb,—
And glowing into day: we may resume
The march of our existence: and thus I,
Still on thy shores, fair Leman! may find room
And food for meditation, nor pass by
Much, that may give us pause, if ponder'd fittingly.

99

Clarens! sweet Clarens, birthplace of deep Love!
Thine air is the young breath of passionate thought;
Thy trees take root in Love; the snows above
The very Glaciers have his colours caught,
And sun-set into rose-hues sees them wrought
By rays which sleep there lovingly: the rocks,
The permanent crags, tell here of Love, who sought
In them a refuge from the worldly shocks,
Which stir and sting the soul with hope that woos, then mocks.

100

Clarens! by heavenly feet thy paths are trod,—
Undying Love's, who here ascends a throne
To which the steps are mountains; where the god
Is a pervading life and light,—so shown
Not on those summits solely, nor alone
In the still cave and forest; o'er the flower
His eye is sparkling, and his breath hath blown,
His soft and summer breath, whose tender power
Passes the strength of storms in their most desolate hour.

101

All things are here of *him;* from the black pines,
Which are his shade on high, and the loud roar
Of torrents, where he listeneth, to the vines
Which slope his green path downward to the shore,
Where the bow'd waters meet him, and adore,
Kissing his feet with murmurs; and the wood,
The covert of old trees, with trunks all hoar,
But light leaves, young as joy, stands where it stood,
Offering to him, and his, a populous solitude.

102

A populous solitude of bees and birds,
And fairy-form'd and many-colour'd things,

Who worship him with notes more sweet than words,
And innocently open their glad wings,
Fearless and full of life: the gush of springs,
And fall of lofty fountains, and the bend
Of stirring branches, and the bud which brings
The swiftest thought of beauty, here extend,
Mingling, and made by Love, unto one mighty end.

103

He who hath loved not, here would learn that lore,
And make his heart a spirit; he who knows
That tender mystery, will love the more;
For this is Love's recess, where vain men's woes,
And the world's waste, have driven him far from those,
For 'tis his nature to advance or die;
He stands not still, but or decays, or grows
Into a boundless blessing, which may vie
With the immortal lights, in its eternity!

104

'Twas not for fiction chose Rousseau this spot,
Peopling it with affections; but he found
It was the scene which Passion must allot
To the Mind's purified beings; 'twas the ground
Where early Love his Psyche's zone unbound,
And hallow'd it with loveliness: 'tis lone,
And wonderful, and deep, and hath a sound,
And sense, and sight of sweetness; here the Rhone
Hath spread himself a couch, the Alps have rear'd a throne.

105

Lausanne! and Ferney! ye have been the abodes
Of names which unto you bequeath'd a name;
Mortals, who sought and found, by dangerous roads,
A path to perpetuity of fame:
They were gigantic minds, and their steep aim
Was, Titan-like, on daring doubts to pile

Thoughts which should call down thunder, and the flame
 Of Heaven again assail'd, if Heaven the while
On man and man's research could deign do more than smile.

106

The one was fire and fickleness, a child
 Most mutable in wishes, but in mind
A wit as various,—gay, grave, sage, or wild,—
 Historian, bard, philosopher, combined;
 He multiplied himself among mankind,
The Proteus of their talents: But his own
 Breathed most in ridicule,—which, as the wind,
 Blew where it listed, laying all things prone,—
Now to o'erthrow a fool, and now to shake a throne.

107

The other, deep and slow, exhausting thought,
 And hiving wisdom with each studious year,
In meditation dwelt, with learning wrought,
 And shaped his weapon with an edge severe,
 Sapping a solemn creed with solemn sneer;
The lord of irony,—that master-spell,
 Which stung his foes to wrath, which grew from fear,
 And doom'd him to the zealot's ready Hell,
Which answers to all doubts so eloquently well.

108

Yet, peace be with their ashes,—for by them,
 If merited, the penalty is paid;
It is not ours to judge,—far less condemn;
 The hour must come when such things shall be made
 Known unto all, or hope and dread allay'd
By slumber, on one pillow, in the dust,
 Which, thus much we are sure, must lie decay'd;
 And when it shall revive, as is our trust,
'Twill be to be forgiven, or suffer what is just.

109

But let me quit man's works, again to read
His Maker's, spread around me, and suspend
This page, which from my reveries I feed,
Until it seems prolonging without end.
The clouds above me to the white Alps tend,
And I must pierce them, and survey whate'er
May be permitted, as my steps I bend
To their most great and growing region, where
The earth to her embrace compels the powers of air.

110

Italia! too, Italia! looking on thee,
Full flashes on the soul the light of ages,
Since the fierce Carthaginian almost won thee,
To the last halo of the chiefs and sages
Who glorify thy consecrated pages;
Thou wert the throne and grave of empires; still,
The fount at which the panting mind assuages
Her thirst of knowledge, quaffing there her fill,
Flows from the eternal source of Rome's imperial hill.

111

Thus far have I proceeded in a theme
Renew'd with no kind auspices:—to feel
We are not what we have been, and to deem
We are not what we should be, and to steel
The heart against itself; and to conceal,
With a proud caution, love, or hate, or aught,—
Passion or feeling, purpose, grief or zeal,—
Which is the tyrant spirit of our thought,
Is a stern task of soul:—No matter,—it is taught.

112

And for these words, thus woven into song,
It may be that they are a harmless wile,—

The colouring of the scenes which fleet along,
Which I would seize, in passing, to beguile
My breast, or that of others, for a while.
Fame is the thirst of youth, but I am not
So young as to regard men's frown or smile,
As loss or guerdon of a glorious lot;
I stood and stand alone,—remember'd or forgot.

113

I have not loved the world, nor the world me;
I have not flatter'd its rank breath, nor bow'd
To its idolatries a patient knee,
Nor coin'd my cheek to smiles, nor cried aloud
In worship of an echo; in the crowd
They could not deem me one of such; I stood
Among them, but not of them; in a shroud
Of thoughts which were not their thoughts, and still could,
Had I not filed my mind, which thus itself subdued.

114

I have not loved the world, nor the world me,—
But let us part fair foes; I do believe,
Though I have found them not, that there may be
Words which are things, hopes which will not deceive,
And virtues which are merciful, nor weave
Snares for the failing; I would also deem
O'er others' griefs that some sincerely grieve;
That two, or one, are almost what they seem,
That goodness is no name, and happiness no dream.

115

My daughter! with thy name this song begun;
My daughter! with thy name thus much shall end;
I see thee not, I hear thee not, but none
Can be so wrapt in thee; thou art the friend
To whom the shadows of far years extend:
Albeit my brow thou never shouldst behold,

My voice shall with thy future visions blend,
    And reach into thy heart, when mine is cold,
A token and a tone, even from thy father's mould.

116

To aid thy mind's development, to watch
    Thy dawn of little joys, to sit and see
    Almost thy very growth, to view thee catch
    Knowledge of objects,—wonders yet to thee!
    To hold thee lightly on a gentle knee,
    And print on thy soft cheek a parent's kiss,—
    This, it should seem, was not reserved for me;
    Yet this was in my nature: as it is,
I know not what is there, yet something like to this.

117

Yet, though dull Hate as duty should be taught,
    I know that thou wilt love me; though my name
    Should be shut from thee, as a spell still fraught
    With desolation, and a broken claim:
    Though the grave closed between us,—'twere the same,
    I know that thou wilt love me; though to drain
    My blood from out thy being were an aim,
    And an attainment,—all would be in vain,—
Still thou wouldst love me, still that more than life retain.

118

The child of love, though born in bitterness,
    And nurtured in convulsion,—of thy sire
    These were the elements, and thine no less.
    As yet such are around thee, but thy fire
    Shall be more temper'd, and thy hope far higher.
    Sweet be thy cradled slumbers! O'er the sea
    And from the mountains where I now respire,
    Fain would I waft such blessing upon thee,
As, with a sigh, I deem thou might'st have been to me.

CANTO THE FOURTH

1

I stood in Venice, on the Bridge of Sighs;
A palace and a prison on each hand:
I saw from out the wave her structures rise
As from the stroke of the enchanter's wand:
A thousand years their cloudy wings expand
Around me, and a dying Glory smiles
O'er the far times, when many a subject land
Look'd to the winged Lion's marble piles,
Where Venice sate in state, throned on her hundred isles!

2

She looks a sea Cybele, fresh from ocean,
Rising with her tiara of proud towers
At airy distance, with majestic motion,
A ruler of the waters and their powers:
And such she was;—her daughters had their dowers
From spoils of nations, and the exhaustless East
Pour'd in her lap all gems in sparkling showers.
In purple was she robed, and of her feast
Monarchs partook, and deem'd their dignity increased.

3

In Venice Tasso's echoes are no more,
And silent rows the songless gondolier;
Her palaces are crumbling to the shore,
And music meets not always now the ear:
Those days are gone—but Beauty still is here.
States fall, arts fade—but Nature doth not die,
Nor yet forget how Venice once was dear,
The pleasant place of all festivity,
The revel of the earth, the masque of Italy!

4

But unto us she hath a spell beyond
Her name in story, and her long array
Of mighty shadows, whose dim forms despond
Above the dogeless city's vanish'd sway;
Ours is a trophy which will not decay
With the Rialto; Shylock and the Moor,
And Pierre, cannot be swept or worn away—
The keystones of the arch! though all were o'er,
For us repeopled were the solitary shore.

5

The beings of the mind are not of clay;
Essentially immortal, they create
And multiply in us a brighter ray
And more beloved existence: that which Fate
Prohibits to dull life, in this our state
Of mortal bondage, by these spirits supplied,
First exiles, then replaces what we hate;
Watering the heart whose early flowers have died,
And with a fresher growth replenishing the void.

6

Such is the refuge of our youth and age,
The first from Hope, the last from Vacancy;
And this worn feeling peoples many a page,
And, may be, that which grows beneath mine eye:
Yet there are things whose strong reality
Outshines our fairy-land; in shape and hues
More beautiful than our fantastic sky,
And the strange constellations which the Muse
O'er her wild universe is skilful to diffuse:

7

I saw or dream'd of such,—but let them go,—
They came like truth, and disappear'd like dreams;
And whatsoe'er they were—are now but so:

I could replace them if I would; still teems
My mind with many a form which aptly seems
Such as I sought for, and at moments found;
Let these too go—for waking Reason deems
Such overweening phantasies unsound,
And other voices speak, and other sights surround.

8

I've taught me other tongues, and in strange eyes
Have made me not a stranger; to the mind
Which is itself, no changes bring surprise;
Nor is it harsh to make, nor hard to find
A country with—ay, or without mankind;
Yet was I born where men are proud to be,—
Not without cause; and should I leave behind
The inviolate island of the sage and free,
And seek me out a home by a remoter sea,

9

Perhaps I loved it well: and should I lay
My ashes in a soil which is not mine,
My spirit shall resume it—if we may
Unbodied choose a sanctuary. I twine
My hopes of being remember'd in my line
With my land's language: if too fond and far
These aspirations in their scope incline,—
If my fame should be, as my fortunes are,
Of hasty growth and blight, and dull Oblivion bar

10

My name from out the temple where the dead
Are honour'd by the nations—let it be—
And light the laurels on a loftier head!
And be the Spartan's epitaph on me—
"Sparta hath many a worthier son than he."
Meantime I seek no sympathies, nor need;
The thorns which I have reap'd are of the tree

I planted: they have torn me, and I bleed:
I should have known what fruit would spring from
      such a seed.

. . . . .

18

I loved her from my boyhood; she to me
Was as a fairy city of the heart,
Rising like water-columns from the sea,
Of joy the sojourn, and of wealth the mart;
And Otway, Radcliffe, Schiller, Shakspeare's art,
Had stamp'd her image in me, and even so,
Although I found her thus, we did not part;
Perchance even dearer in her day of woe,
Than when she was a boast, a marvel, and a show.

19

I can repeople with the past—and of
The present there is still for eye and thought,
And meditation chasten'd down, enough;
And more, it may be, than I hoped or sought;
And of the happiest moments which were wrought
Within the web of my existence, some
From thee, fair Venice! have their colours caught:
There are some feelings Time cannot benumb,
Nor Torture shake, or mine would now be cold and dumb.

20

But from their nature will the Tannen grow
Loftiest on loftiest and least shelter'd rocks,
Rooted in barrenness, where nought below
Of soil supports them 'gainst the Alpine shocks
Of eddying storms; yet springs the trunk, and mocks
The howling tempest, till its height and frame
Are worthy of the mountains from whose blocks
Of bleak, gray granite into life it came,
And grew a giant tree;—the mind may grow the same.

21

Existence may be borne, and the deep root
Of life and sufferance make its firm abode
The bare and desolated bosoms: mute
The camel labours with the heaviest load,
And the wolf dies in silence,—not bestow'd
In vain should such example be; if they,
Things of ignoble or of savage mood,
Endure and shrink not, we of nobler clay
May temper it to bear,—it is but for a day.

22

All suffering doth destroy, or is destroy'd,
Even by the sufferer; and, in each event,
Ends:—Some, with hope replenish'd and rebuoy'd,
Return to whence they came—with like intent,
And weave their web again; some, bow'd and bent,
Wax gray and ghastly, withering ere their time,
And perish with the reed on which they leant;
Some seek devotion, toil, war, good or crime,
According as their souls were form'd to sink or climb.

23

But ever and anon of griefs subdued
There comes a token like a scorpion's sting,
Scarce seen, but with fresh bitterness imbued;
And slight withal may be the things which bring
Back on the heart the weight which it would fling
Aside for ever: it may be a sound—
A tone of music—summer's eve—or spring—
A flower—the wind—the ocean—which shall wound,
Striking the electric chain wherewith we are darkly bound;

24

And how and why we know not, nor can trace
Home to its cloud this lightning of the mind,

But feel the shock renew'd, nor can efface
The blight and blackening which it leaves behind,
Which out of things familiar, undesign'd,
When least we deem of such, calls up to view
The spectres whom no exorcism can bind,—
The cold, the changed, perchance the dead—anew,
The mourn'd, the loved, the lost—too many! yet how few!

25

But my soul wanders; I demand it back
To meditate amongst decay, and stand
A ruin amidst ruins; there to track
Fall'n states and buried greatness, o'er a land
Which *was* the mightiest in its old command,
And *is* the loveliest, and must ever be
The master-mould of Nature's heavenly hand;
Wherein were cast the heroic and the free,
The beautiful, the brave, the lords of earth and sea,

26

The commonwealth of kings, the men of Rome!
And even since, and now, fair Italy!
Thou art the garden of the world, the home
Of all Art yields, and Nature can decree;
Even in thy desert, what is like to thee?
Thy very weeds are beautiful, thy waste
More rich than other climes' fertility;
Thy wreck a glory, and thy ruin graced
With an immaculate charm which cannot be defaced.

27

The moon is up, and yet it is not night;
Sunset divides the sky with her; a sea
Of glory streams along the Alpine height
Of blue Friuli's mountains; Heaven is free
From clouds, but of all colours seems to be,—
Melted to one vast Iris of the West,—

Where the Day joins the past Eternity,
  While, on the other hand, meek Dian's crest
Floats through the azure air—an island of the blest!

28

A single star is at her side, and reigns
  With her o'er half the lovely heaven; but still
Yon sunny sea heaves brightly, and remains
  Roll'd o'er the peak of the far Rhaetian hill,
  As Day and Night contending were, until
Nature reclaim'd her order:—gently flows
  The deep-dyed Brenta, where their hues instil
  The odorous purple of a new-born rose,
Which streams upon her stream, and glass'd within it glows,

29

Fill'd with the face of heaven, which, from afar,
  Comes down upon the waters; all its hues,
From the rich sunset to the rising star,
  Their magical variety diffuse:
  And now they change; a paler shadow strews
Its mantle o'er the mountains; parting day
  Dies like the dolphin, whom each pang imbues
  With a new colour as it gasps away—
The last still loveliest,—till—'tis gone—and all is gray.

.   .   .   .   .

78

Oh Rome! my country! city of the soul!
  The orphans of the heart must turn to thee,
Lone mother of dead empires! and control
  In their shut breasts their petty misery.
What are our woes and sufferance? Come and see
  The cypress, hear the owl, and plod your way
O'er steps of broken thrones and temples, Ye!
  Whose agonies are evils of a day—
A world is at our feet as fragile as our clay.

79

The Niobe of nations! there she stands,
  Childless and crownless, in her voiceless woe;
An empty urn within her wither'd hands,
  Whose holy dust was scatter'd long ago;
  The Scipios' tomb contains no ashes now;
  The very sepulchres lie tenantless
Of their heroic dwellers: dost thou flow,
  Old Tiber! through a marble wilderness?
Rise, with thy yellow waves, and mantle her distress.

80

The Goth, the Christian, Time, War, Flood, and Fire,
  Have dealt upon the seven-hill'd city's pride;
She saw her glories star by star expire,
  And up the steep barbarian monarchs ride,
  Where the car climb'd the Capitol; far and wide
  Temple and tower went down, nor left a site:
Chaos of ruins! who shall trace the void,
  O'er the dim fragments cast a lunar light,
And say, "here was, or is," where all is doubly night?

81

The double night of ages, and of her,
  Night's daughter, Ignorance, hath wrapt and wrap
All round us: we but feel our way to err:
  The ocean hath its chart, the stars their map,
  And Knowledge spreads them on her ample lap;
  But Rome is as the desert, where we steer
Stumbling o'er recollections; now we clap
  Our hands, and cry "Eureka!" it is clear—
When but some false mirage of ruin rises near.

82

Alas! the lofty city! and alas!
  The trebly hundred triumphs! and the day

When Brutus made the dagger's edge surpass
The conqueror's sword in bearing fame away!
Alas, for Tully's voice, and Virgil's lay,
And Livy's pictured page!—but these shall be
Her resurrection; all beside—decay.
Alas, for Earth, for never shall we see
That brightness in her eye she bore when Rome was free!

. . . . .

93

What from this barren being do we reap?
Our senses narrow, and our reason frail,
Life short, and truth a gem which loves the deep,
And all things weigh'd in custom's falsest scale;
Opinion an omnipotence,—whose veil
Mantles the earth with darkness, until right
And wrong are accidents, and men grow pale
Lest their own judgments should become too bright,
And their free thoughts be crimes, and earth have too much light.

94

And thus they plod in sluggish misery,
Rotting from sire to son, and age to age,
Proud of their trampled nature, and so die,
Bequeathing their hereditary rage
To the new race of inborn slaves, who wage
War for their chains, and rather than be free,
Bleed gladiator-like, and still engage
Within the same arena where they see
Their fellows fall before, like leaves of the same tree.

95

I speak not of men's creeds—they rest between
Man and his Maker—but of things allow'd,
Averr'd, and known, and daily, hourly seen—
The yoke that is upon us doubly bow'd,
And the intent of tyranny avow'd,

The edict of Earth's rulers, who are grown
The apes of him who humbled once the proud,
And shook them from their slumbers on the throne:
Too glorious, were this all his mighty arm had done.

96

Can tyrants but by tyrants conquer'd be,
And Freedom find no champion and no child
Such as Columbia saw arise when she
Sprung forth a Pallas, arm'd and undefiled?
Or must such minds be nourish'd in the wild,
Deep in the unpruned forest, 'midst the roar
Of cataracts, where nursing Nature smiled
On infant Washington? Has Earth no more
Such seeds within her breast, or Europe no such shore?

97

But France got drunk with blood to vomit crime,
And fatal have her Saturnalia been
To Freedom's cause, in every age and clime;
Because the deadly days which we have seen,
And vile Ambition, that built up between
Man and his hopes an adamantine wall,
And the base pageant last upon the scene,
Are grown the pretext for the eternal thrall
Which nips life's tree, and dooms man's worst—his second fall.

98

Yet, Freedom! yet thy banner, torn, but flying,
Streams like the thunder-storm *against* the wind;
Thy trumpet voice, though broken now and dying,
The loudest still the tempest leaves behind;
Thy tree hath lost its blossoms, and the rind,
Chopp'd by the axe, looks rough and little worth,
But the sap lasts,—and still the seed we find

Sown deep, even in the bosom of the North;
So shall a better spring less bitter fruit bring forth.

. . . .

107

Cypress and ivy, weed and wallflower grown,
Matted and mass'd together, hillocks heap'd
On what were chambers, arch crush'd, column strown
In fragments, choked up vaults, and frescos steep'd
In subterranean damps, where the owl peep'd,
Deeming it midnight:—Temples, baths, or halls?
Pronounce who can; for all that Learning reap'd
From her research hath been, that these are walls—
Behold the Imperial Mount! 'tis thus the mighty falls.

108

There is the moral of all human tales;
'Tis but the same rehearsal of the past,
First Freedom, and then Glory—when that fails,
Wealth, vice, corruption,—barbarism at last.
And History, with all her volumes vast,
Hath but *one* page,—'tis better written here
Where gorgeous Tyranny hath thus amass'd
All treasures, all delights, that eye or ear,
Heart, soul, could seek, tongue ask—Away with words! draw
    near,

109

Admire, exult, despise, laugh, weep,—for here
There is such matter for all feeling:—Man!
Thou pendulum betwixt a smile and tear,
Ages and realms are crowded in this span,
This mountain, whose obliterated plan
The pyramid of empires pinnacled,
Of Glory's gewgaws shining in the van

Till the sun's rays with added flame were fill'd!
Where are its golden roofs? where those who dared to build?

. . . . .

120

Alas! our young affections run to waste,
Or water but the desert; whence arise
But weeds of dark luxuriance, tares of haste,
Rank at the core, though tempting to the eyes,
Flowers whose wild odours breathe but agonies,
And trees whose gums are poisons; such the plants
Which spring beneath her steps as Passion flies
O'er the world's wilderness, and vainly pants
For some celestial fruit forbidden to our wants.

121

Oh, Love! no habitant of earth thou art—
An unseen seraph, we believe in thee,—
A faith whose martyrs are the broken heart,—
But never yet hath seen, nor e'er shall see
The naked eye, thy form, as it should be;
The mind hath made thee, as it peopled heaven,
Even with its own desiring phantasy,
And to a thought such shape and image given,
As haunts the unquench'd soul—parch'd, wearied, wrung, and
    riven.

122

Of its own beauty is the mind diseased,
And fevers into false creation:—where,
Where are the forms the sculptor's soul hath seiz'd?
In him alone. Can Nature show so fair?
Where are the charms and virtues which we dare
Conceive in boyhood and pursue as men,
The unreach'd Paradise of our despair,
Which o'er-informs the pencil and the pen,
And overpowers the page where it would bloom again?

123

Who loves, raves—'tis youth's frenzy—but the cure
Is bitterer still, as charm by charm unwinds
Which robed our idols, and we see too sure
Nor worth nor beauty dwells from out the mind's
Ideal shape of such; yet still it binds
The fatal spell, and still it draws us on,
Reaping the whirlwind from the oft-sown winds;
The stubborn heart, its alchemy begun,
Seems ever near the prize—wealthiest when most undone.

124

We wither from our youth, we gasp away—
Sick—sick; unfound the boon, unslaked the thirst,
Though to the last, in verge of our decay,
Some phantom lures, such as we sought at first—
But all too late,—so are we doubly curst.
Love, fame, ambition, avarice—'tis the same,
Each idle, and all ill, and none the worst—
For all are meteors with a different name,
And Death the sable smoke where vanishes the flame.

125

Few—none—find what they love or could have loved,
Though accident, blind contact, and the strong
Necessity of loving, have removed
Antipathies—but to recur, ere long,
Envenom'd with irrevocable wrong;
And Circumstance, that unspiritual god
And miscreator, makes and helps along
Our coming evils with a crutch-like rod,
Whose touch turns Hope to dust,—the dust we all have trod.

126

Our life is a false nature: 'tis not in
The harmony of things,—this hard decree,

This uneradicable taint of sin,
This boundless upas, this all-blasting tree,
Whose root is earth, whose leaves and branches be
The skies which rain their plagues on men like dew—
Disease, death, bondage—all the woes we see,
And worse, the woes we see not—which throb through
The immedicable soul, with heart-aches ever new.

127

Yet let us ponder boldly—'tis a base
Abandonment of reason to resign
Our right of thought—our last and only place
Of refuge; this, at least, shall still be mine:
Though from our birth the faculty divine
Is chain'd and tortured—cabin'd, cribb'd, confined,
And bred in darkness, lest the truth should shine
Too brightly on the unprepared mind,
The beam pours in, for time and skill will couch the blind.

128

Arches on arches! as it were that Rome,
Collecting the chief trophies of her line,
Would build up all her triumphs in one dome,
Her Coliseum stands; the moonbeams shine
As 'twere its natural torches, for divine
Should be the light which streams here to illume
This long-explored but still exhaustless mine
Of contemplation; and the azure gloom
Of an Italian night, where the deep skies assume

129

Hues which have words, and speak to ye of heaven,
Floats o'er this vast and wondrous monument,
And shadows forth its glory. There is given
Unto the things of earth, which Time hath bent,
A spirit's feeling, and where he hath leant
His hand, but broke his scythe, there is a power

And magic in the ruin'd battlement,
For which the palace of the present hour
Must yield its pomp, and wait till ages are its dower.

130

Oh Time! the beautifier of the dead,
Adorner of the ruin, comforter
And only healer when the heart hath bled;
Time! the corrector where our judgments err,
The test of truth, love—sole philosopher,
For all beside are sophists—from thy thrift,
Which never loses though it doth defer—
Time, the avenger! unto thee I lift
My hands, and eyes, and heart, and crave of thee a gift:

131

Amidst this wreck, where thou hast made a shrine
And temple more divinely desolate,
Among thy mightier offerings here are mine,
Ruins of years, though few, yet full of fate:
If thou hast ever seen me too elate,
Hear me not; but if calmly I have borne
Good, and reserved my pride against the hate
Which shall not whelm me, let me not have worn
This iron in my soul in vain—shall *they* not mourn?

132

And thou, who never yet of human wrong
Left the unbalanced scale, great Nemesis!
Here, where the ancient paid thee homage long—
Thou who didst call the Furies from the abyss,
And round Orestes bade them howl and hiss
For that unnatural retribution—just,
Had it but been from hands less near—in this
Thy former realm, I call thee from the dust!
Dost thou not hear my heart?—Awake! thou shalt, and must.

133

It is not that I may not have incurr'd
For my ancestral faults or mine the wound
I bleed withal, and, had it been conferr'd
With a just weapon, it had flow'd unbound;
But now my blood shall not sink in the ground;
To thee I do devote it—*thou* shalt take
The vengeance, which shall yet be sought and found,
Which if *I* have not taken for the sake—
But let that pass—I sleep, but thou shalt yet awake.

134

And if my voice break forth, 'tis not that now
I shrink from what is suffer'd: let him speak
Who hath beheld decline upon my brow,
Or seen my mind's convulsion leave it weak;
But in this page a record will I seek.
Not in the air shall these my words disperse,
Though I be ashes; a far hour shall wreak
The deep prophetic fulness of this verse,
And pile on human heads the mountain of my curse!

135

That curse shall be Forgiveness.—Have I not—
Hear me, my mother Earth! behold it, Heaven!
Have I not had to wrestle with my lot?
Have I not suffer'd things to be forgiven?
Have I not had my brain sear'd, my heart riven,
Hopes sapp'd, name blighted, Life's life lied away?
And only not to desperation driven,
Because not altogether of such clay
As rots into the souls of those whom I survey.

136

From mighty wrongs to petty perfidy
Have I not seen what human things could do?

From the loud roar of foaming calumny
To the small whisper of the as paltry few,
And subtler venom of the reptile crew,
The Janus glance of whose significant eye,
Learning to lie with silence, would *seem* true,
And without utterance, save the shrug or sigh,
Deal round to happy fools its speechless obloquy.

137

But I have lived, and have not lived in vain:
My mind may lose its force, my blood its fire,
And my frame perish even in conquering pain;
But there is that within me which shall tire
Torture and Time, and breathe when I expire;
Something unearthly, which they deem not of,
Like the remember'd tone of a mute lyre,
Shall on their soften'd spirits sink, and move
In hearts all rocky now the late remorse of love.

138

The seal is set.—Now welcome, thou dread power!
Nameless, yet thus omnipotent, which here
Walk'st in the shadow of the midnight hour
With a deep awe, yet all distinct from fear;
Thy haunts are ever where the dead walls rear
Their ivy mantles, and the solemn scene
Derives from thee a sense so deep and clear
That we become a part of what has been,
And grow unto the spot, all-seeing but unseen.

139

And here the buzz of eager nations ran,
In murmur'd pity, or loud-roar'd applause,
As man was slaughter'd by his fellowman.
And wherefore slaughter'd? wherefore, but because
Such were the bloody Circus' genial laws,
And the imperial pleasure.—Wherefore not?

What matters where we fall to fill the maws
  Of worms—on battle-plains or listed spot?
Both are but theatres—where the chief actors rot.

140

I see before me the Gladiator lie:
  He leans upon his hand—his manly brow
Consents to death, but conquers agony,
  And his droop'd head sinks gradually low—
And through his side the last drops, ebbing slow
  From the red gash, fall heavy, one by one,
Like the first of a thunder-shower; and now
  The arena swims around him—he is gone,
Ere ceased the inhuman shout which hail'd the
      wretch who won.

141

He heard it, but he heeded not—his eyes
  Were with his heart, and that was far away;
He reck'd not of the life he lost nor prize,
  But where his rude hut by the Danube lay,
There were his young barbarians all at play,
  There was their Dacian mother—he, their sire,
Butcher'd to make a Roman holiday—
  All this rush'd with his blood—Shall he expire
And unavenged? Arise! ye Goths, and glut your ire!

142

But here, where Murder breathed her bloody steam;
  And here, where buzzing nations choked the ways,
And roar'd or murmur'd like a mountain stream
  Dashing or winding as its torrent strays;
Here, where the Roman million's blame or praise
  Was death or life, the playthings of a crowd,
My voice sounds much—and fall the stars' faint rays
  On the arena void—seats crush'd—walls bow'd—
And galleries, where my steps seem echoes strangely loud.

143

A ruin—yet what ruin! from its mass
Walls, palaces, half-cities, have been rear'd;
Yet oft the enormous skeleton ye pass,
And marvel where the spoil could have appear'd.
Hath it indeed been plunder'd, or but clear'd?
Alas! developed, opens the decay,
When the colossal fabric's form is near'd:
It will not bear the brightness of the day,
Which streams too much on all—years—man—have reft away.

144

But when the rising moon begins to climb
Its topmost arch, and gently pauses there;
When the stars twinkle through the loops of time,
And the low night-breeze waves along the air
The garland-forest, which the gray walls wear,
Like laurels on the bald first Caesar's head;
When the light shines serene but doth not glare,
Then in this magic circle raise the dead:
Heroes have trod this spot—'tis on their dust ye tread.

145

"While stands the Coliseum, Rome shall stand;
"When falls the Coliseum, Rome shall fall;
"And when Rome falls—the World." From our own land
Thus spake the pilgrims o'er this mighty wall
In Saxon times, which we are wont to call
Ancient; and these three mortal things are still
On their foundations, and unalter'd all;
Rome and her Ruin past Redemption's skill,
The World, the same wide den—of thieves, or what ye will.

. . . . .

153

But lo! the dome—the vast and wondrous dome,
To which Diana's marvel was a cell—

Christ's mighty shrine above his martyr's tomb!
I have beheld the Ephesian's miracle;—
Its columns strew the wilderness, and dwell
The hyaena and the jackal in their shade;
I have beheld Sophia's bright roofs swell
Their glittering mass i' the sun, and have survey'd
Its sanctuary the while the usurping Moslem pray'd;

154

But thou, of temples old, or altars new,
Standest alone, with nothing like to thee—
Worthiest of God, the holy and the true.
Since Zion's desolation, when that He
Forsook his former city, what could be,
Of earthly structures, in his honour piled,
Of a sublimer aspect? Majesty,
Power, Glory, Strength, and Beauty all are aisled
In this eternal ark of worship undefiled.

155

Enter: its grandeur overwhelms thee not;
And why? It is not lessen'd; but thy mind,
Expanded by the genius of the spot,
Has grown colossal, and can only find
A fit abode wherein appear enshrined
Thy hopes of immortality; and thou
Shalt one day, if found worthy, so defined,
See thy God face to face, as thou dost now
His Holy of Holies, nor be blasted by his brow.

156

Thou movest, but increasing with the advance,
Like climbing some great Alp, which still doth rise,
Deceived by its gigantic elegance;
Vastness which grows, but grows to harmonise—
All musical in its immensities;
Rich marbles, richer painting—shrines where flame

The lamps of gold—and haughty dome which vies
In air with Earth's chief structures, though their frame
Sits on the firm-set ground, and this the clouds must claim.

157

Thou seest not all; but piecemeal thou must break,
To separate contemplation, the great whole;
And as the ocean many bays will make
That ask the eye—so here condense thy soul
To more immediate objects, and control
Thy thoughts until thy mind hath got by heart
Its eloquent proportions, and unroll
In mighty graduations, part by part,
The glory which at once upon thee did not dart,

158

Not by its fault—but thine: Our outward sense
Is but of gradual grasp—and as it is
That what we have of feeling most intense
Outstrips our faint expression; even so this
Outshining and o'erwhelming edifice
Fools our fond gaze, and greatest of the great
Defies at first our Nature's littleness,
Till, growing with its growth, we thus dilate
Our spirits to the size of that they contemplate.

159

Then pause, and be enlighten'd; there is more
In such a survey than the sating gaze
Of wonder pleased, or awe which would adore
The worship of the place, or the mere praise
Of art and its great masters, who could raise
What former time, nor skill, nor thought could plan;
The fountain of sublimity displays
Its depths, and thence may draw the mind of man
Its golden sands, and learn what great conceptions can.

160

Or, turning to the Vatican, go see
Laocoön's torture dignifying pain—
A father's love and mortal's agony
With an immortal's patience blending:—Vain
The struggle; vain, against the coiling strain
And gripe, and deepening of the dragon's grasp,
The old man's clench; the long envenom'd chain
Rivets the living links,—the enormous asp
Enforces pang on pang, and stifles gasp on gasp.

161

Or view the Lord of the unerring bow,
The God of life, and poesy, and light—
The Sun in human limbs array'd, and brow
All radiant from his triumph in the fight;
The shaft hath just been shot—the arrow bright
With an immortal's vengeance; in his eye
And nostrils beautiful disdain, and might
And majesty, flash their full lightnings by,
Developing in that one glance the Deity.

162

But in his delicate form—a dream of Love,
Shaped by some solitary nymph, whose breast
Long'd for a deathless lover from above,
And madden'd in that vision—are exprest
All that ideal beauty ever bless'd
The mind with in its most unearthly mood,
When each conception was a heavenly guest—
A ray of immortality—and stood
Starlike, around, until they gather'd to a god!

163

And if it be Prometheus stole from Heaven
The fire which we endure, it was repaid

By him to whom the energy was given
Which this poetic marble hath array'd
With an eternal glory—which, if made
By human hands, is not of human thought;
And Time himself hath hallow'd it, nor laid
One ringlet in the dust—nor hath it caught
A tinge of years, but breathes the flame with which 'twas wrought.

. . . . .

177

Oh! that the Desert were my dwelling-place,
With one fair Spirit for my minister,
That I might all forget the human race,
And, hating no one, love but only her!
Ye elements!—in whose ennobling stir
I feel myself exalted—Can ye not
Accord me such a being? Do I err
In deeming such inhabit many a spot?
Though with them to converse can rarely be our lot.

178

There is a pleasure in the pathless woods,
There is a rapture on the lonely shore,
There is society, where none intrudes,
By the deep Sea, and music in its roar:
I love not Man the less, but Nature more,
From these our interviews, in which I steal
From all I may be, or have been before,
To mingle with the Universe, and feel
What I can ne'er express, yet cannot all conceal.

179

Roll on, thou deep and dark blue Ocean—roll!
Ten thousand fleets sweep over thee in vain;
Man marks the earth with ruin—his control
Stops with the shore; upon the watery plain
The wrecks are all thy deed, nor doth remain

A shadow of man's ravage, save his own,
    When, for a moment, like a drop of rain,
    He sinks into thy depths with bubbling groan,
Without a grave, unknell'd, uncoffin'd, and unknown.

180

His steps are not upon thy paths,—thy fields
    Are not a spoil for him,—thou dost arise
    And shake him from thee; the vile strength he wields
    For earth's destruction thou dost all despise,
    Spurning him from thy bosom to the skies,
    And send'st him, shivering in thy playful spray
    And howling, to his Gods, where haply lies
    His petty hope in some near port or bay,
And dashest him again to earth:—there let him lay.

181

The armaments which thunderstrike the walls
    Of rock-built cities, bidding nations quake,
    And monarchs tremble in their capitals,
    The oak leviathans, whose huge ribs make
    Their clay creator the vain title take
    Of lord of thee, and arbiter of war—
    These are thy toys, and, as the snowy flake,
    They melt into thy yeast of waves, which mar
Alike the Armada's pride or spoils of Trafalgar.

182

Thy shores are empires, changed in all save thee—
    Assyria, Greece, Rome, Carthage, what are they?
    Thy waters wash'd them power while they were free,
    And many a tyrant since; their shores obey
    The stranger, slave, or savage; their decay
    Has dried up realms to deserts:—not so thou;—
    Unchangeable, save to thy wild waves' play,
    Time writes no wrinkle on thine azure brow:
Such as creation's dawn beheld, thou rollest now.

183

Thou glorious mirror, where the Almighty's form
Glasses itself in tempests; in all time,—
Calm or convulsed, in breeze, or gale, or storm,
Icing the pole, or in the torrid clime
Dark-heaving—boundless, endless, and sublime,
The image of eternity, the throne
Of the Invisible; even from out thy slime
The monsters of the deep are made; each zone
Obeys thee; thou goest forth, dread, fathomless, alone.

184

And I have loved thee, Ocean! and my joy
Of youthful sports was on thy breast to be
Borne, like thy bubbles, onward: from a boy
I wanton'd with thy breakers—they to me
Were a delight; and if the freshening sea
Made them a terror—'twas a pleasing fear,
For I was as it were a child of thee,
And trusted to thy billows far and near,
And laid my hand upon thy mane—as I do here.

185

My task is done, my song hath ceased, my theme
Has died into an echo; it is fit
The spell should break of this protracted dream.
The torch shall be extinguish'd which hath lit
My midnight lamp—and what is writ, is writ;
Would it were worthier! but I am not now
That which I have been—and my visions flit
Less palpably before me—and the glow
Which in my spirit dwelt is fluttering, faint, and low.

186

Farewell! a word that must be, and hath been—
A sound which makes us linger;—yet—farewell!

Ye! who have traced the Pilgrim to the scene
Which is his last, if in your memories dwell
A thought which once was his, if on ye swell
A single recollection, not in vain
He wore his sandal-shoon and scallop-shell;
Farewell! with *him* alone may rest the pain,
If such there were—with *you*, the moral of his strain.

1817   1818

MANFRED

A DRAMATIC POEM

"There are more things in heaven and earth, Horatio,
Than are dreamt of in your philosophy."

DRAMATIS PERSONAE

MANFRED	WITCH OF THE ALPS
CHAMOIS HUNTER	ARIMANES
ABBOT OF ST. MAURICE	NEMESIS
MANUEL	THE DESTINIES
HERMAN	SPIRITS, &C.

The Scene of the Drama is amongst the Higher Alps—partly in the Castle of Manfred, and partly in the Mountains.

ACT I:

SCENE I.—MANFRED *alone.—Scene, a Gothic Gallery.
—Time, Midnight.*

MANFRED. The lamp must be replenish'd, but even then
It will not burn so long as I must watch:
My slumbers—if I slumber—are not sleep,
But a continuance of enduring thought,
Which then I can resist not: in my heart
There is a vigil, and these eyes but close
To look within; and yet I live, and bear
The aspect and the form of breathing men.
But grief should be the instructor of the wise;
Sorrow is knowledge: they who know the most   10
Must mourn the deepest o'er the fatal truth,
The Tree of Knowledge is not that of Life.
Philosophy and science, and the springs
Of wonder, and the wisdom of the world,
I have essay'd, and in my mind there is

A power to make these subject to itself—
But they avail not: I have done men good,
And I have met with good even among men—
But this avail'd not: I have had my foes,
And none have baffled, many fallen before me—   20
But this avail'd not:—Good, or evil, life,
Powers, passions, all I see in other beings,
Have been to me as rain unto the sands,
Since that all-nameless hour. I have no dread,
And feel the curse to have no natural fear,
Nor fluttering throb, that beats with hopes or wishes,
Or lurking love of something on the earth.
Now to my task.—
                    Mysterious agency!
Ye spirits of the unbounded Universe!
Whom I have sought in darkness and in light—   30
Ye, who do compass earth about, and dwell
In subtler essence—ye, to whom the tops
Of mountains inaccessible are haunts,
And earth's and ocean's caves familiar things—
I call upon ye by the written charm
Which gives me power upon you—Rise! Appear!
[*A pause.*]
They come not yet.—Now by the voice of him
Who is the first among you—by this sign,
Which makes you tremble—by the claims of him
Who is undying,—Rise! Appear!——Appear!   40
[*A pause.*]
If it be so—Spirits of earth and air,
Ye shall not thus elude me: by a power,
Deeper than all yet urged, a tyrant-spell,
Which had its birthplace in a star condemn'd,
The burning wreck of a demolish'd world,
A wandering hell in the eternal space;
By the strong curse which is upon my soul,
The thought which is within me and around me,
I do compel ye to my will—Appear!

[*A star is seen at the darker end of the gallery: it is stationary; and a voice is heard singing.*]

FIRST SPIRIT

Mortal! to thy bidding bow'd,   50
From my mansion in the cloud,
Which the breath of twilight builds,
And the summer's sunset gilds
With the azure and vermilion,
Which is mix'd for my pavilion;
Though thy quest may be forbidden,
On a star-beam I have ridden:
To thine adjuration bow'd,
Mortal—be thy wish avow'd!

Voice of the SECOND SPIRIT

Mont Blanc is the monarch of mountains;   60
  They crown'd him long ago
On a throne of rocks, in a robe of clouds,
  With a diadem of snow.
Around his waist are forests braced,
  The Avalanche in his hand;
But ere it fall, that thundering ball
  Must pause for my command.
The Glacier's cold and restless mass
  Moves onward day by day;
But I am he who bids it pass,   70
  Or with its ice delay.
I am the spirit of the place,
  Could make the mountain bow
And quiver to his cavern'd base—
  And what with me wouldst *Thou?*

Voice of the THIRD SPIRIT

In the blue depth of the waters,
  Where the wave hath no strife,
  Where the wind is a stranger,

And the sea-snake hath life,
Where the Mermaid is decking   80
  Her green hair with shells,
Like the storm on the surface   7
  Came the sound of thy spells;
O'er my calm Hall of Coral
  The deep echo roll'd—
To the Spirit of Ocean
  Thy wishes unfold!

FOURTH SPIRIT

Where the slumbering earthquake
  Lies pillow'd on fire,
And the lakes of bitumen   90
  Rise boilingly higher;
Where the roots of the Andes
  Strike deep in the earth,
As their summits to heaven
  Shoot soaringly forth;
I have quitted my birthplace,
  Thy bidding to bide—
Thy spell hath subdued me,
  Thy will be my guide!

FIFTH SPIRIT

I am the Rider of the wind,   100
  The Stirrer of the storm;
The hurricane I left behind
  Is yet with lightning warm;
To speed to thee, o'er shore and sea
  I swept upon the blast:
The fleet I met sail'd well, and yet
  'Twill sink ere night be past.

SIXTH SPIRIT

My dwelling is the shadow of the night,
Why doth thy magic torture me with light?

SEVENTH SPIRIT

The star which rules thy destiny   110
Was ruled, ere earth began, by me:
It was a world as fresh and fair
As e'er revolved round sun in air;
Its course was free and regular,
Space bosom'd not a lovelier star.
The hour arrived—and it became
A wandering mass of shapeless flame,
A pathless comet, and a curse,
The menace of the universe;
Still rolling on with innate force,   120
Without a sphere, without a course,
A bright deformity on high,
The monster of the upper sky!
And thou! beneath its influence born—
Thou worm! whom I obey and scorn—
Forced by a power (which is not thine,
And lent thee but to make thee mine)
For this brief moment to descend,
Where these weak spirits round thee bend
And parley with a thing like thee—   130
What wouldst thou, Child of Clay! with me?

The SEVEN SPIRITS

Earth, ocean, air, night, mountains, winds, thy star,
   Are at thy beck and bidding, Child of Clay!
Before thee at thy quest their spirits are—
   What wouldst thou with us, son of mortals—say?
   MANFRED. Forgetfulness——
   FIRST SPIRIT. Of what—of whom—and why?
   MANFRED. Of that which is within me; read it there—
Ye know it, and I cannot utter it.
   SPIRIT. We can but give thee that which we possess:
Ask of us subjects, sovereignty, the power   140
O'er earth—the whole, or portion—or a sign

Which shall control the elements, whereof
We are the dominators,—each and all,
These shall be thine.

    MANFRED.   Oblivion, self-oblivion!
Can ye not wring from out the hidden realms
Ye offer so profusely what I ask?

    SPIRIT. It is not in our essence, in our skill;
But—thou may'st die.

    MANFRED.   Will death bestow it on me?

    SPIRIT. We are immortal, and do not forget;
We are eternal; and to us the past   150
Is, as the future, present. Art thou answer'd?

    MANFRED. Ye mock me—but the power which brought ye here
Hath made you mine. Slaves, scoff not at my will!
The mind, the spirit, the Promethean spark,
The lightning of my being, is as bright,
Pervading, and far darting as your own,
And shall not yield to yours, though coop'd in clay!
Answer, or I will teach you what I am.

    SPIRIT. We answer as we answer'd; our reply
Is even in thine own words.

    MANFRED.   Why say ye so?   160

    SPIRIT. If, as thou say'st, thine essence be as ours,
We have replied in telling thee, the thing
Mortals call death hath nought to do with us.

    MANFRED. I then have call'd ye from your realms in vain;
Ye cannot, or ye will not, aid me.

    SPIRIT.   Say,
What we possess we offer; it is thine:
Bethink ere thou dismiss us; ask again:
Kingdom, and sway, and strength, and length of days——

    MANFRED. Accursed! what have I to do with days?
They are too long already.—Hence—begone!   170

    SPIRIT. Yet pause: being here, our will would do thee service;
Bethink thee, is there then no other gift
Which we can make not worthless in thine eyes?

    MANFRED. No, none: yet stay—one moment, ere we part,

I would behold ye face to face. I hear
Your voices, sweet and melancholy sounds,
As music on the waters; and I see
The steady aspect of a clear large star;
But nothing more. Approach me as ye are,
Or one, or all, in your accustom'd forms.   180
   SPIRIT. We have no forms, beyond the elements
Of which we are the mind and principle:
But choose a form—in that we will appear.
   MANFRED. I have no choice; there is no form on earth
Hideous or beautiful to me. Let him,
Who is most powerful of ye, take such aspect
As unto him may seem most fitting— Come!
   SEVENTH SPIRIT [*appearing in the shape of a beautiful female fig-*
      ure]. Behold!
   MANFRED. Oh God! if it be thus, and *thou*
Art not a madness and a mockery,
I yet might be most happy, I will clasp thee,   190
And we again will be——

                [*The figure vanishes.*]
                My heart is crush'd!
[MANFRED *falls senseless. A voice is heard in the Incantation which*
        follows.]

      When the moon is on the wave,
        And the glow-worm in the grass,
      And the meteor on the grave,
        And the wisp on the morass;
      When the falling stars are shooting,
      And the answer'd owls are hooting,
      And the silent leaves are still
      In the shadow of the hill,
      Shall my soul be upon thine,   200
      With a power and with a sign.

      Though thy slumber may be deep,
      Yet thy spirit shall not sleep;
      There are shades which will not vanish,

There are thoughts thou canst not banish;
By a power to thee unknown,
Thou canst never be alone;
Thou art wrapt as with a shroud,
Thou art gather'd in a cloud;
And for ever shalt thou dwell   210
In the spirit of this spell.

Though thou seest me not pass by,
Thou shalt feel me with thine eye
As a thing that, though unseen,
Must be near thee, and hath been;
And when in that secret dread
Thou hast turn'd around thy head,
Thou shalt marvel I am not
As thy shadow on the spot,
And the power which thou dost feel   220
Shall be what thou must conceal.

And a magic voice and verse
Hath baptized thee with a curse;
And a spirit of the air
Hath begirt thee with a snare;
In the wind there is a voice
Shall forbid thee to rejoice;
And to thee shall night deny
All the quiet of her sky;
And the day shall have a sun,   230
Which shall make thee wish it done.

From thy false tears I did distil
An essence which hath strength to kill;
From thy own heart I then did wring
The black blood in its blackest spring;
From thy own smile I snatch'd the snake,
For there it coil'd as in a brake;
From thy own lip I drew the charm

Which gave all these their chiefest harm;
In proving every poison known, 240
I found the strongest was thine own.

By thy cold breast and serpent smile,
By thy unfathom'd gulfs of guile,
By that most seeming virtuous eye,
By thy shut soul's hypocrisy;
By the perfection of thine art
Which pass'd for human thine own heart;
By thy delight in others' pain,
And by thy brotherhood of Cain,
I call upon thee! and compel 250
Thyself to be thy proper Hell!

And on thy head I pour the vial
Which doth devote thee to this trial;
Nor to slumber, nor to die,
Shall be in thy destiny;
Though thy death shall still seem near
To thy wish, but as a fear;
Lo! the spell now works around thee,
And the clankless chain hath bound thee;
O'er thy heart and brain together 260
Hath the word been pass'd—now wither!

SCENE II.—*The Mountain of the Jungfrau.—Time, Morning.*
—MANFRED *alone upon the Cliffs.*

MANFRED. The spirits I have raised abandon me,
The spells which I have studied baffle me,
The remedy I reck'd of tortured me;
I lean no more on superhuman aid;
It hath no power upon the past, and for
The future, till the past be gulf'd in darkness,
It is not of my search.—My mother Earth!
And thou fresh breaking Day, and you, ye Mountains,
Why are ye beautiful? I cannot love ye.

And thou, the bright eye of the universe,　　　10
That openest over all, and unto all
Art a delight—thou shin'st not on my heart.
And you, ye crags, upon whose extreme edge
I stand, and on the torrent's brink beneath
Behold the tall pines dwindled as to shrubs
In dizziness of distance; when a leap,
A stir, a motion, even a breath, would bring
My breast upon its rocky bosom's bed
To rest for ever—wherefore do I pause?
I feel the impulse—yet I do not plunge;　　　20
I see the peril—yet do not recede;
And my brain reels—and yet my foot is firm:
There is a power upon me which withholds,
And makes it my fatality to live,—
If it be life to wear within myself
This barrenness of spirit, and to be
My own soul's sepulchre, for I have ceased
To justify my deeds unto myself—
The last infirmity of evil. Ay,
Thou winged and cloud-cleaving minister,　　　30
[*An eagle passes.*]
Whose happy flight is highest into heaven,
Well may'st thou swoop so near me—I should be
Thy prey, and gorge thine eaglets; thou art gone
Where the eye cannot follow thee; but thine
Yet pierces downward, onward, or above,
With a pervading vision.—Beautiful!
How beautiful is all this visible world!
How glorious in its action and itself!
But we, who name ourselves its sovereigns, we,
Half dust, half deity, alike unfit　　　40
To sink or soar, with our mix'd essence make
A conflict of its elements, and breathe
The breath of degradation and of pride,
Contending with low wants and lofty will,
Till our mortality predominates,

And men are—what they name not to themselves,
And trust not to each other. Hark! the note,
[*The Shepherd's pipe in the distance is heard.*]
The natural music of the mountain reed—
For here the patriarchal days are not
A pastoral fable—pipes in the liberal air, 50
Mix'd with the sweet bells of the sauntering herd;
My soul would drink those echoes. Oh, that I were
The viewless spirit of a lovely sound,
A living voice, a breathing harmony,
A bodiless enjoyment—born and dying
With the blest tone which made me!
[*Enter from below a* CHAMOIS HUNTER.]
   CHAMOIS HUNTER.   Even so
This way the chamois leapt: her nimble feet
Have baffled me; my gains to-day will scarce
Repay my break-neck travail.—What is here?
Who seems not of my trade, and yet hath reach'd 60
A height which none even of our mountaineers,
Save our best hunters, may attain: his garb
Is goodly, his mien manly, and his air
Proud as a free-born peasant's, at this distance:
I will approach him nearer.
   MANFRED [*not perceiving the other*]. To be thus—
Grey-hair'd with anguish, like these blasted pines,
Wrecks of a single winter, barkless, branchless,
A blighted trunk upon a cursed root,
Which but supplies a feeling to decay—
And to be thus, eternally but thus, 70
Having been otherwise! Now furrow'd o'er
With wrinkles, plough'd by moments,—not by years,—
And hours, all tortured into ages—hours
Which I outlive!—Ye toppling crags of ice!
Ye avalanches, whom a breath draws down
In mountainous o'erwhelming, come and crush me!
I hear ye momently above, beneath,
Crash with a frequent conflict; but ye pass,

And only fall on things that still would live;
On the young flourishing forest, or the hut   80
And hamlet of the harmless villager.

    CHAMOIS HUNTER. The mists begin to rise from up the valley;
I'll warn him to descend, or he may chance
To lose at once his way and life together.

    MANFRED. The mists boil up around the glaciers; clouds
Rise curling fast beneath me, white and sulphury,
Like foam from the roused ocean of deep Hell,
Whose every wave breaks on a living shore,
Heap'd with the damn'd like pebbles.—I am giddy.

    CHAMOIS HUNTER. I must approach him cautiously; if near,   90
A sudden step will startle him, and he
Seems tottering already.

    MANFRED.   Mountains have fallen,
Leaving a gap in the clouds, and with the shock
Rocking their Alpine brethren; filling up
The ripe green valleys with destruction's splinters;
Damming the rivers with a sudden dash,
Which crush'd the waters into mist and made
Their fountains find another channel—thus,
Thus, in its old age, did Mount Rosenberg—
Why stood I not beneath it?

    CHAMOIS HUNTER.   Friend! have a care,   100
Your next step may be fatal!—for the love
Of him who made you, stand not on that brink!

    MANFRED [*not hearing him*]. Such would have been for me a
        fitting tomb;
My bones had then been quiet in their depth;
They had not then been strewn upon the rocks
For the wind's pastime—as thus—thus they shall be—
In this one plunge.—Farewell, ye opening heavens!
Look not upon me thus reproachfully—
You were not meant for me—Earth! take these atoms!

[*As* MANFRED *is in act to spring from the cliff, the* CHAMOIS HUNTER
      seizes and retains him with a sudden grasp.]

CHAMOIS HUNTER. Hold, madman!—though aweary of
     thy life,   110
Stain not our pure vales with thy guilty blood:
Away with me———I will not quit my hold.
     MANFRED. I am most sick at heart—nay, grasp me not—
I am all feebleness—the mountains whirl
Spinning around me——I grow blind——What art thou?
     CHAMOIS HUNTER. I'll answer that anon. Away with me—
The clouds grow thicker——there—now lean on me—
Place your foot here—here, take this staff, and cling
A moment to that shrub—now give me your hand,
And hold fast by my girdle—softly—well—   120
The Chalet will be gain'd within an hour:
Come on, we'll quickly find a surer footing,
And something like a pathway, which the torrent
Hath wash'd since winter.—Come, 'tis bravely done—
You should have been a hunter.—Follow me.
[*As they descend the rocks with difficulty, the scene closes.*]

ACT II:

SCENE I.—*A Cottage amongst the Bernese Alps.* MANFRED *and the*
CHAMOIS HUNTER.

     CHAMOIS HUNTER. No, no—yet pause—thou must not yet go
          forth:
Thy mind and body are alike unfit
To trust each other, for some hours, at least;
When thou art better, I will be thy guide—
But whither?
     MANFRED.   It imports not: I do know
My route full well, and need no further guidance.
     CHAMOIS HUNTER. Thy garb and gait bespeak thee of high lin-
          eage—
One of the many chiefs, whose castled crags
Look o'er the lower valleys—which of these
May call thee lord? I only know their portals;   10

My way of life leads me but rarely down
To bask by the huge hearths of those old halls,
Carousing with the vassals; but the paths,
Which step from out our mountains to their doors,
I know from childhood—which of these is thine?

    MANFRED. No matter.

    CHAMOIS HUNTER.   Well, sir, pardon me the question,
And be of better cheer. Come, taste my wine;
'Tis of an ancient vintage; many a day
'T has thaw'd my veins among our glaciers, now
Let it do thus for thine—Come, pledge me fairly.   20

    MANFRED. Away, away! there's blood upon the brim!
Will it then never—never sink in the earth?

    CHAMOIS HUNTER. What dost thou mean? thy senses wander from
        thee.

    MANFRED. I say 'tis blood—my blood! the pure warm stream
Which ran in the veins of my fathers, and in ours
When we were in our youth, and had one heart,
And loved each other as we should not love,
And this was shed: but still it rises up,
Colouring the clouds, that shut me out from heaven,
Where thou art not—and I shall never be.   30

    CHAMOIS HUNTER. Man of strange words, and some half-madden-
        ing sin,
Which makes thee people vacancy, whate'er
Thy dread and sufferance be, there's comfort yet—
The aid of holy men, and heavenly patience—

    MANFRED. Patience and patience! Hence—that word was made
For brutes of burthen, not for birds of prey;
Preach it to mortals of a dust like thine,—
I am not of thine order.

    CHAMOIS HUNTER.   Thanks to heaven!
I would not be of thine for the free fame
Of William Tell; but whatsoe'er thine ill,   40
It must be borne, and these wild starts are useless.

    MANFRED. Do I not bear it?—Look on me—I live.

    CHAMOIS HUNTER. This is convulsion, and no healthful life.

MANFRED. I tell thee, man! I have lived many years,
Many long years, but they are nothing now
To those which I must number: ages——ages—
Space and eternity——and consciousness,
With the fierce thirst of death—and still unslaked!

CHAMOIS HUNTER. Why, on thy brow the seal of middle age
Hath scarce been set; I am thine elder far.   50

MANFRED. Think'st thou existence doth depend on time?
It doth; but actions are our epochs: mine
Have made my days and nights imperishable,
Endless, and all alike, as sands on the shore,
Innumerable atoms; and one desert,
Barren and cold, on which the wild waves break,
But nothing rests, save carcasses and wrecks,
Rocks, and the salt-surf weeds of bitterness.

CHAMOIS HUNTER. Alas! he's mad—but yet I must not leave him.

MANFRED. I would I were—for then the things I see   60
Would be but a distemper'd dream.

CHAMOIS HUNTER.   What is it
That thou dost see, or think thou look'st upon?

MANFRED. Myself, and thee—a peasant of the Alps—
Thy humble virtues, hospitable home,
And spirit patient, pious, proud, and free;
Thy self-respect, grafted on innocent thoughts;
Thy days of health, and nights of sleep; thy toils,
By danger dignified, yet guiltless; hopes
Of cheerful old age and a quiet grave,
With cross and garland over its green turf,   70
And thy grandchildren's love for epitaph;
This do I see—and then I look within—
It matters not—my soul was scorch'd already!

CHAMOIS HUNTER. And wouldst thou then exchange thy lot
    for mine?

MANFRED. No, friend! I would not wrong thee, nor exchange
My lot with living being: I can bear—
However wretchedly, 'tis still to bear—
In life what others could not brook to dream,

But perish in their slumber.

CHAMOIS HUNTER.   And with this—   80
This cautious feeling for another's pain,
Canst thou be black with evil?—say not so.
Can one of gentle thoughts have wreak'd revenge
Upon his enemies?

MANFRED.   Oh! no, no, no!
My injuries came down on those who loved me—
On those whom I best loved: I never quell'd
An enemy, save in my just defence—
But my embrace was fatal.

CHAMOIS HUNTER.   Heaven give thee rest!
And penitence restore thee to thyself;
My prayers shall be for thee.

MANFRED.   I need them not—
But can endure thy pity. I depart—   90
'Tis time—farewell!—Here's gold, and thanks for thee—
No words—it is thy due.—Follow me not—
I know my path—the mountain peril's past:
And once again I charge thee, follow not!

[*Exit* MANFRED.]

SCENE II.—*A lower Valley in the Alps.—A Cataract.*
Enter MANFRED.

MANFRED. It is not noon—the sunbow's rays still arch
The torrent with the many hues of heaven,
And roll the sheeted silver's waving column
O'er the crag's headlong perpendicular,
And fling its lines of foaming light along,
And to and fro, like the pale courser's tail,
The Giant steed, to be bestrode by Death,
As told in the Apocalypse. No eyes
But mine now drink this sight of loveliness;
I should be sole in this sweet solitude,   10
And with the Spirit of the place divide
The homage of these waters.—I will call her.

[MANFRED *takes some of the water into the palm of his hand, and*

flings it into the air, muttering the adjuration. After a pause, the
WITCH OF THE ALPS *rises beneath the arch of the sunbow of the*
torrent.]

Beautiful Spirit! with thy hair of light,
And dazzling eyes of glory, in whose form
The charms of earth's least mortal daughters grow
To an unearthly stature, in an essence
Of purer elements; while the hues of youth,—
Carnation'd like a sleeping infant's cheek,
Rock'd by the beating of her mother's heart,
Or the rose tints, which summer's twilight leaves   20
Upon the lofty glacier's virgin snow,
The blush of earth embracing with her heaven,—
Tinge thy celestial aspect, and make tame
The beauties of the sunbow which bends o'er thee.
Beautiful Spirit! in thy calm clear brow,
Wherein is glass'd serenity of soul,
Which of itself shows immortality,
I read that thou wilt pardon to a Son
Of Earth, whom the abstruser powers permit
At times to commune with them—if that he   30
Avail him of his spells—to call thee thus,
And gaze on thee a moment.

   WITCH.   Son of Earth!
I know thee, and the powers which give thee power;
I know thee for a man of many thoughts,
And deeds of good and ill, extreme in both,
Fatal and fated in thy sufferings.
I have expected this—what wouldst thou with me?

   MANFRED. To look upon thy beauty—nothing further.
The face of the earth hath madden'd me, and I
Take refuge in her mysteries, and pierce   40
To the abodes of those who govern her—
But they can nothing aid me. I have sought
From them what they could not bestow, and now
I search no further.

   WITCH.   What could be the quest

Which is not in the power of the most powerful,
The rulers of the invisible?

 MANFRED.   A boon;
But why should I repeat it? 'twere in vain.
 WITCH. I know not that; let thy lips utter it.
 MANFRED. Well, though it torture me, 'tis but the same;
My pang shall find a voice. From my youth upwards   50
My spirit walk'd not with the souls of men,
Nor look'd upon the earth with human eyes;
The thirst of their ambition was not mine,
The aim of their existence was not mine;
My joys, my griefs, my passions, and my powers,
Made me a stranger; though I wore the form,
I had no sympathy with breathing flesh,
Nor midst the creatures of clay that girded me
Was there but one who—but of her anon.
I said with men, and with the thoughts of men,   60
I held but slight communion; but instead,
My joy was in the wilderness,—to breathe
The difficult air of the iced mountain's top,
Where the birds dare not build, nor insect's wing
Flit o'er the herbless granite; or to plunge
Into the torrent, and to roll along
On the swift whirl of the new breaking wave
Of river-stream, or ocean, in their flow.
In these my early strength exulted; or
To follow through the night the moving moon,   70
The stars and their development; or catch
The dazzling lightnings till my eyes grew dim;
Or to look, list'ning, on the scatter'd leaves,
While Autumn winds were at their evening song.
These were my pastimes, and to be alone;
For if the beings, of whom I was one,—
Hating to be so,—cross'd me in my path,
I felt myself degraded back to them,
And was all clay again. And then I dived,
In my lone wanderings, to the caves of death,   80

Searching its cause in its effect; and drew
From wither'd bones, and skulls, and heap'd up dust,
Conclusions most forbidden. Then I pass'd
The nights of years in sciences untaught,
Save in the old time; and with time and toil,
And terrible ordeal, and such penance
As in itself hath power upon the air,
And spirits that do compass air and earth,
Space, and the peopled infinite, I made
Mine eyes familiar with Eternity,   90
Such as, before me, did the Magi, and
He who from out their fountain dwellings raised
Eros and Anteros, at Gadara,
As I do thee;—and with my knowledge grew
The thirst of knowledge, and the power and joy
Of this most bright intelligence, until—
   WITCH. Proceed.
   MANFRED.   Oh! I but thus prolong'd my words,
Boasting these idle attributes, because
As I approach the core of my heart's grief—
But to my task. I have not named to thee   100
Father or mother, mistress, friend, or being,
With whom I wore the chain of human ties;
If I had such, they seem'd not such to me;
Yet there was one—
   WITCH.   Spare not thyself—proceed.
   MANFRED. She was like me in lineaments; her eyes,
Her hair, her features, all, to the very tone
Even of her voice, they said were like to mine;
But soften'd all, and temper'd into beauty:
She had the same lone thoughts and wanderings,
The quest of hidden knowledge, and a mind   110
To comprehend the universe: nor these
Alone, but with them gentler powers than mine,
Pity, and smiles, and tears—which I had not;
And tenderness—but that I had for her;
Humility—and that I never had.

Her faults were mine—her virtues were her own—
I loved her, and destroy'd her!

    WITCH.   With thy hand?

    MANFRED. Not with my hand, but heart, which broke her heart;
It gazed on mine, and wither'd. I have shed
Blood, but not hers—and yet her blood was shed;   120
I saw—and could not stanch it.

    WITCH.   And for this—
A being of the race thou dost despise,
The order, which thine own would rise above,
Mingling with us and ours,—thou dost forego
The gifts of our great knowledge, and shrink'st back
To recreant mortality—Away!

    MANFRED. Daughter of Air! I tell thee, since that hour—
But words are breath—look on me in my sleep,
Or watch my watchings—Come and sit by me!
My solitude is solitude no more,   130
But peopled with the Furies;—I have gnash'd
My teeth in darkness till returning morn,
Then cursed myself till sunset;——I have pray'd
For madness as a blessing—'tis denied me.
I have affronted death—but in the war
Of elements the waters shrunk from me,
And fatal things pass'd harmless; the cold hand
Of an all-pitiless demon held me back,
Back by a single hair, which would not break.
In fantasy, imagination, all   140
The affluence of my soul—which one day was
A Croesus in creation—I plunged deep,
But, like an ebbing wave, it dash'd me back
Into the gulf of my unfathom'd thought.
I plunged amidst mankind—Forgetfulness
I sought in all, save where 'tis to be found.
And that I have to learn; my sciences,
My long-pursued and superhuman art,
Is mortal here: I dwell in my despair—
And live—and live for ever.

WITCH.   It may be 150
That I can aid thee.
   MANFRED.   To do this thy power
Must wake the dead, or lay me low with them.
Do so—in any shape—in any hour—
With any torture—so it be the last.
   WITCH. That is not in my province; but if thou
Wilt swear obedience to my will, and do
My bidding, it may help thee to thy wishes.
   MANFRED. I will not swear—Obey! and whom? the spirits
Whose presence I command, and be the slave
Of those who served me—Never!
   WITCH.   Is this all? 160
Hast thou no gentler answer?—Yet bethink thee,
And pause ere thou rejectest.
   MANFRED.   I have said it.
   WITCH. Enough! I may retire then—say!
   MANFRED.   Retire!
                  [*The* WITCH *disappears.*]
   MANFRED. [*alone*]. We are the fools of time and terror: Days
Steal on us, and steal from us; yet we live,
Loathing our life, and dreading still to die.
In all the days of this detested yoke—
This vital weight upon the struggling heart,
Which sinks with sorrow, or beats quick with pain,
Or joy that ends in agony or faintness—   170
In all the days of past and future, for
In life there is no present, we can number
How few—how less than few—wherein the soul
Forbears to pant for death, and yet draws back
As from a stream in winter, though the chill
Be but a moment's. I have one resource
Still in my science—I can call the dead,
And ask them what it is we dread to be:
The sternest answer can but be the Grave,
And that is nothing. If they answer not——   180
The buried Prophet answered to the Hag

Of Endor; and the Spartan Monarch drew
From the Byzantine maid's unsleeping spirit
An answer and his destiny—he slew
That which he loved, unknowing what he slew,
And died unpardon'd—though he call'd in aid
The Phyxian Jove, and in Phigalia roused
The Arcadian Evocators to compel
The indignant shadow to depose her wrath,
Or fix her term of vengeance—she replied   190
In words of dubious import, but fulfill'd.
If I had never lived, that which I love
Had still been living; had I never loved,
That which I love would still be beautiful,
Happy and giving happiness. What is she?
What is she now?—a sufferer for my sins—
A thing I dare not think upon—or nothing.
Within few hours I shall not call in vain—
Yet in this hour I dread the thing I dare:
Until this hour I never shrunk to gaze   200
On spirit, good or evil—now I tremble,
And feel a strange cold thaw upon my heart.
But I can act even what I most abhor,
And champion human fears.—The night approaches.

                                           [*Exit.*]

SCENE III.—*The Summit of the Jungfrau Mountain.* *Enter* FIRST DESTINY.

    FIRST DESTINY. The moon is rising broad, and round, and bright;
And here on snows, where never human foot
Of common mortal trod, we nightly tread,
And leave no traces: o'er the savage sea,
The glassy ocean of the mountain ice,
We skim its rugged breakers, which put on
The aspect of a tumbling tempest's foam,
Frozen in a moment—a dead whirlpool's image:
And this most steep fantastic pinnacle,
The fretwork of some earthquake—where the clouds   10

Pause to repose themselves in passing by—
Is sacred to our revels, or our vigils;
Here do I wait my sisters, on our way
To the Hall of Arimanes, for to-night
Is our great festival—'tis strange they come not.

A Voice without, singing.

The Captive Usurper,
    Hurl'd down from the throne,
Lay buried in torpor,
    Forgotten and lone;
I broke through his slumbers,   2)
    I shiver'd his chain,
I leagued him with numbers—
    He's Tyrant again!
With the blood of a million he'll answer my care,
With a nation's destruction—his flight and despair.

Second Voice, without.

The ship sail'd on, the ship sail'd fast,
But I left not a sail, and I left not a mast;
There is not a plank of the hull or the deck,
And there is not a wretch to lament o'er his wreck;
Save one, whom I held, as he swam, by the hair,   30
And he was a subject well worthy my care;
A traitor on land, and a pirate at sea—
But I saved him to wreak further havoc for me!

FIRST DESTINY, *answering.*

The city lies sleeping;
    The morn, to deplore it,
May dawn on it weeping: 8
    Sullenly, slowly,
The black plague flew o'er it—
    Thousands lie lowly;
Tens of thousands shall perish;   40
    The living shall fly from

The sick they should cherish;
But nothing can vanquish
The touch that they die from.
Sorrow and anguish,
And evil and dread,
Envelope a nation;
The blest are the dead,
Who see not the sight
Of their own desolation;   50
This work of a night—
This wreck of a realm—this deed of my doing—
For ages I've done, and shall still be renewing!

[*Enter the* SECOND *and* THIRD DESTINIES.]

The Three.

Our hands contain the hearts of men,
Our footsteps are their graves:
We only give to take again
The spirits of our slaves!
FIRST DESTINY. Welcome!—Where's Nemesis?
SECOND DESTINY.   At some great work;
But what I know not, for my hands were full.
THIRD DESTINY. Behold she cometh.   60
[*Enter* NEMESIS.]
FIRST DESTINY. Say, where hast thou been?
My sisters and thyself are slow to-night.
NEMESIS. I was detain'd repairing shatter'd thrones,
Marrying fools, restoring dynasties,
Avenging men upon their enemies,
And making them repent their own revenge;
Goading the wise to madness: from the dull
Shaping out oracles to rule the world
Afresh, for they were waxing out of date,
And mortals dared to ponder for themselves,
To weigh kings in the balance, and to speak   70

Of freedom, the forbidden fruit.—Away!
We have outstay'd the hour—mount we our clouds!

[*Exeunt.*]

SCENE IV.—*The Hall of Arimanes—Arimanes on his Throne, a Globe of Fire, surrounded by the Spirits.*

Hymn of the SPIRITS.

Hail to our Master!—Prince of Earth and Air!
  Who walks the clouds and waters—in his hand
The sceptre of the elements, which tear
  Themselves to chaos at his high command!
He breatheth—and a tempest shakes the sea;
  He speaketh—and the clouds reply in thunder;
He gazeth—from his glance the sunbeams flee;
  He moveth—earthquakes rend the world asunder.
Beneath his footsteps the volcanoes rise;
  His shadow is the Pestilence; his path   10
The comets herald through the crackling skies;
  And planets turn to ashes at his wrath.
To him War offers daily sacrifice;
  To him Death pays his tribute: Life is his,
With all its infinite of agonies—
  And his the spirit of whatever is!
[*Enter the* DESTINIES *and* NEMESIS.]
  FIRST DESTINY. Glory to Arimanes! on the earth
His power increaseth—both my sisters did
His bidding, nor did I neglect my duty!
  SECOND DESTINY. Glory to Arimanes! we who bow   20
The necks of men, bow down before his throne!
  THIRD DESTINY. Glory to Arimanes! we await
His nod!
  NEMESIS. Sovereign of Sovereigns! we are thine,
And all that liveth, more or less, is ours,
And most things wholly so; still to increase

Our power, increasing thine, demands our care,
And we are vigilant. The late commands
Have been fulfill'd to the utmost.
[*Enter* MANFRED.]
   A SPIRIT.   What is here?
A mortal!—Thou most rash and fatal wretch,
Bow down and worship!   30
   SECOND SPIRIT.   I do know the man—
A Magian of great power, and fearful skill!
   THIRD SPIRIT. Bow down and worship, slave!—
                        What, know'st thou not
Thine and our Sovereign?—Tremble, and obey!
   ALL THE SPIRITS. Prostrate thyself, and thy condemned clay,
Child of the Earth! or dread the worst.
   MANFRED.   I know it;
And yet ye see I kneel not.
   FOURTH SPIRIT.   Twill be taught thee.
   MANFRED. 'Tis taught already;—many a night on the earth,
On the bare ground, have I bow'd down my face,
And strew'd my head with ashes; I have known
The fulness of humiliation, for   40
I sunk before my vain despair, and knelt
To my own desolation.
   FIFTH SPIRIT.   Dost thou dare
Refuse to Arimanes on his throne
What the whole earth accords, beholding not
The terror of his glory?—Crouch, I say.
   MANFRED. Bid *him* bow down to that which is above him,
The overruling Infinite—the Maker
Who made him not for worship—let him kneel,
And we will kneel together.
   THE SPIRITS.   Crush the worm!
Tear him in pieces!—
   FIRST DESTINY. Hence! avaunt!—he's mine.   50
Prince of the Powers invisible! This man
Is of no common order, as his port

And presence here denote; his sufferings
Have been of an immortal nature, like
Our own; his knowledge, and his powers and will,
As far as is compatible with clay,
Which clogs the ethereal essence, have been such
As clay hath seldom borne; his aspirations
Have been beyond the dwellers of the earth,
And they have only taught him what we know—   60
That knowledge is not happiness, and science
But an exchange of ignorance for that
Which is another kind of ignorance.
This is not all—the passions, attributes
Of earth and heaven, from which no power, nor being,
Nor breath from the worm upwards is exempt,
Have pierced his heart, and in their consequence
Made him a thing which I, who pity not,
Yet pardon those who pity. He is mine,
And thine, it may be; be it so, or not,   70
No other Spirit in this region hath
A soul like his—or power upon his soul.
  NEMESIS. What doth he here then?
  FIRST DESTINY.   Let him answer that.
  MANFRED. Ye know what I have known; and without power
I could not be amongst ye: but there are
Powers deeper still beyond—I come in quest
Of such, to answer unto what I seek.
  NEMESIS. What wouldst thou?
  MANFRED.   Thou canst not reply to me.
Call up the dead—my question is for them.
  NEMESIS. Great Arimanes, doth thy will avouch   80
The wishes of this mortal?
  ARIMANES.   Yea.
  NEMESIS.   Whom wouldst thou
Uncharnel?
  MANFRED.   One without a tomb—call up
Astarte.

NEMESIS.

Shadow! or Spirit!
    Whatever thou art,
Which still doth inherit
    The whole or a part
Of the form of thy birth,
    Of the mould of thy clay,
Which return'd to the earth,   90
    Re-appear to the day!
Bear what thou borest,
    The heart and the form,
And the aspect thou worest
    Redeem from the worm.
Appear!—Appear!—Appear!
Who sent thee there requires thee here!

[*The Phantom of* ASTARTE *rises and stands in the midst.*]

MANFRED. Can this be death? there's bloom upon her cheek;
But now I see it is no living hue,
But a strange hectic—like the unnatural red   100
Which Autumn plants upon the perish'd leaf.
It is the same! Oh, God! that I should dread
To look upon the same—Astarte!—No,
I cannot speak to her—but bid her speak—
Forgive me or condemn me.

NEMESIS.

By the power which hath broken
    The grave which enthrall'd thee,
Speak to him, who hath spoken,
    Or those who have call'd thee!

MANFRED.   She is silent,   110
And in that silence I am more than answer'd.

NEMESIS. My power extends no further. Prince of Air!
It rests with thee alone—command her voice.

ARIMANES. Spirit—obey this sceptre!

NEMESIS.   Silent still!

She is not of our order, but belongs
To the other powers. Mortal! thy quest is vain,
And we are baffled also.

   MANFRED.   Hear me, hear me—
Astarte! my beloved! speak to me:
I have so much endured—so much endure—
Look on me! the grave hath not changed thee more   120
Than I am changed for thee. Thou lovedst me
Too much, as I loved thee: we were not made
To torture thus each other, though it were
The deadliest sin to love as we have loved.
Say that thou loath'st me not—that I do bear
This punishment for both—that thou wilt be
One of the blessed—and that I shall die;
For hitherto all hateful things conspire
To bind me in existence—in a life
Which makes me shrink from immortality—   130
A future like the past. I cannot rest.
I know not what I ask, nor what I seek:
I feel but what thou art, and what I am;
And I would hear yet once before I perish
The voice which was my music—Speak to me!
For I have call'd on thee in the still night,
Startled the slumbering birds from the hush'd boughs,
And woke the mountain wolves, and made the caves
Acquainted with thy vainly echoed name,
Which answer'd me—many things answer'd me—   140
Spirits and men—but thou wert silent all.
Yet speak to me! I have outwatch'd the stars,
And gazed o'er heaven in vain in search of thee.
Speak to me! I have wander'd o'er the earth,
And never found thy likeness—Speak to me!
Look on the fiends around—they feel for me:
I fear them not, and feel for thee alone—
Speak to me! though it be in wrath;—but say—
I reck not what—but let me hear thee once—
This once—once more!

PHANTOM OF ASTARTE. Manfred!

MANFRED.   Say on, say on— 150
I live but in the sound—it is thy voice!

PHANTOM. Manfred! To-morrow ends thine earthly ills.
Farewell!

MANFRED. Yet one word more—am I forgiven?

PHANTOM. Farewell!

MANFRED.   Say, shall we meet again?

PHANTOM.   Farewell!

MANFRED. One word for mercy! Say, thou lovest me.

PHANTOM. Manfred!

[*The Spirit of* ASTARTE *disappears.*]

NEMESIS. She's gone, and will not be recall'd;
Her words will be fulfill'd. Return to the earth.

A SPIRIT. He is convulsed.—This is to be a mortal
And seek the things beyond mortality.

ANOTHER SPIRIT. Yet, see, he mastereth himself, and makes   160
His torture tributary to his will.
Had he been one of us, he would have made
An awful spirit.

NEMESIS.   Hast thou further question
Of our great sovereign, or his worshipers?

MANFRED. None.

NEMESIS.   Then, for a time, farewell.

MANFRED. We meet then! Where? On the earth?—
Even as thou wilt: and for the grace accorded
I now depart a debtor. Fare ye well!

[*Exit* MANFRED.]

ACT III:

SCENE I.—*A Hall in the Castle of Manfred.* MANFRED *and* HERMAN.

MANFRED. What is the hour?

HERMAN.   It wants but one till sunset,
And promises a lovely twilight.

MANFRED.   Say,
Are all things so disposed of in the tower
As I directed?

HERMAN. All, my lord, are ready:
Here is the key and casket.
MANFRED. It is well:
Thou may'st retire.

[*Exit* HERMAN.]

MANFRED. [*alone.*] There is a calm upon me—
Inexplicable stillness! which till now
Did not belong to what I knew of life.
If that I did not know philosophy
To be of all our vanities the motliest, 10
The merest word that ever fool'd the ear
From out the schoolman's jargon, I should deem
The golden secret, the sought "Kalon", found,
And seated in my soul. It will not last,
But it is well to have known it, though but once:
It hath enlarged my thoughts with a new sense,
And I within my tablets would note down
That there is such a feeling. Who is there?
[*Re-enter* HERMAN.]
HERMAN. My lord, the abbot of St. Maurice craves
To greet your presence.
[*Enter the* ABBOT OF ST. MAURICE.]
ABBOT. Peace be with Count Manfred! 20
MANFRED. Thanks, holy father! welcome to these walls;
Thy presence honours them, and blesseth those
Who dwell within them.
ABBOT. Would it were so, Count!—
But I would fain confer with thee alone.
MANFRED. Herman, retire.—What would my reverend guest?
ABBOT. Thus, without prelude:—Age and zeal, my office,
And good intent, must plead my privilege;
Our near, though not acquainted neighbourhood,
May also be my herald. Rumours strange,
And of unholy nature, are abroad, 30
And busy with thy name; a noble name
For centuries: may he who bears it now
Transmit it unimpair'd!

MANFRED. Proceed,—I listen.

ABBOT. 'Tis said thou holdest converse with the things
Which are forbidden to the search of man;
That with the dwellers of the dark abodes,
The many evil and unheavenly spirits
Which walk the valley of the shade of death,
Thou communest. I know that with mankind,
Thy fellows in creation, thou dost rarely   40
Exchange thy thoughts, and that thy solitude
Is as an anchorite's, were it but holy.

MANFRED. And what are they who do avouch these things?

ABBOT. My pious brethren—the scared peasantry—
Even thy own vassals—who do look on thee
With most unquiet eyes. Thy life's in peril.

MANFRED. Take it.

ABBOT. I come to save, and not destroy:
I would not pry into thy secret soul;
But if these things be sooth, there still is time
For penitence and pity: reconcile thee   50
With the true church, and through the church to heaven.

MANFRED. I hear thee. This is my reply: whate'er
I may have been, or am, doth rest between
Heaven and myself. I shall not choose a mortal
To be my mediator. Have I sinn'd
Against your ordinances? prove and punish!

ABBOT. My son! I did not speak of punishment,
But penitence and pardon;—with thyself
The choice of such remains—and for the last,
Our institutions and our strong belief   60
Have given me power to smooth the path from sin
To higher hope and better thoughts; the first
I leave to heaven,—"Vengeance is mine alone!"
So saith the Lord, and with all humbleness
His servant echoes back the awful word.

MANFRED. Old man! there is no power in holy men,
Nor charm in prayer, nor purifying form
Of penitence, nor outward look, nor fast,

Nor agony—nor, greater than all these,
The innate tortures of that deep despair,   70
Which is remorse without the fear of hell,
But all in all sufficient to itself
Would make a hell of heaven—can exorcise
From out the unbounded spirit the quick sense
Of its own sins, wrongs, sufferance, and revenge
Upon itself; there is no future pang
Can deal that justice on the self-condemn'd
He deals on his own soul.

   ABBOT.   All this is well;
For this will pass away, and be succeeded
By an auspicious hope, which shall look up   80
With calm assurance to that blessed place,
Which all who seek may win, whatever be
Their earthly errors, so they be atoned:
And the commencement of atonement is
The sense of its necessity. Say on—
And all our church can teach thee shall be taught;
And all we can absolve thee shall be pardon'd.

   MANFRED. When Rome's sixth emperor was near his last,
The victim of a self-inflicted wound,
To shun the torments of a public death   90
From senates once his slaves, a certain soldier,
With show of loyal pity, would have stanch'd
The gushing throat with his officious robe;
The dying Roman thrust him back, and said—
Some empire still in his expiring glance—
"It is too late—is this fidelity?"

   ABBOT. And what of this?

   MANFRED.   I answer with the Roman—
"It is too late!"

   ABBOT.   It never can be so,
To reconcile thyself with thy own soul,
And thy own soul with heaven. Hast thou no hope?   100
'Tis strange—even those who do despair above,
Yet shape themselves some fantasy on earth,

To which frail twig they cling, like drowning men.

   MANFRED. Ay—father! I have had those earthly visions,
And noble aspirations in my youth,
To make my own the mind of other men,
The enlightener of nations; and to rise
I knew not whither—it might be to fall;
But fall, even as the mountain-cataract,
Which having leapt from its more dazzling height,   110
Even in the foaming strength of its abyss,
(Which casts up misty columns that become
Clouds raining from the re-ascended skies,)
Lies low but mighty still.—But this is past,
My thoughts mistook themselves.

   ABBOT.   And wherefore so?

   MANFRED. I could not tame my nature down; for he
Must serve who fain would sway; and soothe, and sue,
And watch all time, and pry into all place,
And be a living lie, who would become
A mighty thing amongst the mean, and such   120
The mass are; I disdain'd to mingle with
A herd, though to be leader—and of wolves.
The lion is alone, and so am I.

   ABBOT. And why not live and act with other men?

   MANFRED. Because my nature was averse from life;
And yet not cruel; for I would not make,
But find a desolation. Like the wind,
The red-hot breath of the most lone simoom,
Which dwells but in the desert, and sweeps o'er
The barren sands which bear no shrubs to blast,   130
And revels o'er their wild and arid waves,
And seeketh not, so that it is not sought,
But being met is deadly,—such hath been
The course of my existence; but there came
Things in my path which are no more.

   ABBOT.   Alas!
I 'gin to fear that thou art past all aid

From me and from my calling; yet so young,
I still would—
   MANFRED.   Look on me! there is an order
Of mortals on the earth, who do become
Old in their youth, and die ere middle age,   140
Without the violence of warlike death;
Some perishing of pleasure, some of study,
Some worn with toil, some of mere weariness,
Some of disease, and some insanity,
And some of wither'd or of broken hearts;
For this last is a malady which slays
More than are number'd in the lists of Fate,
Taking all shapes, and bearing many names.
Look upon me! for even of all these things
Have I partaken; and of all these things,   150
One were enough; then wonder not that I
Am what I am, but that I ever was,
Or having been, that I am still on earth.
   ABBOT. Yet, hear me still——
   MANFRED.   Old man! I do respect
Thine order, and revere thine years; I deem
Thy purpose pious, but it is in vain:
Think me not churlish; I would spare thyself,
Far more than me, in shunning at this time
All further colloquy—and so—farewell.

                          [Exit MANFRED.]

   ABBOT. This should have been a noble creature: he   160
Hath all the energy which would have made
A goodly frame of glorious elements,
Had they been wisely mingled; as it is,
It is an awful chaos—light and darkness,
And mind and dust, and passions and pure thoughts
Mix'd, and contending without end or order,—
All dormant or destructive: he will perish,
And yet he must not; I will try once more.
For such are worth redemption; and my duty

Is to dare all things for a righteous end.   170
I'll follow him—but cautiously, though surely.

[*Exit* ABBOT.]

SCENE II.—*Another Chamber.* MANFRED *and* HERMAN.

HERMAN. My lord, you bade me wait on you at sunset:
He sinks behind the mountain.
    MANFRED.   Doth he so?
I will look on him.
[MANFRED *advances to the window of the Hall.*]
                                    Glorious Orb! the idol
Of early nature, and the vigorous race
Of undiseased mankind, the giant sons
Of the embrace of angels, with a sex
More beautiful than they, which did draw down
The erring spirits who can ne'er return.—
Most glorious orb! that wert a worship, ere
The mystery of thy making was reveal'd!   10
Thou earliest minister of the Almighty,
Which gladden'd, on their mountain tops, the hearts
Of the Chaldean shepherds, till they pour'd
Themselves in orisons! Thou material God!
And representative of the Unknown—
Who chose thee for his shadow! Thou chief star!
Centre of many stars! which mak'st our earth
Endurable, and temperest the hues
And hearts of all who walk within thy rays!
Sire of the seasons! Monarch of the climes,   20
And those who dwell in them! for near or far,
Our inborn spirits have a tint of thee
Even as our outward aspects;—thou dost rise,
And shine, and set in glory. Fare thee well!
I ne'er shall see thee more. As my first glance
Of love and wonder was for thee, then take
My latest look; thou wilt not beam on one
To whom the gifts of life and warmth have been

Of a more fatal nature. He is gone:
I follow.

[*Exit* MANFRED.]

SCENE III.—*The Mountains—The Castle of Manfred at some distance—A Terrace before a Tower—Time, Twiilght.* HERMAN,
    MANUEL, *and other Dependants of* MANFRED.

HERMAN. 'Tis strange enough; night after night, for years,
He hath pursued long vigils in this tower,
Without a witness. I have been within it,—
So have we all been oft-times; but from it,
Or its contents, it were impossible
To draw conclusions absolute, of aught
His studies tend to. To be sure, there is
One chamber where none enter: I would give
The fee of what I have to come these three years,
To pore upon its mysteries.
MANUEL.   'Twere dangerous;   10
Content thyself with what thou know'st already.
HERMAN. Ah! Manuel! thou art elderly and wise,
And couldst say much; thou hast dwelt within the castle—
How many years is 't?
MANUEL.   Ere Count Manfred's birth,
I served his father, whom he nought resembles.
HERMAN. There be more sons in like predicament.
But wherein do they differ?
MANUEL.   I speak not
Of features or of form, but mind and habits;
Count Sigismund was proud, but gay and free,—
A warrior and a reveller; he dwelt not   20
With books and solitude, nor made the night
A gloomy vigil, but a festal time,
Merrier than day; he did not walk the rocks
And forests like a wolf, nor turn aside
From men and their delights.
HERMAN.   Beshrew the hour,

But those were jocund times! I would that such
Would visit the old walls again; they look
As if they had forgotten them.

    MANUEL.   These walls
Must change their chieftain first. Oh! I have seen
Some strange things in them, Herman.

    HERMAN.   Come, be friendly; 30
Relate me some to while away our watch:
I've heard thee darkly speak of an event
Which happen'd hereabouts, by this same tower.

    MANUEL. That was a night indeed! I do remember
'Twas twilight, as it may be now, and such
Another evening;—yon red cloud, which rests
On Eigher's pinnacle, so rested then,—
So like that it might be the same; the wind
Was faint and gusty, and the mountain snows
Began to glitter with the climbing moon;   40
Count Manfred was, as now, within his tower,—
How occupied, we know not, but with him
The sole companion of his wanderings
And watchings—her, whom of all earthly things
That lived, the only thing he seem'd to love,—
As he, indeed, by blood was bound to do,
The lady Astarte, his—

                        Hush! who comes here?

[*Enter the* ABBOT.]

    ABBOT. Where is your master?

    HERMAN.   Yonder in the tower.

    ABBOT. I must speak with him.

    MANUEL.   'Tis impossible;
He is most private, and must not be thus
Intruded on.

    ABBOT.   Upon myself I take
The forfeit of my fault, if fault there be—
But I must see him.

    HERMAN.   Thou hast seen him once
This eve already.

ABBOT.   Herman! I command thee,
Knock, and apprize the Count of my approach.
HERMAN. We dare not.
ABBOT. Then it seems I must be herald
Of my own purpose.
MANUEL.   Reverend father, stop—
I pray you pause.
ABBOT.   Why so?
MANUEL.   But step this way,
And I will tell you further.

[*Exeunt.*]

SCENE IV.—*Interior of the Tower*. MANFRED *alone*.

The stars are forth, the moon above the tops
Of the snow-shining mountains.—Beautiful!
I linger yet with Nature, for the Night
Hath been to me a more familiar face
Than that of man; and in her starry shade
Of dim and solitary loveliness,
I learn'd the language of another world.
I do remember me, that in my youth,
When I was wandering,—upon such a night
I stood within the Coliseum's wall,   10
'Midst the chief relics of almighty Rome;
The trees which grew along the broken arches
Waved dark in the blue midnight, and the stars
Shone through the rents of ruin; from afar
The watch-dog bay'd beyond the Tiber; and
More near from out the Caesars' palace came
The owls long cry, and, interruptedly,
Of distant sentinels the fitful song
Begun and died upon the gentle wind.
Some cypresses beyond the time-worn breach   20
Appear'd to skirt the horizon, yet they stood
Within a bowshot. Where the Caesars dwelt,
And dwell the tuneless birds of night, amidst
A grove which springs through levell'd battlements,

And twines its roots with the imperial hearths,
Ivy usurps the laurel's place of growth;
But the gladiators' bloody Circus stands,
A noble wreck in ruinous perfection,
While Caesar's chambers, and the Augustan halls,
Grovel on earth in indistinct decay.   30
And thou didst shine, thou rolling moon, upon
All this, and cast a wide and tender light,
Which soften'd down the hoar austerity
Of rugged desolation, and fill'd up,
As 'twere anew, the gaps of centuries;
Leaving that beautiful which still was so,
And making that which was not, till the place
Became religion, and the heart ran o'er
With silent worship of the great of old,—
The dead but sceptred sovereigns, who still rule   40
Our spirits from their urns.

                                      'Twas such a night!
'Tis strange that I recall it at this time;
But I have found our thoughts take wildest flight
Even at the moment when they should array
Themselves in pensive order.
[*Enter the* ABBOT.]

    ABBOT.   My good lord!
I crave a second grace for this approach;
But yet let not my humble zeal offend
By its abruptness—all it hath of ill
Recoils on me; its good in the effect
May light upon your head—could I say *heart*—   50
Could I touch *that*, with words or prayers, I should
Recall a noble spirit which hath wander'd;
But is not yet all lost.

    MANFRED.   Thou know'st me not;
My days are number'd, and my deeds recorded:
Retire, or 'twill be dangerous—Away!

    ABBOT.   Thou dost not mean to menace me?

MANFRED.   Not I;
I simply tell thee peril is at hand,
And would preserve thee.

ABBOT.   What dost thou mean?

MANFRED.   Look there!
What dost thou see?

ABBOT.   Nothing.

MANFRED.   Look there I say,
And steadfastly;—now tell me what thou seest?   60

ABBOT. That which should shake me, but I fear it not:
I see a dusk and awful figure rise,
Like an infernal god, from out the earth;
His face wrapt in a mantle, and his form
Robed as with angry clouds: he stands between
Thyself and me—but I do fear him not.

MANFRED. Thou hast no cause—he shall not harm thee—but
His sight may shock thine old limbs into palsy.
I say to thee—Retire!

ABBOT.   And I reply—
Never—till I have battled with this fiend:—   70
What doth he here?

MANFRED. Why—ay—what doth he here?
I did not send for him,—he is unbidden.

ABBOT. Alas! lost mortal! what with guests like these
Hast thou to do? I tremble for thy sake:
Why doth he gaze on thee, and thou on him?
Ah! he unveils his aspect: on his brow
The thunder-scars are graven: from his eye
Glares forth the immortality of hell—
Avaunt!—

MANFRED. Pronounce—what is thy mission?

SPIRIT.   Come!

ABBOT. What art thou, unknown being? answer!—speak!   80

SPIRIT. The genius of this mortal.—Come! 'tis time.

MANFRED. I am prepared for all things, but deny
The power which summons me. Who sent thee here?

SPIRIT. Thou'lt know anon—Come! come!

MANFRED.   I have commanded
Things of an essence greater far than thine,
And striven with thy masters. Get thee hence!

SPIRIT. Mortal! thine hour is come—Away! I say.

MANFRED. I knew, and know my hour is come, but **not**
To render up my soul to such as thee:
Away! I'll die as I have lived—alone.   90

SPIRIT. Then I must summon up my brethren.—Rise!
[*Other Spirits rise up.*]

ABBOT. Avaunt! ye evil ones!—Avaunt! I say;
Ye have no power where piety hath power,
And I do charge ye in the name——

SPIRIT.   Old man!
We know ourselves, our mission, and thine order;
Waste not thy holy words on idle uses,
It were in vain: this man is forfeited.
Once more I summon him—Away! Away!

MANFRED. I do defy ye,—though I feel my soul
Is ebbing from me, yet I do defy ye;   100
Nor will I hence, while I have earthly breath
To breathe my scorn upon ye—earthly strength
To wrestle, though with spirits; what ye take
Shall be ta'en limb by limb.

SPIRIT.   Reluctant mortal!
Is this the Magian who would so pervade
The world invisible, and make himself
Almost our equal? Can it be that thou
Art thus in love with life? the very life
Which made thee wretched!

MANFRED.   Thou false fiend, thou liest!
My life is in its last hour,—*that* I know,   110
Nor would redeem a moment of that hour;
I do not combat against death, but thee
And thy surrounding angels; my past power,
Was purchased by no compact with thy crew,
But by superior science—penance, daring,

And length of watching, strength of mind, and skill
In knowledge of our fathers—when the earth
Saw men and spirits walking side by side,
And gave ye no supremacy: I stand
Upon my strength—I do defy—deny—   120
Spurn back, and scorn ye!—
    SPIRIT.   But thy many crimes
Have made thee————
    MANFRED. What are they to such as thee?
Must crimes be punish'd but by other crimes,
And greater criminals?—Back to thy hell!
Thou hast no power upon me, *that* I feel;
Thou never shalt possess me, *that* I know:
What I have done is done; I bear within
A torture which could nothing gain from thine:
The mind which is immortal makes itself
Requital for its good or evil thoughts,—   130
Is its own origin of ill and end—
And its own place and time: its innate sense,
When stripp'd of this mortality, derives
No colour from the fleeting things without,
But is absorb'd in sufferance or in joy,
Born from the knowledge of its own desert.
Thou didst not tempt me, and thou couldst not tempt me;
I have not been thy dupe, nor am thy prey—
But was my own destroyer, and will be
My own hereafter.—Back, ye baffled fiends!—   140
The hand of death is on me—but not yours!
                      [*The Demons disappear.*]
    ABBOT. Alas! how pale thou art—thy lips are white—
And thy breast heaves—and in thy gasping throat
The accents rattle: Give thy prayers to heaven—
Pray—albeit but in thought,—but die not thus.
    MANFRED. 'Tis over—my dull eyes can fix thee not;
But all things swim around me, and the earth
Heaves as it were beneath me. Fare thee well!
Give me thy hand.

ABBOT. Cold—cold—even to the heart—
But yet one prayer—Alas! how fares it with thee?   150
MANFRED. Old man! 'tis not so difficult to die.

[MANFRED *expires*.]

ABBOT. He's gone—his soul hath ta'en its earthless flight;
Whither? I dread to think—but he is gone.

1816-1817   1817

THE VISION OF
JUDGMENT

[When George III died in 1820, Robert Southey, the Poet Laureate, wrote an eulogy entitled *A Vision of Judgment* in which he described the king's arrival and reception in heaven. In the introduction to the poem, Southey attacked Byron as one of the founders of a "Satanic School" of poetry. This poem is Byron's satiric reply.]

I

Saint Peter sat by the celestial gate:
  His keys were rusty, and the lock was dull,
So little trouble had been given of late;
  Not that the place by any means was full,
But since the Gallic era "eighty-eight"
  The devils had ta'en a longer, stronger pull,
And "a pull altogether," as they say
At sea—which drew most souls another way.

2

The angels all were singing out of tune,
  And hoarse with having little else to do,
Excepting to wind up the sun and moon,
  Or curb a runaway young star or two,
Or wild colt of a comet, which too soon
  Broke out of bounds o'er th' ethereal blue,
Splitting some planet with its playful tail,
As boats are sometimes by a wanton whale.

3

The guardian seraphs had retired on high,
  Finding their charges past all care below;

Terrestrial business fill'd nought in the sky
　　Save the recording angel's black bureau;
Who found, indeed, the facts to multiply
　　With such rapidity of vice and woe,
That he had stripp'd off both his wings in quills,
And yet was in arrear of human ills.

4

His business so augmented of late years,
　　That he was forced, against his will no doubt,
(Just like those cherubs, earthly ministers,)
　　For some resource to turn himself about,
And claim the help of his celestial peers,
　　To aid him ere he should be quite worn out
By the increased demand for his remarks:
Six angels and twelve saints were named his clerks.

5

This was a handsome board—at least for heaven;
　　And yet they had even then enough to do,
So many conquerors' cars were daily driven,
　　So many kingdoms fitted up anew;
Each day too slew its thousands six or seven,
　　Till at the crowning carnage, Waterloo,
They threw their pens down in divine disgust—
The page was so besmear'd with blood and dust.

6

This by the way; 'tis not mine to record
　　What angels shrink from: even the very devil
On this occasion his own work abhorr'd,
　　So surfeited with the infernal revel:
Though he himself had sharpen'd every sword,
　　It almost quench'd his innate thirst of evil.
(Here Satan's sole good work deserves insertion—
'Tis, that he has both generals in reversion.)

7

Let's skip a few short years of hollow peace,
    Which peopled earth no better, hell as wont,
And heaven none—they form the tyrant's lease,
    With nothing but new names subscribed upon't;
'Twill one day finish: meantime they increase,
    "With seven heads and ten horns," and all in front,
Like Saint John's foretold beast; but ours are born
Less formidable in the head than horn.

8

In the first year of freedom's second dawn
    Died George the Third; although no tyrant, one
Who shielded tyrants, till each sense withdrawn
    Left him nor mental nor external sun:
A better farmer ne'er brush'd dew from lawn,
    A worse king never left a realm undone!
He died—but left his subjects still behind,
One half as mad—and t'other no less blind.

9

He died! his death made no great stir on earth:
    His burial made some pomp; there was profusion
Of velvet, gilding, brass, and no great dearth
    Of aught but tears—save those shed by collusion.
For these things may be bought at their true worth;
    Of elegy there was the due infusion—
Bought also; and the torches, cloaks, and banners,
Heralds, and relics of old Gothic manners,

10

Form'd a sepulchral melodrame. Of all
    The fools who flock'd to swell or see the show,
Who cared about the corpse? The funeral
    Made the attraction, and the black the woe.
There throbb'd not there a thought which pierced the pall;

And when the gorgeous coffin was laid low,
It seem'd the mockery of hell to fold
The rottenness of eighty years in gold.

11

So mix his body with the dust! It might
    Return to what it *must* far sooner, were
The natural compound left alone to fight
    Its way back into earth, and fire, and air;
But the unnatural balsams merely blight
    What nature made him at his birth, as bare
As the mere million's base unmummied clay—
Yet all his spices but prolong decay.

12

He's dead—and upper earth with him has done;
    He's buried; save the undertaker's bill,
Or lapidary scrawl, the world is gone
    For him, unless he left a German will:
But where's the proctor who will ask his son?
    In whom his qualities are reigning still,
Except that household virtue, most uncommon,
Of constancy to a bad, ugly woman.

13

"God save the king!" It is a large economy
    In God to save the like; but if he will
Be saving, all the better; for not one am I
    Of those who think damnation better still:
I hardly know too if not quite alone am I
    In this small hope of bettering future ill
By circumscribing, with some slight restriction,
The eternity of hell's hot jurisdiction.

14

I know this is unpopular; I know
    'Tis blasphemous; I know one may be damn'd

For hoping no one else may e'er be so;
   I know my catechism; I know we're cramm'd
With the best doctrines till we quite o'erflow;
   I know that all save England's church have shamm'd,
And that the other twice two hundred churches
And synagogues have made a *damn'd* bad purchase.

15

God help us all! God help me too! I am,
   God knows, as helpless as the devil can wish,
And not a whit more difficult to damn,
   Than is to bring to land a late-hook'd fish,
Or to the butcher to purvey the lamb;
   Not that I'm fit for such a noble dish,
As one day will be that immortal fry
Of almost everybody born to die.

16

Saint Peter sat by the celestial gate,
   And nodded o'er his keys; when, lo! there came
A wondrous noise he had not heard of late—
   A rushing sound of wind, and stream, and flame;
In short, a roar of things extremely great,
   Which would have made aught save a saint exclaim;
But he, with first a start and then a wink,
Said, "There's another star gone out, I think!"

17

But ere he could return to his repose,
   A cherub flapp'd his right wing o'er his eyes—
At which St. Peter yawn'd, and rubb'd his nose:
   "Saint porter," said the angel, "prithee rise!"
Waving a goodly wing, which glow'd, as glows
   An earthly peacock's tail, with heavenly dyes:
To which the saint replied, "Well, what's the matter?
"Is Lucifer come back with all this clatter?"

18

"No," quoth the cherub; "George the Third is dead."
   "And who *is* George the Third?" replied the apostle:
"What George? what Third?" "The king of England," said
   The angel. "Well! he won't find kings to jostle
Him on his way; but does he wear his head?
   Because the last we saw here had a tustle,
And ne'er would have got into heaven's good graces,
Had he not flung his head in all our faces.

19

"He was, if I remember, king of France;
   That head of his, which could not keep a crown
On earth, yet ventured in my face to advance
   A claim to those of martyrs—like my own:
If I had had my sword, as I had once
   When I cut ears off, I had cut him down;
But having but my *keys*, and not my brand,
I only knock'd his head from out his hand.

20

"And then he set up such a headless howl,
   That all the saints came out and took him in;
And there he sits by St. Paul, cheek by jowl;
   That fellow Paul—the parvenu! The skin
Of St. Bartholomew, which makes his cowl
   In heaven, and upon earth redeem'd his sin,
So as to make a martyr, never sped
Better than did this weak and wooden head.

21

"But had it come up here upon its shoulders,
   There would have been a different tale to tell:
The fellow-feeling in the saint's beholders
   Seems to have acted on them like a spell,
And so this very foolish head heaven solders

Back on its trunk: it may be very well,
And seems the custom here to overthrow
Whatever has been wisely done below."

22

The angel answer'd, "Peter! do not pout:
  The king who comes has head and all entire,
And never knew much what it was about—
  He did as doth the puppet—by its wire,
And will be judged like all the rest, no doubt:
  My business and your own is not to inquire
Into such matters, but to mind our cue—
Which is to act as we are bid to do."

23

While thus they spake, the angelic caravan,
  Arriving like a rush of mighty wind,
Cleaving the fields of space, as doth the swan
  Some silver stream (say Ganges, Nile, or Inde,
Or Thames, or Tweed), and 'midst them an old man
  With an old soul, and both extremely blind,
Halted before the gate, and in his shroud
Seated their fellow traveller on a cloud.

24

But bringing up the rear of this bright host
  A Spirit of a different aspect waved
His wings, like thunder-clouds above some coast
  Whose barren beach with frequent wrecks is paved;
His brow was like the deep when tempest-toss'd;
  Fierce and unfathomable thoughts engraved
Eternal wrath on his immortal face,
And *where* he gazed a gloom pervaded space.

25

As he drew near, he gazed upon the gate
  Ne'er to be enter'd more by him or Sin,

With such a glance of supernatural hate,
  As made Saint Peter wish himself within;
He patter'd with his keys at a great rate,
  And sweated through his apostolic skin:
Of course his perspiration was but ichor,
Or some such other spiritual liquor.

26

The very cherubs huddled all together,
  Like birds when soars the falcon; and they felt
A tingling to the tip of every feather,
  And form'd a circle like Orion's belt
Around their poor old charge; who scarce knew whither
  His guards had led him, though they gently dealt
With royal manes (for by many stories,
And true, we learn the angels all are Tories).

27

As things were in this posture, the gate flew
  Asunder, and the flashing of its hinges
Flung over space an universal hue
  Of many-colour'd flame, until its tinges
Reach'd even our speck of earth, and made a new
  Aurora borealis spread its fringes
O'er the North Pole; the same seen, when ice-bound,
By Captain Parry's crew, in "Melville's Sound."

28

And from the gate thrown open issued beaming
  A beautiful and mighty Thing of Light,
Radiant with glory, like a banner streaming
  Victorious from some world-o'erthrowing fight:
My poor comparisons must needs be teeming
  With earthly likenesses, for here the night
Of clay obscures our best conceptions, saving
Johanna Southcote, or Bob Southey raving.

29

'Twas the archangel Michael; all men know
   The make of angels and archangels, since
There's scarce a scribbler has not one to show,
   From the fiends' leader to the angels' prince;
There also are some altar-pieces, though
   I really can't say that they much evince
One's inner notions of immortal spirits;
But let the connoisseurs explain *their* merits.

30

Michael flew forth in glory and in good;
   A goodly work of him from whom all glory
And good arise; the portal past—he stood;
   Before him the young cherubs and saints hoary—
(I say *young*, begging to be understood
   By looks, not years; and should be very sorry
To state, they were not older than St. Peter,
But merely that they seem'd a little sweeter).

31

The cherubs and the saints bow'd down before
   That arch-angelic hierarch, the first
Of essences angelical, who wore
   The aspect of a god; but this ne'er nursed
Pride in his heavenly bosom, in whose core
   No thought, save for his Master's service, durst
Intrude, however glorified and high;
He knew him but the viceroy of the sky.

32

He and the sombre, silent Spirit met—
   They knew each other both for good and ill;
Such was their power, that neither could forget
   His former friend and future foe; but still
There was a high, immortal, proud regret

In either's eye, as if 'twere less their will
Than destiny to make the eternal years
Their date of war, and their "champ clos" the spheres.

33

But here they were in neutral space: we know
   From Job, that Satan hath the power to pay
A heavenly visit thrice a year or so;
   And that the "sons of God", like those of clay,
Must keep him company; and we might show
   From the same book, in how polite a way
The dialgoue is held between the Powers
Of Good and Evil—but 'twould take up hours

34

And this is not a theologic tract,
   To prove with Hebrew and with Arabic,
If Job be allegory or a fact,
   But a true narrative; and thus I pick
From out the whole but such and such an act
   As sets aside the slightest thought of trick.
'Tis every tittle true, beyond suspicion,
And accurate as any other vision.

35

The spirits were in neutral space, before
   The gate of heaven; like eastern thresholds is
The place where Death's grand cause is argued o'er,
   And souls despatch'd to that world or to this;
And therefore Michael and the other wore
   A civil aspect: though they did not kiss,
Yet still between his Darkness and his Brightness
There pass'd a mutual glance of great politeness.

36

The Archangel bow'd, not like a modern beau,
   But with a graceful Oriental bend,

Pressing one radiant arm just where below
    The heart in good men is supposed to tend;
He turn'd as to an equal, not too low,
    But kindly; Satan met his ancient friend
With more hauteur, as might an old Castilian
Poor noble meet a mushroom rich civilian.

37

He merely bent his diabolic brow
    An instant; and then raising it, he stood
In act to assert his right or wrong, and show
    Cause why King George by no means could or should
Make out a case to be exempt from woe
    Eternal, more than other kings, endued
With better sense and hearts, whom history mentions,
Who long have "paved hell with their good intentions."

38

Michael began: "What wouldst thou with this man,
    Now dead, and brought before the Lord? What ill
Hath he wrought since his mortal race began,
    That thou canst claim him? Speak! and do thy will,
If it be just: if in this earthly span
    He hath been greatly failing to fulfil
His duties as a king and mortal, say,
And he is thine; if not, let him have way."

39

"Michael!" replied the Prince of Air, "even here,
    Before the Gate of him thou servest, must
I claim my subject: and will make appear
    That as he was my worshipper in dust,
So shall he be in spirit, although dear
    To thee and thine, because nor wine nor lust
Were of his weaknesses; yet on the throne
He reign'd o'er millions to serve me alone.

40

"Look to *our* earth, or rather *mine;* it was,
　Once, *more* thy master's: but I triumph not
In this poor planet's conquest; nor, alas!
　Need he thou servest envy me my lot:
With all the myriads of bright worlds which pass
　In worship round him, he may have forgot
Yon weak creation of such paltry things:
I think few worth damnation save their kings,—

41

"And these but as a kind of quit-rent, to
　Assert my right as lord: and even had
I such an inclination, 'twere (as you
　Well know) superfluous; they are grown so bad,
That hell has nothing better left to do
　Than leave them to themselves: so much more mad
And evil by their own internal curse,
Heaven cannot make them better, nor I worse.

42

"Look to the earth, I said, and say again:
　When this old, blind, mad, helpless, weak, poor worm
Began in youth's first bloom and flush to reign,
　The world and he both wore a different form,
And much of earth and all the watery plain
　Of ocean call'd him king: through many a storm
His isles had floated on the abyss of time;
For the rough virtues chose them for their clime.

43

"He came to his sceptre young; he leaves it old:
　Look to the state in which he found his realm,
And left it; and his annals too behold,
　How to a minion first he gave the helm;
How grew upon his heart a thirst for gold,

The beggar's vice, which can but overwhelm
The meanest hearts; and for the rest, but glance
Thine eye along America and France.

44

" 'Tis true, he was a tool from first to last
    (I have the workmen safe); but as a tool
So let him be consumed. From out the past
    Of ages, since mankind have known the rule
Of monarchs—from the bloody rolls amass'd
    Of sin and slaughter—from the Caesar's school,
Take the worst pupil; and produce a reign
More drench'd with gore, more cumber'd with the slain.

45

"He ever warr'd with freedom and the free:
    Nations as men, home subjects, foreign foes,
So that they utter'd the word 'Liberty!'
    Found George the Third their first opponent. Whose
History was ever stain'd as his will be
    With national and individual woes?
I grant his household abstinence; I grant
His neutral virtues, which most monarchs want;

46

"I know he was a constant consort; own
    He was a decent sire, and middling lord.
All this is much, and most upon a throne;
    As temperance, if at Apicius' board,
Is more than at an anchorite's supper shown.
    I grant him all the kindest can accord;
And this was well for him, but not for those
Millions who found him what oppression chose.

47

"The New World shook him off; the Old yet groans
    Beneath what he and his prepared, if not

Completed: he leaves heirs on many thrones
　To all his vices, without what begot
Compassion for him—his tame virtues; drones
　Who sleep, or despots who have now forgot
A lesson which shall be re-taught them, wake
Upon the thrones of earth; but let them quake!

48

"Five millions of the primitive, who hold
　The faith which makes ye great on earth, implored
A *part* of that vast *all* they held of old,—
　Freedom to worship—not alone your Lord,
Michael, but you, and you, Saint Peter! Cold
　Must be your souls, if you have not abhorr'd
The foe to Catholic participation
In all the license of a Christian nation.

49

"True! he allow'd them to pray God; but as
　A consequence of prayer, refused the law
Which would have placed them upon the same base
　With those who did not hold the saints in awe."
But here Saint Peter started from his place,
　And cried, "You may the prisoner withdraw:
Ere heaven shall ope her portals to this Guelph,
While I am guard, may I be damn'd myself!

50

"Sooner will I with Cerberus exchange
　My office (and *his* is no sinecure)
Than see this royal Bedlam bigot range
　The azure fields of heaven, of that be sure!"
"Saint!" replied Satan, "you do well to avenge
　The wrongs he made your satellites endure;
And if to this exchange you should be given,
I'll try to coax *our* Cerberus up to heaven!"

51

Here Michael interposed: "Good saint! and devil!
  Pray, not so fast; you both outrun discretion.
Saint Peter! you were wont to be more civil!
  Satan! excuse this warmth of his expression,
And condescension to the vulgar's level:
  Even saints sometimes forget themselves in session.
Have you got more to say?"—"No."—"If you please,
I'll trouble you to call your witnesses."

52

Then Satan turn'd and waved his swarthy hand,
  Which stirr'd with its electric qualities
Clouds farther off than we can understand,
  Although we find him sometimes in our skies;
Infernal thunder shook both sea and land
  In all the planets, and hell's batteries
Let off the artillery, which Milton mentions
As one of Satan's most sublime inventions.

53

This was a signal unto such damn'd souls
  As have the privilege of their damnation
Extended far beyond the mere controls
  Of worlds past, present, or to come; no station
Is theirs particularly in the rolls
  Of hell assign'd; but where their inclination
Or business carries them in search of game,
They may range freely—being damn'd the same.

54

They're proud of this—as very well they may,
  It being a sort of knighthood, or gilt key
Stuck in their loins; or like to an "entré"
  Up the back stairs, or such free-masonry.
I borrow my comparisons from clay,

Being clay myself. Let not those spirits be
Offended with such base low likenesses;
We know their posts are nobler far than these.

55

When the great signal ran from heaven to hell—
  About ten million times the distance reckon'd
From our sun to its earth, as we can tell
  How much time it takes up, even to a second,
For every ray that travels to dispel
  The fogs of London, through which, dimly beacon'd,
The weathercocks are gilt some thrice a year,
If that the *summer* is not too severe:

56

I say that I can tell—'twas half a minute;
  I know the solar beams take up more time
Ere, pack'd up for their journey, they begin it;
  But then their telegraph is less sublime,
And if they ran a race, they would not win it
  'Gainst Satan's couriers bound for their own clime.
The sun takes up some years for every ray
To reach its goal—the devil not half a day.

57

Upon the verge of space, about the size
  Of half-a-crown, a little speck appear'd
(I've seen a something like it in the skies
  In the Aegean, ere a squall); it near'd,
And, growing bigger, took another guise;
  Like an aërial ship it tack'd, and steer'd,
Or *was* steer'd (I am doubtful of the grammar
Of the last phrase, which makes the stanza stammer;—

58

But take your choice): and then it grew a cloud;
  And so it was—a cloud of witnesses.

But such a cloud! No land e'er saw a crowd
   Of locusts numerous as the heavens saw these;
They shadow'd with their myriads space; their loud
   And varied cries were like those of wild geese
(If nations may be liken'd to a goose),
And realised the phrase of "hell broke loose."

59

Here crash'd a sturdy oath of stout John Bull,
   Who damn'd away his eyes as heretofore:
There Paddy brogued "By Jasus!"—"What's your wull?"
   The temperate Scot exclaim'd: the French ghost swore
In certain terms I shan't translate in full,
   As the first coachman will; and 'midst the war,
The voice of Jonathan was heard to express,
"*Our* president is going to war, I guess."

60

Besides there was the Spaniard, Dutch, and Dane;
   In short, an universal shoal of shades,
From Otaheite's isle to Salisbury Plain,
   Of all climes and professions, years and trades,
Ready to swear against the good king's reign,
   Bitter as clubs in cards are against spades:
All summon'd by this grand "subpoena," to
Try if kings mayn't be damn'd like me or you.

61

When Michael saw this host, he first grew pale,
   As angels can; next, like Italian twilight,
He turn'd all colours—as a peacock's tail,
   Or sunset streaming through a Gothic skylight
In some old abbey, or a trout not stale,
   Or distant lightning on the horizon *by* night,
Or a fresh rainbow, or a grand review
Of thirty regiments in red, green, and blue.

62

Then he address'd himself to Satan: "Why—
  My good old friend, for such I deem you, though
Our different parties make us fight so shy,
  I ne'er mistake you for a *personal* foe;
Our difference is *political,* and I
  Trust that, whatever may occur below,
You know my great respect for you: and this
Makes me regret whate'er you do amiss—

63

"Why, my dear Lucifer, would you abuse
  My call for witnesses? I did not mean
That you should half of earth and hell produce;
  'Tis even superfluous, since two honest, clean,
True testimonies are enough: we lose
  Our time, nay, our eternity, between
The accusation and defence: if we
Hear both, 'twill stretch our immortality."

64

Satan replied, "To me the matter is
  Indifferent, in a personal point of view:
I can have fifty better souls than this
  With far less trouble than we have gone through
Already; and I merely argued his
  Late majesty of Britain's case with you
Upon a point of form: you may dispose
Of him; I've kings enough below, God knows!"

65

Thus spoke the Demon (late call'd "multi-faced"
  By multo-scribbling Southey). "Then we'll call
One or two persons of the myriads placed
  Around our congress, and dispense with all
The rest," quoth Michael: "Who may be so graced

As to speak first? there's choice enough—who shall
It be?" Then Satan answer'd, "There are many;
But you may choose Jack Wilkes as well as any."

66

A merry, cock-eyed, curious-looking sprite
    Upon the instant started from the throng,
Dress'd in a fashion now forgotten quite;
    For all the fashions of the flesh stick long
By people in the next world; where unite
    All the costumes since Adam's, right or wrong,
From Eve's fig-leaf down to the petticoat,
Almost as scanty, of days less remote.

67

The spirit look'd around upon the crowds
    Assembled, and exclaim'd, "My friends of all
The spheres, we shall catch cold amongst these clouds;
    So let's to business: why this general call?
If those are freeholders I see in shrouds,
    And 'tis for an election that they bawl,
Behold a candidate with unturn'd coat!
Saint Peter, may I count upon your vote?"

68

"Sir," replied Michael, "you mistake; these things
    Are of a former life, and what we do
Above is more august; to judge of kings
    Is the tribunal met: so now you know."
"Then I presume those gentlemen with wings,"
    Said Wilkes, "are cherubs; and that soul below
Looks much like George the Third, but to my mind
A good deal older—Bless me! is he blind?"

69

"He is what you behold him, and his doom
    Depends upon his deeds," the Angel said;

"If you have aught to arraign in him, the tomb
  Gives licence to the humblest beggar's head
To lift itself against the loftiest."—"Some,"
  Said Wilkes, "don't wait to see them laid in lead,
For such a liberty—and I, for one,
Have told them what I thought beneath the sun."

70

"*Above* the sun repeat, then, what thou hast
  To urge against him," said the Archangel. "Why,"
Replied the spirit, "since old scores are past,
  Must I turn evidence? In faith, not I.
Besides, I beat him hollow at the last,
  With all his Lords and Commons: in the sky
I don't like ripping up old stories, since
His conduct was but natural in a prince.

71

"Foolish, no doubt, and wicked, to oppress
  A poor unlucky devil without a shilling;
But then I blame the man himself much less
  Than Bute and Grafton, and shall be unwilling
To see him punish'd here for their excess,
  Since they were both damn'd long ago, and still in
Their place below: for me, I have forgiven,
And vote his 'habeas corpus' into heaven."

72

"Wilkes," said the devil, "I understand all this;
  You turn'd to half a courtier ere you died,
And seem to think it would not be amiss
  To grow a whole one on the other side
Of Charon's ferry; you forget that *his*
  Reign is concluded; whatsoe'er betide,
He won't be sovereign more: you've lost your labour,
For at the best he will but be your neighbour.

73

'However, I knew what to think of it,
  When I beheld you in your jesting way,
Flitting and whispering round about the spit
  Where Belial, upon duty for the day,
With Fox's lard was basting William Pitt,
  His pupil; I knew what to think, I say:
That fellow even in hell breeds farther ills;
I'll have him *gagg'd*—'twas one of his own bills.

74

"Call Junius!" From the crowd a shadow stalk'd,
  And at the name there was a general squeeze,
So that the very ghosts no longer walk'd
  In comfort, at their own aërial ease,
But were all ramm'd, and jamm'd (but to be balk'd,
  As we shall see), and jostled hands and knees,
Like wind compress'd and pent within a bladder,
Or like a human colic, which is sadder.

75

The shadow came—a tall, thin, grey-hair'd figure,
  That look'd as it had been a shade on earth;
Quick in its motions, with an air of vigour,
  But nought to mark its breeding or its birth;
Now it wax'd little, then again grew bigger,
  With now an air of gloom, or savage mirth;
But as you gazed upon its features, they
Changed every instant—to *what*, none could say.

76

The more intently the ghosts gazed, the less
  Could they distinguish whose the features were;
The Devil himself seem'd puzzled even to guess;
  They varied like a dream—now here, now there;
And several people swore from out the press,

They knew him perfectly; and one could swear
He was his father: upon which another
Was sure he was his mother's cousin's brother:

77

Another, that he was a duke, or knight,
   An orator, a lawyer, or a priest,
A nabob, a man-midwife; but the wight
   Mysterious changed his countenance at least
As oft as they their minds; though in full sight
   He stood, the puzzle only was increased;
The man was a phantasmagoria in
Himself—he was so volatile and thin.

78

The moment that you had pronounced him *one*,
   Presto! his face changed, and he was another;
And when that change was hardly well put on,
   It varied, till I don't think his own mother
(If that he had a mother) would her son
   Have known, he shifted so from one to t'other;
Till guessing from a pleasure grew a task,
At this epistolary "Iron Mask."

79

For sometimes he like Cerberus would seem—
   "Three gentlemen at once" (as sagely says
Good Mrs. Malaprop); then you might deem
   That he was not even *one*; now many rays
Were flashing round him; and now a thick steam
   Hid him from sight—like fogs on London days:
Now Burke, now Tooke, he grew to people's fancies,
And certes often like Sir Philip Francis.

80

I've an hypothesis—'tis quite my own;
   I never let it out till now, for fear

Of doing people harm about the throne,
   And injuring some minister or peer,
On whom the stigma might perhaps be blown;
   It is—my gentle public, lend thine ear!
'Tis, that what Junius we are wont to call
Was *really*, *truly*, nobody at all.

81

I don't see wherefore letters should not be
   Written without hands, since we daily view
Them written without heads; and books, we see,
   Are fill'd as well without the latter too:
And reålly till we fix on somebody
   For certain sure to claim them as his due,
Their author, like the Niger's mouth, will bother
The world to say if *there* be mouth or author.

82

"And who and what art thou?" the Archangel said.
   "For *that* you may consult my title-page,"
Replied this mighty shadow of a shade:
   "If I have kept my secret half an age,
I scarce shall tell it now."—"Canst thou upbraid,"
   Continued Michael, "George Rex, or allege
Aught further?" Junius answer'd, "You had better
First ask him for *his* answer to my letter:

83

"My charges upon record will outlast
   The brass of both his epitaph and tomb."
"Repent'st thou not," said Michael, "of some past
   Exaggeration? something which may doom
Thyself if false, as him if true? Thou wast
   Too bitter—is it not so?—in thy gloom
Of passion?"—"Passion!" cried the phantom dim,
"I loved my country, and I hated him.

84

"What I have written, I have written: let
    The rest be on his head or mine!" So spoke
Old "Nominis Umbra"; and while speaking yet,
    Away he melted in celestial smoke.
Then Satan said to Michael, "Don't forget
    To call George Washington, and John Horne Tooke,
And Franklin;"—but at this time there was heard
A cry for room, though not a phantom stirr'd.

85

At length with jostling, elbowing, and the aid
    Of cherubim appointed to that post,
The devil Asmodeus to the circle made
    His way, and look'd as if his journey cost
Some trouble. When his burden down he laid,
    "What's this?" cried Michael; "why, 'tis not a ghost?"
"I know it," quoth the incubus; "but he
Shall be one, if you leave the affair to me.

86

"Confound the renegado! I have sprain'd
    My left wing, he's so heavy; one would think
Some of his works about his neck were chain'd.
    But to the point; while hovering o'er the brink
Of Skiddaw (where as usual it still rain'd),
    I saw a taper, far below me, wink,
And stooping, caught this fellow at a libel—
No less on history than the Holy Bible.

87

"The former is the devil's scripture, and
    The latter yours, good Michael: so the affair
Belongs to all of us, you understand.
    I snatch'd him up just as you see him there,
And brought him off for sentence out of hand:

I've scarcely been ten minutes in the air—
At least a quarter it can hardly be:
I dare say that his wife is still at tea."

88

Here Satan said, "I know this man of old,
    And have expected him for some time here;
A sillier fellow you will scarce behold,
    Or more conceited in his petty sphere:
But surely it was not worth while to fold
    Such trash below your wing, Asmodeus dear:
We had the poor wretch safe (without being bored
With carriage) coming of his own accord.

89

"But since he's here, let's see what he has done."
    "Done!" cried Asmodeus, "he anticipates
The very business you are now upon,
    And scribbles as if head clerk to the Fates.
Who knows to what his ribaldry may run,
    When such an ass as this, like Balaam's, prates?"
"Let's hear," quoth Michael, "what he has to say:
You know we're bound to that in every way."

90

Now the bard, glad to get an audience, which
    By no means often was his case below,
Began to cough, and hawk, and hem, and pitch
    His voice into that awful note of woe
To all unhappy hearers within reach
    Of poets when the tide of rhyme's in flow;
But stuck fast with his first hexameter,
Not one of all whose gouty feet would stir.

91

But ere the spavin'd dactyls could be spurr'd
    Into recitative, in great dismay

Both cherubim and seraphim were heard
  To murmur loudly through their long array;
And Michael rose ere he could get a word
  Of all his founder'd verses under way,
And cried, "For God's sake stop, my friend! 'twere best—
Non Di, non homines—you know the rest."

92

A general bustle spread throughout the throng,
  Which seem'd to hold all verse in detestation;
The angels had of course enough of song
  When upon service; and the generation
Of ghosts had heard too much in life, not long
  Before, to profit by a new occasion:
The monarch, mute till then, exclaim'd, "What! what!
Pye come again? No more—no more of that!"

93

The tumult grew; an universal cough
  Convulsed the skies, as during a debate,
When Castlereagh has been up long enough
  (Before he was first minister of state,
I mean—the *slaves hear now*); some cried "Off, off!"
  As at a farce; till, grown quite desperate,
The bard Saint Peter pray'd to interpose
(Himself an author) only for his prose.

94

The varlet was not an ill-favour'd knave;
  A good deal like a vulture in the face,
With a hook nose and a hawk's eye, which gave
  A smart and sharper-looking sort of grace
To his whole aspect, which, though rather grave,
  Was by no means so ugly as his case;
But that, indeed, was hopeless as can be,
Quite a poetic felony "*de se.*"

95

Then Michael blew his trump, and still'd the noise
  With one still greater, as is yet the mode
On earth besides; except some grumbling voice,
  Which now and then will make a slight inroad
Upon decorous silence, few will twice
  Lift up their lungs when fairly overcrow'd;
And now the bard could plead his own bad cause,
With all the attitudes of self-applause.

96

He said—(I only give the heads)—he said,
  He meant no harm in scribbling; 'twas his way
Upon all topics; 'twas, besides, his bread,
  Of which he butter'd both sides; 'twould delay
Too long the assembly (he was pleased to dread),
  And take up rather more time than a day,
To name his works—he would but cite a few—
"Wat Tyler"—"Rhymes on Blenheim"—"Waterloo."

97

He had written praises of a regicide;
  He had written praises of all kings whatever;
He had written for republics far and wide,
  And then against them bitterer than ever;
For pantisocracy he once had cried
  Aloud, a scheme less moral than 'twas clever;
Then grew a hearty anti-jacobin—
Had turn'd his coat—and would have turn'd his skin.

98

He had sung against all battles, and again
  In their high praise and glory; he had call'd
Reviewing "the ungentle craft," and then
  Become as base a critic as e'er crawl'd—
Fed, paid, and pamper'd by the very men

By whom his muse and morals had been maul'd:
He had written much blank verse, and blanker prose,
And more of both than anybody knows.

99

He had written Wesley's life:—here turning round
    To Satan, "Sir, I'm ready to write yours,
In two octavo volumes, nicely bound,
    With notes and preface, all that most allures
The pious purchaser; and there's no ground
    For fear, for I can choose my own reviewers:
So let me have the proper documents,
That I may add you to my other saints."

100

Satan bow'd, and was silent. "Well, if you,
    With amiable modesty, decline
My offer, what says Michael? There are few
    Whose memoirs could be render'd more divine.
Mine is a pen of all work; not so new
    As it was once, but I would make you shine
Like your own trumpet. By the way, my own
Has more brass in it, and is as well blown.

101

"But talking about trumpets, here's my Vision!
    Now you shall judge, all people; yes, you shall
Judge with my judgment, and by my decision
    Be guided who shall enter heaven or fall.
I settle all these things by intuition,
    Times present, past, to come, heaven, hell, and all,
Like King Alfonso. When I thus see double,
I save the Deity some worlds of trouble."

102

He ceased, and drew forth an MS.; and no
    Persuasion on the part of devils, saints,

Or angels, now could stop the torrent; so
   He read the first three lines of the contents;
But at the fourth, the whole spiritual show
   Had vanish'd, with variety of scents,
Ambrosial and sulphureous, as they sprang,
Like lightning, off from his "melodious twang."

103

Those grand heroics acted as a spell:
   The angels stopp'd their ears and plied their pinions;
The devils ran howling, deafen'd, down to hell;
   The ghosts fled, gibbering, for their own dominions—
(For 'tis not yet decided where they dwell,
   And I leave every man to his opinions);
Michael took refuge in his trump—but lo!
His teeth were set on edge, he could not blow!

104

Saint Peter, who has hitherto been known
   For an impetuous saint, upraised his keys,
And at the fifth line knock'd the poet down;
   Who fell like Phaeton, but more at ease,
Into his lake, for there he did not drown;
   A different web being by the Destinies
Woven for the Laureate's final wreath, whene'er
Reform shall happen either here or there.

105

He first sank to the bottom—like his works,
   But soon rose to the surface—like himself;
For all corrupted things are buoy'd like corks,
   By their own rottenness, light as an elf,
Or wisp that flits o'er a morass: he lurks,
   It may be, still, like dull books on a shelf,
In his own den, to scrawl some "Life" or "Vision,"
As Welborn says—"the devil turn'd precisian."

106

As for the rest, to come to the conclusion
    Of this true dream, the telescope is gone
Which kept my optics free from all delusion,
    And show'd me what I in my turn have shown;
All I saw farther, in the last confusion,
    Was, that King George slipp'd into heaven for one;
And when the tumult dwindled to a calm,
I left him practising the hundredth psalm.

1821   1822

DON JUAN

'Difficile est propriè communia dicere.'—HORACE.

'Dost thou think, because thou art virtuous, there shall be no more cakes and ale?
Yes, by Saint Anne, and ginger shall be hot i' the mouth, too!'—SHAKESPEARE,
Twelfth Night, or What You Will.

CANTO THE FIRST

FRAGMENT

On the back of the Poet's MS. of Canto I.

I would to heaven that I were so much clay,
  As I am blood, bone, marrow, passion, feeling—
Because at least the past were pass'd away—
  And for the future—(but I write this reeling,
Having got drunk exceedingly to-day,
  So that I seem to stand upon the ceiling)
I say—the future is a serious matter—
And so—for God's sake—hock and soda-water!

DEDICATION

I

Bob Southey! You're a poet—Poet-laureate,
  And representative of all the race;
Although 'tis true that you turn'd out a Tory at
  Last,—yours has lately been a common case;
And now, my Epic Renegade! what are ye at?
  With all the Lakers, in and out of place?
A nest of tuneful persons, to my eye
Like "four and twenty Blackbirds in a pye;

2

"Which pye being open'd they began to sing"
  (This old song and new simile holds good),

187

"A dainty dish to set before the King,"
　　Or Regent, who admires such kind of food;—
And Coleridge, too, has lately taken wing,
　　But like a hawk encumber'd with his hood,—
Explaining metaphysics to the nation—
I wish he would explain his Explanation.

3

You, Bob! are rather insolent, you know,
　　At being disappointed in your wish
To supersede all warblers here below,
　　And be the only Blackbird in the dish;
And then you overstrain yourself, or so,
　　And tumble downward like the flying fish
Gasping on deck, because you soar too high, Bob,
And fall, for lack of moisture quite a-dry, Bob!

4

And Wordsworth, in a rather long "Excursion"
　　(I think the quarto holds five hundred pages),
Has given a sample from the vasty version
　　Of his new system to perplex the sages;
'Tis poetry—at least by his assertion,
　　And may appear so when the dog-star rages—
And he who understands it would be able
To add a story to the Tower of Babel.

5

You—Gentlemen! by dint of long seclusion
　　From better company, have kept your own
At Keswick, and, through still continued fusion
　　Of one another's minds, at last have grown
To deem as a most logical conclusion,
　　That Poesy has wreaths for you alone:
There is a narrowness in such a notion,
Which makes me wish you'd change your lakes for ocean.

6

I would not imitate the petty thought,
　　Nor coin my self-love to so base a vice,
For all the glory your conversion brought,
　　Since gold alone should not have been its price.
You have your salary: was't for that you wrought?
　　And Wordsworth has his place in the Excise.
You're shabby fellows—true—but poets still,
And duly seated on the immortal hill.

7

Your bays may hide the baldness of your brows—
　　Perhaps some virtuous blushes;—let them go—
To you I envy neither fruit nor boughs—
　　And for the fame you would engross below,
The field is universal, and allows
　　Scope to all such as feel the inherent glow:
Scott, Rogers, Campbell, Moore, and Crabbe, will try
'Gainst you the question with posterity.

8

For me, who, wandering with pedestrian Muses,
　　Contend not with you on the winged steed,
I wish your fate may yield ye, when she chooses,
　　The fame you envy, and the skill you need;
And recollect a poet nothing loses
　　In giving to his brethren their full meed
Of merit, and complaint of present days
Is not the certain path to future praise.

9

He that reserves his laurels for posterity
　　(Who does not often claim the bright reversion)
Has generally no great crop to spare it, he
　　Being only injured by his own assertion;
And although here and there some glorious rarity

Arise like Titan from the sea's immersion,
The major part of such appellants go
To—God knows where—for no one else can know.

10

If, fallen in evil days on evil tongues,
    Milton appealed to the Avenger, Time,
If Time, the Avenger, execrates his wrongs,
    And makes the word "Miltonic" mean "*sublime*,"
He deign'd not to belie his soul in songs,
    Nor turn his very talent to a crime;
He did not loathe the Sire to laud the Son,
But closed the tyrant-hater he begun.

11

Think'st thou, could he—the blind Old Man—arise,
    Like Samuel from the grave, to freeze once more
The blood of monarchs with his prophecies,
    Or be alive again—again all hoar
With time and trials, and those helpless eyes,
    And heartless daughters—worn—and pale—and poor;
Would *he* adore a sultan? *he* obey
The intellectual eunuch Castlereagh?

12

Cold-blooded, smooth-faced, placid miscreant!
    Dabbling its sleek young hands in Erin's gore,
And thus for wider carnage taught to pant,
    Transferr'd to gorge upon a sister shore,
The vulgarest tool that Tyranny could want,
    With just enough of talent, and no more,
To lengthen fetters by another fix'd,
And offer poison long already mix'd.

13

An orator of such set trash of phrase
    Ineffably—legitimately vile,

That even its grossest flatterers dare not praise,
    Nor foes—all nations—condescend to smile;
Not even a sprightly blunder's spark can blaze
    From that Ixion grindstone's ceaseless toil,
That turns and turns to give the world a notion
Of endless torments and perpetual motion.

14

A bungler even in its disgusting trade,
    And botching, patching, leaving still behind
Something of which its masters are afraid,
    States to be curb'd, and thoughts to be confined,
Conspiracy or Congress to be made—
    Cobbling at manacles for all mankind—
A tinkering slave-maker, who mends old chains,
With God and man's abhorrence for its gains.

15

If we may judge of matter by the mind,
    Emasculated to the marrow *It*
Hath but two objects, how to serve, and bind,
    Deeming the chain it wears even men may fit,
Eutropius of its many masters,—blind
    To worth as freedom, wisdom as to wit,
Fearless—because *no* feeling dwells in ice,
Its very courage stagnates to a vice.

16

Where shall I turn me not to *view* its bonds,
    For I will never *feel* them;—Italy!
Thy late reviving Roman soul desponds
    Beneath the lie this State-thing breathed o'er thee—
Thy clanking chain, and Erin's yet green wounds,
    Have voices—tongues to cry aloud for me.
Europe has slaves, allies, kings, armies still,
And Southey lives to sing them very ill.

17

Meantime, Sir Laureate, I proceed to dedicate,
  In honest simple verse, this song to you.
And, if in flattering strains I do not predicate,
  'Tis that I still retain my "buff and blue;"
My politics as yet are all to educate:
  Apostasy's so fashionable, too,
To keep *one* creed's a task grown quite Herculean:
Is it not so, my Tory, ultra-Julian?

Venice, September 16, 1818.

CANTO THE FIRST

1

I want a hero: an uncommon want,
  When every year and month sends forth a new one,
Till, after cloying the gazettes with cant,
  The age discovers he is not the true one:
Of such as these I should not care to vaunt,
  I'll therefore take our ancient friend Don Juan—
We all have seen him, in the pantomime,
Sent to the devil somewhat ere his time.

2

Vernon, the butcher Cumberland, Wolfe, Hawke,
  Prince Ferdinand, Granby, Burgoyne, Keppel, Howe,
Evil and good, have had their tithe of talk,
  And fill'd their sign-posts then, like Wellesley now;
Each in their turn like Banquo's monarchs stalk,
  Followers of fame, "nine farrow" of that sow:
France, too, had Buonaparté and Dumourier
Recorded in the Moniteur and Courier.

3

Barnave, Brissot, Condorcet, Mirabeau,
    Pétion, Clootz, Danton, Marat, La Fayette,
Were French, and famous people, as we know;
    And there were others, scarce forgotten yet,
Joubert, Hoche, Marceau, Lannes, Desaix, Moreau,
    With many of the military set,
Exceedingly remarkable at times,
But not at all adapted to my rhymes.

4

Nelson was once Britannia's god of war,
    And still should be so, but the tide is turn'd;
There's no more to be said of Trafalgar,
    'Tis with our hero quietly inurn'd;
Because the army's grown more popular,
    At which the naval people are concern'd,
Besides, the prince is all for the land-service,
Forgetting Duncan, Nelson, Howe, and Jervis.

5

Brave men were living before Agamemnon
    And since, exceeding valorous and sage,
A good deal like him too, though quite the same none;
    But then they shone not on the poet's page,
And so have been forgotten:—I condemn none,
    But can't find any in the present age
Fit for my poem (that is, for my new one);
So, as I said, I'll take my friend Don Juan.

6

Most epic poets plunge "in medias res"
    (Horace makes this the heroic turnpike road),
And then your hero tells, whene'er you please,
    What went before—by way of episode,
While seated after dinner at his ease.

Beside his mistress in some soft abode,
Palace, or garden, paradise, or cavern,
Which serves the happy couple for a tavern.

7

That is the usual method, but not mine—
  My way is to begin with the beginning;
The regularity of my design
  Forbids all wandering as the worst of sinning,
And therefore I shall open with a line
  (Although it cost me half an hour in spinning)
Narrating somewhat of Don Juan's father,
And also of his mother, if you'd rather.

8

In Seville was he born, a pleasant city,
  Famous for oranges and women—he
Who has not seen it will be much to pity,
  So says the proverb—and I quite agree;
Of all the Spanish towns is none more pretty,
  Cadiz, perhaps—but that you soon may see:—
Don Juan's parents lived beside the river,
A noble stream, and call'd the Guadalquivir.

9

His father's name was José—*Don*, of course,
  A true Hidalgo, free from every stain
Of Moor or Hebrew blood, he traced his source
  Through the most Gothic gentlemen of Spain;
A better cavalier ne'er mounted horse,
  Or, being mounted, e'er got down again,
Than José, who begot our hero, who
Begot—but that's to come——Well, to renew:

10

His mother was a learned lady, famed
  For every branch of every science known—

[margin annotations: break all rules; burlesque — ancestry — hero to have supernatural ancestors]

In every Christian language ever named,
    With virtues equall'd by her wit alone:
She made the cleverest people quite ashamed,
    And even the good with inward envy groan,
Finding themselves so very much exceeded
In their own way by all the things that she did.

11

Her memory was a mine: she knew by heart
    All Calderon and greater part of Lopé,
So that if any actor miss'd his part
    She could have served him for the prompter's copy;
For her Feinagle's were an useless art,
    And he himself obliged to shut up shop—he
Could never make a memory so fine as
That which adorn'd the brain of Donna Inez.

12

Her favorite science was the mathematical,
    Her noblest virtue was her magnanimity;
Her wit (she sometimes tried at wit) was Attic all,
    Her serious sayings darken'd to sublimity;
In short, in all things she was fairly what I call
    A prodigy—her morning dress was dimity,
Her evening silk, or, in the summer, muslin,
And other stuffs, with which I won't stay puzzling.

13

She knew the Latin—that is, "the Lord's prayer,"
    And Greek—the alphabet—I'm nearly sure;
She read some French romances here and there,
    Although her mode of speaking was not pure;
For native Spanish she had no great care,
    At least her conversation was obscure;
Her thoughts were theorems, her words a problem,
As if she deem'd that mystery would ennoble 'em.

14

She liked the English and the Hebrew tongue,
　　And said there was analogy between 'em;
She proved it somehow out of sacred song,
　　But I must leave the proofs to those who've seen 'em,
But this I heard say, and can't be wrong,
　　And all may think which way their judgments lean 'em,
" 'Tis strange—the Hebrew noun which means 'I am,'
The English always use to govern d—n."

15

Some women use their tongues—she *look'd* a lecture,
　　Each eye a sermon, and her brow a homily,
An all-in-all sufficient self-director,
　　Like the lamented late Sir Samuel Romilly,
The Law's expounder, and the State's corrector,
　　Whose suicide was almost an anomaly—
One sad example more, that "All is vanity,"—
(The jury brought their verdict in "Insanity.")

16

In short, she was a walking calculation,
　　Miss Edgeworth's novels stepping from their covers,
Or Mrs. Trimmer's books on education,
　　Or "Coelebs' Wife" set out in quest of lovers,
Morality's prim personification,
　　In which not Envy's self a flaw discovers;
To others' share let "female errors fall,"
For she had not even one—the worst of all.

17

Oh! she was perfect past all parallel—
　　Of any modern female saint's comparison;
So far above the cunning powers of hell,
　　Her guardian angel had given up his garrison;
Even her minutest motions went as well

As those of the best time-piece made by Harrison:
In virtues nothing earthly could surpass her,
Save thine "incomparable oil," Macassar!

18

Perfect she was, but as perfection is
    Insipid in this naughty world of ours,
Where our first parents never learn'd to kiss
    Till they were exiled from their earlier bowers,
Where all was peace, and innocence, and bliss
    (I wonder how they got through the twelve hours),
Don José, like a lineal son of Eve,
Went plucking various fruit without her leave.

19

He was a mortal of the careless kind,
    With no great love for learning, or the learn'd,
Who chose to go where'er he had a mind,
    And never dream'd his lady was concern'd;
The world, as usual, wickedly inclined
    To see a kingdom or a house o'erturn'd,
Whisper'd he had a mistress, some said *two*,
But for domestic quarrels *one* will do.

20

Now Donna Inez had, with all her merit,
    A great opinion of her own good qualities;
Neglect, indeed, requires a saint to bear it,
    And such, indeed, she was in her moralities;
But then she had a devil of a spirit,
    And sometimes mix'd up fancies with realities,
And let few opportunities escape
Of getting her liege lord into a scrape.

21

This was an easy matter with a man
    Oft in the wrong, and never on his guard;

And even the wisest, do the best they can,
  Have moments, hours, and days, so unprepared,
That you might "brain them with their lady's fan";
  And sometimes ladies hit exceeding hard,
And fans turn into falchions in fair hands,
And why and wherefore no one understands.

22

'Tis pity learned virgins ever wed
  With persons of no sort of education,
Or gentlemen, who, though well born and bred,
  Grow tired of scientific conversation;
I don't choose to say much upon this head,
  I'm a plain man, and in a single station,
But—Oh! ye lords of ladies intellectual,
Inform us truly, have they not hen-peck'd you all?

23

Don José and his lady quarrell'd—*why*,
  Not any of the many could divine,
Though several thousand people chose to try,
  'Twas surely no concern of theirs nor mine;
I loathe that low vice—curiosity;
  But if there's anything in which I shine,
'Tis in arranging all my friends' affairs,
Not having, of my own, domestic cares.

24

And so I interfered, and with the best
  Intentions, but their treatment was not kind;
I think the foolish people were possess'd,
  For neither of them could I ever find,
Although their porter afterwards confess'd—
  But that's no matter, and the worst's behind,
For little Juan o'er me threw, down stairs
A pail of housemaid's water unawares.

25

A little curly-headed, good-for-nothing,
    And mischief-making monkey from his birth;
His parents ne'er agreed except in doting
    Upon the most unquiet imp on earth;
Instead of quarrelling, had they been but both in
    Their senses, they'd have sent young master forth
To school, or had him soundly whipp'd at home,
To teach him manners for the time to come.

26

Don José and the Donna Inez led
    For some time an unhappy sort of life,
Wishing each other, not divorced, but dead;
    They lived respectably as man and wife,
Their conduct was exceedingly well-bred,
    And gave no outward signs of inward strife,
Until at length the smother'd fire broke out,
And put the business past all kind of doubt.

27

For Inez call'd some druggists and physicians,
    And tried to prove her loving lord was *mad*,
But as he had some lucid intermissions,
    She next decided he was only *bad;*
Yet when they ask'd her for her depositions,
    No sort of explanation could be had,
Save that her duty both to man and God
Required this conduct—which seem'd very odd.

28

She kept a journal, where his faults were noted,
    And open'd certain trunks of books and letters,
All which might, if occasion served, be quoted;
    And then she had all Seville for abettors,
Besides her good old grandmother (who doted);

The hearers of her case became repeaters,
Then advocates, inquisitors, and judges,
Some for amusement, others for old grudges.

29

And then this best and meekest woman bore
    With such serenity her husband's woes,
Just as the Spartan ladies did of yore,
    Who saw their spouses kill'd, and nobly chose
Never to say a word about them more—
    Calmly she heard each calumny that rose,
And saw *his* agonies with such sublimity,
That all the world exclaim'd, "What magnanimity!"

30

No doubt this patience, when the world is damning us,
    Is philosophic in our former friends;
'Tis also pleasant to be deem'd magnanimous,
    The more so in obtaining our own ends;
And what the lawyers call a *"malus animus"*
    Conduct like this by no means comprehends:
Revenge in person's certainly no virtue,
But then 'tis not *my* fault, if *others* hurt you.

31

And if our quarrels should rip up old stories,
    And help them with a lie or two additional,
I'm not to blame, as you well know—no more is
    Any one else—they were become traditional;
Besides, their resurrection aids our glories
    By contrast, which is what we just were wishing all:
And science profits by this resurrection—
Dead scandals form good subjects for dissection.

32

Their friends had tried at reconciliation,
    Then their relations, who made matters worse

('Twere hard to tell upon a like occasion
    To whom it may be best to have recourse—
I can't say much for friend or yet relation):
    The lawyers did their utmost for divorce,
But scarce a fee was paid on either side
Before, unluckily, Don José died.

33

He died: and most unluckily, because,
    According to all hints I could collect
From counsel learned in those kinds of laws
    (Although their talk's obscure and circumspect),
His death contrived to spoil a charming cause;
    A thousand pities also with respect
To public feeling, which on this occasion
Was manifested in a great sensation.

34

But ah! he died; and buried with him lay
    The public feeling and the lawyers' fees:
His house was sold, his servants sent away,
    A Jew took one of his two mistresses,
A priest the other—at least so they say:
    I ask'd the doctors after his disease—
He died of the slow fever called the tertian,
And left his widow to her own aversion.

35

Yet José was an honourable man,
    That I must say, who knew him very well;
Therefore his frailties I'll no further scan,
    Indeed there were not many more to tell:
And if his passions now and then outran
    Discretion, and were not so peaceable
As Numa's (who was also named Pompilius),
He had been ill brought up, and was born bilious.

36

Whate'er might be his worthlessness or worth,
  Poor fellow! he had many things to wound him,
Let's own—since it can do no good on earth—
  It was a trying moment that which found him
Standing alone beside his desolate hearth,
  Where all his household gods lay shiver'd round him:
No choice was left his feelings or his pride,
Save death or Doctors' Commons—so he died.

37

Dying intestate, Juan was sole heir
  To a chancery suit, and messuages and lands,
Which, with a long minority and care,
  Promised to turn out well in proper hands:
Inez became sole guardian, which was fair,
  And answer'd but to nature's just demands;
An only son left with an only mother
Is brought up much more wisely than another.

38

Sagest of women, even of widows, she
  Resolved that Juan should be quite a paragon,
And worthy of the noblest pedigree:
  (His sire was of Castile, his dam from Aragon).
Then for accomplishments of chivalry,
  In case our lord the king should go to war again,
He learn'd the arts of riding, fencing, gunnery,
And how to scale a fortress—or a nunnery.

39

But that which Donna Inez most desired,
  And saw into herself each day before all
The learned tutors whom for him she hired,
  Was, that his breeding should be strictly moral:
Much into all his studies she inquired,

And so they were submitted first to her, all,
Arts, sciences, no branch was made a mystery
To Juan's eyes, excepting natural history.

40

The languages, especially the dead,
   The sciences, and most of all the abstruse,
The arts, at least all such as could be said
   To be the most remote from common use,
In all these he was much and deeply read:
   But not a page of anything that's loose,
Or hints continuation of the species,
Was ever suffer'd, lest he should grow vicious.

41

His classic studies made a little puzzle,
   Because of filthy loves of gods and goddesses,
Who in the earlier ages raised a bustle,
   But never put on pantaloons or bodices;
His reverend tutors had at times a tussle,
   And for their Aeneids, Iliads, and Odysseys,
Were forced to make an odd sort of apology,
For Donna Inez dreaded the Mythology.

42

Ovid's a rake, as half his verses show him,
   Anacreon's morals are a still worse sample,
Catullus scarcely has a decent poem,
   I don't think Sappho's Ode a good example,
Although Longinus tells us there is no hymn
   Where the sublime soars forth on wings more ample;
But Virgil's songs are pure, except that horrid one
Beginning with "Formosum Pastor Corydon."

43

Lucretius' irreligion is too strong
   For early stomachs, to prove wholesome food;

I can't help thinking Juvenal was wrong,
  Although no doubt his real intent was good,
For speaking out so plainly in his song,
  So much indeed as to be downright rude;
And then what proper person can be partial
To all those nauseous epigrams of Martial?

44

Juan was taught from out the best edition,
  Expurgated by learned men, who place,
Judiciously, from out the schoolboy's vision,
  The grosser parts; but, fearful to deface
Too much their modest bard by this omission,
  And pitying sore this mutilated case,
They only add them all in an appendix,
Which saves, in fact, the trouble of an index;

45

For there we have them all "at one fell swoop,"
  Instead of being scatter'd through the pages;
They stand forth marshall'd in a handsome troop,
  To meet the ingenuous youth of future ages,
Till some less rigid editor shall stoop
  To call them back into their separate cages,
Instead of standing staring all together,
Like garden gods—and not so decent either.

46

The Missal too (it was the family Missal)
  Was ornamented in a sort of way
Which ancient mass-books often are, and this all
  Kinds of grotesques illumined; and how they,
Who saw those figures on the margin kiss all,
  Could turn their optics to the text and pray,
Is more than I know—But Don Juan's mother
Kept this herself, and gave her son another.

47

Sermons he read, and lectures he endured,
  And homilies, and lives of all the saints;
To Jerome and to Chrysostom inured,
  He did not take such studies for restraints;
But how faith is acquired, and then insured,
  So well not one of the aforesaid paints
As Saint Augustine in his fine Confessions,
Which make the reader envy his transgressions.

48

This, too, was a seal'd book to little Juan—
  I can't but say that his mamma was right,
If such an education was the true one.
  She scarcely trusted him from out her sight;
Her maids were old, and if she took a new one,
  You might be sure she was a perfect fright,
She did this during even her husband's life—
I recommend as much to every wife.

49

Young Juan wax'd in goodliness and grace,
  At six a charming child, and at eleven
With all the promise of as fine a face
  As e'er to man's maturer growth was given.
He studied steadily and grew apace,
  And seem'd, at least, in the right road to heaven,
For half his days were pass'd at church, the other
Between his tutors, confessor, and mother.

50

At six, I said, he was a charming child,
  At twelve he was a fine, but quiet boy;
Although in infancy a little wild,
  They tamed him down amongst them: to destroy
His natural spirit not in vain they toil'd,

At least it seem'd so; and his mother's joy
Was to declare how sage, and still, and steady,
Her young philosopher was grown already.

51

I had my doubts, perhaps I have them still,
   But what I say is neither here nor there:
I knew his father well, and have some skill
   In character—but it would not be fair
From sire to son to augur good or ill:
   He and his wife were an ill sorted pair—
But scandal's my aversion—I protest
Against all evil speaking, even in jest.

52

For my part I say nothing—nothing—but
   This I will say—my reasons are my own—
That if I had an only son to put
   To school (as God be praised that I have none),
'Tis not with Donna Inez I would shut
   Him up to learn his catechism alone,
No—no—I'd send him out betimes to college,
For there it was I pick'd up my own knowledge.

53

For there one learns—'tis not for me to boast,
   Though I acquired—but I pass over *that*,
As well as all the Greek I since have lost:
   I say that there's the place—but *"Verbum sat,"*
I think I pick'd up too, as well as most,
   Knowledge of matters—but no matter *what*—
I never married—but, I think, I know
That sons should not be educated so.

54

Young Juan now was sixteen years of age,
   Tall, handsome, slender, but well knit: he seem'd

Active, though not so sprightly, as a page;
  And everybody but his mother deem'd
Him almost man; but she flew in a rage
  And bit her lips (for else she might have scream'd)
If any said so, for to be precocious
Was in her eyes a thing the most atrocious.

55

Amongst her numerous acquaintance, all
  Selected for discretion and devotion,
There was the Donna Julia, whom to call
  Pretty were but to give a feeble notion
Of many charms in her as natural
  As sweetness to the flower, or salt to ocean,
Her zone to Venus, or his bow to Cupid
(But this last simile is trite and stupid).

56

The darkness of her Oriental eye
  Accorded with her Moorish origin;
(Her blood was not all Spanish, by the by;
  In Spain, you know, this is a sort of sin).
When proud Granada fell, and, forced to fly,
  Boabdil wept, of Donna Julia's kin
Some went to Africa, some stay'd in Spain,
Her great great grandmamma chose to remain.

57

She married (I forget the pedigree)
  With an Hidalgo, who transmitted down
His blood less noble than such blood should be;
  At such alliances his sires would frown,
In that point so precise in each degree
  That they bred *in and in*, as might be shown,
Marrying their cousins—nay, their aunts, and nieces,
Which always spoils the breed, if it increases.

58

This heathenish cross restored the breed again,
   Ruin'd its blood, but much improved its flesh;
For from a root the ugliest in old Spain
   Sprung up a branch as beautiful as fresh;
The sons no more were short, the daughters plain:
   But there's a rumour which I fain would hush,
'Tis said that Donna Julia's grandmamma
Produced her Don more heirs at love than law.

59

However this might be, the race went on
   Improving still through every generation,
Until it centred in an only son,
   Who left an only daughter: my narration
May have suggested that this single one
   Could be but Julia (whom on this occasion
I shall have much to speak about), and she
Was married, charming, chaste, and twenty-three.

60

Her eye (I'm very fond of handsome eyes)
   Was large and dark, suppressing half its fire
Until she spoke, then through its soft disguise
   Flash'd an expression more of pride than ire,
And love than either; and there would arise
   A something in them which was not desire,
But would have been, perhaps, but for the soul
Which struggled through and chasten'd down the whole.

61

Her glossy hair was cluster'd o'er a brow
   Bright with intelligence, and fair, and smooth;
Her eyebrow's shape was like the aërial bow,
   Her cheek all purple with the beam of youth,
Mounting, at times, to a transparent glow,

As if her veins ran lightning; she, in sooth,
Possess'd an air and grace by no means common:
Her stature tall—I hate a dumpy woman.

62

Wedded she was some years, and to a man
   Of fifty, and such husbands are in plenty;
And yet, I think, instead of such a *one*
   'Twere better to have *two* of five-and-twenty,
Especially in countries near the sun:
   And now I think on't, "mi vien in mente,"
Ladies even of the most uneasy virtue
Prefer a spouse whose age is short of thirty.

63

'Tis a sad thing, I cannot choose but say,
   And all the fault of that indecent sun,
Who cannot leave alone our helpless clay,
   But will keep baking, broiling, burning on,
That howsoever people fast and pray,
   The flesh is frail, and so the soul undone:
What men call gallantry, and gods adultery,
Is much more common where the climate's sultry.

64

Happy the nations of the moral North!
   Where all is virtue, and the winter season
Sends sin, without a rag on, shivering forth
   ('Twas snow that brought St. Anthony to reason);
Where juries cast up what a wife is worth,
   By laying whate'er sum, in mulct, they please on
The lover, who must pay a handsome price,
Because it is a marketable vice.

65

Alfonso was the name of Julia's lord,
   A man well looking for his years, and who

Was neither much beloved nor yet abhorr'd:
  They lived together as most people do,
Suffering each other's foibles by accord,
  And not exactly either *one* or *two;*
Yet he was jealous, though he did not show it,
For jealousy dislikes the world to know it.

66

Julia was—yet I never could see why—
  With Donna Inez quite a favourite friend;
Between their tastes there was small sympathy,
  For not a line had Julia ever penn'd:
Some people whisper (but, no doubt, they lie,
  For malice still imputes some private end)
That Inez had, ere Don Alfonso's marriage,
Forgot with him her very prudent carriage;

67

And that still keeping up the old connexion,
  Which time had lately render'd much more chaste,
She took his lady also in affection,
  And certainly this course was much the best:
She flatter'd Julia with her sage protection,
  And complimented Don Alfonso's taste;
And if she could not (who can?) silence scandal,
At least she left it a more slender handle.

68

I can't tell whether Julia saw the affair
  With other people's eyes, or if her own
Discoveries made, but none could be aware
  Of this, at least no symptom e'er was shown;
Perhaps she did not know, or did not care,
  Indifferent from the first, or callous grown:
I'm really puzzled what to think or say,
She kept her counsel in so close a way.

69

Juan she saw, and, as a pretty child,
    Caress'd him often—such a thing might be
Quite innocently done, and harmless styled,
    When she had twenty years, and thirteen he;
But I am not so sure I should have smiled
    When he was sixteen, Julia twenty-three;
These few short years make wondrous alterations,
Particularly amongst sun-burnt nations.

70

Whate'er the cause might be, they had become
    Changed; for the dame grew distant, the youth shy,
Their looks cast down, their greetings almost dumb,
    And much embarrassment in either eye;
There surely will be little doubt with some
    That Donna Julia knew the reason why,
But as for Juan, he had no more notion
Than he who never saw the sea of ocean.

71

Yet Julia's very coldness still was kind,
    And tremulously gentle her small hand
Withdrew itself from his, but left behind
    A little pressure, thrilling, and so bland
And slight, so very slight, that to the mind
    'Twas but a doubt; but ne'er magician's wand
Wrought change with all Armida's fairy art
Like what this light touch left on Juan's heart.

72

And if she met him, though she smiled no more,
    She look'd a sadness sweeter than her smile,
As if her heart had deeper thoughts in store
    She must not own, but cherish'd more the while
For that compression in its burning core;

Even innocence itself has many a wile,
And will not dare to trust itself with truth,
And love is taught hypocrisy from youth.

73

But passion most dissembles, yet betrays
    Even by its darkness; as the blackest sky
Foretells the heaviest tempest, it displays
    Its workings through the vainly guarded eye,
And in whatever aspect it arrays
    Itself, 'tis still the same hypocrisy:
Coldness or anger, even disdain or hate,
Are masks it often wears, and still too late.

74

Then there were sighs, the deeper for suppression,
    And stolen glances, sweeter for the theft,
And burning blushes, though for no transgression,
    Tremblings when met, and restlessness when left;
All these are little preludes to possession,
    Of which young passion cannot be bereft,
And merely tend to show how greatly love is
Embarrass'd at first starting with a novice.

75

Poor Julia's heart was in an awkward state;
    She felt it going, and resolved to make
The noblest efforts for herself and mate,
    For honour's, pride's, religion's, virtue's sake.
Her resolutions were most truly great,
    And almost might have made a Tarquin quake:
She pray'd the Virgin Mary for her grace,
As being the best judge of a lady's case.

76

She vow'd she never would see Juan more,
    And next day paid a visit to his mother,

And look'd extremely at the opening door,
   Which, by the Virgin's grace, let in another;
Grateful she was, and yet a little sore—
   Again it opens, it can be no other,
'Tis surely Juan now—No! I'm afraid
That night the Virgin was no further pray'd.

77

She now determined that a virtuous woman
   Should rather face and overcome temptation,
That flight was base and dastardly, and no man
   Should ever give her heart the least sensation;
That is to say, a thought beyond the common
   Preference, that we must feel upon occasion,
For people who are pleasanter than others,
But then they only seem so many brothers.

78

And even if by chance—and who can tell?
   The devil's so very sly—she should discover
That all within was not so very well,
   And, if still free, that such or such a lover
Might please perhaps, a virtuous wife can quell
   Such thoughts, and be the better when they're over;
And if the man should ask, 'tis but denial:
I recommend young ladies to make trial.

79

And then there are such things as love divine,
   Bright and immaculate, unmix'd and pure,
Such as the angels think so very fine,
   And matrons, who would be no less secure,
Platonic, perfect, "just such love as mine":
   Thus Julia said—and thought so, to be sure;
And so I'd have her think, were I the man
On whom her reveries celestial ran.

80

Such love is innocent, and may exist
   Between young persons without any danger:
A hand may first, and then a lip be kist;
   For my part, to such doings I'm a stranger,
But *hear* these freedoms form the utmost list
   Of all o'er which such love may be a ranger:
If people go beyond, 'tis quite a crime,
But not my fault—I tell them all in time.

81

Love, then, but love within its proper limits
   Was Julia's innocent determination
In young Don Juan's favour, and to him its
   Exertion might be useful on occasion;
And, lighted at too pure a shrine to dim its
   Ethereal lustre, with what sweet persuasion
He might be taught, by love and her together—
I really don't know what, nor Julia either.

82

Fraught with this fine intention, and well fenced
   In mail of proof—her purity of soul,
She, for the future of her strength convinced,
   And that her honour was a rock, or mole,
Exceeding sagely from that hour dispensed
   With any kind of troublesome control;
But whether Julia to the task was equal
Is that which must be mention'd in the sequel.

83

Her plan she deem'd both innocent and feasible,
   And, surely, with a stripling of sixteen
Not scandal's fangs could fix on much that's seizable,
   Or if they did so, satisfied to mean
Nothing but what was good, her breast was peaceable:

A quiet conscience makes one so serene!
Christians have burnt each other, quite persuaded
That all the Apostles would have done as they did.

84

And if in the mean time her husband died,
  But Heaven forbid that such a thought should cross
Her brain, though in a dream! (and then she sigh'd)
  Never could she survive that common loss;
But just suppose that moment should betide,
  I only say suppose it—*inter nos*.
(This should be *entre nous*, for Julia thought
In French, but then the rhyme would go for nought.)

85

I only say, suppose this supposition:
  Juan being then grown up to man's estate
Would fully suit a widow of condition,
  Even seven years hence it would not be too late;
And in the interim (to pursue this vision)
  The mischief, after all, could not be great,
For he would learn the rudiments of love,
I mean the seraph way of those above.

86

So much for Julia. Now we'll turn to Juan.
  Poor little fellow! he had no idea
Of his own case, and never hit the true one;
  In feelings quick as Ovid's Miss Medea,
He puzzled over what he found a new one,
  But not as yet imagined it could be a
Thing quite in course, and not at all alarming,
Which, with a little patience, might grow charming.

87

Silent and pensive, idle, restless, slow,
  His home deserted for the lonely wood.

Tormented with a wound he could not know,
   His, like all deep grief, plunged in solitude:
I'm fond myself of solitude or so,
   But then, I beg it may be understood,
By solitude I mean a Sultan's, not
A hermit's, with a haram for a grot.

88

"Oh Love! in such a wilderness as this,
   Where transport and security entwine,
Here is the empire of thy perfect bliss,
   And here thou art a god indeed divine."
The bard I quote from does not sing amiss,
   With the exception of the second line,
For that same twining "transport and security"
Are twisted to a phrase of some obscurity.

89

The poet meant, no doubt, and thus appeals
   To the good sense and senses of mankind,
The very thing which everybody feels,
   As all have found on trial, or may find,
That no one likes to be disturb'd at meals
   Or love.—I won't say more about "entwined"
Or "transport," as we knew all that before,
But beg "Security" will bolt the door.

90

Young Juan wander'd by the glassy brooks,
   Thinking unutterable things; he threw
Himself at length within the leafy nooks
   Where the wild branch of the cork forest grew;
There poets find materials for their books,
   And every now and then we read them through,
So that their plan and prosody are eligible,
Unless, like Wordsworth, they prove unintelligible.

91

He, Juan (and not Wordsworth), so pursued
  His self-communion with his own high soul,
Until his mighty heart, in its great mood,
  Had mitigated part, though not the whole
Of its disease; he did the best he could
  With things not very subject to control,
And turn'd, without perceiving his condition,
Like Coleridge, into a metaphysician.

92

He thought about himself, and the whole earth,
  Of man the wonderful, and of the stars,
And how the deuce they ever could have birth;
  And then he thought of earthquakes, and of wars.
How many miles the moon might have in girth,
  Of air-balloons, and of the many bars
To perfect knowledge of the boundless skies;—
And then he thought of Donna Julia's eyes.

93

In thoughts like these true wisdom may discern
  Longings sublime, and aspirations high,
Which some are born with, but the most part learn
  To plague themselves withal, they know not why:
'Twas strange that one so young should thus concern
  His brain about the action of the sky;
If *you* think 'twas philosophy that this did,
I can't help thinking puberty assisted.

94

He pored upon the leaves, and on the flowers,
  And heard a voice in all the winds; and then
He thought of wood-nymphs and immortal bowers,
  And how the goddesses came down to men:
He miss'd the pathway, he forgot the hours,

And when he look'd upon his watch again,
He found how much old Time had been a winner—
He also found that he had lost his dinner.

95

Sometimes he turn'd to gaze upon his book,
    Boscan, or Garcilasso;—by the wind
Even as the page is rustled while we look,
    So by the poesy of his own mind
Over the mystic leaf his soul was shook,
    As if 'twere one whereon magicians bind
Their spells, and give them to the passing gale
According to some good old woman's tale.

96

Thus would he while his lonely hours away
    Dissatisfied, nor knowing what he wanted;
Nor glowing reverie, nor poet's lay,
    Could yield his spirit that for which it panted,
A bosom whereon he his head might lay,
    And hear the heart beat with the love it granted,
With——several other things, which I forget,
Or which, at least, I need not mention yet.

97

Those lonely walks, and lengthening reveries,
    Could not escape the gentle Julia's eyes;
She saw that Juan was not at his ease;
    But that which chiefly may, and must surprise,
Is, that the Donna Inez did not tease
    Her only son with question or surmise;
Whether it was she did not see, or would not,
Or, like all very clever people, could not.

98

This may seem strange, but yet 'tis very common;
    For instance—gentlemen, whose ladies take

Leave to o'erstep the written rights of woman,
    And break the——Which commandment is't they break?
(I have forgot the number, and think no man
    Should rashly quote, for fear of a mistake.)
I say, when these same gentlemen are jealous,
They make some blunder, which their ladies tell us.

99

A real husband always is suspicious,
    But still no less suspects in the wrong place,
Jealous of some one who had no such wishes,
    Or pandering blindly to his own disgrace,
By harbouring some dear friend extremely vicious;
    The last indeed's infallibly the case:
And when the spouse and friend are gone off wholly,
He wonders at their vice, and not his folly.

100

Thus parents also are at times short-sighted;
    Though watchful as the lynx, they ne'er discover,
The while the wicked world beholds delighted,
    Young Hopeful's mistress, or Miss Fanny's lover,
Till some confounded escapade has blighted
    The plan of twenty years, and all is over;
And then the mother cries, the father swears,
And wonders why the devil he got heirs.

101

But Inez was so anxious, and so clear
    Of sight, that I must think, on this occasion,
She had some other motive much more near
    For leaving Juan to this new temptation,
But what that motive was, I shan't say here;
    Perhaps to finish Juan's education,
Perhaps to open Don Alfonso's eyes,
In case he thought his wife too great a prize.

102

It was upon a day, a summer's day;—
  Summer's indeed a very dangerous season,
And so is spring about the end of May;
  The sun, no doubt, is the prevailing reason;
But whatsoe'er the cause is, one may say,
  And stand convicted of more truth than treason,
That there are months which nature grows more merry in,—
March has its hares, and May must have its heroine.

103

'Twas on a summer's day—the sixth of June:—
  I like to be particular in dates,
Not only of the age, and year, but moon;
  They are a sort of post-house, where the Fates
Change horses, making history change its tune,
  Then spur away o'er empires and o'er states,
Leaving at last not much besides chronology,
Excepting the post-obits of theology.

104

'Twas on the sixth of June, about the hour
  Of half-past six—perhaps still nearer seven—
When Julia sate within as pretty a bower
  As e'er held houri in that heathenish heaven
Described by Mahomet, and Anacreon Moore,
  To whom the lyre and laurels have been given,
With all the trophies of triumphant song—
He won them well, and may he wear them long!

105

She sate, but not alone; I know not well
  How this same interview had taken place,
And even if I knew, I should not tell—
  People should hold their tongues in any case;
No matter how or why the thing befell,

But there were she and Juan, face to face—
When two such faces are so, 'twould be wise,
But very difficult, to shut their eyes.

106

How beautiful she look'd! her conscious heart
    Glow'd in her cheek, and yet she felt no wrong.
Oh Love! how perfect is thy mystic art,
    Strengthening the weak, and trampling on the strong!
How self-deceitful is the sagest part
    Of mortals whom thy lure hath led along!—
The precipice she stood on was immense,
So was her creed in her own innocence.

107

She thought of her own strength, and Juan's youth,
    And of the folly of all prudish fears,
Victorious virtue, and domestic truth,
    And then of Don Alfonso's fifty years:
I wish these last had not occurr'd, in sooth,
    Because that number rarely much endears,
And through all climes, the snowy and the sunny,
Sounds ill in love, what'er it may in money.

108

When people say, "I've told you *fifty* times,"
    They mean to scold, and very often do;
When poets say, "I've written *fifty* rhymes,"
    They make you dread that they'll recite them too;
In gangs of *fifty*, thieves commit their crimes;
    At *fifty* love for love is rare, 'tis true,
But then, no doubt, it equally as true is,
A good deal may be bought for *fifty* Louis.

109

Julia had honour, virtue, truth, and love
    For Don Alfonso; and she inly swore,

By all the vows below to powers above,
　She never would disgrace the ring she wore,
Nor leave a wish which wisdom might reprove;
　And while she ponder'd this, besides much more,
One hand on Juan's carelessly was thrown,
Quite by mistake—she thought it was her own;

110

Unconsciously she lean'd upon the other,
　Which play'd within the tangles of her hair;
And to contend with thoughts she could not smother
　She seem'd, by the distraction of her air.
'Twas surely very wrong in Juan's mother
　To leave together this imprudent pair,
She who for many years had watch'd her son so—
I'm very certain *mine* would not have done so.

111

The hand which still held Juan's, by degrees
　Gently, but palpably confirm'd its grasp,
As if it said, "Detain me, if you please";
　Yet there's no doubt she only meant to clasp
His fingers with a pure Platonic squeeze;
　She would have shrunk as from a toad, or asp,
Had she imagined such a thing could rouse
A feeling dangerous to a prudent spouse.

112

I cannot know what Juan thought of this,
　But what he did, is much what you would do;
His young lip thank'd it with a grateful kiss,
　And then, abash'd at its own joy, withdrew
In deep despair, lest he had done amiss,—
　Love is so very timid when 'tis new:
She blush'd, and frown'd not, but she strove to speak,
And held her tongue, her voice was grown so weak.

113

The sun set, and up rose the yellow moon:
  The devil's in the moon for mischief; they
Who call'd her *chaste*, methinks, began too soon
  Their nomenclature; there is not a day,
The longest, not the twenty-first of June,
  Sees half the business in a wicked way,
On which three single hours of moonshine smile—
And then she looks so modest all the while.

114

There is a dangerous silence in that hour,
  A stillness, which leaves room for the full soul
To open all itself, without the power
  Of calling wholly back its self-control;
The silver light which, hallowing tree and tower,
  Sheds beauty and deep softness o'er the whole,
Breathes also to the heart, and o'er it throws
A loving languor, which is not repose.

115

And Julia sate with Juan, half embraced
  And half retiring from the glowing arm,
Which trembled like the bosom where 'twas placed;
  Yet still she must have thought there was no harm,
Or else 'twere easy to withdraw her waist;
  But then the situation had its charm,
And then——God knows what next—I can't go on;
I'm almost sorry that I e'er begun.

116

Oh Plato! Plato! you have paved the way,
  With your confounded fantasies, to more
Immoral conduct by the fancied sway
  Your system feigns o'er the controlless core
Of human hearts, than all the long array

Of poets and romancers:—You're a bore,
A charlatan, a coxcomb—and have been,
At best, no better than a go-between.

117

And Julia's voice was lost, except in sighs,
  Until too late for useful conversation;
The tears were gushing from her gentle eyes,
  I wish, indeed, they had not had occasion;
But who, alas! can love, and then be wise?
  Not that remorse did not oppose temptation;
A little still strove, and much repented,
And whispering "I will ne'er consent"—consented.

118

'Tis said that Xerxes offer'd a reward
  To those who could invent him a new pleasure.
Methinks the requisition's rather hard,
  And must have cost his majesty a treasure:
For my part, I'm a moderate-minded bard,
  Fond of a little love (which I call leisure);
I care not for new pleasures, as the old
Are quite enough for me, so they but hold.

119

Oh Pleasure! you're indeed a pleasant thing,
  Although one must be damn'd for you, no doubt:
I make a resolution every spring
  Of reformation, ere the year run out,
But somehow, this my vestal vow takes wing,
  Yet still, I trust, it may be kept throughout:
I'm very sorry, very much ashamed,
And mean, next winter, to be quite reclaim'd.

120

Here my chaste Muse a liberty must take—
  Start not! still chaster reader—she'll be nice hence-

Forward, and there is no great cause to quake;
    This liberty is a poetic licence,
Which some irregularity may make
    In the design, and as I have a high sense
Of Aristotle and the Rules, 'tis fit
To beg his pardon when I err a bit.

121

This licence is to hope the reader will
    Suppose from June the sixth (the fatal day
Without whose epoch my poetic skill
    For want of facts would all be thrown away),
But keeping Julia and Don Juan still
    In sight, that several months have pass'd; we'll say
'Twas in November, but I'm not so sure
About the day—the era's more obscure.

122

We'll talk of that anon.—'Tis sweet to hear
    At midnight on the blue and moonlit deep
The song and oar of Adria's gondolier,
    By distance mellow'd, o'er the waters sweep;
'Tis sweet to see the evening star appear;
    'Tis sweet to listen as the night-winds creep
From leaf to leaf; 'tis sweet to view on high
The rainbow, based on ocean, span the sky.

123

'Tis sweet to hear the watch-dog's honest bark
    Bay deep-mouth'd welcome as we draw near home;
'Tis sweet to know there is an eye will mark
    Our coming, and look brighter when we come;
'Tis sweet to be awaken'd by the lark,
    Or lull'd by falling waters; sweet the hum
Of bees, the voice of girls, the song of birds,
The lisp of children, and their earliest words.

124

Sweet is the vintage, when the showering grapes
   In Bacchanal profusion reel to earth,
Purple and gushing; sweet are our escapes
   From civic revelry to rural mirth;
Sweet to the miser are his glittering heaps,
   Sweet to the father is his first-born's birth,
Sweet is revenge—especially to women,
Pillage to soldiers, prize-money to seamen.

125

Sweet is a legacy, and passing sweet
   The unexpected death of some old lady
Or gentleman of seventy years complete,
   Who've made "us youth" wait too—too long already
For an estate, or cash, or country seat,
   Still breaking, but with stamina so steady
That all the Israelites are fit to mob its
Next owner for their double-damn'd post-obits.

126

'Tis sweet to win, no matter how, one's laurels,
   By blood or ink; 'tis sweet to put an end
To strife; 'tis sometimes sweet to have our quarrels,
   Particularly with a tiresome friend:
Sweet is old wine in bottles, ale in barrels;
   Dear is the helpless creature we defend
Against the world; and dear the schoolboy spot
We ne'er forget, though there we are forgot.

127

But sweeter still than this, than these, than all,
   Is first and passionate love—it stands alone,
Like Adam's recollection of his fall;
   The tree of knowledge has been pluck'd—all's known—
And life yields nothing further to recall

Worthy of this ambrosial sin, so shown,
No doubt in fable, as the unforgiven
Fire which Prometheus filch'd for us from heaven.

128

Man's a strange animal, and makes strange use
  Of his own nature, and the various arts,
And likes particularly to produce
  Some new experiment to show his parts;
This is the age of oddities let loose,
  Where different talents find their different marts;
You'd best begin with truth, and when you've lost your
Labour, there's a sure market for imposture.

129

What opposite discoveries we have seen!
  (Signs of true genius, and of empty pockets.)
One makes new noses, one a guillotine,
  One breaks your bones, one sets them in their sockets;
But vaccination certainly has been
  A kind antithesis to Congreve's rockets,
With which the Doctor paid off an old pox,
By borrowing a new one from an ox.

130

Bread has been made (indifferent) from potatoes;
  And galvanism has set some corpses grinning,
But has not answer'd like the apparatus
  Of the Humane Society's beginning,
By which men are unsuffocated gratis:
  What wondrous new machines have late been spinning!
I said the small pox has gone out of late;
Perhaps it may be follow'd by the great.

131

'Tis said the great came from America;
  Perhaps it may set out on its return,—

The population there so spreads, they say
  'Tis grown high time to thin it in its turn,
With war, or plague, or famine, any way,
  So that civilisation they may learn;
And which in ravage the more loathsome evil is—
Their real lues, or our pseudo-syphilis?

132

This is the patent age of new inventions
  For killing bodies, and for saving souls,
All propagated with the best intentions;
  Sir Humphry Davy's lantern, by which coals
Are safely mined for in the mode he mentions,
  Tombuctoo travels, voyages to the Poles,
Are ways to benefit mankind, as true,
Perhaps, as shooting them at Waterloo.

133

Man's a phenomenon, one knows not what,
  And wonderful beyond all wondrous measure;
'Tis pity though, in this sublime world, that
  Pleasure's a sin, and sometimes sin's a pleasure;
Few mortals know what end they would be at,
  But whether glory, power, or love, or treasure,
The path is through perplexing ways, and when
The goal is gain'd, we die, you know—and then——

134

What then?—I do not know, no more do you—
  And so good night.—Return we to our story:
'Twas in November, when fine days are few,
  And the far mountains wax a little hoary,
And clap a white cape on their mantles blue;
  And the sea dashes round the promontory,
And the loud breaker boils against the rock,
And sober suns must set at five o'clock.

135

'Twas, as the watchmen say, a cloudy night;
  No moon, no stars, the wind was low or loud
By gusts, and many a sparkling hearth was bright
  With the piled wood, round which the family crowd;
There's something cheerful in that sort of light,
  Even as a summer sky's without a cloud:
I'm fond of fire, and crickets, and all that,
A lobster salad, and champagne, and chat.

136

'Twas midnight—Donna Julia was in bed,
  Sleeping, most probably,—when at her door
Arose a clatter might awake the dead,
  If they had never been awoke before,
And that they have been so we all have read,
  And are to be so, at the least, once more;—
The door was fasten'd, but with voice and fist
First knocks were heard, then "Madam—Madam—hist!

137

"For God's sake, Madam—Madam—here's my master,
  With more than half the city at his back—
Was ever heard of such a curst disaster!
  'Tis not my fault—I kept good watch—Alack!
Do pray undo the bolt a little faster—
  They're on the stair just now, and in a crack
Will all be here; perhaps he yet may fly—
Surely the window's not so *very* high!"

138

By this time Don Alfonso was arrived,
  With torches, friends, and servants in great number;
The major part of them had long been wived,
  And therefore paused not to disturb the slumber
Of any wicked woman, who contrived

By stealth her husband's temples to encumber:
Examples of this kind are so contagious,
Were *one* not punish'd, *all* would be outrageous.

139

I can't tell how, or why, or what suspicion
   Could enter into Don Alfonso's head;
But for a cavalier of his condition
   It surely was exceedingly ill-bred,
Without a word of previous admonition,
   To hold a levee round his lady's bed,
And summon lackeys, arm'd with fire and sword,
To prove himself the thing he most abhorr'd.

140

Poor Donna Julia! starting as from sleep
   (Mind—that I do not say—she had not slept),
Began at once to scream, and yawn, and weep;
   Her maid, Antonia, who was an adept,
Contrived to fling the bed-clothes in a heap,
   As if she had just now from out them crept:
I can't tell why she should take all this trouble
To prove her mistress had been sleeping double.

141

But Julia mistress, and Antonia maid,
   Appear'd like two poor harmless women, who
Of goblins, but still more of men afraid,
   Had thought one man might be deterr'd by two,
And therefore side by side were gently laid,
   Until the hours of absence should run through,
And truant husband should return, and say,
"My dear, I was the first who came away."

142

Now Julia found at length a voice, and cried,
   "In heaven's name, Don Alfonso, what d'ye mean?

Has madness seized you? would that I had died
    Ere such a monster's victim I had been!
What may this midnight violence betide,
    A sudden fit of drunkenness or spleen?
Dare you suspect me, whom the thought would kill?
Search, then, the room!"—Alfonso said, "I will."

143

He search'd, *they* search'd, and rummaged everywhere,
    Closet and clothes-press, chest and window-seat,
And found much linen, lace, and several pair
    Of stockings, slippers, brushes, combs, complete,
With other articles of ladies fair,
    To keep them beautiful, or leave them neat:
Arras they prick'd and curtains with their swords,
And wounded several shutters, and some boards.

144

Under the bed they search'd, and there they found—
    No matter what—it was not that they sought;
They open'd windows, gazing if the ground
    Had signs or footmarks, but the earth said nought;
And then they stared each other's faces round:
    'Tis odd, not one of all these seekers thought,
And seems to me almost a sort of blunder,
Of looking *in* the bed as well as under.

145

During this inquisition Julia's tongue
    Was not asleep—"Yes, search and search," she cried,
"Insult on insult heap, and wrong on wrong!
    It was for this that I became a bride!
For this in silence I have suffer'd long
    A husband like Alfonso at my side;
But now I'll bear no more, nor here remain,
If there be law or lawyers in all Spain.

146

"Yes, Don Alfonso! husband now no more,
  If ever you indeed deserved the name,
Is't worthy of your years?—you have threescore—
  Fifty, or sixty, it is all the same—
Is't wise or fitting, causeless to explore
  For facts against a virtuous woman's fame?
Ungrateful, perjured, barbarous Don Alfonso,
How dare you think your lady would go on so?

147

"Is it for this I have disdain'd to hold
  The common privileges of my sex?
That I have chosen a confessor so old
  And deaf, that any other it would vex,
And never once he has had cause to scold,
  But found my very innocence perplex
So much, he always doubted I was married—
How sorry you will be when I've miscarried!

148

"Was it for this that no Cortejo e'er
  I yet have chosen from out the youth of Seville?
Is it for this I scarce went anywhere,
  Except to bull-fights, mass, play, rout, and revel?
Is it for this, whate'er my suitors were,
  I favour'd none—nay, was almost uncivil?
Is it for this that General Count O'Reilly,
Who took Algiers, declares I used him vilely?

149

"Did not the Italian Musico Cazzani
  Sing at my heart six months at least in vain?
Did not his countryman, Count Corniani,
  Call me the only virtuous wife in Spain?
Were there not also Russians, English, many?

The Count Strongstroganoff I put in pain,
And Lord Mount Coffeehouse, the Irish peer,
Who kill'd himself for love (with wine) last year.

150

"Have I not had two bishops at my feet?
    The Duke of Ichar, and Don Fernan Nunez?
And is it thus a faithful wife you treat?
    I wonder in what quarter now the moon is:
I praise your vast forbearance not to beat
    Me also, since the time so opportune is—
Oh, valiant man! with sword drawn and cock'd trigger,
Now, tell me, don't you cut a pretty figure?

151

"Was it for this you took your sudden journey,
    Under pretence of business indispensable,
With that sublime of rascals your attorney,
    Whom I see standing there, and looking sensible
Of having play'd the fool? though both I spurn, he
    Deserves the worst, his conduct's less defensible,
Because, no doubt, 'twas for his dirty fee,
And not from any love to you nor me.

152

"If he comes here to take a deposition,
    By all means let the gentleman proceed;
You've made the apartment in a fit condition:—
    There's pen and ink for you, sir, when you need—
Let everything be noted with precision,
    I would not you for nothing should be fee'd—
But as my maid's undrest, pray turn your spies out."
"Oh!" sobb'd Antonia, "I could tear their eyes out."

153

"There is the closet, there the toilet, there
    The antechamber—search them under, over;

There is the sofa, there the great armchair,
   The chimney—which would really hold a lover.
' wish to sleep, and beg you will take care
   And make no further noise, till you discover
The secret cavern of this lurking treasure—
And when 'tis found, let me, too, have that pleasure.

154

"And now, Hidalgo! now that you have thrown
   Doubt upon me, confusion over all,
Pray have the courtesy to make it known
   Who is the man you search for? how d'ye call
Him? what's his lineage? let him but be shown—
   I hope he's young and handsome—is he tall?
Tell me—and be assured, that since you stain
Mine honour thus, it shall not be in vain.

155

"At least, perhaps, he has not sixty years,
   At that age he would be too old for slaughter,
Or for so young a husband's jealous fears—
   (Antonia! let me have a glass of water.)
I am ashamed of having shed these tears,
   They are unworthy of my father's daughter;
My mother dream'd not in my natal hour,
That I should fall into a monster's power.

156

"Perhaps 'tis of Antonia you are jealous,
   You saw that she was sleeping by my side,
When you broke in upon us with your fellows;
   Look where you please—we've nothing, sir, to hide;
Only another time, I trust, you'll tell us,
   Or for the sake of decency abide
A moment at the door, that we may be
Drest to receive so much good company.

157

"And now, sir, I have done, and say no more;
    The little I have said may serve to show
The guileless heart in silence may grieve o'er
    The wrongs to whose exposure it is slow:—
I leave you to your conscience as before,
    'Twill one day ask you, *why* you used me so?
God grant you feel not then the bitterest grief!
Antonia! where's my pocket-handkerchief?"

158

She ceased, and turn'd upon her pillow; pale
    She lay, her dark eyes flashing through their tears,
Like skies that rain and lighten; as a veil,
    Waved and o'ershading her wan cheek, appears
Her streaming hair; the black curls strive, but fail,
    To hide the glossy shoulder, which uprears
Its snow through all;—her soft lips lie apart,
And louder than her breathing beats her heart.

159

The Senhor Don Alfonso stood confused;
    Antonia bustled round the ransack'd room,
And, turning up her nose, with looks abused
    Her master, and his myrmidons, of whom
Not one, except the attorney, was amused;
    He, like Achates, faithful to the tomb,
So there were quarrels, cared not for the cause,
Knowing they must be settled by the laws.

160

With prying snub-nose, and small eyes, he stood,
    Following Antonia's motions here and there,
With much suspicion in his attitude;
    For reputations he had little care;
So that a suit or action were made good,

Small pity had he for the young and fair,
And ne'er believed in negatives, till these
Were proved by competent false witnesses.

161

But Don Alfonso stood with downcast looks,
  And, truth to say, he made a foolish figure;
When, after searching in five hundred nooks,
  And treating a young wife with so much rigour,
He gain'd no point, except some self-rebukes,
  Added to those his lady with such vigour
Had pour'd upon him for the last half hour,
Quick, thick, and heavy—as a thundershower.

162

At first he tried to hammer an excuse,
  To which the sole reply was tears and sobs,
And indications of hysterics, whose
  Prologue is always certain throes, and throbs,
Gasps, and whatever else the owners choose:
  Alfonso saw his wife, and thought of Job's;
He saw too, in perspective, her relations,
And then he tried to muster all his patience.

163

He stood in act to speak, or rather stammer,
  But sage Antonia cut him short before
The anvil of his speech received the hammer,
  With "Pray, sir, leave the room, and say no more,
Or madam dies."—Alfonso mutter'd, "D—n her,"
  But nothing else, the time of words was o'er;
He cast a rueful look or two, and did,
He knew not wherefore, that which he was bid.

164

With him retired his *"posse comitatus,"*
  The attorney last, who linger'd near the door

Reluctantly, still tarrying there as late as
    Antonia let him—not a little sore
At this most strange and unexplain'd *"hiatus"*
    In Don Alfonso's facts, which just now wore
An awkward look; as he revolved the case,
The door was fasten'd in his legal face.

165

No sooner was it bolted, than—Oh shame!
    Oh sin! Oh sorrow! and Oh womankind!
How can you do such things and keep your fame,
    Unless this world, and t'other too, be blind?
Nothing so dear as an unfilch'd good name!
    But to proceed—for there is more behind:
With much heartfelt reluctance be it said,
Young Juan slipp'd, half-smother'd, from the bed.

166

He had been hid—I don't pretend to say
    How, nor can I indeed describe the where—
Young, slender, and pack'd easily, he lay,
    No doubt, in little compass, round or square;
But pity him I neither must nor may
    His suffocation by that pretty pair;
'Twere better, sure, to die so, than be shut
With maudlin Clarence in his Malmsey butt.

167

And, secondly, I pity not, because
    He had no business to commit a sin,
Forbid by heavenly, fined by human laws;
    At least 'twas rather early to begin;
But at sixteen the conscience rarely gnaws
    So much as when we call our old debts in
At sixty years, and draw the accompts of evil,
And find a deuced balance with the devil.

168

Of his position I can give no notion:
　'Tis written in the Hebrew Chronicle,
How the physicians, leaving pill and potion,
　Prescribed, by way of blister, a young belle,
When old King David's blood grew dull in motion,
　And that the medicine answer'd very well;
Perhaps 'twas in a different way applied,
For David lived, but Juan nearly died.

169

What's to be done? Alfonso will be back
　The moment he has sent his fools away.
Antonia's skill was put upon the rack,
　But no device could be brought into play—
And how to parry the renew'd attack?
　Besides, it wanted but few hours of day:
Antonia puzzled; Julia did not speak,
But press'd her bloodless lip to Juan's cheek.

170

He turn'd his lip to hers, and with his hand
　Call'd back the tangles of her wandering hair;
Even then their love they could not all command,
　And half forgot their danger and despair:
Antonia's patience now was at a stand—
　"Come, come, 'tis no time now for fooling there,"
She whisper'd, in great wrath—"I must deposit
This pretty gentleman within the closet:

171

"Pray, keep your nonsense for some luckier night—
　Who can have put my master in this mood?
What will become on't—I'm in such a fright,
　The devil's in the urchin, and no good—
Is this a time for giggling? this a plight?

Why, don't you know that it may end in blood?
You'll lose your life, and I shall lose my place,
My mistress all, for that half-girlish face.

172

"Had it but been for a stout cavalier
    Of twenty-five or thirty—(come, make haste)
But for a child, what piece of work is here!
    I really, madam, wonder at your taste—
(Come, sir, get in)—my master must be near:
    There, for the present, at the least, he's fast,
And if we can but till the morning keep
Our counsel—(Juan, mind, you must not sleep)."

173

Now, Don Alfonso entering, but alone,
    Closed the oration of the trusty maid:
She loiter'd, and he told her to be gone,
    An order somewhat sullenly obey'd;
However, present remedy was none,
    And no great good seem'd answer'd if she staid;
Regarding both with slow and sidelong view,
She snuff'd the candle, curtsied, and withdrew.

174

Alfonso paused a minute—then begun
    Some strange excuses for his late proceeding:
He would not justify what he had done,
    To say the best, it was extreme ill-breeding;
But there were ample reasons for it, none
    Of which he specified in this his pleading:
His speech was a fine sample, on the whole,
Of rhetoric, which the learn'd call *"rigmarole."*

175

Julia said nought; though all the while there rose
    A ready answer, which at once enables

A matron, who her husband's foible knows,
    By a few timely words to turn the tables,
Which, if it does not silence, still must pose,—
    Even if it should comprise a pack of fables;
'Tis to retort with firmness, and when he
Suspects with *one*, do you reproach with *three*.

176

Julia, in fact, had tolerable grounds,—
    Alfonso's loves with Inez were well known;
But whether 'twas that one's own guilt confounds—
    But that can't be, as has been often shown,
A lady with apologies abounds;—
    It might be that her silence sprang alone
From delicacy to Don Juan's ear,
To whom she knew his mother's fame was dear.

177

There might be one more motive, which makes two,
    Alfonso ne'er to Juan had alluded,—
Mentioned his jealousy, but never who
    Had been the happy lover, he concluded,
Conceal'd amongst his premises; 'tis true,
    His mind the more o'er this its mystery brooded
To speak of Inez now were, one may say,
Like throwing Juan in Alfonso's way.

178

A hint, in tender cases, is enough;
    Silence is best: besides there is a *tact*—
(That modern phrase appears to me sad stuff,
    But it will serve to keep my verse compact)—
Which keeps, when push'd by questions rather rough,
    A lady always distant from the fact:
The charming creatures lie with such a grace,
There's nothing so becoming to the face.

179

They blush, and we believe them, at least I
　　Have always done so; 'tis of no great use,
In any case, attempting a reply,
　　For then their eloquence grows quite profuse;
And when at length they're out of breath, they sigh,
　　And cast their languid eyes down, and let loose
A tear or two, and then we make it up;
And then—and then—and then—sit down and sup.

180

Alfonso closed his speech, and begg'd her pardon,
　　Which Julia half withheld, and then half granted,
And laid conditions, he thought very hard, on,
　　Denying several little things he wanted:
He stood like Adam lingering near his garden,
　　With useless penitence perplex'd and haunted,
Beseeching she no further would refuse,
When, lo! he stumbled o'er a pair of shoes.

181

A pair of shoes!—what then? not much, if they
　　Are such as fit with ladies' feet, but these
(No one can tell how much I grieve to say)
　　Were masculine; to see them, and to seize,
Was but a moment's act.—Ah! well-a-day!
　　My teeth begin to chatter, my veins freeze—
Alfonso first examined well their fashion,
And then flew out into another passion.

182

He left the room for his relinquish'd sword,
　　And Julia instant to the closet flew.
"Fly, Juan, fly! for heaven's sake—not a word—
　　The door is open—you may yet slip through
The passage you so often have explored—

Here is the garden-key—Fly—fly—Adieu!
Haste—haste! I hear Alfonso's hurrying feet—
Day has not broke—there's no one in the street."

183

None can say that this was not good advice,
   The only mischief was, it came too late;
Of all experience 'tis the usual price,
   A sort of income-tax laid on by fate:
Juan had reach'd the room-door in a trice,
   And might have done so by the garden-gate,
But met Alfonso in his dressing-gown,
Who threaten'd death—so Juan knock'd him down.

184

Dire was the scuffle, and out went the light;
   Antonia cried out "Rape!" and Julia "Fire!"
But not a servant stirr'd to aid the fight.
   Alfonso, pommell'd to his heart's desire,
Swore lustily he'd be revenged this night;
   And Juan, too, blasphemed an octave higher;
His blood was up: though young, he was a Tartar,
And not at all disposed to prove a martyr.

185

Alfonso's sword had dropp'd ere he could draw it,
   And they continued battling hand to hand,
For Juan very luckily ne'er saw it;
   His temper not being under great command,
If at that moment he had chanced to claw it,
   Alfonso's days had not been in the land
Much longer.—Think of husbands', lovers' lives!
And how ye may be doubly widows—wives!

186

Alfonso grappled to detain the foe,
   And Juan throttled him to get away,

And blood ('twas from the nose) began to flow;
   At last, as they more faintly wrestling lay,
Juan contrived to give an awkward blow,
   And then his only garment quite gave way;
He fled, like Joseph, leaving it; but there,
I doubt, all likeness ends between the pair.

187

Lights came at length, and men, and maids, who found
   An awkward spectacle their eyes before;
Antonia in hysterics, Julia swoon'd,
   Alfonso leaning, breathless, by the door;
Some half-torn drapery scatter'd on the ground,
   Some blood, and several footsteps, but no more:
Juan the gate gain'd, turn'd the key about,
And liking not the inside, lock'd the out.

188

Here ends this canto.—Need I sing, or say,
   How Juan, naked, favour'd by the night,
Who favours what she should not, found his way,
   And reach'd his home in an unseemly plight?
The pleasant scandal which arose next day,
   The nine days' wonder which was brought to light,
And how Alfonso sued for a divorce,
Were in the English newspapers, of course.

189

If you would like to see the whole proceedings,
   The depositions and the cause at full,
The names of all the witnesses, the pleadings
   Of counsel to nonsuit, or to annul,
There's more than one edition, and the readings
   Are various, but they none of them are dull;
The best is that in short-hand ta'en by Gurney,
Who to Madrid on purpose made a journey.

190

But Donna Inez, to divert the train
   Of one of the most circulating scandals
That had for centuries been known in Spain,
   At least since the retirement of the Vandals,
First vow'd (and never had she vow'd in vain)
   To Virgin Mary several pounds of candles;
And then, by the advice of some old ladies,
She sent her son to be shipp'd off from Cadiz.

191

She had resolved that he should travel through
   All European climes, by land or sea,
To mend his former morals, and get new,
   Especially in France and Italy
(At least this is the thing most people do).
   Julia was sent into a convent: she
Grieved, but, perhaps, her feelings may be better
Shown in the following copy of her Letter:—

192

"They tell me 'tis decided you depart:
   'Tis wise—'tis well, but not the less a pain;
I have no further claim on your young heart,
   Mine is the victim, and would be again:
To love too much has been the only art
   I used;—I write in haste, and if a stain
Be on this sheet, 'tis not what it appears;
My eyeballs burn and throb, but have no tears.

193

"I loved, I love you, for this love have lost
   State, station, heaven, mankind's, my own esteem,
And yet cannot regret what it hath cost,
   So dear is still the memory of that dream;
Yet, if I name my guilt, 'tis not to boast,

None can deem harshlier of me than I deem:
I trace this scrawl because I cannot rest—
I've nothing to reproach or to request.

194

"Man's love is of man's life a thing apart,
    'Tis woman's whole existence; man may range
The court, camp, church, the vessel, and the mart;
    Sword, gown, gain, glory, offer in exchange
Pride, fame, ambition, to fill up his heart,
    And few there are whom these cannot estrange;
Men have all these resources, we but one,
To love again, and be again undone.

195

"You will proceed in pleasure, and in pride,
    Beloved and loving many; all is o'er
For me on earth, except some years to hide
    My shame and sorrow deep in my heart's core:
These I could bear, but cannot cast aside
    The passion which still rages as before,—
And so farewell—forgive me, love me—No,
That word is idle now—but let it go.

196

"My breast has been all weakness, is so yet;
    But still I think I can collect my mind;
My blood still rushes where my spirit's set,
    As roll the waves before the settled wind;
My heart is feminine, nor can forget—
    To all, except one image, madly blind;
So shakes the needle, and so stands the pole,
As vibrates my fond heart to my fix'd soul.

197

"I have no more to say, but linger still,
    And dare not set my seal upon this sheet,

And yet I may as well the task fulfil,
   My misery can scarce be more complete:
I had not lived till now, could sorrow kill;
   Death shuns the wretch who fain the blow would meet,
And I must even survive this last adieu,
And bear with life to love and pray for you!"

198

This note was written upon gilt-edged paper
   With a neat little crow-quill, slight and new;
Her small white hand could hardly reach the taper,
   It trembled as magnetic needles do,
And yet she did not let one tear escape her;
   The seal a sun-flower; *"Elle vous suit partout,"*
The motto, cut upon a white cornelian;
The wax was superfine, its hue vermilion.

199

This was Don Juan's earliest scrape; but whether
   I shall proceed with his adventures is
Dependent on the public altogether;
   We'll see, however, what they say to this,
Their favour in an author's cap's a feather,
   And no great mischief's done by their caprice;
And if their approbation we experience,
Perhaps they'll have some more about a year hence.

200

My poem's epic, and is meant to be
   Divided in twelve books; each book containing,
With love, and war, a heavy gale at sea,
   A list of ships, and captains, and kings reigning,
New characters; the episodes are three:
   A panoramic view of hell's in training,
After the style of Virgil and of Homer,
So that my name of Epic's no misnomer.

201

All these things will be specified in time,
    With strict regard to Aristotle's rules,
The *Vade Mecum* of the true sublime,
    Which makes so many poets, and some fools:
Prose poets like blank-verse, I'm fond of rhyme,
    Good workmen never quarrel with their tools;
I've got new mythological machinery,
And very handsome supernatural scenery.

202

There's only one slight difference between
    Me and my epic brethren gone before,
And here the advantage is my own, I ween
    (Not that I have not several merits more,
But this will more peculiarly be seen);
    They so embelish, that 'tis quite a bore
Their labyrinth of fables to thread through,
Whereas this story's actually true.

203

If any person doubt it, I appeal
    To history, tradition, and to facts,
To newspapers, whose truth all know and feel,
    To plays in five, and operas in three acts;
All these confirm my statement a good deal,
    But that which more completely faith exacts
Is, that myself, and several now in Seville,
Saw Juan's last elopement with the devil.

204

If ever I should condescend to prose,
    I'll write poetical commandments, which
Shall supersede beyond all doubt all those
    That went before; in these I shall enrich
My text with many things that no one knows,

And carry precept to the highest pitch:
I'll call the work "Longinus o'er a Bottle,
Or, Every Poet his *own* Aristotle."

205

Thou shalt believe in Milton, Dryden, Pope;
    Thou shalt not set up Wordsworth, Coleridge, Southey;
Because the first is crazed beyond all hope,
    The second drunk, the third so quaint and mouthy:
With Crabbe it may be difficult to cope,
    And Campbell's Hippocrene is somewhat drouthy:
Thou shalt not steal from Samuel Rogers, nor
Commit—flirtation with the muse of Moore.

206

Thou shalt not covet Mr. Sotheby's Muse,
    His Pegasus, nor anything that's his;
Thou shalt not bear false witness like "the Blues"—
    (There's *one*, at least, is very fond of this);
Thou shalt not write, in short, but what I choose;
    This is true criticism, and you may kiss—
Exactly as you please, or not,—the rod;
But if you don't, I'll lay it on, by G—d!

207

If any person should presume to assert
    This story is not moral, first, I pray,
That they will not cry out before they're hurt,
    Then that they'll read it o'er again, and say
(But, doubtless, nobody will be so pert),
    That this is not a moral tale, though gay;
Besides, in Canto Twelfth, I mean to show
The very place where wicked people go.

208

If; after all, there should be some so blind
    To their own good this warning to despise.

Let by some tortuosity of mind,
   Not to believe my verse and their own eyes,
And cry that they "the moral cannot find,"
   I tell him, if a clergyman, he lies;
Should captains the remark, or critics, make,
They also lie too—under a mistake.

209

The public approbation I expect,
   And beg they'll take my word about the moral,
Which I with their amusement will connect
   (So children cutting teeth receive a coral);
Meantime they'll doubtless please to recollect
   My epical pretensions to the laurel:
For fear some prudish readers should grow skittish,
I've bribed my Grandmother's Review—the British.

210

I sent it in a letter to the Editor,
   Who thank'd me duly by return of post—
I'm for a handsome article his creditor;
   Yet, if my gentle Muse he please to roast,
And break a promise after having made it her,
   Denying the receipt of what it cost,
And smear his page with gall instead of honey,
All I can say is—that he had the money.

211

I think that with this holy new alliance
   I may ensure the public, and defy
All other magazines of art or science,
   Daily, or monthly, or three monthly; I
Have not essay'd to multiply their clients,
   Because they tell me 'twere in vain to try,
And that the Edinburgh Review and Quarterly
Treat a dissenting author very martyrly.

212

"*Non ego hoc ferrem calidus juventa*
　　Consule Planco," Horace said, and so
Say I; by which quotation there is meant a
　　Hint that some six or seven good years ago
(Long ere I dreamt of dating from the Brenta)
　　I was most ready to return a blow,
And would not brook at all this sort of thing
In my hot youth—when George the Third was King.

213

But now at thirty years my hair is gray—
　　(I wonder what it will be like at forty?
I thought of a peruke the other day—)
　　My heart is not much greener; and, in short, I
Have squander'd my whole summer while 'twas May,
　　And feel no more the spirit to retort; I
Have spent my life, both interest and principal,
And deem not, what I deem'd, my soul invincible.

214

No more—no more—Oh! never more on me
　　The freshness of the heart can fall like dew,
Which out of all the lovely things we see
　　Extracts emotions beautiful and new;
Hived in our bosoms like the bag o' the bee.
　　Think'st thou the honey with those objects grew?
Alas! 'twas not in them, but in thy power
To double even the sweetness of a flower.

215

No more—no more—Oh! never more, my heart,
　　Canst thou be my sole world, my universe!
Once all in all, but now a thing apart,
　　Thou canst not be my blessing or my curse:
The illusion's gone for ever, and thou art

Insensible, I trust, but none the worse,
And in thy stead I've got a deal of judgment,
Though heaven knows how it ever found a lodgment.

216

My days of love are over; me no more
   The charms of maid, wife, and still less of widow,
Can make the fool of which they made before,—
   In short, I must not lead the life I did do;
The credulous hope of mutual minds is o'er,
   The copious use of claret is forbid too,
So for a good old-gentlemanly vice,
I think I must take up with avarice.

217

Ambition was my idol, which was broken
   Before the shrines of Sorrow, and of Pleasure;
And the two last have left me many a token
   O'er which reflection may be made at leisure;
Now, like Friar Bacon's brazen head, I've spoken,
   "Time is, Time was, Time's past":—a chymic treasure
Is glittering youth, which I have spent betimes—
My heart in passion, and my head on rhymes.

218

What is the end of fame? 'tis but to fill
   A certain portion of uncertain paper:
Some liken it to climbing up a hill,
   Whose summit, like all hills, is lost in vapour;
For this men write, speak, preach, and heroes kill,
   And bards burn what they call their "midnight taper,"
To have, when the original is dust,
A name, a wretched picture, and worse bust.

219

What are the hopes of man? Old Egypt's King
   Cheops erected the first pyramid

And largest, thinking it was just the thing
  To keep his memory whole, and mummy hid:
But somebody or other rummaging,
  Burglariously broke his coffin's lid:
Let not a monument give you or me hopes,
Since not a pinch of dust remains of Cheops.

220

But I, being fond of true philosophy,
  Say very often to myself, "Alas!
All things that have been born were born to die,
  And flesh (which Death mows down to hay) is grass;
You've pass'd your youth not so unpleasantly,
  And if you had it o'er again—'twould pass—
So thank your stars that matters are no worse,
And read your Bible, sir, and mind your purse."

221

But for the present, gentle reader! and
  Still gentler purchaser! the bard—that's I—
Must, with permission, shake you by the hand,
  And so your humble servant, and goodbye!
We meet again, if we should understand
  Each other; and if not, I shall not try
Your patience further than by this short sample—
'Twere well if others follow'd my example.

222

"Go, little book, from this my solitude!
  I cast thee on the waters—go thy ways!
And if, as I believe, thy vein be good,
  The world will find thee after many days."
When Southey's read, and Wordsworth understood,
  I can't help putting in my claim to praise—
The four first rhymes are Southey's, every line:
For God's sake, reader! take them not for mine!

1818   1819

CANTO THE SECOND

1

Oh ye! who teach the ingenuous youth of nations,
    Holland, France, England, Germany, or Spain,
I pray ye flog them upon all occasions,
    It mends their morals, never mind the pain:
The best of mothers and of educations
    In Juan's case were but employ'd in vain,
Since, in a way that's rather of the oddest, he
Became divested of his native modesty.

2

Had he but been placed at a public school,
    In the third form or even in the fourth,
His daily task had kept his fancy cool,
    At least, had he been nurtured in the north;
Spain may prove an exception to the rule,
    But then exceptions always prove its worth—
A lad of sixteen causing a divorce
Puzzled his tutors very much, of course.

3

I can't say that it puzzles me at all,
    If all things be consider'd; first, there was
His lady-mother, mathematical,
    A——never mind;—his tutor, an old ass;
A pretty woman—(that's quite natural,
    Or else the thing had hardly come to pass)
A husband rather old, not much in unity
With his young wife—a time, and opportunity.

4

Well—well; the world must turn upon its axis,
    And all mankind turn with it, heads or tails,

And live and die, make love and pay our taxes,
　　And as the veering wind shifts, shift our sails;
The king commands us, and the doctor quacks us,
　　The priest instructs, and so our life exhales,
A little breath, love, wine, ambition, fame,
Fighting, devotion, dust,—perhaps a name.

5

I said, that Juan had been sent to Cadiz—
　　A pretty town, I recollect it well—
'Tis there the mart of the colonial trade is,
　　(Or was, before Peru learn'd to rebel,)
And such sweet girls—I mean, such graceful ladies,
　　Their very walk would make your bosom swell;
I can't describe it, though so much it strike,
Nor liken it—I never saw the like:

6

An Arab horse, a stately stag, a barb
　　New broke, a camel-leopard, a gazelle,
No—none of these will do;—and then their garb,
　　Their veil and petticoat—Alas! to dwell
Upon such things would very near absorb
　　A canto—then their feet and ankles,—well,
Thank Heaven I've got no metaphor quite ready,
(And so, my sober Muse—come, let's be steady—

7

Chaste Muse!—well, if you must, you must)—the veil
　　Thrown back a moment with the glancing hand,
While the o'erpowering eye, that turns you pale,
　　Flashes into the heart:—All sunny land
Of love! when I forget you, may I fail
　　To——say my prayers—but never was there plann'd
A dress through which the eyes give such a volley,
Excepting the Venetian Fazzioli.

8

But to our tale: the Donna Inez sent
  Her son to Cadiz only to embark;
To stay there had not answer'd her intent,
  But why?—we leave the reader in the dark—
'Twas for a voyage the young man was meant,
  As if a Spanish ship were Noah's ark,
To wean him from the wickedness of earth,
And send him like a dove of promise forth.

9

Don Juan bade his valet pack his things
  According to direction, then received
A lecture and some money: for four springs
  He was to travel; and though Inez grieved
(As every kind of parting has its stings),
  She hoped he would improve—perhaps believed:
A letter, too, she gave (he never read it)
Of good advice—and two or three of credit.

10

In the mean time, to pass her hours away,
  Brave Inez now set up a Sunday school
For naughty children, who would rather play
  (Like truant rogues) the devil, or the fool;
Infants of three years old were taught that day,
  Dunces were whipt, or set upon a stool:
The great success of Juan's education
Spurr'd her to teach another generation.

11

Juan embark'd—the ship got under way,
  The wind was fair, the water passing rough;
A devil of a sea rolls in that bay,
  As I, who've cross'd it oft, know well enough;
And, standing upon deck, the dashing spray

Flies in one's face, and makes it weather-tough:
And there he stood to take, and take again,
His first—perhaps his last—farewell of Spain.

12

I can't but say it is an awkward sight
　　To see one's native land receding through
The growing waters; it unmans one quite,
　　Especially when life is rather new:
I recollect Great Britain's coast looks white,
　　But almost every other country's blue,
When gazing on them, mystified by distance,
We enter on our nautical existence.

13

So Juan stood, bewilder'd on the deck:
　　The wind sung, cordage strain'd, and sailors swore,
And the ship creak'd, the town became a speck,
　　From which away so fair and fast they bore.
The best of remedies is a beef-steak
　　Against sea-sickness: try it, sir, before
You sneer, and I assure you this is true,
For I have found it answer—so may you.

14

Don Juan stood, and, gazing from the stern,
　　Beheld his native Spain receding far:
First partings form a lesson hard to learn,
　　Even nations feel this when they go to war;
There is a sort of unexprest concern,
　　A kind of shock that sets one's heart ajar:
At leaving even the most unpleasant people
And places, one keeps looking at the steeple.

15

But Juan had got many things to leave,
　　His mother, and a mistress, and no wife,

So that he had much better cause to grieve
 Than many persons more advanced in life;
And if we now and then a sigh must heave
 At quitting even those we quit in strife,
No doubt we weep for those the heart endears—
That is, till deeper griefs congeal our tears.

16

So Juan wept, as wept the captive Jews
 By Babel's waters, still remembering Sion:
I'd weep,—but mine is not a weeping Muse,
 And such light griefs are not a thing to die on;
Young men should travel, if but to amuse
 Themselves; and the next time their servants tie on
Behind their carriages their new portmanteau,
Perhaps it may be lined with this my canto.

17

And Juan wept, and much he sigh'd and thought,
 While his salt tears dropp'd into the salt sea,
"Sweets to the sweet;" (I like so much to quote;
 You must excuse this extract,—'tis where she,
The Queen of Denmark, for Ophelia brought
 Flowers to the grave;) and, sobbing often, he
Reflected on his present situation,
And seriously resolved on reformation.

18

"Farewell, my Spain! a long farewell!" he cried,
 "Perhaps I may revisit thee no more,
But die, as many an exiled heart hath died,
 Of its own thirst to see again thy shore:
Farewell, where Guadalquivir's waters glide!
 Farewell, my mother! and, since all is o'er,
Farewell, too, dearest Julia!—(here he drew
Her letter out again, and read it through.)

19

"And oh! if e'er I should forget, I swear—
  But that's impossible, and cannot be—
Sooner shall this blue ocean melt to air,
  Sooner shall earth resolve itself to sea,
Than I resign thine image, oh, my fair!
  Or think of anything, excepting thee;
A mind diseased no remedy can physic—
(Here the ship gave a lurch, and he grew sea-sick.)

20

"Sooner shall heaven kiss earth—(here he fell sicker)
  Oh, Julia! what is every other woe?—
(For God's sake let me have a glass of liquor;
  Pedro, Battista, help me down below.)
Julia, my love—(you rascal, Pedro, quicker)—
  Oh, Julia!—(this curst vessel pitches so)—
Beloved Julia, hear me still beseeching!"
(Here he grew inarticulate with retching.)

21

He felt that chilling heaviness of heart,
  Or rather stomach, which, alas! attends,
Beyond the best apothecary's art,
  The loss of love, the treachery of friends,
Or death of those we dote on, when a part
  Of us dies with them as each fond hope ends:
No doubt he would have been much more pathetic,
But the sea acted as a strong emetic.

22

Love's a capricious power: I've known it hold
  Out through a fever caused by its own heat,
But be much puzzled by a cough and cold,
  And find a quinsy very hard to treat;
Against all noble maladies he's bold,

But vulgar illnesses don't like to meet,
Nor that a sneeze should interrupt his sigh,
Nor inflammations redden his blind eye.

23

But worst of all is nausea, or a pain
   About the lower region of the bowels;
Love, who heroically breathes a vein,
   Shrinks from the application of hot towels,
And purgatives are dangerous to his reign,
   Sea-sickness death: his love was perfect, how else
Could Juan's passion, while the billows roar,
Resist his stomach, ne'er at sea before?

24

The ship, call'd the most holy "Trinidada,"
   Was steering duly for the port Leghorn;
For there the Spanish family Moncada
   Were settled long ere Juan's sire was born:
They were relations, and for them he had a
   Letter of introduction, which the morn
Of his departure had been sent him by
His Spanish friends for those in Italy.

25

His suite consisted of three servants and
   A tutor, the licentiate Pedrillo,
Who several languages did understand,
   But now lay sick and speechless on his pillow,
And, rocking in his hammock, long'd for land,
   His headache being increased by every billow;
And the waves oozing through the porthole made
His berth a little damp, and him afraid.

26

'Twas not without some reason, for the wind
   Increased at night, until it blew a gale;

And though 'twas not much to a naval mind,
  Some landsmen would have look'd a little pale,
For sailors are, in fact, a different kind:
  At sunset they began to take in sail,
For the sky show'd it would come on to blow,
And carry away, perhaps, a mast or so.

27

At one o'clock the wind with sudden shift
  Threw the ship right into the trough of the sea,
Which struck her aft, and made an awkward rift,
  Started the stern-post, also shatter'd the
Whole of her stern-frame, and, ere she could lift
  Herself from out her present jeopardy,
The rudder tore away: 'twas time to sound
The pumps, and there were four feet water found.

28

One gang of people instantly was put
  Upon the pumps, and the remainder set
To get up part of the cargo, and what not;
  But they could not come at the leak as yet;
At last they did get at it really, but
  Still their salvation was an even bet:
The water rush'd through in a way quite puzzling,
While they thrust sheets, shirts, jackets, bales of muslin,

29

Into the opening; but all such ingredients
  Would have been vain, and they must have gone down,
Despite of all their efforts and expedients,
  But for the pumps: I'm glad to make them known
To all the brother tars who may have need hence,
  For fifty tons of water were upthrown
By them per hour, and they all had been undone,
But for the maker, Mr. Mann, of London.

30

As day advanced the weather seem'd to abate,
    And then the leak they reckon'd to reduce,
And keep the ship afloat, though three feet yet
    Kept two hand- and one chain-pump still in use.
The wind blew fresh again: as it grew late
    A squall came on, and while some guns broke loose,
A gust—which all descriptive power transcends—
Laid with one blast the ship on her beam ends.

31

There she lay, motionless, and seem'd upset;
    The water left the hold, and wash'd the decks,
And made a scene men do not soon forget;
    For they remember battles, fires, and wrecks,
Or any other thing that brings regret,
    Or breaks their hopes, or hearts, or heads, or necks;
Thus drownings are much talk'd of by the divers,
And swimmers, who may chance to be survivors.

32

Immediately the masts were cut away,
    Both main and mizen: first the mizen went,
The main-mast follow'd; but the ship still lay
    Like a mere log, and baffled our intent.
Foremast and bowsprit were cut down, and they
    Eased her at last (although we never meant
To part with all till every hope was blighted),
And then with violence the old ship righted.

33

It may be easily supposed, while this
    Was going on, some people were unquiet,
That passengers would find it much amiss
    To lose their lives, as well as spoil their diet;
That even the able seaman, deeming his

Days nearly o'er, might be disposed to riot,
As upon such occasions tars will ask
For grog, and sometimes drink rum from the cask.

34

There's nought, no doubt, so much the spirit calms
    As rum and true religion: thus it was,
Some plunder'd, some drank spirits, some sung psalms,
    The high wind made the treble, and as bass
The hoarse harsh waves kept time; fright cured the qualms
    Of all the luckless landsmen's sea-sick maws:
Strange sounds of wailing, blasphemy, devotion,
Clamour'd in chorus to the roaring ocean.

35

Perhaps more mischief had been done, but for
    Our Juan, who, with sense beyond his years,
Got to the spirit-room, and stood before
    It with a pair of pistols; and their fears,
As if Death were more dreadful by his door
    Of fire than water, spite of oaths and tears,
Kept still aloof the crew, who, ere they sunk,
Thought it would be becoming to die drunk.

36

"Give us more grog," they cried, "for it will be
    All one an hour hence." Juan answer'd, "No!
'Tis true that death awaits both you and me,
    But let us die like men, not sink below
Like brutes":—and thus his dangerous post kept he,
    And none liked to anticipate the blow;
And even Pedrillo, his most reverend tutor,
Was for some rum a disappointed suitor.

37

The good old gentleman was quite aghast,
    And made a loud and pious lamentation;

Repented all his sins, and made a last
   Irrevocable vow of reformation;
Nothing should tempt him more (this peril past)
   To quit his academic occupation,
In cloisters of the classic Salamanca,
To follow Juan's wake, like Sancho Panca.

38

But now there came a flash of hope once more;
   Day broke, and the wind lull'd: the masts were gone;
The leak increased; shoals round her, but no shore,
   The vessel swam, yet still she held her own.
They tried the pumps again, and though before
   Their desperate efforts seem'd all useless grown,
A glimpse of sunshine set some hands to bale—
The stronger pump'd, the weaker thrumm'd a sail.

39

Under the vessel's keel the sail was pass'd,
   And for a moment it had some effect;
But with a leak, and not a stick of mast,
   Nor rag of canvas, what could they expect?
But still 'tis best to struggle to the last,
   'Tis never too late to be wholly wreck'd:
And though 'tis true that man can only die once,
'Tis not so pleasant in the Gulf of Lyons.

40

There winds and waves had hurl'd them, and from thence,
   Without their will, they carried them away;
For they were forced with steering to dispense,
   And never had as yet a quiet day
On which they might repose, or even commence
   A jurymast or rudder, or could say
The ship would swim an hour, which, by good luck,
Still swam—though not exactly like a duck.

41

The wind, in fact, perhaps, was rather less,
  But the ship labour'd so, they scarce could hope
To weather out much longer; the distress
  Was also great with which they had to cope
For want of water, and their solid mess
  Was scant enough: in vain the telescope
Was used—nor sail nor shore appear'd in sight,
Nought but the heavy sea, and coming night.

42

Again the weather threaten'd,—again blew
  A gale, and in the fore and after hold
Water appear'd; yet, though the people knew
  All this, the most were patient, and some bold,
Until the chains and leathers were worn through
  Of all our pumps:—a wreck complete she roll'd,
At mercy of the waves, whose mercies are
Like human beings during civil war.

43

Then came the carpenter, at last, with tears
  In his rough eyes, and told the captain, he
Could do no more: he was a man in years,
  And long had voyaged through many a stormy sea,
And if he wept at length, they were not fears
  That made his eyelids as a woman's be,
But he, poor fellow, had a wife and children,
Two things for dying people quite bewildering.

44

The ship was evidently settling now
  Fast by the head; and, all distinction gone,
Some went to prayers again, and made a vow
  Of candles to their saints—but there were none
To pay them with; and some look'd o'er the bow;

Some hoisted out the boats; and there was one
That begg'd Pedrillo for an absolution,
Who told him to be damn'd—in his confusion.

45

Some lash'd them in their hammocks; some put on
    Their best clothes, as if going to a fair;
Some cursed the day on which they saw the sun,
    And gnash'd their teeth, and howling, tore their hair;
And others went on as they had begun,
    Getting the boats out, being well aware
That a tight boat will live in a rough sea,
Unless with breakers close beneath her lee.

46

The worst of all was, that in their condition,
    Having been several days in great distress,
'Twas difficult to get out such provision
    As now might render their long suffering less:
Men, even when dying, dislike inanition;
    Their stock was damaged by the weather's stress:
Two casks of biscuit, and a keg of butter,
Were all that could be thrown into the cutter.

47

But in the long-boat they contrived to stow
    Some pounds of bread, though injured by the wet;
Water, a twenty-gallon cask or so;
    Six flasks of wine: and they contrived to get
A portion of their beef up from below,
    And with a piece of pork, moreover, met,
But scarce enough to serve them for a luncheon—
Then there was rum, eight gallons in a puncheon.

48

The other boats, the yawl and pinnace, had
    Been stove in the beginning of the gale;

And the long-boat's condition was but bad,
  As there were but two blankets for a sail,
And one oar for a mast, which a young lad
  Threw in by good luck over the ship's rail;
And two boats could not hold, far less be stored,
To save one half the people then on board.

49

'Twas twilight, and the sunless day went down
  Over the waste of waters; like a veil,
Which, if withdrawn, would but disclose the frown
  Of one whose hate is mask'd but to assail.
Thus to their hopeless eyes the night was shown,
  And grimly darkled o'er the faces pale,
And the dim desolate deep: twelve days had Fear
Been their familiar, and now Death was here.

50

Some trial had been making at a raft,
  With little hope in such a rolling sea,
A sort of thing at which one would have laugh'd,
  If any laughter at such times could be,
Unless with people who too much have quaff'd,
  And have a kind of wild and horrid glee,
Half epileptical, and half hysterical:—
Their preservation would have been a miracle.

51

At half-past eight o'clock, booms, hencoops, spars,
  And all things, for a chance, had been cast loose
That still could keep afloat the struggling tars,
  For yet they strove, although of no great use:
There was no light in heaven but a few stars,
  The boats put off o'ercrowded with their crews;
She gave a heel, and then a lurch to port,
And, going down head foremost—sunk, in short.

52

Then rose from sea to sky the wild farewell—
   Then shriek'd the timid, and stood still the brave—
Then some leap'd overboard with dreadful yell,
   As eager to anticipate their grave;
And the sea yawn'd around her like a hell,
   And down she suck'd with her the whirling wave,
Like one who grapples with his enemy,
And strives to strangle him before he die.

53

And first one universal shriek there rush'd,
   Louder than the loud ocean, like a crash
Of echoing thunder; and then all was hush'd,
   Save the wild wind and the remorseless dash
Of billows; but at intervals there gush'd,
   Accompanied with a convulsive splash,
A solitary shriek, the bubbling cry
Of some strong swimmer in his agony.

54

The boats, as stated, had got off before,
   And in them crowded several of the crew;
And yet their present hope was hardly more
   Than what it had been, for so strong it blew
There was slight chance of reaching any shore;
   And then they were too many, though so few—
Nine in the cutter, thirty in the boat,
Were counted in them when they got afloat.

55

All the rest perish'd; near two hundred souls
   Had left their bodies; and what's worse, alas!
When over Catholics the ocean rolls,
   They must wait several weeks before a mass
Takes off one peck of purgatorial coals,

Because, till people know what's come to pass,
They won't lay out their money on the dead—
It costs three francs for every mass that's said.

56

Juan got into the long-boat, and there
   Contrived to help Pedrillo to a place;
It seem'd as if they had exchanged their care,
   For Juan wore the magisterial face
Which courage gives, while poor Pedrillo's pair
   Of eyes were crying for their owner's case:
Battista, though (a name call'd shortly Tita),
Was lost by getting at some aqua-vita.

57

Pedro, his valet, too, he tried to save,
   But the same cause, conducive to his loss,
Left him so drunk, he jump'd into the wave,
   As o'er the cutter's edge he tried to cross,
And so he found a wine-and-watery grave;
   They could not rescue him although so close,
Because the sea ran higher every minute,
And for the boat—the crew kept crowding in it.

58

A small old spaniel—which had been Don José's,
   His father's, whom he loved, as ye may think,
For on such things the memory reposes
   With tenderness—stood howling on the brink,
Knowing, (dogs have such intellectual noses!)
   No doubt, the vessel was about to sink;
And Juan caught him up, and ere he stepp'd
Off threw him in, then after him he leap'd.

59

He also stuff'd his money where he could
   About his person, and Pedrillo's too.

Who let him do, in fact, whate'er he would,
    Not knowing what himself to say, or do,
As every rising wave his dread renew'd;
    But Juan, trusting they might still get through,
And deeming there were remedies for any ill,
Thus re-embark'd his tutor and his spaniel.

60

'Twas a rough night, and blew so stiffly yet,
    That the sail was becalm'd between the seas,
Though on the wave's high top too much to set,
    They dared not take it in for all the breeze:
Each sea curl'd o'er the stern, and kept them wet,
    And made them bale without a moment's ease,
So that themselves as well as hopes were damp'd,
And the poor little cutter quickly swamp'd.

61

Nine souls more went in her: the long-boat still
    Kept above water, with an oar for mast,
Two blankets stitch'd together, answering ill
    Instead of sail, were to the oar made fast:
Though every wave roll'd menacing to fill,
    And present peril all before surpass'd,
They grieved for those who perish'd with the cutter,
And also for the biscuit-casks and butter.

62

The sun rose red and fiery, a sure sign
    Of the continuance of the gale: to run
Before the sea until it should grow fine,
    Was all that for the present could be done:
A few tea-spoonfuls of their rum and wine
    Were served out to the people, who begun
To faint, and damaged bread wet through the bags,
And most of them had little clothes but rags.

63

They counted thirty, crowded in a space
    Which left scarce room for motion or exertion;
They did their best to modify their case,
    One half sate up, though numb'd with the immersion,
While t'other half were laid down in their place,
    At watch and watch; thus, shivering like the tertian
Ague in its cold fit, they fill'd their boat,
With nothing but the sky for a great coat.

64

'Tis very certain the desire of life
    Prolongs it: this is obvious to physicians,
When patients, neither plagued with friends nor wife,
    Survive through very desperate conditions,
Because they still can hope, nor shines the knife
    Nor shears of Atropos before their visions:
Despair of all recovery spoils longevity,
And makes men's miseries of alarming brevity.

65

'Tis said that persons living on annuities
    Are longer lived than others,—God knows why,
Unless to plague the grantors,—yet so true it is,
    That some, I really think, *do* never die;
Of any creditors the worst a Jew it is,
    And *that's* their mode of furnishing supply:
In my young days they lent me cash that way,
Which I found very troublesome to pay.

66

'Tis thus with people in an open boat,
    They live upon the love of life, and bear
More than can be believed, or even thought,
    And stand like rocks the tempest's wear and tear;
And hardship still has been the sailor's lot,

Since Noah's ark went cruising here and there;
She had a curious crew as well as cargo,
Like the first old Greek privateer, the Argo.

67

But man is a carnivorous production,
  And must have meals, at least one meal a day;
He cannot live, like woodcocks, upon suction,
  But, like the shark and tiger, must have prey;
Although his anatomical construction
  Bears vegetables, in a grumbling way,
Your labouring people think beyond all question
Beef, veal, and mutton, better for digestion.

68

And thus it was with this our hapless crew;
  For on the third day there came on a calm,
And though at first their strength it might renew,
  And lying on their weariness like balm,
Lull'd them like turtles sleeping on the blue
  Of ocean, when they woke they felt a qualm,
And fell all ravenously on their provision,
Instead of hoarding it with due precision.

69

The consequence was easily foreseen—
  They ate up all they had, and drank their wine,
In spite of all remonstrances, and then
  On what, in fact, next day were they to dine?
They hoped the wind would rise, these foolish men!
  And carry them to shore; these hopes were fine,
But as they had but one oar, and that brittle,
It would have been more wise to save their victual.

70

The fourth day came, but not a breath of air,
  And Ocean slumber'd like an unwean'd child:

The fifth day, and their boat lay floating there,
　　The sea and sky were blue, and clear, and mild—
With their one oar (I wish they had had a pair)
　　What could they do? and hunger's rage grew wild:
So Juan's spaniel, spite of his entreating,
Was kill'd, and portion'd out for present eating.

71

On the sixth day they fed upon his hide,
　　And Juan, who had still refused, because
The creature was his father's dog that died,
　　Now feeling all the vulture in his jaws,
With some remorse received (though first denied)
　　As a great favour one of the fore-paws,
Which he divided with Pedrillo, who
Devour'd it, longing for the other too.

72

The seventh day, and no wind—the burning sun
　　Blister'd and scorch'd, and, stagnant on the sea,
They lay like carcasses; and hope was none,
　　Save in the breeze that came not: savagely
They glared upon each other—all was done,
　　Water, and wine, and food,—and you might see
The longings of the cannibal arise
(Although they spoke not) in their wolfish eyes.

73

At length one whisper'd his companion, who
　　Whisper'd another, and thus it went round,
And then into a hoarser murmur grew,
　　An ominous, and wild, and desperate sound;
And when his comrade's thought each sufferer knew,
　　'Twas but his own, suppress'd till now, he found:
And out they spoke of lots for flesh and blood,
And who should die to be his fellow's food.

74

But ere they came to this, they that day shared
　　Some leathern caps, and what remain'd of shoes;
And then they look'd around them, and despair'd,
　　And none to be the sacrifice would choose;
At length the lots were torn up, and prepared,
　　But of materials that must shock the Muse—
Having no paper, for the want of better,
They took by force from Juan Julia's letter.

75

Then lots were made, and mark'd, and mix'd, and handed
　　In silent horror, and their distribution
Lull'd even the savage hunger which demanded,
　　Like the Promethean vulture, this pollution;
None in particular had sought or plann'd it,
　　'Twas Nature gnaw'd them to this resolution,
By which none were permitted to be neuter—
And the lot fell on Juan's luckless tutor.

76

He but requested to be bled to death:
　　The surgeon had his instruments, and bled
Pedrillo, and so gently ebb'd his breath,
　　You hardly could perceive when he was dead.
He died as born, a Catholic in faith,
　　Like most in the belief in which they're bred,
And first a little crucifix he kiss'd,
And then held out his jugular and wrist.

77

The surgeon, as there was no other fee,
　　Had his first choice of morsels for his pains;
But being thirstiest at the moment, he
　　Preferr'd a draught from the fast-flowing veins:
Part was divided. part thrown in the sea,

And such things as the entrails and the brains
Regaled two sharks, who follow'd o'er the billow—
The sailors ate the rest of poor Pedrillo.

78

The sailors ate him, all save three or four,
  Who were not quite so fond of animal food;
To these was added Juan, who, before
  Refusing his own spaniel, hardly could
Feel now his appetite increased much more;
  'Twas not to be expected that he should,
Even in extremity of their disaster,
Dine with them on his pastor and his master.

79

'Twas better that he did not; for, in fact,
  The consequence was awful in the extreme;
For they, who were most ravenous in the act,
  Went raging mad—Lord! how they did blaspheme!
And foam, and roll, with strange convulsions rack'd,
  Drinking salt-water like a mountain-stream;
Tearing, and grinning, howling, screeching, swearing,
And, with hyaena-laughter, died despairing.

80

Their numbers were much thinn'd by this infliction,
  And all the rest were thin enough, Heaven knows;
And some of them had lost their recollection,
  Happier than they who still perceived their woes;
But others ponder'd on a new dissection,
  As if not warn'd sufficently by those
Who had already perish'd, suffering madly,
For having used their appetites so sadly.

81

And next they thought upon the master's mate,
  As fattest: but he saved himself, because,

Besides being much averse from such a fate,
    There were some other reasons: the first was,
He had been rather indisposed of late;
    And that which chiefly proved his saving clause,
Was a small present made to him at Cadiz,
By general subscription of the ladies.

82

Of poor Pedrillo something still remain'd,
    But was used sparingly,—some were afraid,
And others still their appetites constrain'd,
    Or but at times a little supper made;
All except Juan, who throughout abstain'd,
    Chewing a piece of bamboo, and some lead:
At length they caught two boobies, and a noddy,
And then they left off eating the dead body.

83

And if Pedrillo's fate should shocking be,
    Remember Ugolino condescends
To eat the head of his arch-enemy
    The moment after he politely ends
His tale: if foes be food in hell, at sea
    'Tis surely fair to dine upon our friends,
When shipwreck's short allowance grows too scanty,
Without being much more horrible than Dante.

84

And the same night there fell a shower of rain,
    For which their mouths gaped, like the cracks of earth
When dried to summer dust; till taught by pain,
    Men really know not what good water's worth;
If you had been in Turkey or in Spain,
    Or with a famish'd boat's-crew had your berth,
Or in the desert heard the camel's bell,
You'd wish yourself where Truth is—in a well.

85

It pour'd down torrents, but they were no richer,
  Until they found a ragged piece of sheet,
Which served them as a sort of spongy pitcher,
  And when they deem'd its moisture was complete,
They wrung it out, and though a thirsty ditcher
  Might not have thought the scanty draught so sweet
As a full pot of porter, to their thinking
They ne'er till now had known the joys of drinking.

86

And their baked lips, with many a bloody crack,
  Suck'd in the moisture, which like nectar stream'd;
Their throats were ovens, their swoln tongues were black
  As the rich man's in hell, who vainly scream'd
To beg the beggar, who could not rain back
  A drop of dew, when every drop had seem'd
To taste of heaven—If this be true, indeed,
Some Christians have a comfortable creed.

87

There were two fathers in this ghastly crew,
  And with them their two sons, of whom the one
Was more robust and hardy to the view,
  But he died early; and when he was gone,
His nearest messmate told his sire, who threw
  One glance at him, and said, "Heaven's will be done!
I can do nothing," and he saw him thrown
Into the deep without a tear or groan.

88

The other father had a weaklier child,
  Of a soft cheek, and aspect delicate;
But the boy bore up long, and with a mild
  And patient spirit held aloof his fate;
Little he said, and now and then he smiled,

As if to win a part from off the weight
He saw increasing on his father's heart,
With the deep deadly thought, that they must part.

89

And o'er him bent his sire, and never raised
    His eyes from off his face, but wiped the foam
From his pale lips, and ever on him gazed,
    And when the wish'd-for shower at length was come,
And the boy's eyes, which the dull film half glazed,
    Brighten'd, and for a moment seem'd to roam,
He squeezed from out a rag some drops of rain
Into his dying child's mouth—but in vain.

90

The boy expired—the father held the clay,
    And look'd upon it long, and when at last
Death left no doubt, and the dead burthen lay
    Stiff on his heart, and pulse and hope were past,
He watch'd it wistfully, until away
    'Twas borne by the rude wave wherein 'twas cast;
Then he himself sunk down all dumb and shivering,
And gave no sign of life, save his limbs quivering.

91

Now overhead a rainbow, bursting through
    The scattering clouds, shone, spanning the dark sea,
Resting its bright base on the quivering blue;
    And all within its arch appear'd to be
Clearer than that without, and its wide hue
    Wax'd broad and waving, like a banner free,
Then changed like to a bow that's bent, and then
Forsook the dim eyes of these shipwreck'd men.

92

It changed, of course; a heavenly chameleon,
    The airy child of vapour and the sun,

Brought forth in purple, cradled in vermilion,
   Baptized in molten gold, and swathed in dun,
Glittering like crescents o'er a Turk's pavilion,
   And blending every colour into one,
Just like a black eye in a recent scuffle
(For sometimes we must box without the muffle).

93

Our shipwreck'd seamen thought it a good omen—
   It is as well to think so, now and then;
'Twas an old custom of the Greek and Roman,
   And may become of great advantage when
Folks are discouraged; and most surely no men
   Had greater need to nerve themselves again
Than these, and so this rainbow look'd like hope—
Quite a celestial kaleidoscope.

94

About this time a beautiful white bird,
   Web-footed, not unlike a dove in size
And plumage (probably it might have err'd
   Upon its course), pass'd oft before their eyes,
And tried to perch, although it saw and heard
   The men within the boat, and in this guise
It came and went, and flutter'd round them till
Night fell:—this seem'd a better omen still.

95

But in this case I also must remark,
   'Twas well this bird of promise did not perch,
Because the tackle of our shatter'd bark
   Was not so safe for roosting as a church;
And had it been the dove from Noah's ark,
   Returning there from her successful search,
Which in their way that moment chanced to fall,
They would have eat her, olive-branch and all.

96

With twilight it again came on to blow,
  But not with violence; the stars shone out,
The boat made way; yet now they were so low,
  They knew not where nor what they were about;
Some fancied they saw land, and some said 'No!'
  The frequent fog-banks gave them cause to doubt—
Some swore that they heard breakers, others guns,
And all mistook about the latter once.

97

As morning broke, the light wind died away,
  When he who had the watch sung out and swore,
If 'twas not land that rose with the sun's ray,
  He wish'd that land he never might see more:
And the rest rubb'd their eyes, and saw a bay,
  Or thought they saw, and shaped their course for shore;
For shore it was, and gradually grew
Distinct, and high, and palpable to view.

98

And then of these some part burst into tears,
  And others, looking with a stupid stare,
Could not yet separate their hopes from fears,
  And seem'd as if they had no further care;
While a few pray'd—(the first time for some years)—
  And at the bottom of the boat three were
Asleep: they shook them by the hand and head,
And tried to awaken them, but found them dead.

99

The day before, fast sleeping on the water,
  They found a turtle of the hawk's-bill kind,
And by good fortune, gliding softly, caught her,
  Which yielded a day's life, and to their mind
Proved even still a more nutritious matter,

Because it left encouragement behind:
They thought that in such perils, more than chance
Had sent them this for their deliverance.

100

The land appear'd a high and rocky coast,
  And higher grew the mountains as they drew,
Set by a current, toward it: they were lost
  In various conjectures, for none knew
To what part of the earth they had been tost,
  So changeable had been the winds that blew;
Some thought it was Mount Aetna, some the highlands
Of Candia, Cyprus, Rhodes, or other islands.

101

Meantime the current, with a rising gale,
  Still set them onwards to the welcome shore,
Like Charon's bark of spectres, dull and pale:
  Their living freight was now reduced to four,
And three dead, whom their strength could not avail
  To heave into the deep with those before,
Though the two sharks still follow'd them, and dash'd
The spray into their faces as they splash'd.

102

Famine, despair, cold, thirst, and heat, had done
  Their work on them by turns, and thinn'd them to
Such things a mother had not known her son
  Amidst the skeletons of that gaunt crew;
By night chill'd, by day scorch'd, thus one by one
  They perish'd, until wither'd to these few,
But chiefly by a species of self-slaughter,
In washing down Pedrillo with salt water.

103

As they drew nigh the land, which now was seen
  Unequal in its aspect here and there,

They felt the freshness of its growing green,
   That waved in forest-tops, and smooth'd the air,
And fell upon their glazed eyes like a screen
   From glistening waves, and skies so hot and bare—
Lovely seem'd any object that should sweep
Away the vast, salt, dread, eternal deep.

104

The shore look'd wild, without a trace of man,
   And girt by formidable waves; but they
Were mad for land, and thus their course they ran,
   Though right ahead the roaring breakers lay:
A reef between them also now began
   To show its boiling surf and bounding spray,
But finding no place for their landing better,
They ran the boat for shore,—and overset her.

105

But in his native stream, the Guadalquivir,
   Juan to lave his youthful limbs was wont;
And having learnt to swim in that sweet river,
   Had often turn'd the art to some account:
A better swimmer you could scarce see ever,
   He could, perhaps, have pass'd the Hellespont,
As once (a feat on which ourselves we prided)
Leander, Mr. Ekenhead, and I did.

106

So here, though faint, emaciated, and stark,
   He buoy'd his boyish limbs, and strove to ply
With the quick wave, and gain, ere it was dark,
   The beach which lay before him, high and dry:
The greatest danger here was from a shark,
   That carried off his neighbour by the thigh;
As for the other two, they could not swim,
So nobody arrived on shore but him.

107

Nor yet had he arrived but for the oar,
    Which, providentially for him, was wash'd
Just as his feeble arms could strike no more,
    And the hard wave o'erwhelm'd him as 'twas dash'd
Within his grasp; he clung to it, and sore
    The waters beat while he thereto was lash'd;
At last, with swimming, wading, scrambling, he
Roll'd on the beach, half senseless, from the sea:

108

There, breathless, with his digging nails he clung
    Fast to the sand, lest the returning wave,
From whose reluctant roar his life he wrung,
    Should suck him back to her insatiate grave:
And there he lay, full length, where he was flung,
    Before the entrance of a cliff-worn cave,
With just enough of life to feel its pain,
And deem that it was saved, perhaps in vain.

109

With slow and staggering effort he arose,
    But sunk again upon his bleeding knee
And quivering hand; and then he look'd for those
    Who long had been his mates upon the sea;
But none of them appear'd to share his woes,
    Save one, a corpse, from out the famish'd three,
Who died two days before, and now had found
An unknown barren beach for burial-ground.

110

And as he gazed, his dizzy brain spun fast,
    And down he sunk; and as he sunk, the sand
Swam round and round, and all his senses pass'd:
    He fell upon his side, and his stretch'd hand
Droop'd dripping on the oar (their jurymast),

And, like a wither'd lily, on the land
His slender frame and pallid aspect lay,
As fair a thing as e'er was form'd of clay.

III

How long in his damp trance young Juan lay
  He knew not, for the earth was gone for him,
And time had nothing more of night nor day
  For his congealing blood, and senses dim;
And how this heavy faintness pass'd away
  He knew not, till each painful pulse and limb,
And tingling vein, seem'd throbbing back to life,
For Death, though vanquish'd, still retired with strife.

112

His eyes he open'd, shut, again unclosed,
  For all was doubt and dizziness; he thought
He still was in the boat, and had but dozed,
  And felt again with his despair o'er-wrought,
And wish'd it death in which he had reposed,
  And then once more his feelings back were brought,
And slowly by his swimming eyes was seen
A lovely female face of seventeen.

113

'Twas bending close o'er his, and the small mouth
  Seem'd almost prying into his for breath;
And chafing him, the soft warm hand of youth
  Recall'd his answering spirits back from death;
And, bathing his chill temples, tried to soothe
  Each pulse to animation, till beneath
Its gentle touch and trembling care, a sigh
To these kind efforts made a low reply.

114

Then was the cordial pour'd, and mantle flung
  Around his scarce-clad limbs; and the fair arm

Raised higher the faint head which o'er it hung;
   And her transparent cheek, all pure and warm,
Pillow'd his death-like forehead; then she wrung
   His dewy curls, long drench'd by every storm;
And watch'd with eagerness each throb that drew
A sigh from his heaved bosom—and hers, too.

115

And lifting him with care into the cave,
   The gentle girl, and her attendant,—one
Young, yet her elder, and of brow less grave,
   And more robust of figure—then begun
To kindle fire, and as the new flames gave
   Light to the rocks that roof'd them, which the sun
Had never seen, the maid, or whatsoe'er
She was, appear'd distinct, and tall, and fair.

116

Her brow was overhung with coins of gold,
   That sparkled o'er the auburn of her hair,
Her clustering hair, whose longer locks were roll'd
   In braids behind; and though her stature were
Even of the highest for a female mould,
   They nearly reach'd her heel; and in her air
There was a something which bespoke command,
As one who was a lady in the land.

117

Her hair, I said, was auburn; but her eyes
   Were black as death, their lashes the same hue,
Of downcast length, in whose silk shadow lies
   Deepest attraction; for when to the view
Forth from its raven fringe the full glance flies,
   Ne'er with such force the swiftest arrow flew;
'Tis as the snake late coil'd, who pours his length,
And hurls at once his venom and his strength.

118

Her brow was white and low, her cheek's pure dye
   Like twilight rosy still with the set sun;
Short upper lip—sweet lips! that make us sigh
   Ever to have seen such; for she was one
Fit for the model of a statuary
   (A race of mere impostors, when all's done—
I've seen much finer women, ripe and real,
Than all the nonsense of their stone ideal).

119

I'll tell you why I say so, for 'tis just
   One should not rail without a decent cause:
There was an Irish lady, to whose bust
   I ne'er saw justice done, and yet she was
A frequent model; and if e'er she must
   Yield to stern Time and Nature's wrinkling laws,
They will destroy a face which mortal thought
Ne'er compass'd, nor less mortal chisel wrought.

120

And such was she, the lady of the cave:
   Her dress was very different from the Spanish,
Simpler, and yet of colours not so grave;
   For, as you know, the Spanish women banish
Bright hues when out of doors, and yet, while wave
   Around them (what I hope will never vanish)
The basquina and the mantilla, they
Seem at the same time mystical and gay.

121

But with our damsel this was not the case:
   Her dress was many-colour'd, finely spun;
Her locks curl'd negligently round her face,
   But through them gold and gems profusely shone:
Her girdle sparkled, and the richest lace

Flow'd in her veil, and many a precious stone
Flash'd on her little hand; but, what was shocking,
Her small snow feet had slippers, but no stocking.

122

The other female's dress was not unlike,
   But of inferior materials: she
Had not so many ornaments to strike,
   Her hair had silver only, bound to be
Her dowry; and her veil, in form alike,
   Was coarser; and her air, though firm, less free;
Her hair was thicker, but less long; her eyes
As black, but quicker, and of smaller size.

123

And these two tended him, and cheer'd him both
   With food and raiment, and those soft attentions,
Which are—(as I must own)—of female growth,
   And have ten thousand delicate inventions:
They made a most superior mess of broth,
   A thing which poesy but seldom mentions,
But the best dish that e'er was cook'd since Homer's
Achilles order'd dinner for new comers.

124

I'll tell you who they were, this female pair,
   Lest they should seem princesses in disguise;
Besides, I hate all mystery, and that air
   Of clap-trap, which your recent poets prize;
And so, in short, the girls they really were
   They shall appear before your curious eyes,
Mistress and maid; the first was only daughter
Of an old man, who lived upon the water.

125

A fisherman he had been in his youth,
   And still a sort of fisherman was he;

But other speculations were, in sooth,
    Added to his connexion with the sea,
Perhaps not so respectable, in truth:
    A little smuggling, and some piracy,
Left him, at last, the sole of many masters
Of an ill-gotten million of piastres.

126

A fisher, therefore, was he,—though of men,
    Like Peter the Apostle,—and he fish'd
For wandering merchant vessels, now and then,
    And sometimes caught as many as he wish'd;
The cargoes he confiscated, and gain
    He sought in the slave-market too, and dish'd
Full many a morsel for that Turkish trade,
By which, no doubt, a good deal may be made.

127

He was a Greek, and on his isle had built
    (One of the wild and smaller Cyclades)
A very handsome house from out his guilt,
    And there he lived exceedingly at ease;
Heaven knows what cash he got, or blood he spilt,
    A sad old fellow was he, if you please;
But this I know, it was a spacious building,
Full of barbaric carving, paint, and gilding.

128

He had an only daughter, call'd Haidée,
    The greatest heiress of the Eastern Isles;
Besides, so very beautiful was she,
    Her dowry was as nothing to her smiles:
Still in her teens, and like a lovely tree
    She grew to womanhood, and between whiles
Rejected several suitors, just to learn
How to accept a better in his turn.

129

And walking out upon the beach, below
   The cliff,—towards sunset, on that day she found,
Insensible,—not dead, but nearly so,—
   Don Juan, almost famish'd, and half drown'd;
But being naked, she was shock'd, you know,
   Yet deem'd herself in common pity bound,
As far as in her lay, "to take him in,
A stranger" dying, with so white a skin.

130

But taking him into her father's house
   Was not exactly the best way to save,
But like conveying to the cat the mouse,
   Or people in a trance into their grave
Because the good old man had so much *"vous,"*
   Unlike the honest Arab thieves so brave,
He would have hospitably cured the stranger
And sold him instantly when out of danger.

131

And therefore, with her maid, she thought it best
   (A virgin always on her maid relies)
To place him in the cave for present rest:
   And when, at last, he open'd his black eyes,
Their charity increased about their guest;
   And their compassion grew to such a size,
It open'd half the turnpike gates to heaven—
(St. Paul says, 'tis the toll which must be given).

132

They made a fire,—but such a fire as they
   Upon the moment could contrive with such
Materials as were cast up round the bay,—
   Some broken planks, and oars, that to the touch
Were nearly tinder, since so long they lay,

A mast was almost crumbled to a crutch;
But, by God's grace, here wrecks were in such plenty,
That there was fuel to have furnish'd twenty.

133

He had a bed of furs, and a pelisse,
    For Haidée stripp'd her sables off to make
His couch; and, that he might be more at ease,
    And warm, in case by chance he should awake,
They also gave a petticoat apiece,
    She and her maid,—and promised by daybreak
To pay him a fresh visit, with a dish
For breakfast, of eggs, coffee, bread, and fish.

134

And thus they left him to his lone repose:
    Juan slept like a top, or like the dead,
Who sleep at last, perhaps (God only knows),
    Just for the present; and in his lull'd head
Not even a vision of his former woes
    Throbb'd in accursed dreams, which sometimes spread
Unwelcome visions of our former years,
Till the eye, cheated, opens thick with tears.

135

Young Juan slept all dreamless:—but the maid,
    Who smooth'd his pillow, as she left the den
Look'd back upon him, and a moment stayed,
    And turn'd, believing that he call'd again.
He slumber'd; yet she thought, at least she said
    (The heart will slip, even as the tongue and pen),
He had pronounced her name—but she forgot
That at this moment Juan knew it not.

136

And pensive to her father's house she went,
    Enjoining silence strict to Zoe, who

Better than her knew what, in fact, she meant,
  She being wiser by a year or two:
A year or two's an age when rightly spent,
  And Zoe spent hers, as most women do,
In gaining all that useful sort of knowledge
Which is acquired in Nature's good old college.

137

The morn broke, and found Juan slumbering still
  Fast in his cave, and nothing clash'd upon
His rest: the rushing of the neighbouring rill,
  And the young beams of the excluded sun,
Troubled him not, and he might sleep his fill;
  And need he had of slumber yet, for none
Had suffer'd more—his hardships were comparative
To those related in my grand-dad's "Narrative."

138

Not so Haidée: she sadly toss'd and tumbled,
  And started from her sleep, and, turning o'er,
Dream'd of a thousand wrecks, o'er which she stumbled,
  And handsome corpses strew'd upon the shore;
And woke her maid so early that she grumbled,
  And call'd her father's old slaves up, who swore
In several oaths—Armenian, Turk, and Greek—
They knew not what to think of such a freak.

139

But up she got, and up she made them get,
  With some pretence about the sun, that makes
Sweet skies just when he rises, or is set;
  And 'tis, no doubt, a sight to see when breaks
Bright Phoebus, while the mountains still are wet
  With mist, and every bird with him awakes,
And night is flung off like a mourning suit
Worn for a husband,—or some other brute.

140

I say, the sun is a most glorious sight:
  I've seen him rise full oft, indeed of late
I have sat up on purpose all the night,
  Which hastens, as physicians say, one's fate;
And so all ye, who would be in the right
  In health and purse, begin your day to date
From daybreak, and when coffin'd at fourscore
Engrave upon the plate, you rose at four.

141

And Haidée met the morning face to face;
  Her own was freshest, though a feverish flush
Had dyed it with the headlong blood, whose race
  From heart to cheek is curb'd into a blush,
Like to a torrent which a mountain's base,
  That overpowers some Alpine river's rush,
Checks to a lake, whose waves in circles spread;
Or the Red Sea—but the sea is not red.

142

And down the cliff the island virgin came,
  And near the cave her quick light footsteps drew,
While the sun smiled on her with his first flame,
  And young Aurora kiss'd her lips with dew,
Taking her for a sister; just the same
  Mistake you would have made on seeing the two,
Although the mortal, quite as fresh and fair,
Had all the advantage, too, of not being air.

143

And when into the cavern Haidée stepp'd
  All timidly, yet rapidly, she saw
That like an infant Juan sweetly slept;
  And then she stopp'd, and stood as if in awe
(For sleep is awful), and on tiptoe crept

And wrapt him closer, lest the air, too raw,
Should reach his blood, then o'er him still as death
Bent, with hush'd lips, that drank his scarce-drawn breath.

144

And thus like to an angel o'er the dying
　　Who die in righteousness, she lean'd; and there
All tranquilly the shipwreck'd boy was lying,
　　As o'er him lay the calm and stirless air:
But Zoe the meantime some eggs was frying,
　　Since, after all, no doubt the youthful pair
Must breakfast, and betimes—lest they should ask it,
She drew out her provision from the basket.

145

She knew that the best feelings must have victual,
　　And that a shipwreck'd youth would hungry be;
Besides, being less in love, she yawn'd a little,
　　And felt her veins chill'd by the neighbouring sea;
And so, she cook'd their breakfast to a tittle;
　　I can't say that she gave them any tea,
But there were eggs, fruit, coffee, bread, fish, honey,
With Scio wine,—and all for love, not money.

146

And Zoe, when the eggs were ready, and
　　The coffee made, would fain have waken'd Juan;
But Haidée stopp'd her with her quick small hand,
　　And without word, a sign her finger drew on
Her lip, which Zoe needs must understand;
　　And, the first breakfast spoilt, prepared a new one,
Because her mistress would not let her break
That sleep which seem'd as it would ne'er awake.

147

For still he lay, and on his thin worn cheek
　　A purple hectic play'd like dying day

On the snow-tops of distant hills; the streak
   Of sufferance yet upon his forehead lay,
Where the blue veins look'd shadowy, shrunk, and weak;
   And his black curls were dewy with the spray,
Which weigh'd upon them yet, all damp and salt,
Mix'd with the stony vapours of the vault.

148

And she bent o'er him, and he lay beneath,
   Hush'd as the babe upon its mother's breast,
Droop'd as the willow when no winds can breathe,
   Lull'd like the depth of ocean when at rest,
Fair as the crowning rose of the whole wreath,
   Soft as the callow cygnet in its nest;
In short, he was a very pretty fellow,
Although his woes had turn'd him rather yellow.

149

He woke and gazed, and would have slept again,
   But the fair face which met his eyes forbade
Those eyes to close, though weariness and pain
   Had further sleep a further pleasure made;
For woman's face was never form'd in vain
   For Juan, so that even when he pray'd
He turn'd from grisly saints, and martyrs hairy,
To the sweet portraits of the Virgin Mary.

150

And thus upon his elbow he arose,
   And look'd upon the lady, in whose cheek
The pale contended with the purple rose,
   As with an effort she began to speak;
Her eyes were eloquent, her words would pose,
   Although she told him, in good modern Greek,
With an Ionian accent, low and sweet,
That he was faint, and must not talk, but eat.

151

Now Juan could not understand a word,
  Being no Grecian; but he had an ear,
And her voice was the warble of a bird,
  So soft, so sweet, so delicately clear,
That finer, simpler music ne'er was heard;
  The sort of sound we echo with a tear,
Without knowing why—an overpowering tone,
Whence melody descends as from a throne.

152

And Juan gazed as one who is awoke
  By a distant organ, doubting if he be
Not yet a dreamer, till the spell is broke
  By the watchman, or some such reality,
Or by one's early valet's cursed knock;
  At least it is a heavy sound to me,
Who like a morning slumber—for the night
Shows stars and women in a better light.

153

And Juan, too, was help'd out from his dream,
  Or sleep, or whatsoe'er it was, by feeling
A most prodigious appetite; the steam
  Of Zoe's cookery no doubt was stealing
Upon his senses, and the kindling beam
  Of the new fire, which Zoe kept up, kneeling,
To stir her viands, made him quite awake
And long for food, but chiefly a beef-steak.

154

But beef is rare within these oxless isles;
  Goat's flesh there is, no doubt, and kid, and mutton,
And, when a holiday upon them smiles,
  A joint upon their barbarous spits they put on:
But this occurs but seldom, between whiles,

For some of these are rocks with scarce a hut on;
Others are fair and fertile, among which
This, though not large, was one of the most rich.

155

I say that beef is rare, and can't help thinking
   That the old fable of the Minotaur—
From which our modern morals, rightly shrinking,
   Condemn the royal lady's taste who wore
A cow's shape for a mask—was only (sinking
   The allegory) a mere type, no more,
That Pasiphae promoted breeding cattle,
To make the Cretans bloodier in battle.

156

For we all know that English people are
   Fed upon beef—I won't say much of beer,
Because 'tis liquor only, and being far
   From this my subject, has no business here;
We know, too, they are very fond of war,
   A pleasure—like all pleasures—rather dear;
So were the Cretans—from which I infer
That beef and battles both were owing to her.

157

But to resume. The languid Juan raised
   His head upon his elbow, and he saw
A sight on which he had not lately gazed,
   As all his latter meals had been quite raw,
Three or four things, for which the Lord he praised,
   And, feeling still the famish'd vulture gnaw,
He fell upon whate'er was offer'd, like
A priest, a shark, an alderman, or pike.

158

He ate, and he was well supplied; and she,
   Who watch'd him like a mother, would have fed

Him past all bounds, because she smiled to see
    Such appetite in one she had deem'd dead:
But Zoe, being older than Haidée,
    Knew (by tradition, for she ne'er had read)
That famish'd people must be slowly nurst,
And fed by spoonfuls, else they always burst.

159

And so she took the liberty to state,
    Rather by deeds than words, because the case
Was urgent, that the gentleman, whose fate
    Had made her mistress quit her bed to trace
The sea-shore at this hour, must leave his plate,
    Unless he wish'd to die upon the place—
She snatch'd it, and refused another morsel,
Saying, he had gorged enough to make a horse ill.

160

Next they—he being naked, save a tatter'd
    Pair of scarce decent trowsers—went to work,
And in the fire his recent rags they scatter'd,
    And dress'd him, for the present, like a Turk,
Or Greek—that is, although it not much matter'd,
    Omitting turban, slippers, pistols, dirk,—
They furnish'd him, entire, except some stitches,
With a clean shirt, and very spacious breeches.

161

And then fair Haidée tried her tongue at speaking,
    But not a word could Juan comprehend,
Although he listen'd so that the young Greek in
    Her earnestness would ne'er have made an end;
And, as he interrupted not, went eking
    Her speech out to her protégé and friend,
Till pausing at the last her breath to take,
She saw he did not understand Romaic.

162

And then she had recourse to nods, and signs,
  And smiles, and sparkles of the speaking eye,
And read (the only book she could) the lines
  Of his fair face, and found, by sympathy,
The answer eloquent, where the soul shines
  And darts in one quick glance a long reply;
And thus in every look she saw exprest
A world of words, and things at which she guess'd.

163

And now, by dint of fingers and of eyes,
  And words repeated after her, he took
A lesson in her tongue; but by surmise,
  No doubt, less of her language than her look:
As he who studies fervently the skies
  Turns oftener to the stars than to his book,
Thus Juan learn'd his alpha beta better
From Haidée's glance than any graven letter.

164

'Tis pleasing to be school'd in a strange tongue
  By female lips and eyes—that is, I mean,
When both the teacher and the taught are young,
  As was the case, at least, where I have been;
They smile so when one's right, and when one's wrong
  They smile still more, and then there intervene
Pressure of hands, perhaps even a chaste kiss;—
I learn'd the little that I know by this:

165

That is, some words of Spanish, Turk, and Greek,
  Italian not at all, having no teachers;
Much English I cannot pretend to speak,
  Learning that language chiefly from its preachers,
Barrow, South, Tillotson, whom every week

I study, also Blair, the highest reachers
Of eloquence in piety and prose—
I hate your poets, so read none of those.

166

As for the ladies, I have nought to say,
  A wanderer from the British world of fashion,
Where I, like other "dogs, have had my day,"
  Like other men, too, may have had my passion—
But that, like other things, has pass'd away,
  And all her fools whom I *could* lay the lash on:
Foes, friends, men, women, now are nought to me
But dreams of what has been, no more to be.

167

Return we to Don Juan. He begun
  To hear new words, and to repeat them; but
Some feelings, universal as the sun,
  Were such as could not in his breast be shut
More than within the bosom of a nun:
  He was in love,—as you would be, no doubt,
With a young benefactress,—so was she,
Just in the way we very often see.

168

And every day by daybreak—rather early
  For Juan, who was somewhat fond of rest—
She came into the cave, but it was merely
  To see her bird reposing in his nest;
And she would softly stir his locks so curly,
  Without disturbing her yet slumbering guest,
Breathing all gently o'er his cheek and mouth,
As o'er a bed of roses the sweet south.

169

And every morn his colour freshlier came,
  And every day help'd on his convalescence;

'Twas well, because health in the human frame
  Is pleasant, besides being true love's essence,
For health and idleness to passion's flame
  Are oil and gunpowder; and some good lessons
Are also learnt from Ceres and from Bacchus,
Without whom Venus will not long attack us.

170

While Venus fills the heart (without heart really
  Love, though good always, is not quite so good),
Ceres presents a plate of vermicelli,—
  For love must be sustain'd like flesh and blood,
While Bacchus pours out wine, or hands a jelly:
  Eggs, oysters, too, are amatory food;
But who is their purveyor from above
Heaven knows,—it may be Neptune, Pan, or Jove.

171

When Juan woke he found some good things ready,
  A bath, a breakfast, and the finest eyes
That ever made a youthful heart less steady,
  Besides her maid's, as pretty for their size;
But I have spoken of all this already—
  And repetition's tiresome and unwise,—
Well—Juan, after bathing in the sea,
Came always back to coffee and Haidée.

172

Both were so young, and one so innocent,
  That bathing pass'd for nothing: Juan seem'd
To her, as 'twere, the kind of being sent,
  Of whom these two years she had nightly dream'd,
A something to be loved, a creature meant
  To be her happiness, and whom she deem'd
To render happy: all who joy would win
Must share it,—Happiness was born a twin.

173

It was such pleasure to behold him, such
　　Enlargement of existence to partake
Nature with him, to thrill beneath his touch,
　　To watch him slumbering, and to see him wake;
To live with him for ever were too much;
　　But then the thought of parting made her quake:
He was her own, her ocean-treasure, cast
Like a rich wreck—her first love, and her last.

174

And thus a moon roll'd on, and fair Haidée
　　Paid daily visits to her boy, and took
Such plentiful precautions, that still he
　　Remain'd unknown within his craggy nook;
At last her father's prows put out to sea,
　　For certain merchantmen upon the look,
Not as of yore to carry off an Io,
But three Ragusan vessels bound for Scio.

175

Then came her freedom, for she had no mother,
　　So that, her father being at sea, she was
Free as a married woman, or such other
　　Female, as where she likes may freely pass,
Without even the encumbrance of a brother,
　　The freest she that ever gazed on glass:
I speak of Christian lands in this comparison,
Where wives, at least, are seldom kept in garrison.

176

Now she prolong'd her visits and her talk
　　(For they must talk), and he had learnt to say
So much as to propose to take a walk,—
　　For little had he wander'd since the day
On which, like a young flower snapp'd from the stalk,

Drooping and dewy on the beach he lay,—
And thus they walk'd out in the afternoon,
And saw the sun set opposite the moon.

177

It was a wild and breaker-beaten coast,
    With cliffs above, and a broad sandy shore,
Guarded by shoals and rocks as by an host,
    With here and there a creek, whose aspect wore
A better welcome to the tempest-tost;
    And rarely ceased the haughty billow's roar,
Save on the dead long summer days, which make
The outstretch'd ocean glitter like a lake.

178

And the small ripple spilt upon the beach
    Scarcely o'erpass'd the cream of your champagne,
When o'er the brim the sparkling bumpers reach,
    That spring-dew of the spirit! the heart's rain!
Few things surpass old wine; and they may preach
    Who please,—the more because they preach in vain,—
Let us have wine and women, mirth and laughter,
Sermons and soda-water the day after.

179

Man, being reasonable, must get drunk;
    The best of life is but intoxication:
Glory, the grape, love, gold, in these are sunk
    The hopes of all men, and of every nation;
Without their sap, how branchless were the trunk
    Of life's strange tree, so fruitful on occasion!
But to return,—Get very drunk; and when
You wake with headache, you shall see what then.

180

Ring for your valet—bid him quickly bring
    Some hock and soda-water, then you'll know

A pleasure worthy Xerxes the great king;
   For not the blest sherbet, sublimed with snow,
Nor the first sparkle of the desert spring,
   Nor Burgundy in all its sunset glow,
After long travel, ennui, love, or slaughter,
Vie with that draught of hock and soda-water.

181

The coast—I think it was the coast that I
   Was just describing—Yes, it *was* the coast—
Lay at this period quiet as the sky,
   The sands untumbled, the blue waves untost,
And all was stillness, save the sea-bird's cry,
   And dolphin's leap, and little billow crost
By some low rock or shelve, that made it fret
Against the boundary it scarcely wet.

182

And forth they wander'd, her sire being gone,
   As I have said, upon an expedition;
And mother, brother, guardian, she had none,
   Save Zoe, who, although with due precision
She waited on her lady with the sun,
   Thought daily service was her only mission,
Bringing warm water, wreathing her long tresses,
And asking now and then for cast-off dresses.

183

It was the cooling hour, just when the rounded
   Red sun sinks down behind the azure hill,
Which then seems as if the whole earth it bounded,
   Circling all nature, hush'd, and dim, and still,
With the far mountain-crescent half surrounded
   On one side, and the deep sea calm and chill,
Upon the other, and the rosy sky,
With one star sparkling through it like an eye.

184

And thus they wander'd forth, and hand in hand,
  Over the shining pebbles and the shells,
Glided along the smooth and harden'd sand,
  And in the worn and wild receptacles
Work'd by the storms, yet work'd as it were plann'd,
  In hollow halls, with sparry roofs and cells,
They turn'd to rest; and, each clasp'd by an arm,
Yielded to the deep twilight's purple charm.

185

They look'd up to the sky, whose floating glow
  Spread like a rosy ocean, vast and bright;
They gazed upon the glittering sea below,
  Whence the broad moon rose circling into sight;
They heard the waves splash, and the wind so low,
  And saw each other's dark eyes darting light
Into each other—and, beholding this,
Their lips drew near, and clung into a kiss;

186

A long, long kiss, a kiss of youth, and love,
  And beauty, all concentrating like rays
Into one focus, kindled from above;
  Such kisses as belong to early days,
Where heart, and soul, and sense, in concert move,
  And the blood's lava, and the pulse a blaze,
Each kiss a heart-quake,—for a kiss's strength,
I think it must be reckon'd by its length.

187

By length I mean duration; theirs endured
  Heaven knows how long—no doubt they never reckon'd;
And if they had, they could not have secured
  The sum of their sensations to a second:
They had not spoken; but they felt allured,

As if their souls and lips each other beckon'd,
Which, being join'd, like swarming bees they clung—
Their hearts the flowers from whence the honey sprung.

188

They were alone, but not alone as they
    Who shut in chambers think it loneliness;
The silent ocean, and the starlight bay,
    The twilight glow, which momently grew less,
The voiceless sands, and dropping caves, that lay
    Around them, made them to each other press,
As if there were no life beneath the sky
Save theirs, and that their life could never die.

189

They fear'd no eyes nor ears on that lone beach,
    They felt no terrors from the night; they were
All in all to each other; though their speech
    Was broken words, they *thought* a language there,—
And all the burning tongues the passions teach
    Found in one sigh the best interpreter
Of nature's oracle—first love,—that all
Which Eve has left her daughters since her fall.

190

Haidée spoke not of scruples, ask'd no vows,
    Nor offer'd any; she had never heard
Of plight and promises to be a spouse,
    Or perils by a loving maid incurr'd;
She was all which pure ignorance allows,
    And flew to her young mate like a young bird,
And never having dreamt of falsehood, she
Had not one word to say of constancy.

191

She loved, and was beloved—she adored,
    And she was worshipp'd; after nature's fashion,

Their intense souls, into each other pour'd,
    If souls could die, had perish'd in that passion,—
But by degrees their senses were restored,
    Again to be o'ercome, again to dash on;
And, beating 'gainst *his* bosom, Haidée's heart
Felt as if never more to beat apart.

192

Alas! they were so young, so beautiful,
    So lonely, loving, helpless, and the hour
Was that in which the heart is always full,
    And, having o'er itself no further power,
Prompts deeds eternity cannot annul,
    But pays off moments in an endless shower
Of hell-fire—all prepared for people giving
Pleasure or pain to one another living.

193

Alas! for Juan and Haidée! they were
    So loving and so lovely—till then never,
Excepting our first parents, such a pair
    Had run the risk of being damn'd for ever;
And Haidée, being devout as well as fair,
    Had, doubtless, heard about the Stygian river,
And hell and purgatory—but forgot
Just in the very crisis she should not.

194

They look upon each other, and their eyes
    Gleam in the moonlight; and her white arm clasps
Round Juan's head, and his around her lies
    Half buried in the tresses which it grasps:
She sits upon his knee, and drinks his sighs,
    He hers, until they end in broken gasps;
And thus they form a group that's quite antique,
Half naked, loving, natural, and Greek.

195

And when those deep and burning moments pass'd,
   And Juan sunk to sleep within her arms,
She slept not, but all tenderly, though fast,
   Sustain'd his head upon her bosom's charms;
And now and then her eye to heaven is cast,
   And then on the pale cheek her breast now warms,
Pillow'd on her o'erflowing heart, which pants
With all it granted, and with all it grants.

196

An infant when it gazes on a light,
   A child the moment when it drains the breast,
A devotee when soars the Host in sight,
   An Arab with a stranger for a guest,
A sailor when the prize has struck in fight,
   A miser filling his most hoarded chest,
Feel rapture; but not such true joy are reaping
As they who watch o'er what they love while sleeping.

197

For there it lies so tranquil, so beloved,
   All that it hath of life with us is living;
So gentle, stirless, helpless, and unmoved,
   And all unconscious of the joy 'tis giving;
All it hath felt, inflicted, pass'd, and proved,
   Hush'd into depths beyond the watcher's diving;
There lies the thing we love with all its errors
And all its charms, like death without its terrors.

198

The lady watch'd her lover—and that hour
   Of Love's, and Night's, and Ocean's solitude,
O'erflow'd her soul with their united power;
   Amidst the barren sand and rocks so rude
She and her wave-worn love had made their bower,

Where nought upon their passion could intrude,
And all the stars that crowded the blue space
Saw nothing happier than her glowing face.

199

Alas! the love of women! it is known
  To be a lovely and a fearful thing;
For all of theirs upon that die is thrown,
  And if 'tis lost, life hath no more to bring
To them but mockeries of the past alone,
  And their revenge is as the tiger's spring,
Deadly, and quick, and crushing; yet, as real
Torture is theirs, what they inflict they feel.

200

They are right; for man, to man so oft unjust,
  Is always so to women; one sole bond
Awaits them, treachery is all their trust;
  Taught to conceal, their bursting hearts despond
Over their idol, till some wealthier lust
  Buys them in marriage—and what rests beyond?
A thankless husband, next a faithless lover,
Then dressing, nursing, praying, and all's over.

201

Some take a lover, some take drams or prayers,
  Some mind their household, others dissipation,
Some run away, and but exchange their cares,
  Losing the advantage of a virtuous station;
Few changes e'er can better their affairs,
  Theirs being an unnatural situation,
From the dull palace to the dirty hovel:
Some play the devil, and then write a novel.

202

Haidée was Nature's bride, and knew not this:
  Haidée was Passion's child, born where the sun

Showers triple light, and scorches even the kiss
   Of his gazelle-eyed daughters; she was one
Made but to love, to feel that she was his
   Who was her chosen: what was said or done
Elsewhere was nothing. She had nought to fear,
Hope, care, nor love beyond,—her heart beat *here*.

203

And oh! that quickening of the heart, that beat!
   How much it costs us! yet each rising throb
Is in its cause as its effect so sweet,
   That Wisdom, ever on the watch to rob
Joy of its alchemy, and to repeat
   Fine truths; even Conscience, too, has a tough job
To make us understand each good old maxim,
So good—I wonder Castlereagh don't tax 'em.

204

And now 'twas done—on the lone shore were plighted
   Their hearts; the stars, their nuptial torches, shed
Beauty upon the beautiful they lighted:
   Ocean their witness, and the cave their bed,
By their own feelings hallow'd and united,
   Their priest was Solitude, and they were wed:
And they were happy, for to their young eyes
Each was an angel, and earth paradise.

205

Oh, Love! of whom great Caesar was the suitor,
   Titus the master, Antony the slave,
Horace, Catullus, scholars, Ovid tutor,
   Sappho the sage blue-stocking, in whose grave
All those may leap who rather would be neuter—
   (Leucadia's rock still overlooks the wave)—
Oh, Love! thou art the very god of evil,
For, after all, we cannot call thee devil.

206

Thou mak'st the chaste connubial state precarious,
  And jestest with the brows of mightiest men:
Caesar and Pompey, Mahomet, Belisarius,
  Have much employ'd the muse of history's pen:
Their lives and fortunes were extremely various,
  Such worthies Time will never see again;
Yet to these four in three things the same luck holds,
They all were heroes, conquerors, and cuckolds.

207

Thou mak'st philosophers; there's Epicurus
  And Aristippus, a material crew!
Who to immoral courses would allure us
  By theories quite practicable too;
If only from the devil they would insure us,
  How pleasant were the maxim (not quite new),
"Eat, drink, and love; what can the rest avail us?"
So said the royal sage Sardanapalus.

208

But Juan! had he quite forgotten Julia?
  And should he have forgotten her so soon?
I can't but say it seems to me most truly a
  Perplexing question; but, no doubt, the moon
Does these things for us, and whenever newly a
  Strong palpitation rises, 'tis her boon,
Else how the devil is it that fresh features
Have such a charm for us poor human creatures?

209

I hate inconstancy—I loathe, detest,
  Abhor, condemn, abjure the mortal made
Of such quicksilver clay that in his breast
  No permanent foundations can be laid;
Love, constant love, has been my constant guest,

And yet last night, being at a masquerade,
I saw the prettiest creature, fresh from Milan,
Which gave me some sensations like a villain.

210

But soon Philosophy came to my aid,
   And whisper'd, "Think of every sacred tie!"
"I will, my dear Philosophy!" I said,
   "But then her teeth, and then, oh, Heaven! her eye!
I'll just inquire if she be wife or maid,
   Or neither—out of curiosity."
"Stop!" cried Philosophy, with air so Grecian
(Though she was masqued then as a fair Venetian);

211

"Stop!" so I stopp'd.—But to return: that which
   Men call inconstancy is nothing more
Than admiration due where nature's rich
   Profusion with young beauty covers o'er
Some favour'd object; and as in the niche
   A lovely statue we almost adore,
This sort of adoration of the real
Is but a heightening of the *beau idéal*.

212

'Tis the perception of the beautiful,
   A fine extension of the faculties,
Platonic, universal, wonderful,
   Drawn from the stars, and filter'd through the skies,
Without which life would be extremely dull;
   In short, it is the use of our own eyes,
With one or two small senses added, just
To hint that flesh is form'd of fiery dust.

213

Yet 'tis a painful feeling, and unwilling,
   For surely if we always could perceive

In the same object graces quite as killing
    As when she rose upon us like an Eve,
'Twould save us many a heart-ache, many a shilling
    (For we must get them any how, or grieve),
Whereas, if one sole lady pleased for ever,
How pleasant for the heart, as well as liver!

214

The heart is like the sky, a part of heaven,
    But changes night and day, too, like the sky;
Now o'er it clouds and thunder must be driven,
    And darkness and destruction as on high:
But when it hath been scorch'd, and pierced, and riven,
    Its storms expire in water-drops; the eye
Pours forth at last the heart's blood turn'd to tears,
Which make the English climate of our years.

215

The liver is the lazaret of bile,
    But very rarely executes its function,
For the first passion stays there such a while,
    That all the rest creep in and form a junction,
Like knots of vipers on a dunghill's soil,
    Rage, fear, hate, jealousy, revenge, compunction,
So that all mischiefs spring up from this entrail,
Like earthquakes from the hidden fire call'd "central."

216

In the mean time, without proceeding more
    In this anatomy, I've finish'd now
Two hundred and odd stanzas as before,
    That being about the number I'll allow
Each canto of the twelve, or twenty-four;
    And, laying down my pen, I make my bow,
Leaving Don Juan and Haidée to plead
For them and theirs with all who deign to read.

1819   1819

CANTO THE THIRD

1

Hail, Muse! *et cetera.*—We left Juan sleeping,
   Pillow'd upon a fair and happy breast,
And watch'd by eyes that never yet knew weeping,
   And loved by a young heart, too deeply blest
To feel the poison through her spirit creeping,
   Or know who rested there, a foe to rest,
Had soil'd the current of her sinless years,
And turn'd her pure heart's purest blood to tears!

2

Oh, Love! what is it in this world of ours
   Which makes it fatal to be loved? Ah why
With cypress branches hast thou wreathed thy bowers,
   And made thy best interpreter a sigh?
As those who dote on odours pluck the flowers,
   And place them on their breast—but place to die—
Thus the frail beings we would fondly cherish
Are laid within our bosoms but to perish.

3

In her first passion woman loves her lover,
   In all the others all she loves is love,
Which grows a habit she can ne'er get over
   And fits her loosely—like an easy glove,
As you may find, whene'er you like to prove her:
   One man alone at first her heart can move;
She then prefers him in the plural number,
Not finding that the additions much encumber.

4

I know not if the fault be men's or theirs;
   But one thing's pretty sure; a woman planted

(Unless at once she plunge for life in prayers)—
   After a decent time must be gallanted;
Although, no doubt, her first of love affairs
   Is that to which her heart is wholly granted;
Yet there are some, they say, who have had *none*,
But those who have ne'er end with only *one*.

5

'Tis melancholy, and a fearful sign
   Of human frailty, folly, also crime,
That love and marriage rarely can combine,
   Although they both are born in the same clime;
Marriage from love, like vinegar from wine—
   A sad, sour, sober beverage—by time
Is sharpen'd from its high celestial flavour,
Down to a very homely household savour.

6

There's something of antipathy, as 'twere,
   Between their present and their future state;
A kind of flattery that's hardly fair
   Is used until the truth arrives too late—
Yet what can people do, except despair?
   The same things change their names at such a rate;
For instance—passion in a lover's glorious,
But in a husband is pronounced uxorious.

7

Men grow ashamed of being so very fond;
   They sometimes also get a little tired
(But that, of course, is rare), and then despond:
   The same things cannot always be admired,
Yet 'tis 'so nominated in the bond,'
   That both are tied till one shall have expired.
Sad thought! to lose the spouse that was adorning
Our days, and put one's servants into mourning.

8

There's doubtless something in domestic doings
    Which forms, in fact, true love's antithesis;
Romances paint at full length people's wooings,
    But only give a bust of marriages;
For no one cares for matrimonial cooings,
    There's nothing wrong in a connubial kiss:
Think you, if Laura had been Petrarch's wife,
He would have written sonnets all his life?

9

All tragedies are finish'd by a death,
    All comedies are ended by a marriage;
The future states of both are left to faith,
    For authors fear description might disparage
The worlds to come of both, or fall beneath,
    And then both worlds would punish their miscarriage;
So leaving each their priest and prayerbook ready,
They say no more of Death or of the Lady.

10

The only two that in my recollection
    Have sung of heaven and hell, or marriage, are
Dante and Milton, and of both the affection
    Was hapless in their nuptials, for some bar
Of fault or temper ruin'd the connexion
    (Such things, in fact, it don't ask much to mar);
But Dante's Beatrice and Milton's Eve
Were not drawn from their spouses, you conceive.

11

Some persons say that Dante meant theology
    By Beatrice, and not a mistress—I,
Although my opinion may require apology,
    Deem this a commentator's phantasy,
Unless indeed it was from his own knowledge he

Decided thus, and show'd good reason why;
I think that Dante's more abstruse ecstatics
Meant to personify the mathematics.

12

Haidée and Juan were not married, but
    The fault was theirs, not mine: it is not fair,
Chaste reader, then, in any way to put
    The blame on me, unless you wish they were;
Then if you'd have them wedded, please to shut
    The book which treats of this erroneous pair,
Before the consequences grow too awful;
'Tis dangerous to read of loves unlawful.

13

Yet they were happy,—happy in the illicit
    Indulgence of their innocent desires;
But more imprudent grown with every visit,
    Haidée forgot the island was her sire's:
When we have what we like, 'tis hard to miss it,
    At least in the beginning, ere one tires;
Thus she came often, not a moment losing,
Whilst her piratical papa was cruising.

14

Let not his mode of raising cash seem strange,
    Although he fleeced the flags of every nation,
For into a prime minister but change
    His title, and 'tis nothing but taxation;
But he, more modest, took an humbler range
    Of life, and in an honester vocation
Pursued o'er the high seas his watery journey,
And merely practised as a sea-attorney.

15

The good old gentleman had been detain'd
    By winds and waves, and some important captures;

And, in the hope of more, at sea remain'd,
   Although a squall or two had damp'd his raptures,
By swamping one of the prizes; he had chain'd
   His prisoners, dividing them like chapters
In number'd lots; they all had cuffs and collars,
And averaged each from ten to a hundred dollars.

16

Some he disposed of off Cape Matapan,
   Among his friends the Mainots; some he sold
To his Tunis correspondents, save one man
   Toss'd overboard unsaleable (being old):
The rest—save here and there some richer one,
   Reserved for future ransom—in the hold,
Were link'd alike, as for the common people he
Had a large order from the Dey of Tripoli.

17

The merchandise was served in the same way,
   Pieced out for different marts in the Levant,
Except some certain portions of the prey,
   Light classic articles of female want,
French stuffs, lace, tweezers, toothpicks, teapot, tray,
   Guitars and castanets from Alicant,
All which selected from the spoil he gathers,
Robb'd for his daughter by the best of fathers.

18

A monkey, a Dutch mastiff, a mackaw,
   Two parrots, with a Persian cat and kittens,
He chose from several animals he saw—
   A terrier, too, which once had been a Briton's,
Who dying on the coast of Ithaca,
   The peasants gave the poor dumb thing a pittance.
These to secure in this strong blowing weather,
He caged in one huge hamper all together.

19

Then having settled his marine affairs,
  Despatching single cruisers here and there,
His vessel having need of some repairs,
  He shaped his course to where his daughter fair
Continued still her hospitable cares;
  But that part of the coast being shoal and bare,
And rough with reefs which ran out many a mile,
His port lay on the other side o' the isle.

20

And there he went ashore without delay,
  Having no custom-house nor quarantine
To ask him awkward questions on the way,
  About the time and place where he had been:
He left his ship to be hove down next day,
  With orders to the people to careen;
So that all hands were busy beyond measure,
In getting out goods, ballast, guns, and treasure.

21

Arriving at the summit of a hill
  Which overlook'd the white walls of his home,
He stopp'd.—What singular emotions fill
  Their bosoms who have been induced to roam!
With fluttering doubts if all be well or ill—
  With love for many, and with fears for some;
All feelings which o'erleap the years long lost,
And bring our hearts back to their starting-post.

22

The approach of home to husbands and to sires,
  After long travelling by land or water,
Most naturally some small doubt inspires—
  A female family's a serious matter;
(None trusts the sex more, or so much admires—

But they hate flattery, so I never flatter;)
Wives in their husbands' absences grow subtler,
And daughters sometimes run off with the butler.

23

An honest gentleman at his return
   May not have the good fortune of Ulysses;
Not all lone matrons for their husbands mourn,
   Or show the same dislike to suitors' kisses;
The odds are that he finds a handsome urn
   To his memory—and two or three young misses
Born to some friend, who holds his wife and riches;—
And that *his* Argus bites him by—the breeches.

24

If single, probably his plighted fair
   Has in his absence wedded some rich miser;
But all the better, for the happy pair
   May quarrel, and the lady growing wiser,
He may resume his amatory care
   As cavalier servente, or despise her;
And that his sorrow may not be a dumb one,
Write odes on the Inconstancy of Woman.

25

And oh! ye gentlemen who have already
   Some chaste *liaison* of the kind—I mean
An honest friendship with a married lady—
   The only thing of this sort ever seen
To last—of all connexions the most steady,
   And the true Hymen, (the first's but a screen)—
Yet for all that keep not too long away;
I've known the absent wrong'd four times a day.

26

Lambro, our sea-solicitor, who had
   Much less experience of dry land than ocean,

On seeing his own chimney-smoke, felt glad;
  But not knowing metaphysics, had no notion
Of the true reason of his not being sad,
  Or that of any other strong emotion;
He loved his child, and would have wept the loss of her,
But knew the cause no more than a philosopher.

27

He saw his white walls shining in the sun,
  His garden trees all shadowy and green;
He heard his rivulet's light bubbling run,
  The distant dog-bark; and perceived between
The umbrage of the wood so cool and dun,
  The moving figures, and the sparkling sheen
Of arms (in the East all arm)—and various dyes
Of colour'd garbs, as bright as butterflies.

28

And as the spot where they appear he nears,
  Surprised at these unwonted signs of idling,
He hears—alas! no music of the spheres,
  But an unhallow'd, earthly sound of fiddling!
A melody which made him doubt his ears,
  The cause being past his guessing or unriddling;
A pipe, too, and a drum, and shortly after,
A most unoriental roar of laughter.

29

And still more nearly to the place advancing,
  Descending rather quickly the declivity,
Through the waved branches, o'er the greensward glancing,
  'Midst other indications of festivity,
Seeing a troop of his domestics dancing
  Like dervises, who turn as on a pivot, he
Perceived it was the Pyrrhic dance so martial,
To which the Levantines are very partial.

30

And further on a group of Grecian girls,
   The first and tallest her white kerchief waving,
Were strung together like a row of pearls,
   Link'd hand in hand, and dancing: each too having
Down her white neck long floating auburn curls—
   (The least of which would set ten poets raving);
Their leader sang—and bounded to her song,
With choral step and voice, the virgin throng.

31

And here, assembled cross-legg'd round their trays,
   Small social parties just begun to dine;
Pilaus and meats of all sorts met the gaze,
   And flasks of Samian and of Chian wine,
And sherbet cooling in the porous vase;
   Above them their dessert grew on its vine,
The orange and pomegranate nodding o'er
Dropp'd in their laps, scarce pluck'd, their mellow store.

32

A band of children, round a snow-white ram,
   There wreathe his venerable horns with flowers
While peaceful as if still an unwean'd lamb,
   The patriarch of the flock all gently cowers
His sober head, majestically tame,
   Or eats from out the palm, or playful lowers
His brow, as if in act to butt, and then
Yielding to their small hands, draws back again.

33

Their classical profiles, and glittering dresses,
   Their large black eyes, and soft seraphic cheeks,
Crimson as cleft pomegranates, their long tresses,
   The gesture which enchants, the eye that speaks,
The innocence which happy childhood blesses,

Made quite a picture of these little Greeks;
So that the philosophical beholder
Sigh'd for their sakes—that they should e'er grow older.

34

Afar, a dwarf buffoon stood telling tales
    To a sedate grey circle of old smokers,
Of secret treasures found in hidden vales,
    Of wonderful replies from Arab jokers,
Of charms to make good gold and cure bad ails,
    Of rocks bewitch'd that open to the knockers,
Of magic ladies who, by one sole act,
Transform'd their lords to beasts (but that's a fact).

35

Here was no lack of innocent diversion
    For the imagination or the senses,
Song, dance, wine, music, stories from the Persian,
    All pretty pastimes in which no offence is;
But Lambro saw all these things with aversion,
    Perceiving in his absence such expenses,
Dreading that climax of all human ills
The inflammation of his weekly bills.

36

Ah! what is man? what perils still environ
    The happiest mortals even after dinner!
A day of gold from out an age of iron
    Is all that life allows the luckiest sinner;
Pleasure (whene'er she sings, at least)'s a siren,
    That lures, to flay alive, the young beginner;
Lambro's reception at his people's banquet
Was such as fire accords to a wet blanket.

37

He—being a man who seldom used a word
    Too much, and wishing gladly to surprise

(In general he surprised men with the sword)
   His daughter—had not sent before to advise
Of his arrival, so that no one stirr'd;
   And long he paused to reassure his eyes,
In fact much more astonish'd than delighted,
To find so much good company invited.

38

He did not know (alas! how men will lie!)
   That a report (especially the Greeks)
Avouch'd his death (such people never die),
   And put his house in mourning several weeks,—
But now their eyes and also lips were dry;
   The bloom, too, had return'd to Haidée's cheeks.
Her tears, too, being return'd into their fount,
She now kept house upon her own account.

39

Hence all this rice, meat, dancing, wine, and fiddling,
   Which turn'd the isle into a place of pleasure;
The servants all were getting drunk or idling.
   A life which made them happy beyond measure.
Her father's hospitality seem'd middling,
   Compared with what Haidée did with his treasure;
'Twas wonderful how things went on improving,
While she had not one hour to spare from loving.

40

Perhaps you think, in stumbling on this feast,
   He flew into a passion, and in fact
There was no mighty reason to be pleased;
   Perhaps you prophesy some sudden act,
The whip, the rack, or dungeon at the least,
   To teach his people to be more exact,
And that, proceeding at a very high rate,
He show'd the royal *penchants* of a pirate.

41

You're wrong.—He was the mildest manner'd man
  That ever scuttled ship or cut a throat,
With such true breeding of a gentleman,
  You never could divine his real thought;
No courtier could, and scarcely woman can
  Gird more deceit within a petticoat;
Pity he loved adventurous life's variety,
He was so great a loss to good society.

42

Advancing to the nearest dinner tray,
  Tapping the shoulder of the nighest guest,
With a peculiar smile, which, by the way,
  Boded no good, whatever it express'd,
He asked the meaning of this holiday;
  The vinous Greek to whom he had address'd
His question, much too merry to divine
The questioner, fill'd up a glass of wine,

43

And without turning his facetious head,
  Over his shoulder, with a Bacchant air,
Presented the o'erflowing cup, and said,
  "Talking's dry work, I have no time to spare."
A second hiccup'd, "Our old master's dead,
  You'd better ask our mistress who's his heir."
"Our mistress!" quoth a third: "Our mistress!—pooh—
You mean our master—not the old, but new."

44

These rascals, being new comers, knew not whom
  They thus address'd—and Lambro's visage fell—
And o'er his eye a momentary gloom
  Pass'd, but he strove quite courteously to quell
The expression, and endeavouring to resume

His smile, requested one of them to tell
The name and quality of his new patron,
Who seem'd to have turn'd Haidée into a matron.

45

"I know not," quoth the fellow, "who or what
  He is, nor whence he came—and little care;
But this I know, that this roast capon's fat,
  And that good wine ne'er wash'd down better fare;
And if you are not satisfied with that,
  Direct your questions to my neighbour there;
He'll answer all for better or for worse,
For none likes more to hear himself converse."

46

I said that Lambro was a man of patience,
  And certainly he show'd the best of breeding,
Which scarce even France, the paragon of nations,
  E'er saw her most polite of sons exceeding;
He bore these sneers against his near relations,
  His own anxiety, his heart, too, bleeding,
The insults, too, of every servile glutton,
Who all the time was eating up his mutton.

47

Now in a person used to much command—
  To bid men come, and go, and come again—
To see his orders done, too, out of hand—
  Whether the word was death, or but the chain—
It may seem strange to find his manners bland;
  Yet such things are, which I cannot explain,
Though doubtless he who can command himself
Is good to govern—almost as a Guelf.

48

Not that he was not sometimes rash or so,
  But never in his real and serious mood;

Then calm, concentrated, and still, and slow,
    He lay coil'd like the boa in the wood;
With him it never was a word and blow,
    His angry word once o'er, he shed no **blood,**
But in his silence there was much to rue,
And his *one* blow left little work for two.

49

He ask'd no further questions, and proceeded
    On to the house, but by a private way,
So that the few who met him hardly heeded,
    So little they expected him that day;
If love paternal in his bosom pleaded
    For Haidée's sake, is more than I can say,
But certainly to one deem'd dead returning,
This revel seem'd a curious mode of mourning.

50

If all the dead could now return to life,
    (Which God forbid!) or some, or a great many,
For instance, if a husband or his wife
    (Nuptial examples are as good as any),
No doubt, whate'er might be their former strife,
    The present weather would be much more **rainy—**
Tears shed into the grave of the connexion
Would share most probably its resurrection.

51

He enter'd in the house no more his home,
    A thing to human feelings the most trying,
And harder for the heart to overcome,
    Perhaps, than even the mental pangs of dying;
To find our hearthstone turn'd into a tomb,
    And round its once warm precincts palely **lying**
The ashes of our hopes, is a deep grief,
Beyond a single gentleman's belief.

52

He enter'd in the house—his home no more,
    For without hearts there is no home;—and felt
The solitude of passing his own door
    Without a welcome: *there* he long had dwelt,
There his few peaceful days Time had swept o'er,
    There his warm bosom and keen eye would melt
Over the innocence of that sweet child,
His only shrine of feelings undefiled.

53

He was a man of a strange temperament,
    Of mild demeanour though of savage mood,
Moderate in all his habits, and content
    With temperance in pleasure, as in food,
Quick to perceive, and strong to bear, and meant
    For something better, if not wholly good;
His country's wrongs and his despair to save her
Had stung him from a slave to an enslaver.

54

The love of power, and rapid gain of gold,
    The hardness by long habitude produced,
The dangerous life in which he had grown old,
    The mercy he had granted oft abused,
The sights he was accustom'd to behold,
    The wild seas, and wild men with whom he cruised,
Had cost his enemies a long repentance,
And made him a good friend, but bad acquaintance.

55

But something of the spirit of old Greece
    Flash'd o'er his soul a few heroic rays,
Such as lit onward to the Golden Fleece
    His predecessors in the Colchian days;
'Tis true he had no ardent love for peace—

Alas! his country show'd no path to praise:
Hate to the world and war with every nation
He waged, in vengeance of her degradation.

56

Still o'er his mind the influence of the clime
    Shed its Ionian elegance, which show'd
Its power unconsciously full many a time,—
    A taste seen in the choice of his abode,
A love of music and of scenes sublime,
    A pleasure in the gentle stream that flow'd
Past him in crystal, and a joy in flowers,
Bedew'd his spirit in his calmer hours.

57

But whatsoe'er he had of love reposed
    On that beloved daughter; she had been
The only thing which kept his heart unclosed
    Amidst the savage deeds he had done and seen,
A lonely pure affection unopposed:
    There wanted but the loss of this to wean
His feelings from all milk of human kindness,
And turn him like the Cyclops mad with blindness.

58

The cubless tigress in her jungle raging
    Is dreadful to the shepherd and the flock;
The ocean when its yeasty war is waging
    Is awful to the vessel near the rock;
But violent things will sooner bear assuaging,
    Their fury being spent by its own shock,
Than the stern, single, deep, and wordless ire
Of a strong human heart, and in a sire.

59

It is a hard although a common case
    To find our children running restive—they

In whom our brightest days we would retrace,
　　Our little selves re-formed in finer clay,
Just as old age is creeping on apace,
　　And clouds come o'er the sunset of our day,
They kindly leave us, though not quite alone,
But in good company—the gout or stone.

60

Yet a fine family is a fine thing
　　(Provided they don't come in after dinner);
'Tis beautiful to see a matron bring
　　Her children up (if nursing them don't thin her);
Like cherubs round an altar-piece they cling
　　To the fire-side (a sight to touch a sinner).
A lady with her daughters or her nieces
Shine like a guinea and seven-shilling pieces.

61

Old Lambro pass'd unseen a private gate,
　　And stood within his hall at eventide;
Meantime the lady and her lover sate
　　At wassail in their beauty and their pride:
An ivory inlaid table spread with state
　　Before them, and fair slaves on every side;
Gems, gold, and silver, form'd the service mostly,
Mother of pearl and coral the less costly.

62

The dinner made about a hundred dishes;
　　Lamb and pistachio nuts—in short, all meats,
And saffron soups, and sweetbreads; and the fishes
　　Were of the finest that e'er flounced in nets,
Drest to a Sybarite's most pamper'd wishes;
　　The beverage was various sherbets
Of raisin, orange, and pomegranate juice,
Squeezed through the rind, which makes it best for use.

63

These were ranged round, each in its crystal ewer,
  And fruits, and date-bread loaves closed the repast,
And Mocha's berry, from Arabia pure,
  In small fine China cups, came in at last;
Gold cups of filigree made to secure
  The hand from burning underneath them placed;
Cloves, cinnamon, and saffron too were boil'd
Up with the coffee, which (I think) they spoil'd.

64

The hangings of the room were tapestry, made
  Of velvet panels, each of different hue,
And thick with damask flowers of silk inlaid;
  And round them ran a yellow border too;
The upper border, richly wrought, display'd,
  Embroider'd delicately o'er with blue,
Soft Persian sentences, in lilac letters,
From poets, or the moralists their betters.

65

These Oriental writings on the wall,
  Quite common in those countries, are a kind
Of monitors adapted to recall,
  Like skulls at Memphian banquets, to the mind
The words which shook Belshazzar in his hall,
  And took his kingdom from him: You will find,
Though sages may pour out their wisdom's treasure,
There is no sterner moralist than Pleasure.

66

A beauty at the season's close grown hectic,
  A genius who has drunk himself to death,
A rake turn'd methodistic, or Eclectic—
  (For that's the name they like to pray beneath)—
But most. an alderman struck apoplectic,

Are things that really take away the breath,—
And show that late hours, wine, and love are able
To do not much less damage than the table.

67

Haidée and Juan carpeted their feet
 On crimson satin, border'd with pale blue;
Their sofa occupied three parts complete
 Of the apartment—and appear'd quite new;
The velvet cushions (for a throne more meet)
 Were scarlet, from whose glowing centre grew
A sun emboss'd in gold, whose rays of tissue,
Meridian-like, were seen all light to issue.

68

Crystal and marble, plate and porcelain,
 Had done their work of splendour; Indian mats
And Persian carpets, which the heart bled to stain,
 Over the floors were spread; gazelles and cats,
And dwarfs and blacks, and such like things that gain
 Their bread as ministers and favourites—(that's
To say, by degradation)—mingled there
As plentiful as in a court or fair.

69

There was no want of lofty mirrors, and
 The tables, most of ebony inlaid
With mother of pearl or ivory, stood at hand,
 Or were of tortoise-shell or rare woods made,
Fretted with gold or silver:—by command,
 The greater part of these were ready spread
With viands and sherbets in ice—and wine—
Kept for all comers at all hours to dine.

70

Of all the dresses I select Haidée's:
 She wore two jelicks—one was of pale yellow;

Of azure, pink, and white was her chemise—
  'Neath which her breast heaved like a little billow,
With buttons form'd of pearls as large as peas,
  All gold and crimson shone her jelick's fellow,
And the striped white gauze baracan that bound her,
Like fleecy clouds about the moon, flow'd round her.

71

One large gold bracelet clasp'd each lovely arm,
  Lockless—so pliable from the pure gold
That the hand stretch'd and shut it without harm,
  The limb which it adorn'd its only mould;
So beautiful—its very shape would charm,
  And clinging as if loath to lose its hold,
The purest ore enclosed the whitest skin
That e'er by precious metal was held in.

72

Around, as princess of her father's land,
  A like gold bar above her instep roll'd
Announced her rank; twelve rings were on her hand;
  Her hair was starr'd with gems; her veil's fine fold
Below her breasts was fasten'd with a band
  Of lavish pearls, whose worth could scarce be told;
Her orange silk full Turkish trousers furl'd
About the prettiest ankle in the world.

73

Her hair's long auburn waves down to her heel
  Flow'd like an Alpine torrent which the sun
Dyes with his morning light,—and would conceal
  Her person if allow'd at large to run,
And still they seem'd resentfully to feel
  The silken fillet's curb, and sought to shun
Their bonds whene'er some Zephyr caught began
To offer his young pinion as her fan.

74

Round her she made an atmosphere of life,
   The very air seem'd lighter from her eyes,
They were so soft and beautiful, and rife
   With all we can imagine of the skies,
And pure as Psyche ere she grew a wife—
   Too pure even for the purest human ties;
Her overpowering presence made you feel
It would not be idolatry to kneel.

75

Her eyelashes, though dark as night, were tinged
   (It is the country's custom), but in vain;
For those large black eyes were so blackly fringed,
   The glossy rebels mock'd the jetty stain,
And in their native beauty stood avenged:
   Her nails were touch'd with henna; but again
The power of art was turn'd to nothing, for
They could not look more rosy than before.

76

The henna should be deeply dyed to make
   The skin relieved appear more fairly fair;
She had no need of this, day ne'er will break
   On mountain-tops more heavenly white than her:
The eye might doubt if it were well awake,
   She was so like a vision; I might err,
But Shakspeare also says, 'tis very silly
"To gild refined gold, or paint the lily."

77

Juan had on a shawl of black and gold,
   But a white baracan, and so transparent
The sparkling gems beneath you might behold,
   Like small stars through the milky way apparent;
His turban furl'd in many a graceful fold,

An emerald aigrette with Haidée's hair in't
Surmounted, as its clasp, a glowing crescent,
Whose rays shone ever trembling, but incessant.

78

And now they were diverted by their suite,
    Dwarfs, dancing-girls, black eunuchs, and a poet,
Which made their new establishment complete;
    The last was of great fame, and liked to show it;
His verses rarely wanted their due feet—
    And for his theme—he seldom sung below it,
He being paid to satirise or flatter,
As the psalm says, "inditing a good matter."

79

He praised the present, and abused the past,
    Reversing the good custom of old days,
An Eastern anti-jacobin at last
    He turn'd, preferring pudding to *no* praise—
For some few years his lot had been o'ercast
    By his seeming independent in his lays,
But now he sung the Sultan and the Pacha
With truth like Southey, and with verse like Crashaw.

80

He was a man who had seen many changes,
    And always changed as true as any needle;
His polar star being one which rather ranges,
    And not the fix'd—he knew the way to wheedle:
So vile he 'scaped the doom which oft avenges;
    And being fluent (save indeed when fee'd ill),
He lied with such a fervour of intention—
There was no doubt he earn'd his laureate pension.

81

But he had genius,—when a turncoat has it,
    The "Vates irritabilis" takes care

That without notice few full moons shall pass it;
Even good men like to make the public stare:—
But to my subject—let me see—what was it?—
Oh!—the third canto—and the pretty pair—
Their loves, and feasts, and house, and dress, and mode
Of living in their insular abode.

82

Their poet, a sad trimmer, but no less
In company a very pleasant fellow,
Had been the favourite of full many a mess
Of men, and made them speeches when half mellow;
And though his meaning they could rarely guess,
Yet still they deign'd to hiccup or to bellow
The glorious meed of popular applause,
Of which the first ne'er knows the second cause.

83

But now being lifted into high society,
And having pick'd up several odds and ends
Of free thoughts in his travels, for variety,
He deem'd, being in a lone isle, among friends,
That without any danger of a riot, he
Might for long lying make himself amends;
And singing as he sung in his warm youth,
Agree to a short armistice with truth.

84

He had travell'd 'mongst the Arabs, Turks, and Franks,
And knew the self-loves of the different nations;
And having lived with people of all ranks,
Had something ready upon most occasions—
Which got him a few presents and some thanks.
He varied with some skill his adulations;
To "do at Rome as Romans do," a piece
Of conduct was which he observed in Greece.

85

Thus, usually, when he was asked to sing,
　　He gave the different nations something national;
'Twas all the same to him—"God save the king,"
　　Or "*Ça ira*," according to the fashion all:
His muse made increment of anything,
　　From the high lyric down to the low rational:
If Pindar sang horse-races, what should hinder
Himself from being as pliable as Pindar?

86

In France, for instance, he would write a chanson;
　　In England a six-canto quarto tale;
In Spain he'd make a ballad or romance on
　　The last war—much the same in Portugal;
In Germany, the Pegasus he'd prance on
　　Would be old Goethe's—(see what says De Staël);
In Italy he'd ape the "Trecentisti";
In Greece, he'd sing some sort of hymn like this t' ye:

undercuts poem before he writes it

I

The isles of Greece, the isles of Greece!
　　Where burning Sappho loved and sung,
Where grew the arts of war and peace,
　　Where Delos rose, and Phoebus sprung!
Eternal summer gilds them yet,
But all, except their sun, is set.

II

The Scian and the Teian muse,
　　The hero's harp, the lover's lute,
Have found the fame your shores refuse:
　　Their place of birth alone is mute
To sounds which echo further west
Than your sires' "Islands of the Blest."

III

The mountains look on Marathon—
   And Marathon looks on the sea;
And musing there an hour alone,
   I dream'd that Greece might still be free;
For standing on the Persians' grave,
I could not deem myself a slave.

IV

A king sate on the rocky brow
   Which looks o'er sea-born Salamis;
And ships, by thousands, lay below,
   And men in nations;—all were his!
He counted them at break of day—
And when the sun set where were they?

V

And where are they? and where art thou,
   My country? On thy voiceless shore
The heroic lay is tuneless now—
   The heroic bosom beats no more!
And must thy lyre, so long divine,
Degenerate into hands like mine?

VI

'Tis something, in the dearth of fame,
   Though link'd among a fetter'd race,
To feel at least a patriot's shame,
   Even as I sing, suffuse my face;
For what is left the poet here?
For Greeks a blush—for Greece a tear.

VII

Must *we* but weep o'er days more blest?
   Must *we* but blush?—Our fathers bled.

Earth! render back from out thy breast
 A remnant of our Spartan dead!
Of the three hundred grant but three,
To make a new Thermopylae!

VIII

What, silent still? and silent all?
 Ah! no;—the voices of the dead
Sound like a distant torrent's fall,
 And answer, "Let one living head,
But one arise,—we come, we come!"
'Tis but the living who are dumb.

IX

In vain—in vain: strike other chords;
 Fill high the cup with Samian wine!
Leave battles to the Turkish hordes,
 And shed the blood of Scio's vine!
Hark! rising to the ignoble call—
How answers each bold Bacchanal!

X

You have the Pyrrhic dance as yet;
 Where is the Pyrrhic phalanx gone?
Of two such lessons, why forget
 The nobler and the manlier one?
You have the letters Cadmus gave—
Think ye he meant them for a slave?

XI

Fill high the bowl with Samian wine.
 We will not think of themes like these!
It made Anacreon's song divine:
 He served—but served Polycrates—
A tyrant; but our masters then
Were still, at least, our countrymen.

XII

The tyrant of the Chersonese
  Was freedom's best and bravest friend;
That tyrant was Miltiades!
  Oh! that the present hour would lend
Another despot of the kind!
Such chains as his were sure to bind.

XIII

Fill high the bowl with Samian wine!
  On Suli's rock, and Parga's shore,
Exists the remnant of a line
  Such as the Doric mothers bore;
And there, perhaps, some seed is sown,
The Heracleidan blood might own.

XIV

Trust not for freedom to the Franks—
  They have a king who buys and sells;
In native swords, and native ranks,
  The only hope of courage dwells:
But Turkish force, and Latin fraud,
Would break your shield, however broad.

XV

Fill high the bowl with Samian wine!
  Our virgins dance beneath the shade—
I see their glorious black eyes shine;
  But gazing on each glowing maid,
My own the burning tear-drop laves,
To think such breasts must suckle slaves.

XVI

Place me on Sunium's marbled steep,
  Where nothing, save the waves and I,
May hear our mutual murmurs sweep;

There, swan-like, let me sing and die:
A land of slaves shall ne'er be mine—
Dash down yon cup of Samian wine!

87

Thus sung, or would, or could, or should have sung,
   The modern Greek, in tolerable verse;
If not like Orpheus quite, when Greece was young,
   Yet in these times he might have done much worse:
His strain display'd some feeling—right or wrong;
   And feeling, in a poet, is the source
Of others' feeling; but they are such liars,
And take all colours—like the hands of dyers.

88

But words are things, and a small drop of ink,
   Falling like dew, upon a thought, produces
That which makes thousands, perhaps millions, think;
   'Tis strange, the shortest letter which man uses
Instead of speech, may form a lasting link
   Of ages; to what straits old Time reduces
Frail man, when paper—even a rag like this,
Survives himself, his tomb, and all that's his!

89

And when his bones are dust, his grave a blank,
   His station, generation, even his nation,
Become a thing, or nothing, save to rank
   In chronological commemoration,
Some dull MS. oblivion long has sank,
   Or graven stone found in a barrack's station
In digging the foundation of a closet,
May turn his name up, as a rare deposit.

90

And glory long has made the sages smile;
   'Tis something, nothing, words, illusion, wind—

Depending more upon the historian's style
   Than on the name a person leaves behind:
Troy owes to Homer what whist owes to Hoyle:
   The present century was growing blind
To the great Marlborough's skill in giving knocks,
Until his late Life by Archdeacon Coxe.

91

Milton's the prince of poets—so we say;
   A little heavy, but no less divine:
An independent being in his day—
   Learn'd, pious, temperate in love and wine;
But his life falling into Johnson's way,
   We're told this great high priest of all the Nine
Was whipt at college—a harsh sire—odd spouse,
For the first Mrs. Milton left his house.

92

All these are, *certes*, entertaining facts,
   Like Shakespeare's stealing deer, Lord Bacon's bribes;
Like Titus' youth, and Caesar's earliest acts;
   Like Burns (whom Doctor Currie well describes);
Like Cromwell's pranks;—but although truth exacts
   These amiable descriptions from the scribes,
As most essential to their hero's story,
They do not much contribute to his glory.

93

All are not moralists, like Southey, when
   He prated to the world of "Pantisocracy";
Or Wordsworth unexcised, unhired, who then
   Season'd his pedlar poems with democracy;
Or Coleridge, long before his flighty pen
   Let to the Morning Post its aristocracy;
When he and Southey, following the same path,
Espoused two partners (milliners of Bath).

94

Such names at present cut a convict figure,
    The very Botany Bay in moral geography;
Their loyal treason, renegado rigour,
    Are good manure for their more bare biography,
Wordsworth's last quarto, by the way, is bigger
    Than any since the birthday of typography;
A drowsy frowzy poem, call'd the "Excursion."
Writ in a manner which is my aversion.

95

He there builds up a formidable dyke
    Between his own and others' intellect:
But Wordsworth's poem, and his followers, like
    Joanna Southcote's Shiloh, and her sect,
Are things which, in this century don't strike
    The public mind,—so few are the elect;
And the new births of both their stale virginities
Have proved but dropsies, taken for divinities.

96

But let me to my story: I must own,
    If I have any fault, it is digression,
Leaving my people to proceed alone,
    While I soliloquize beyond expression:
But these are my addresses from the throne,
    Which put off business to the ensuing session:
Forgetting each omission is a loss to
The world, not quite so great as Ariosto.

97

I know that what our neighbours call "*longueurs*,"
    (We've not so good a *word*, but have the *thing*,
In that complete perfection which insures
    An epic from Bob Southey every Spring—)
Form not the true temptation which allures

The reader; but 'twould not be hard to bring
Some fine examples of the *epopée*,
To prove its grand ingredient is *ennui*.

98

We learn from Horace, "Homer sometimes sleeps;"
    We feel without him, Wordsworth sometimes wakes,—
To show with what complacency he creeps,
    With his dear "*Waggoners*," around his lakes.
He wishes for "a boat" to sail the deeps—
    Of ocean?—No, of air; and then he makes
Another outcry for "a little boat,"
And drivels seas to set it well afloat.

99

If he must fain sweep o'er the ethereal plain,
    And Pegasus runs restive in his "Waggon,"
Could he not beg the loan of Charles's Wain?
    Or pray Medea for a single dragon?
Or if, too classic for his vulgar brain,
    He fear'd his neck to venture such a nag on,
And he must needs mount nearer to the moon,
Could not the blockhead ask for a balloon?

100

"Pedlars," and "Boats," and "Waggons!" Oh! ye shades
    Of Pope and Dryden, are we come to this?
That trash of such sort not alone evades
    Contempt, but from the bathos' vast abyss
Floats scumlike uppermost, and these Jack Cades
    Of sense and song above your graves may hiss—
The "little boatman" and his "Peter Bell"
Can sneer at him who drew "Achitophel"!

101

Γ' our tale.—The feast was over, the slaves gone,
    The dwarfs and dancing girls had all retired;

The Arab lore and poet's song were done,
   And every sound of revelry expired;
The lady and her lover, left alone,
   The rosy flood of twilight's sky admired;—
Ave Maria! o'er the earth and sea,
That heavenliest hour of Heaven is worthiest thee!

102

Ave Maria! blessed be the hour!
   The time, the clime, the spot, where I so oft
Have felt that moment in its fullest power
   Sink o'er the earth so beautiful and soft,
While swung the deep bell in the distant tower,
   Or the faint dying day-hymn stole aloft,
And not a breath crept through the rosy air,
And yet the forest leaves seem'd stirr'd with prayer.

103

Ave Maria! 'tis the hour of prayer!
   Ave Maria! 'tis the hour of love!
Ave Maria! may our spirits dare
   Look up to thine and to thy Son's above!
Ave Maria! oh that face so fair!
   Those downcast eyes beneath the Almighty dove—
What though 'tis but a pictured image?—strike,
That painting is no idol,—'tis too like.

104

Some kinder casuists are pleased to say,
   In nameless print—that I have no devotion;
But set those persons down with me to pray,
   And you shall see who has the properest notion
Of getting into heaven the shortest way;
   My altars are the mountains and the ocean,
Earth, air, stars,—all that springs from the great Whole,
Who hath produced, and will receive the soul.

105

Sweet hour of twilight!—in the solitude
  Of the pine forest, and the silent shore
Which bounds Ravenna's immemorial wood,
  Rooted where once the Adrian wave flow'd o'er,
To where the last Caesarean fortress stood,
  Evergreen forest! which Boccaccio's lore
And Dryden's lay made haunted ground to me,
How have I loved the twilight hour and thee!

106

The shrill cicalas, people of the pine,
  Making their summer lives one ceaseless song,
Were the sole echoes, save my steed's and mine,
  And vesper bell's that rose the boughs along;
The spectre huntsman of Onesti's line,
  His hell-dogs, and their chase, and the fair throng
Which learn'd from this example not to fly
From a true lover,—shadow'd my mind's eye.

107

Oh, Hesperus! thou bringest all good things—
  Home to the weary, to the hungry cheer,
To the young bird the parent's brooding wings,
  The welcome stall to the o'erlabour'd steer;
Whate'er of peace about our hearthstone clings,
  Whate'er our household gods protect of dear,
Are gather'd round us by thy look of rest;
Thou bring'st the child, too, to the mother's breast.

108

Soft hour! which wakes the wish and melts the heart
  Of those who sail the seas, on the first day
When they from their sweet friends are torn apart;
  Or fills with love the pilgrim on his way

As the far bell of vesper makes him start,
  Seeming to weep the dying day's decay;
Is this a fancy which our reason scorns?
Ah! Surely nothing dies but something mourns!

109

When Nero perish'd by the justest doom
  Which ever the destroyer yet destroy'd,
Amidst the roar of liberated Rome,
  Of nations freed, and the world overjoy'd,
Some hands unseen strew'd flowers upon his tomb:
  Perhaps the weakness of a heart not void
Of feeling for some kindness done, when power
Had left the wretch an uncorrupted hour.

110

But I'm digressing; what on earth has Nero,
  Or any such like sovereign buffoons,
To do with the transactions of my hero,
  More than such madmen's fellow man—the moon's?
Sure my invention must be down at zero,
  And I grown one of many "wooden spoons"
Of verse (the name with which we Cantabs please
To dub the last of honours in degrees).

111

I feel this tediousness will never do—
  'Tis being *too* epic, and I must cut down
(In copying) this long canto into two;
  They'll never find it out, unless I own
The fact, excepting some experienced few;
  And then as an improvement 'twill be shown:
I'll prove that such the opinion of the critic is
From Aristotle *passim*.—See Ποιητικῆς

1819   1821

CANTO THE FOURTH

1

Nothing so difficult as a beginning
  In poesy, unless perhaps the end;
For oftentimes when Pegasus seems winning
  The race, he sprains a wing, and down we tend,
Like Lucifer when hurl'd from heaven for sinning;
  Our sin the same, and hard as his to mend,
Being pride, which leads the mind to soar too far,
Till our own weakness shows us what we are.

2

But time, which brings all beings to their level,
  And sharp Adversity, will teach at last
Man,—and, as we would hope,—perhaps the devil,
  That neither of their intellects are vast:
While youth's hot wishes in our red veins revel,
  We know not this—the blood flows on too fast:
But as the torrent widens towards the ocean,
We ponder deeply on each past emotion.

3

As boy, I thought myself a clever fellow,
  And wish'd that others held the same opinion;
They took it up when my days grew more mellow,
  And other minds acknowledged my dominion:
Now my sere fancy "falls into the yellow
  Leaf," and Imagination droops her pinion,
And the sad truth which hovers o'er my desk
Turns what was once romantic to burlesque.

4

And if I laugh at any mortal thing,
  'Tis that I may not weep; and if I weep,

'Tis that our nature cannot always bring
  Itself to apathy, for we must steep
Our hearts first in the depths of Lethe's spring,
  Ere what we least wish to behold will sleep:
Thetis baptized her mortal son in Styx;
A mortal mother would on Lethe fix.

5

Some have accused me of a strange design
  Against the creed and morals of the land,
And trace it in this poem every line;
  I don't pretend that I quite understand
My own meaning when I would be *very* fine;
  But the fact is that I have nothing plann'd,
Unless it were to be a moment merry,
A novel word in my vocabulary.

6

To the kind reader of our sober clime
  This way of writing will appear exotic;
Pulci was sire of the half-serious rhyme,
  Who sang when chivalry was more Quixotic,
And revell'd in the fancies of the time,
  True knights, chaste dames, huge giant kings despotic:
But all these, save the last, being obsolete,
I chose a modern subject as more meet.

7

How I have treated it, I do not know;
  Perhaps no better than they have treated me,
Who have imputed such designs as show
  Not what they saw, but what they wish'd to see;
But if it gives them pleasure, be it so,
  This is a liberal age, and thoughts are free:
Meantime Apollo plucks me by the ear,
And tells me to resume my story here.

8

Young Juan and his lady-love were left
  To their own hearts' most sweet society;
Even Time the pitiless in sorrow cleft
  With his rude scythe such gentle bosoms; he
Sigh'd to behold them of their hours bereft,
  Though foe to love; and yet they could not be
Meant to grow old, but die in happy spring,
Before one charm or hope had taken wing.

9

Their faces were not made for wrinkles, their
  Pure blood to stagnate, their great hearts to fail;
The blank grey was not made to blast their hair,
  But like the climes that know nor snow nor hail,
They were all summer; lightning might assail
  And shiver them to ashes, but to trail
A long and snake-like life of dull decay
Was not for them—they had too little clay.

10

They were alone once more; for them to be
  Thus was another Eden; they were never
Weary, unless when separate: the tree
  Cut from its forest root of years—the river
Damm'd from its fountain—the child from the knee
  And breast maternal wean'd at once for ever,—
Would wither less than these two torn apart;
Alas! there is no instinct like the heart—

11

The heart—which may be broken: happy they!
  Thrice fortunate! who of that fragile mould,
The precious porcelain of human clay,
  Break with the first fall: they can ne'er behold
The long year link'd with heavy day on day,

And all which must be borne, and never told;
While life's strange principle will often lie
Deepest in those who long the most to die.

12

"Whom the gods love die young" was said of yore,
    And many deaths do they escape by this:
The death of friends, and that which slays even more—
    The death of friendship, love, youth, all that is,
Except mere breath; and since the silent shore
    Awaits at last even those who longest miss
The old archer's shafts, perhaps the early grave
Which men weep over may be meant to save.

13

Haidée and Juan thought not of the dead.
    The heavens, and earth, and air, seem'd made for them:
They found no fault with Time, save that he fled;
    They saw not in themselves aught to condemn;
Each was the other's mirror, and but read
    Joy sparkling in their dark eyes like a gem,
And knew such brightness was but the reflection
Of their exchanging glances of affection.

14

The gentle pressure, and the thrilling touch,
    The least glance better understood than words,
Which still said all, and ne'er could say too much;
    A language, too, but like to that of birds,
Known but to them, at least appearing such
    As but to lovers a true sense affords;
Sweet playful phrases, which would seem absurd
To those who have ceased to hear such, or ne'er heard.

15

All these were theirs, for they were children still,
    And children still they should have ever been;

They were not made in the real world to fill
   A busy character in the dull scene,
But like two beings born from out a rill,
   A nymph and her beloved, all unseen
To pass their lives in fountains and on flowers,
And never know the weight of human hours.

16

Moons changing had roll'd on, and changeless found
   Those their bright rise had lighted to such joys
As rarely they beheld throughout their round;
   And these were not of the vain kind which cloys,
For theirs were buoyant spirits, never bound
   By the mere senses; and that which destroys
Most love, possession, unto them appear'd
A thing which each endearment more endear'd.

17

Oh beautiful! and rare as beautiful!
   But theirs was love in which the mind delights
To lose itself, when the old world grows dull,
   And we are sick of its hack sounds and sights,
Intrigues, adventures of the common school,
   Its petty passions, marriages, and flights,
Where Hymen's torch but brands one strumpet more,
Whose husband only knows her not a whore.

18

Hard words; harsh truth; a truth which many know.
   Enough.—The faithful and the fairy pair,
Who never found a single hour too slow,
   What was it made them thus exempt from care?
Young innate feelings all have felt below,
   Which perish in the rest, but in them were
Inherent; what we mortals call romantic,
And always envy, though we deem it frantic.

19

This is in others a factitious state,
  An opium dream of too much youth and reading,
But was in them their nature or their fate:
  No novels e'er had set their young hearts bleeding,
For Haidée's knowledge was by no means great,
  And Juan was a boy of saintly breeding;
So that there was no reason for their loves
More than for those of nightingales or doves.

20

They gazed upon the sunset; 'tis an hour
  Dear unto all, but dearest to *their* eyes,
For it had made them what they were: the power
  Of love had first o'erwhelm'd them from such skies,
When happiness had been their only dower,
  And twilight saw them link'd in passion's ties;
Charm'd with each other, all things charm'd that brought
The past still welcome as the present thought.

21

I know not why, but in that hour to-night,
  Even as they gazed, a sudden tremor came,
And swept, as 'twere, across their hearts' delight,
  Like the wind o'er a harp-string, or a flame,
When one is shook in sound, and one in sight:
  And thus some boding flash'd through either frame,
And call'd from Juan's breast a faint low sigh,
While one new tear arose in Haidée's eye.

22

That large black prophet eye seem'd to dilate
  And follow far the disappearing sun,
As if their last day of a happy date
  With his broad, bright, and dropping orb were gone.
Juan gazed on her as to ask his fate—

He felt a grief, but knowing cause for none,
His glance inquired of hers for some excuse
For feelings causeless, or at least abstruse.

23

She turn'd to him, and smiled, but in that sort
    Which makes not others smile; then turn'd aside:
Whatever feeling shook her, it seem'd short,
    And master'd by her wisdom or her pride;
When Juan spoke, too—it might be in sport—
    Of this their mutual feeling, she replied—
"If it should be so,—but—it cannot be—
Or I at least shall not survive to see."

24

Juan would question further, but she press'd
    His lips to hers, and silenced him with this,
And then dismiss'd the omen from her breast,
    Defying augury with that fond kiss;
And no doubt of all methods 'tis the best:
    Some people prefer wine—'tis not amiss;
I have tried both; so those who would a part take
May choose between the headache and the heartache.

25

One of the two according to your choice,
    Woman or wine, you'll have to undergo:
Both maladies are taxes on our joys:
    But which to choose, I really hardly know;
And if I had to give a casting voice,
    For both sides I could many reasons show,
And then decide, without great wrong to either,
It were much better to have both than neither.

26

Juan and Haidée gazed upon each other
    With swimming looks of speechless tenderness,

Which mix'd all feelings, friend, child, lover, brother;
  All that the best can mingle and express
When two pure hearts are pour'd in one another,
  And love too much, and yet cannot love less;
But almost sanctify the sweet excess
By the immortal wish and power to bless.

27

Mix'd in each other's arms, and heart in heart,
  Why did they not then die?—they had lived too long
Should an hour come to bid them breathe apart;
  Years could but bring them cruel things or wrong;
The world was not for them, nor the world's art
  For beings passionate as Sappho's song;
Love was born *with* them, *in* them, so intense,
It was their very spirit—not a sense.

28

They should have lived together deep in woods,
  Unseen as sings the nightingale; they were
Unfit to mix in these thick solitudes
  Call'd social, haunts of Hate, and Vice, and Care;
How lonely every freeborn creature broods!
  The sweetest song-birds nestle in a pair;
The eagle soars alone; the gull and crow
Flock o'er their carrion, just like men below.

29

Now pillow'd cheek to cheek, in loving sleep,
  Haidée and Juan their siesta took,
A gentle slumber, but it was not deep,
  For ever and anon a something shook
Juan, and shuddering o'er his frame would creep;
  And Haidée's sweet lips murmur'd like a brook
A wordless music, and her face so fair
Stirr'd with her dream, as rose-leaves with the air;

30

Or as the stirring of a deep clear stream
   Within an Alpine hollow, when the wind
Walks o'er it, was she shaken by the dream,
   The mystical usurper of the mind—
O'erpowering us to be whate'er may seem
   Good to the soul which we no more can bind:
Strange state of being! (for 'tis still to be),
Senseless to feel, and with seal'd eyes to see.

31

She dream'd of being alone on the sea-shore,
   Chain'd to a rock; she knew not how, but stir
She could not from the spot, and the loud roar
   Grew, and each wave rose roughly threatening her;
And o'er her upper lip they seem'd to pour,
   Until she sobb'd for breath, and soon they were
Foaming o'er her lone head, so fierce and high—
Each broke to drown her, yet she could not die.

32

Anon—she was released, and then she stray'd
   O'er the sharp shingles with her bleeding feet,
And stumbled almost every step she made;
   And something roll'd before her in a sheet,
Which she must still pursue howe'er afraid:
   'Twas white and indistinct, nor stopp'd to meet
Her glance nor grasp, for still she gazed and grasp'd,
And ran, but it escaped her as she clasp'd.

33

The dream changed:—in a cave she stood, its walls
   Were hung with marble icicles; the work
Of ages on its water-fretted halls,
   Where waves might wash, and seals might breed and lurk;
Her hair was dripping, and the very balls

Of her black eyes seem'd turn'd to tears, and mirk
The sharp rocks look'd below each drop they caught,
Which froze to marble as it fell,—she thought.

34

And wet, and cold, and lifeless at her feet,
    Pale as the foam that froth'd on his dead brow,
Which she essay'd in vain to clear, (how sweet
    Were once her cares, how idle seem'd they now!)
Lay Juan, nor could aught renew the beat
    Of his quench'd heart; and the sea dirges low
Rang in her sad ears like a mermaid's song,
And that brief dream appear'd a life too long.

35

And gazing on the dead, she thought his face
    Faded, or alter'd into something new—
Like to her father's features, till each trace
    More like and like to Lambro's aspect grew—
With all his keen worn look and Grecian grace;
    And starting, she awoke, and what to view?
Oh! Powers of Heaven! what dark eye meets she there?
'Tis—'tis her father's—fix'd upon the pair!

36

Then shrieking, she arose, and shrieking fell,
    With joy and sorrow, hope and fear, to see
Him whom she deem'd a habitant where dwell
    The ocean-buried, risen from death, to be
Perchance the death of one she loved too well:
    Dear as her father had been to Haidée,
It was a moment of that awful kind—
I have seen such—but must not call to mind.

37

Up Juan sprang to Haidée's bitter shriek,
    And caught her falling, and from off the wall

Snatch'd down his sabre, in hot haste to wreak
    Vengeance on him who was the cause of all:
Then Lambro, who till now forbore to speak,
    Smiled scornfully, and said, "Within my call,
A thousand scimitars await the word;
Put up, young man, put up your silly sword."

38

And Haidée clung around him; "Juan, 'tis—
    'Tis Lambro—'tis my father! Kneel with me—
He will forgive us—yes—it must be—yes.
    Oh! dearest father, in this agony
Of pleasure and of pain—even while I kiss
    Thy garment's hem with transport, can it be
That doubt should mingle with my filial joy?
Deal with me as thou wilt, but spare this boy."

39

High and inscrutable the old man stood,
    Calm in his voice, and calm within his eye—
Not always signs with him of calmest mood:
    He look'd upon her, but gave no reply;
Then turn'd to Juan, in whose cheek the blood
    Oft came and went, as there resolved to die;
In arms, at least, he stood, in act to spring
On the first foe whom Lambro's call might bring.

40

"Young man, your sword;" so Lambro once more said:
    Juan replied, "Not while this arm is free."
The old man's cheek grew pale, but not with dread,
    And drawing from his belt a pistol, he
Replied, "Your blood be then on your own head."
    Then look'd close at the flint, as if to see
'Twas fresh—for he had lately used the lock—
And next proceeded quietly to cock.

41

It has a strange quick jar upon the ear,
  That cocking of a pistol, when you know
A moment more will bring the sight to bear
  Upon your person, twelve yards off, or so;
A gentlemanly distance, not too near,
  If you have got a former friend for foe;
But after being fired at once or twice,
The ear becomes more Irish, and less nice.

42

Lambro presented, and one instant more
  Had stopp'd this Canto, and Don Juan's breath,
When Haidée threw herself her boy before;
  Stern as her sire: "On me," she cried, "let death
Descend—the fault is mine; this fatal shore
  He found—but sought not. I have pledged my faith;
I love him—I will die with him: I knew
Your nature's firmness—know your daughter's too."

43

A minute past, and she had been all tears,
  And tenderness, and infancy; but now
She stood as one who champion'd human fears—
  Pale, statue-like, and stern, she woo'd the blow;
And tall beyond her sex, and their compeers,
  She drew up to her height, as if to show
A fairer mark; and with a fix'd eye scann'd
Her father's face—but never stopp'd his hand.

44

He gazed on her, and she on him; 'twas strange
  How like they look'd! the expression was the same;
Serenely savage, with a little change
  In the large dark eye's mutual-darted flame;
For she, too, was as one who could avenge,

If cause should be—a lioness, though tame;
Her father's blood before her father's face
Boil'd up, and proved her truly of his race.

45

I said they were alike, their features and
    Their stature, differing but in sex and years:
Even to the delicacy of their hand
    There was resemblance, such as true blood wears;
And now to see them, thus divided, stand
    In fix'd ferocity, when joyous tears,
And sweet sensations, should have welcomed both,
Show what the passions are in their full growth.

46

The father paused a moment, then withdrew
    His weapon, and replaced it; but stood still,
And looking on her, as to look her through,
    "Not *I*," he said, "have sought this stranger's ill;
Not *I* have made this desolation: few
    Would bear such outrage, and forbear to kill;
But I must do my duty—how thou hast
Done thine, the present vouches for the past.

47

"Let him disarm; or, by my father's head,
    His own shall roll before you like a ball!"
He raised his whistle as the word he said,
    And blew; another answer'd to the call,
And rushing in disorderly, though led,
    And arm'd from boot to turban, one and all,
Some twenty of his train came, rank on rank;
He gave the word, "Arrest or slay the Frank."

48

Then, with a sudden movement, he withdrew
    His daughter; while compress'd within his clasp,

'Twixt her and Juan interposed the crew;
　　In vain she struggled in her father's grasp—
His arms were like a serpent's coil: then flew
　　Upon their prey, as darts an angry asp,
The file of pirates: save the foremost, who
Had fallen, with his right shoulder half cut through.

49

The second had his cheek laid open; but
　　The third, a wary, cool old sworder, took
The blows upon his cutlass, and then put
　　His own well in; so well, ere you could look,
His man was floor'd, and helpless at his foot,
　　With the blood running like a little brook
From two smart sabre gashes, deep and red—
One on the arm, the other on the head.

50

And then they bound him where he fell, and bore
　　Juan from the apartment: with a sign
Old Lambro bade them take him to the shore,
　　Where lay some ships which were to sail at nine.
They laid him in a boat, and plied the oar
　　Until they reach'd some galliots, placed in line;
On board of one of these, and under hatches,
They stow'd him, with strict orders to the watches.

51

The world is full of strange vicissitudes,
　　And here was one exceedingly unpleasant:
A gentleman so rich in the world's goods,
　　Handsome and young, enjoying all the present,
Just at the very time when he least broods
　　On such a thing, is suddenly to sea sent,
Wounded and chain'd, so that he cannot move,
And all because a lady fell in love.

52

Here I must leave him, for I grow pathetic,
  Moved by the Chinese nymph of tears, green tea!
Than whom Cassandra was not more prophetic;
  For if my pure libations exceed three,
I feel my heart become so sympathetic,
  That I must have recourse to black Bohea:
'Tis pity wine should be so deleterious,
For tea and coffee leave us much more serious,

53

Unless when qualified with thee, Cogniac!
    Sweet Naïad of the Phlegethontic rill!
Ah! why the liver wilt thou thus attack,
  And make, like other nymphs, thy lovers ill?
I would take refuge in weak punch, but *rack*
  (In each sense of the word), whene'er I fill
My mild and midnight beakers to the brim,
Wakes me next morning with its synonym.

54

I leave Don Juan for the present, safe—
  Not sound, poor fellow, but severely wounded;
Yet could his corporal pangs amount to half
  Of those with which his Haidée's bosom bounded!
She was not one to weep, and rave, and chafe,
  And then give way, subdued because surrounded;
Her mother was a Moorish maid from Fez,
Where all is Eden, or a wilderness.

55

There the large olive rains its amber store
  In marble fonts; there grain, and flour, and fruit,
Gush from the earth until the land runs o'er;
  But there, too, many a poison-tree has root,
And midnight listens to the lion's roar,

And long, long deserts scorch the camel's foot,
Or heaving whelm the helpless caravan;
And as the soil is, so the heart of man.

56

Afric is all the sun's, and as her earth
   Her human clay is kindled; full of power
For good or evil, burning from its birth,
   The Moorish blood partakes the planet's hour,
And like the soil beneath it will bring forth:
   Beauty and love were Haidée's mother's dower;
But her large dark eye show'd deep Passion's force.
Though sleeping like a lion near a source.

57

Her daughter, temper'd with a milder ray,
   Like summer clouds all silvery, smooth, and fair,
Till slowly charged with thunder they display
   Terror to earth, and tempest to the air,
Had held till now her soft and milky way;
   But overwrought with passion and despair,
The fire burst forth from her Numidian veins,
Even as the Simoom sweeps the blasted plains.

58

The last sight which she saw was Juan's gore,
   And he himself o'ermaster'd and cut down;
His blood was running on the very floor
   Where late he trod, her beautiful, her own;
Thus much she view'd an instant and no more,—
   Her struggles ceased with one convulsive groan;
On her sire's arm, which until now scarce held
Her writhing, fell she like a cedar fell'd.

59

A vein had burst, and her sweet lips' pure dyes
   Were dabbled with the deep blood which ran o'er;

And her head droop'd, as when the lily lies
  O'ercharged with rain: her summon'd handmaids bore
Their lady to her couch with gushing eyes;
  Of herbs and cordials they produced their store,
But she defied all means they could employ,
Like one life could not hold, nor death destroy.

60

Days lay she in that state unchanged, though chill—
  With nothing livid, still her lips were red;
She had no pulse, but death seem'd absent still;
  No hideous sign proclaim'd her surely dead;
Corruption came not in each mind to kill
  All hope; to look upon her sweet face bred
New thoughts of life, for it seem'd full of soul—
She had so much, earth could not claim the whole.

61

The ruling passion, such as marble shows
  When exquisitely chisell'd, still lay there,
But fix'd as marble's unchanged aspect throws
  O'er the fair Venus, but for ever fair;
O'er the Laocoön's all eternal throes,
  And ever-dying Gladiator's air,
Their energy like life forms all their fame,
Yet looks not life, for they are still the same.

62

She woke at length, but not as sleepers wake,
  Rather the dead, for life seem'd something new,
A strange sensation which she must partake
  Perforce, since whatsoever meet her view
Struck not on memory, though a heavy ache
  Lay at her heart, whose earliest beat still true
Brought back the sense of pain without the cause,
For, for a while, the furies made a pause.

63

She look'd on many a face with vacant eye,
　　On many a token without knowing what;
She saw them watch her without asking why,
　　And reck'd not who around her pillow sat;
Not speechless, though she spoke not; not a sigh
　　Relieved her thoughts; dull silence and quick chat
Were tried in vain by those who served; she gave
No sign, save breath, of having left the grave.

64

Her handmaids tended, but she heeded not;
　　Her father watch'd, she turn'd her eyes away;
She recognised no being, and no spot,
　　However dear or cherish'd in their day;
They changed from room to room, but all forgot,
　　Gentle, but without memory she lay;
At length those eyes, which they would fain be weaning
Back to old thoughts, wax'd full of fearful meaning.

65

And then a slave bethought her of a harp;
　　The harper came, and tuned his instrument;
At the first notes, irregular and sharp,
　　On him her flashing eyes a moment bent,
Then to the wall she turn'd as if to warp
　　Her thoughts from sorrow through her heart re-sent;
And he began a long low island song
Of ancient days, ere tyranny grew strong.

66

Anon her thin wan fingers beat the wall
　　In time to his old tune; he changed the theme,
And sung of love; the fierce name struck through all
　　Her recollection; on her flash'd the dream
Of what she was, and is, if ye could call

To be so being; in a gushing stream
The tears rush'd forth from her o'erclouded brain,
Like mountain mists at length dissolved in rain.

67

Short solace, vain relief!—thought came too quick,
   And whirl'd her brain to madness; she arose
As one who ne'er had dwelt among the sick,
   And flew at all she met, as on her foes;
But no one ever heard her speak or shriek,
   Although her paroxysm drew towards its close;—
Hers was a phrensy which disdain'd to rave,
Even when they smote her, in the hope to save.

68

Yet she betray'd at times a gleam of sense;
   Nothing could make her meet her father's face,
Though on all other things with looks intense
   She gazed, but none she ever could retrace;
Food she refused, and raiment; no pretence
   Avail'd for either; neither change of place,
Nor time, nor skill, nor remedy, could give her
Senses to sleep—the power seem'd gone for ever.

69

Twelve days and nights she wither'd thus; at last
   Without a groan, or sigh, or glance, to show
A parting pang, the spirit from her passed:
   And they who watch'd her nearest could not know
The very instant, till the change that cast
   Her sweet face into shadow, dull and slow,
Glazed o'er her eyes—the beautiful, the black—
Oh! to possess such lustre—and then lack!

70

She died, but not alone; she held within
   A second principle of life, which might

Have dawn'd a fair and sinless child of sin;
  But closed its little being without light,
And went down to the grave unborn, wherein
  Blossom and bough lie wither'd with one blight;
In vain the dews of Heaven descend above
The bleeding flower and blasted fruit of love.

71

Thus lived—thus died she; never more on her
  Shall sorrow light, or shame. She was not made
Through years or moons the inner weight to bear,
  Which colder hearts endure till they are laid
By age in earth: her days and pleasures were
  Brief, but delightful—such as had not stayed
Long with her destiny; but she sleeps well
By the sea-shore, whereon she loved to dwell.

72

That isle is now all desolate and bare,
  Its dwellings down, its tenants pass'd away;
None but her own and father's grave is there,
  And nothing outward tells of human clay;
Ye could not know where lies a thing so fair,
  No stone is there to show, no tongue to say,
What was; no dirge, except the hollow sea's,
Mourns o'er the beauty of the Cyclades.

73

But many a Greek maid in a loving song
  Sighs o'er her name; and many an islander
With her sire's story makes the night less long;
  Valour was his, and beauty dwelt with her;
If she loved rashly, her life paid for wrong—
  A heavy price must all pay who thus err,
In some shape; let none think to fly the danger,
For soon or late Love is his own avenger.

. . . . .

1819   1821

[In Canto V, Juan is sold as a slave to the Turkish Sultana, Gulbeyaz. His experiences in the Harem are related in Cantos V and VI. In Canto VII he escapes from the Harem and makes his way into the lines of the Russian army which is about to attack the Turkish city of Ismail, situated near the mouth of the Danube in what is today Rumania. Juan joins the Russian army and takes part in the attack.]

CANTO THE SEVENTH

. . . . .

80

Oh, thou eternal Homer! I have now
   To paint a siege, wherein more men were slain,
With deadlier engines and a speedier blow,
   Than in thy Greek gazette of that campaign;
And yet, like all men else, I must allow,
   To vie with thee would be about as vain
As for a brook to cope with ocean's flood;
But still we moderns equal you in blood;

81

If not in poetry, at least in fact;
   And fact is truth, the grand desideratum!
Of which, howe'er the Muse describes each act,
   There should be ne'ertheless a slight substratum.
But now the town is going to be attack'd;
   Great deeds are doing—how shall I relate 'em?
Souls of immortal generals! Phoebus watches
To colour up his rays from your despatches.

82

Oh, ye great bulletins of Bonaparte!
   Oh, ye less grand long lists of kill'd and wounded!
Shade of Leonidas, who fought so hearty,
   When my poor Greece was once, as now, surrounded!

Oh, Caesar's Commentaries! now impart, ye
  Shadows of glory! (lest I be confounded),
A portion of your fading twilight hues,
So beautiful, so fleeting, to the Muse.

83

When I call "fading" martial immortality,
  I mean, that every age and every year,
And almost every day, in sad reality,
  Some sucking hero is compell'd to rear,
Who, when we come to sum up the totality
  Of deeds to human happiness most dear,
Turns out to be a butcher in great business,
Afflicting young folks with a sort of dizziness.

84

Medals, rank, ribands, lace, embroidery, scarlet,
  Are things immortal to immortal man,
As purple to the Babylonian harlot:
  An uniform to boys is like a fan
To women; there is scarce a crimson varlet
  But deems himself the first in Glory's van.
But Glory's glory; and if you would find
What *that* is—ask the pig who sees the wind!

1822   1823

CANTO THE EIGHTH

. . . . .

6

The night was dark, and the thick mist allow'd
  Nought to be seen save the artillery's flame,
Which arch'd the horizon like a fiery cloud,
  And in the Danube's waters shone the same—

A mirror'd hell! the volleying roar, and loud
  Long booming of each peal on peal, o'ercame
The ear far more than thunder; for Heaven's flashes
Spare, or smite rarely—man's make millions ashes!

7

The column order'd on the assault scarce pass'd
  Beyond the Russian batteries a few toises,
When up the bristling Moslem rose at last,
  Answering the Christian thunders with like voices:
Then one vast fire, air, earth, and stream embraced,
  Which rock'd as 'twere beneath the mighty noises;
While the whole rampart blazed like Etna, when
The restless Titan hiccups in his den;

8

And one enormous shout of "Allah!" rose
  In the same moment, loud as even the roar
Of war's most mortal engines, to their foes
  Hurling defiance: city, stream, and shore
Resounded "Allah!" and the clouds which close
  With thick'ning canopy the conflict o'er
Vibrate to the Eternal name. Hark! through
All sounds it pierceth, "Allah! Allah! Hu!"

9

The columns were in movement one and all,
  But of the portion which attack'd by water,
Thicker than leaves the lives began to fall,
  Though led by Arseniew, that great son of slaughter,
As brave as ever faced both bomb and ball.
  "Carnage, (so Wordsworth tells you) is God's daughter:"
If *he* speak truth, she is Christ's sister, and
Just now behaved as in the Holy Land.

10

The Prince de Ligne was wounded in the knee;
  Count Chapeau-Bras, too, had a ball between

His cap and head, which proves the head to be
   Aristocratic as was ever seen,
Because it then received no injury
   More than the cap; in fact, the ball could mean
No harm unto a right legitimate head;
"Ashes to ashes"—why not lead to lead?

11

Also the General Markow, Brigadier,
   Insisting on removal of the *prince*
Amidst some groaning thousands dying near,—
   All common fellows, who might writhe and wince,
And shriek for water into a deaf ear,—
   The General Markow, who could thus evince
His sympathy for rank, by the same token,
To teach him greater, had his own leg broken.

12

Three hundred cannon threw up their emetic,
   And thirty thousand muskets flung their pills
Like hail, to make a bloody diuretic.
   Mortality! thou hast thy monthly bills:
Thy plagues, thy famines, thy physicians, yet tick,
   Like the death-watch, within our ears the ills
Past, present, and to come;—but all may yield
To the true portrait of one battle-field;

13

There the still varying pangs, which multiply
   Until their very number makes men hard
By the infinities of agony,
   Which meet the gaze, whate'er it may regard—
The groan, the roll in dust, the all-*white* eye
   Turn'd back within its socket,—these reward
Your rank and file by thousands, while the rest
May win perhaps a riband at the breast!

14

Yet I love glory;—glory's a great thing:—
   Think what it is to be in your old age
Maintain'd at the expense of your good king:
   A moderate pension shakes full many a sage,
And heroes are but made for bards to sing,
   Which is still better; thus in verse to wage
Your wars eternally, besides enjoying
Half-pay for life, make mankind worth destroying.

15

The troops, already disembark'd, push'd on
   To take a battery on the right: the others,
Who landed lower down, their landing done,
   Had set to work as briskly as their brothers:
Being grenadiers, they mounted one by one,
   Cheerful as children climb the breasts of mothers,
O'er the intrenchment and the palisade,
Quite orderly, as if upon parade.

16

And this was admirable; for so hot
   The fire was, that were red Vesuvius loaded,
Besides its lava, with all sorts of shot
   And shells or hells, it could not more have goaded.
Of officers a third fell on the spot,
   A thing which victory by no means boded
To gentlemen engaged in the assault:
Hounds, when the huntsman tumbles, are at fault.

17

But here I leave the general concern,
   To track our hero on his path of fame:
He must his laurels separately earn;
   For fifty thousand heroes, name by name,
Though all deserving equally to turn
   A couplet, or an elegy to claim,

Would form a lengthy lexicon of glory,
And what is worse still, a much longer story:

18

And therefore we must give the greater number
  To the Gazette—which doubtless fairly dealt
By the deceased, who lie in famous slumber
  In ditches, fields, or whereso'er they felt
Their clay for the last time their souls encumber;—
  Thrice happy he whose name has been well spelt
In the despatch: I knew a man whose loss
Was printed *Grove*, although his name was Grose.

· · · · ·

82

The city's taken—only part by part—
  And death is drunk with gore: there's not a street
Where fights not to the last some desperate heart
  For those for whom it soon shall cease to beat.
Here War forgot his own destructive art
  In more destroying Nature; and the heat
Of carnage, like the Nile's sun-sodden slime,
Engender'd monstrous shapes of every crime.

83

A Russian officer, in martial tread
  Over a heap of bodies, felt his heel
Seized fast, as if 'twere by the serpent's head
  Whose fangs Eve taught her human seed to feel:
In vain he kick'd, and swore, and writhed, and bled,
  And howl'd for help as wolves do for a meal—
The teeth still kept their gratifying hold,
As do the subtle snakes described of old.

84

A dying Moslem, who had felt the foot
  Of a foe o'er him, snatch'd at it, and bit

The very tendon which is most acute—
  (That which some ancient Muse or modern wit
Named after thee, Achilles) and quite through't
  He made the teeth meet, nor relinquish'd it
Even with his life—for (but they lie) 'tis said
To the live leg still clung the sever'd head.

85

However this may be, 'tis pretty sure
  The Russian officer for life was lamed,
For the Turk's teeth stuck faster than a skewer,
  And left him 'midst the invalid and maim'd:
The regimental surgeon could not cure
  His patient, and perhaps was to be blamed
More than the head of the inveterate foe,
Which was cut off, and scarce even then let go.

86

But then the fact's a fact—and 'tis the part
  Of a true poet to escape from fiction
Whene'er he can; for there is little art
  In leaving verse more free from the restriction
Of truth than prose, unless to suit the mart
  For what is sometimes call'd poetic diction
And that outrageous appetite for lies
Which Satan angles with for souls, like flies.

87

The city's taken, but not render'd!—No!
  There's not a Moslem that hath yielded sword:
The blood may gush out, as the Danube's flow
  Rolls by the city wall; but deed nor word
Acknowledge aught of dread of death or foe:
  In vain the yell of victory is roar'd
By the advancing Muscovite—the groan
Of the last foe is echoed by his own.

88

The bayonet pierces and the sabre cleaves,
  And human lives are lavish'd everywhere,
As the year closing whirls the scarlet leaves
  When the stripp'd forest bows to the bleak air,
And groans; and thus the peopled city grieves,
  Shorn of its best and loveliest, and left bare;
But still it falls in vast and awful splinters,
As oaks blown down with all their thousand winters.

89

It is an awful topic—but 'tis not
  My cue for any time to be terrific:
For checker'd as is seen our human lot
  With good, and bad, and worse, alike prolific
Of melancholy merriment, to quote
  Too much of one sort would be soporific;—
Without, or with, offence to friends or foes,
I sketch your world exactly as it goes.

90

And one good action in the midst of crimes
  Is "quite refreshing," in the affected phrase
Of these ambrosial, Pharisaic times,
  With all their pretty milk-and-water ways,
And may serve therefore to bedew these rhymes,
  A little scorch'd at present with the blaze
Of conquest and its consequences, which
Make epic poesy so rare and rich.

91

Upon a taken bastion, where there lay
  Thousands of slaughter'd men, a yet warm group
Of murder'd women, who had found their way
  To this vain refuge, made the good heart droop
And shudder;—while, as beautiful as May,

A female child of ten years tried to stoop
And hide her little palpitating breast
Amidst the bodies lull'd in bloody rest.

92

Two villainous Cossacques pursued the child
  With flashing eyes and weapons: match'd with *them*,
The rudest brute that roams Siberia's wild
  Has feelings pure and polish'd as a gem,—
The bear is civilised, the wolf is mild:
  And whom for this at last must we condemn?
Their natures? or their sovereigns, who employ
All arts to teach their subjects to destroy?

93

Their sabres glitter'd o'er her little head,
  Whence her fair hair rose twining with affright,
Her hidden face was plunged amidst the dead:
  When Juan caught a glimpse of this sad sight,
I shall not say exactly what he *said*,
  Because it might not solace "ears polite";
But what he *did*, was to lay on their backs,
The readiest way of reasoning with Cossacques.

94

One's hip he slash'd, and split the other's shoulder,
  And drove them with their brutal yells to seek
If there might be chirurgeons who could solder
  The wounds they richly merited, and shriek
Their baffled rage and pain; while waxing colder
  As he turn'd o'er each pale and gory cheek,
Don Juan raised his little captive from
The heap a moment more had made her tomb.

95

And she was chill as they, and on her face
  A slender streak of blood announced how near

Her fate had been to that of all her race;
  For the same blow which laid her mother here
Had scarr'd her brow, and left its crimson trace,
  As the last link with all she had held dear;
But else unhurt, she open'd her large eyes,
And gazed on Juan with a wild surprise.

          . . . . .

120

But the stone bastion still kept up its fire,
  Where the chief pacha calmly held his post:
Some twenty times he made the Russ retire,
  And baffled the assaults of all their host;
At length he condescended to inquire,
  If yet the city's rest were won or lost;
And being told the latter, sent a bey
To answer Ribas' summons to give way.

121

In the mean time, cross-legg'd, with great sang-froid,
  Among the scorching ruins he sat smoking
Tobacco on a little carpet;—Troy
  Saw nothing like the scene around;—yet looking
With martial stoicism, nought seem'd to annoy
  His stern philosophy; but gently stroking
His beard, he puff'd his pipe's ambrosial gales,
As if he had three lives, as well as tails.

122

The town was taken—whether he might yield
  Himself or bastion, little matter'd now:
His stubborn valour was no future shield.
  Ismail's no more! The crescent's silver bow
Sunk, and the crimson cross glared o'er the field,
  But red with no *redeeming* gore: the glow
Of burning streets, like moonlight on the water,
Was imaged back in blood, the sea of slaughter.

123

All that the mind would shrink from of excesses;
  All that the body perpetrates of bad;
All that we read, hear, dream, of man's distresses;
  All that the devil would do if run stark mad;
All that defies the worst which pen expresses;
  All by which hell is peopled, or as sad
As hell—mere mortals who their power abuse—
Was here (as heretofore and since) let loose.

124

If here and there some transient trait of pity
  Was shown, and some more noble heart broke through
Its bloody bond, and saved, perhaps, some pretty
  Child, or an aged, helpless man or two—
What's this in one annihilated city,
  Where thousand loves, and ties, and duties grew?
Cockneys of London! Muscadins of Paris!
Just ponder what a pious pastime war is.

125

Think how the joys of reading a Gazette
  Are purchased by all agonies and crimes:
Or if these do not move you, don't forget
  Such doom may be your own in aftertimes.
Meantime the Taxes, Castlereagh, and Debt,
  Are hints as good as sermons, or as rhymes.
Read your own hearts and Ireland's present story,
Then feed her famine fat with Wellesley's glory.

126

But still there is unto a patriot nation,
  Which loves so well its country and its king,
A subject of sublimest exultation—
  Bear it, ye Muses, on your brightest wing!
Howe'er the mighty locust, Desolation,

Strip your green fields, and to your harvest cling,
Gaunt famine never shall approach the throne—
Though Ireland starve, great George weighs twenty stone.

127

But let me put an end unto my theme:
    There was an end of Ismail—hapless town!
Far flash'd her burning towers o'er Danube's stream,
    And redly ran his blushing waters down.
The horrid war-whoop and the shriller scream
    Rose still; but fainter were the thunders grown:
Of forty thousand who had mann'd the wall,
Some hundreds breathed—the rest were silent all!

. . . . .

1822   1823

[Juan emerges from the battle a hero and in Canto IX is sent as
emissary to the Court of Russia where he immediately becomes
the newest favorite of Catherine the Great. But he falls ill and
Catherine in the hope that a change of climate will restore his
health sends him on a secret mission to England.]

CANTO THE TENTH

. . . . .

66

I've no great cause to love that spot of earth,
    Which holds what *might have been* the noblest nation;
But though I owe it little but my birth,
    I feel a mix'd regret and veneration
For its decaying fame and former worth.
    Seven years (the usual term of transportation)
Of absence lay one's old resentments level,
When a man's country's going to the devil.

67

Alas! could she but fully, truly, know
  How her great name is now throughout abhorr'd;
How eager all the earth is for the blow
  Which shall lay bare her bosom to the sword;
How all the nations deem her their worst foe,
  That worse than *worst of foes*, the once adored
False friend, who held out freedom to mankind,
And now would chain them, to the very *mind*;—

68

Would she be proud, or boast herself the free,
  Who is but first of slaves? The nations are
In prison,—but the gaoler, what is he?
  No less a victim to the bolt and bar.
Is the poor privilege to turn the key
  Upon the captive, freedom? He's as far
From the enjoyment of the earth and air
Who watches o'er the chain, as they who wear.

69

Don Juan now saw Albion's earliest beauties,
  Thy cliffs, *dear* Dover! harbour, and hotel;
Thy custom-house, with all its delicate duties;
  Thy waiters running mucks at every bell;
Thy packets, all whose passengers are booties
  To those who upon land or water dwell;
And last, not least, to strangers uninstructed,
Thy long, long bills, whence nothing is deducted.

70

Juan, though careless, young, and *magnifique*,
  And rich in rubles, diamonds, cash, and credit,
Who did not limit much his bills per week,
  Yet stared at this a little, though he paid it—
(His Maggior Duomo, a smart, subtle Greek,

Before him summ'd the awful scroll and read it):
But, doubtless, as the air, though seldom sunny,
Is free, the respiration's worth the money.

71

On with the horses! Off to Canterbury!
　　Tramp, tramp o'er pebble, and splash, splash through puddle;
Hurrah! how swiftly speeds the post so merry!
　　Not like slow Germany, wherein they muddle
Along the road, as if they went to bury
　　Their fare; and also pause besides, to fuddle,
With "schnapps"—sad dogs! whom "Hundsfot," or "Verflucter,"
Affect no more than lightning a conductor.

72

Now there is nothing gives a man such spirits,
　　Leavening his blood as cayenne doth a curry,
As going at full speed—no matter where its
　　Direction be, so 'tis but in a hurry,
And merely for the sake of its own merits;
　　For the less cause there is for all this flurry,
The greater is the pleasure in arriving
At the great *end* of travel—which is driving.

73

They saw at Canterbury the cathedral;
　　Black Edward's helm, and Becket's bloody stone,
Were pointed out as usual by the bedral,
　　In the same quaint, uninterested tone:—
There's glory again for you, gentle reader! All
　　Ends in a rusty casque and dubious bone,
Half-solved into these sodas or magnesias,
Which form that bitter draught, the human species.

74

The effect on Juan was of course sublime:
　　He breathed a thousand Cressys, as he saw

That casque, which never stoop'd except to Time.
  Even the bold Churchman's tomb excited awe,
Who died in the then great attempt to climb
  O'er kings, who *now* at least *must talk* of law
Before they butcher. Little Leila gazed,
And ask'd why such a structure had been raised;

75

And being told it was "God's house," she said
  He was well lodged, but only wonder'd how
He suffer'd Infidels in his homestead,
  The cruel Nazarenes, who had laid low
His holy temples in the lands which bred
  The True Believers;—and her infant brow
Was bent with grief that Mahomet should resign
A mosque so noble, flung like pearls to swine.

76

On! on! through meadows, managed like a garden,
  A paradise of hops and high production;
For, after years of travel by a bard in
  Countries of greater heat, but lesser suction,
A green field is a sight which makes him pardon
  The absence of that more sublime construction
Which mixes up vines, olives, precipices,
Glaciers, volcanos, oranges, and ices.

77

And when I think upon a pot of beer—
  But I won't weep!—and so drive on, postillions!
As the smart boys spurr'd fast in their career,
  Juan admired these highways of free millions;
A country in all senses the most dear
  To foreigner or native, save some silly ones,
Who "kick against the pricks" just at this juncture,
And for their pains get only a fresh puncture.

78

What a delightful thing's a turnpike road!
  So smooth, so level, such a mode of shaving
The earth, as scarce the eagle in the broad
  Air can accomplish, with his wide wings waving.
Had such been cut in Phaeton's time, the god
  Had told his son to satisfy his craving
With the York mail;—but onward as we roll,
Surgit amari aliquid—the toll!

79

Alas! how deeply painful is all payment!
  Take lives, take wives, take aught except men's purses.
As Machiavel shows those in purple raiment,
  Such is the shortest way to general curses.
They hate a murderer much less than a claimant
  On that sweet ore which everybody nurses.—
Kill a man's family, and he may brook it,
But keep your hands out of his breeches' pocket:

80

So said the Florentine; ye monarchs, hearken
  To your instructor. Juan now was borne,
Just as the day began to wane and darken,
  O'er the high hill, which looks with pride or scorn
Toward the great city.—Ye who have a spark in
  Your veins of Cockney spirit, smile or mourn
According as you take things well or ill;
Bold Britons, we are now on Shooter's Hill!

81

The sun went down, the smoke rose up, as from
  A half-unquench'd volcano o'er a space
Which well beseem'd the "Devil's drawingroom,"
  As some have qualified that wondrous place:
But Juan felt, though not approaching *home*,

As one who, though he were not of the race,
Revered the soil, of those true sons the mother,
Who butcher'd half the earth, and bullied t'other.

82

A mighty mass of brick, and smoke, and shipping,
  Dirty and dusky, but as wide as eye
Could reach, with here and there a sail just skipping
  In sight, then lost amidst the forestry
Of masts; a wilderness of steeples peeping
  On tiptoe through their sea-coal canopy;
A huge, dun cupola, like a foolscap crown
On a fool's head—and there is London Town.

83

But Juan saw not this: each wreath of smoke
  Appear'd to him but as the magic vapour
Of some alchymic furnace, from whence broke
  The wealth of worlds (a wealth of tax and paper):
The gloomy clouds, which o'er it as a yoke
  Are bow'd, and put the sun out like a taper,
Were nothing but the natural atmosphere,
Extremely wholesome, though but rarely clear.

· · · · ·

1822   1823

CANTO THE ELEVENTH

I

When Bishop Berkeley said "there was no matter,"
  And proved it—'twas no matter what he said:
They say his system 'tis in vain to batter,
  Too subtle for the airiest human head;
And yet who can believe it? I would shatter

Gladly all matters down to stone or lead,
Or adamant, to find the world a spirit,
And wear my head, denying that I wear it.

2

What a sublime discovery 'twas to make the
    Universe universal egotism,
That all's ideal—*all ourselves!* I'll stake the
    World (be it what you will) that *that's* no schism:
Oh Doubt!—if thou be'st Doubt, for which some take thee,
    But which I doubt extremely—thou sole prism
Of the Truth's rays, spoil not my draught of spirit!
Heaven's brandy, though our brain can hardly bear it.

3

For ever and anon comes Indigestion
    (Not the most "dainty Ariel"), and perplexes
Our soarings with another sort of question:
    And that which after all my spirit vexes,
Is, that I find no spot where man can rest eye on,
    Without confusion of the sorts and sexes,
Of beings, stars, and this unriddled wonder,
The world, which at the worst's a *glorious* blunder—

4

If it be chance; or if it be according
    To the old text, still better:—lest it should
Turn out so, we'll say nothing 'gainst the wording,
    As several people think such hazards rude.
They're right; our days are too brief for affording
    Space to dispute what *no one* ever could
Decide, and *everybody one day* will
Know very clearly—or at least lie still.

5

And therefore will I leave off metaphysical
    Discussion, which is neither here nor there:

If I agree that what is, is; then this I call
   Being quite perspicuous and extremely fair;
The truth is, I've grown lately rather phthisical:
   I don't know what the reason is—the air
Perhaps; but as I suffer from the shocks
Of illness, I grow much more orthodox.

6

The first attack at once proved the Divinity
   (But *that* I never doubted, nor the Devil);
The next, the Virgin's mystical virginity;
   The third, the usual Origin of Evil;
The fourth at once establish'd the whole Trinity
   On so uncontrovertible a level,
That I devoutly wish'd the three were four
On purpose to believe so much the more.

7

To our theme.—The man who has stood on the Acropolis
   And look'd down over Attica; or he
Who has sail'd where picturesque Constantinople is,
   Or seen Timbuctoo, or hath taken tea
In small-eyed China's crockery-ware metropolis,
   Or sat amidst the bricks of Nineveh,
May not think much of London's first appearance—
But ask him what he thinks of it a year hence?

8

Don Juan had got out on Shooter's Hill;
   Sunset the time, the place the same declivity
Which looks along that vale of good and ill
   Where London streets ferment in full activity;
While everything around was calm and still,
   Except the creak of wheels, which on their pivot he
Heard,—and that bee-like, bubbling, busy hum
Of cities, that boil over with their scum:—

9

I say, Don Juan, wrapt in contemplation,
  Walk'd on behind his carriage, o'er the summit,
And lost in wonder of so great a nation,
  Gave way to 't, since he could not overcome it.
"And here," he cried, "is Freedom's chosen station;
  Here peals the people's voice, nor can entomb it
Racks, prisons, inquisitions; resurrection
Awaits it, each new meeting or election.

10

"Here are chaste wives, pure lives; here people pay
  But what they please; and if that things be dear,
'Tis only that they love to throw away
  Their cash, to show how much they have a year.
Here laws are all inviolate; none lay
  Traps for the traveller; every highway's clear;
Here"—he was interrupted by a knife,
With—"Damn your eyes! your money or your life!"—

11

These freeborn sounds proceeded from four pads
  In ambush laid, who had perceived him loiter
Behind his carriage; and, like handy lads,
  Had seized the lucky hour to reconnoitre,
In which the heedless gentleman who gads
  Upon the road, unless he prove a fighter,
May find himself within that isle of riches
Exposed to lose his life as well as breeches.

12

Juan, who did not understand a word
  Of English, save their shibboleth, "God damn!"
And even that he had so rarely heard,
  He sometimes thought 'twas only their "Salām,"
Or "God be with you!"—and 'tis not absurd

To think so: for half English as I am
(To my misfortune), never can I say
I heard them wish "God with you," save that way;—

13

Juan yet quickly understood their gesture,
   And being somewhat choleric and sudden,
Drew forth a pocket-pistol from his vesture,
   And fired it into one assailant's pudding—
Who fell, as rolls an ox o'er in his pasture,
   And roar'd out, as he writhed his native mud in,
Unto his nearest follower or henchman,
"Oh Jack! I'm floor'd by that 'ere bloody Frenchman!"

14

On which Jack and his train set off at speed,
   And Juan's suite, late scatter'd at a distance,
Came up, all marvelling at such a deed,
   And offering, as usual, late assistance.
Juan, who saw the moon's late minion bleed
   As if his veins would pour out his existence,
Stood calling out for bandages and lint,
And wish'd he had had been less hasty with his flint.

15

"Perhaps," thought he, "it is the country's wont
   To welcome foreigners in this way: now
I recollect some innkeepers who don't
   Differ, except in robbing with a bow,
In lieu of a bare blade and brazen front.
   But what is to be done? I can't allow
The fellow to lie groaning on the road:
So take him up; I'll help you with the load."

16

But ere they could perform this pious duty,
   The dying man cried, "Hold! I've got my gruel!

Oh! for a glass of *max!* We've miss'd our booty;
  Let me die where I am!" And as the fuel
Of life shrunk in his heart, and thick and sooty
  The drops fell from his death-wound, and he drew ill
His breath,—he from his swelling throat untied
A kerchief, crying "Give Sal that!"—and died.

17

The cravat stain'd with bloody drops fell down
  Before Don Juan's feet: he could not tell
Exactly why it was before him thrown,
  Nor what the meaning of the man's farewell.
Poor Tom was once a kiddy upon town,
  A thorough varmit, and a *real* swell,
Full flash, all fancy, until fairly diddled,
His pockets first and then his body riddled.

18

Don Juan, having done the best he could
  In all the circumstances of the case,
As soon as "Crowner's quest" allow'd, pursued
  His travels to the capital apace;—
Esteeming it a little hard he should
  In twelve hours' time, and very little space,
Have been obliged to slay a free-born native
In self-defence: this made him meditative.

19

He from the world had cut off a great man,
  Who in his time had made heroic bustle.
Who in a row like Tom could lead the van,
  Booze in the ken, or at the spellken hustle?
Who queer a flat? Who (spite of Bowstreet's ban)
  On the high toby-spice so flash the muzzle?
Who on a lark, with black-eyed Sal (his blowing),
So prime, so swell, so nutty, and so knowing?

20

But Tom's no more—and so no more of Tom.
  Heroes must die; and by God's blessing 'tis
Not long before the most of them go home.
  Hail! Thamis, hail! Upon thy verge it is
That Juan's chariot, rolling like a drum
  In thunder, holds the way it can't well miss,
Through Kennington and all the other "tons,"
Which make us wish ourselves in town at once;—

. . . . .

45

In the great world,—which, being interpreted,
  Meaneth the west or worst end of a city,
And about twice two thousand people bred
  By no means to be very wise or witty,
But to sit up while others lie in bed,
  And look down on the universe with pity,—
Juan, as an inveterate patrician,
Was well received by persons of condition.

46

He was a bachelor, which is a matter
  Of import both to virgin and to bride,
The former's hymeneal hopes to flatter;
  And (should she not hold fast by love or pride)
'Tis also of some moment to the latter:
  A rib's a thorn in a wed gallant's side,
Requires decorum, and is apt to double
The horrid sin—and what's still worse, the trouble.

47

But Juan was a bachelor—of arts,
  And parts, and hearts: he danced and sung, and had
An air as sentimental as Mozart's
  Softest of melodies; and could be sad
Or cheerful, without any "flaws or starts,"

Just at the proper time: and though a lad,
Had seen the world—which is a curious sight,
And very much unlike what people write.

48

Fair virgins blush'd upon him; wedded dames
   Bloom'd also in less transitory hues;
For both commodities dwell by the Thames,
   The painting and the painted; youth, ceruse,
Against his heart preferr'd their usual claims,
   Such as no gentleman can quite refuse;
Daughters admired his dress, and pious mothers
Inquired his income, and if he had brothers.

49

The milliners who furnish "drapery Misses"
   Throughout the season, upon speculation
Of payment ere the honeymoon's last kisses
   Have waned into a crescent's coruscation,
Thought such an opportunity as this is,
   Of a rich foreigner's initiation,
Not to be overlook'd—and gave such credit,
That future bridegrooms swore, and sigh'd, and paid it.

50

The Blues, that tender tribe, who sigh o'er sonnets,
   And with the pages of the last Review
Line the interior of their heads or bonnets,
   Advanced in all their azure's highest hue:
They talk'd bad French or Spanish, and upon its
   Late authors ask'd him for a hint or two;
And which was softest, Russian or Castilian?
And whether in his travels he saw Ilion?

51

Juan, who was a little superficial,
   And not in literature a great Drawcansir,

Examined by this learned and especial
    Jury of matrons, scarce knew what to answer:
His duties warlike, loving, or official,
    His steady application as a dancer,
Had kept him from the brink of Hippocrene,
Which now he found was blue instead of green.

52

However, he replied at hazard, with
    A modest confidence and calm assurance,
Which lent his learned lucubrations pith,
    And pass'd for arguments of good endurance.
That prodigy, Miss Araminta Smith
    (Who at sixteen translated "Hercules Furens"
Into as furious English), with her best look,
Set down his sayings in her commonplace book.

53

Juan knew several languages—as well
    He might—and brought them up with skill, in time
To save his fame with each accomplish'd belle,
    Who still regretted that he did not rhyme.
There wanted but this requisite to swell
    His qualities (with them) into sublime:
Lady Fitz-Frisky, and Miss Maevia Mannish,
Both long'd extremely to be sung in Spanish.

54

However, he did pretty well, and was
    Admitted as an aspirant to all
The coteries, and, as in Banquo's glass,
    At great assemblies or in parties small,
He saw ten thousand living authors pass,
    That being about their average numeral;
Also the eighty "greatest living poets,"
As every paltry magazine can show its.

55

In twice five years the "greatest living poet,"
    Like to the champion in the fisty ring,
Is call'd on to support his claim, or show it,
    Although 'tis an imaginary thing.
Even I—albeit I'm sure I did not know it,
    Nor sought of foolscap subjects to be king,—
Was reckon'd, a considerable time,
The grand Napoleon of the realms of rhyme.

56

But Juan was my Moscow, and Faliero
    My Leipsic, and my Mont Saint Jean seems Cain:
La Belle Alliance of dunces down at zero,
    Now that the Lion's fall'n, may rise again:
But I will fall at least as fell my hero;
    Nor reign at all, or as a monarch reign;
Or to some lonely isle of gaolers go,
With turncoat Southey for my turnkey Lowe.

57

Sir Walter reign'd before me; Moore and Campbell
    Before and after: but now grown more holy,
The Muses upon Sion's hill must ramble
    With poets almost clergymen, or wholly:
And Pegasus has a psalmodic amble
    Beneath the very Reverend Rowley Powley,
Who shoes the glorious animal with stilts,
A modern Ancient Pistol—by the hilts!

58

Still he excels that artificial hard
    Labourer in the same vineyard, though the vine
Yields him but vinegar for his reward,—
    That neutralized dull Dorus of the Nine;
That swarthy Sporus, neither man nor bard:

That ox of verse, who *ploughs* for every line:—
Cambyses' roaring Romans beat at least
The howling Hebrews of Cybele's priest.—

59

Then there's my gentle Euphues; who, they say,
   Sets up for being a sort of *moral me*;
He'll find it rather difficult some day
   To turn out both, or either, it may be.
Some persons think that Coleridge hath the sway;
   And Wordsworth has supporters, two or three;
And that deep-mouth'd Boeotian "Savage Landor"
Has taken for a swan rogue Southey's gander.

60

John Keats, who was kill'd off by one critique,
   Just as he really promised something great,
If not intelligible, without Greek
   Contrived to talk about the Gods of late,
Much as they might have been supposed to speak.
   Poor fellow! His was an untoward fate;
'Tis strange the mind, that very fiery particle,
Should let itself be snuff'd out by an article.

61

The list grows long of live and dead pretenders
   To that which none will gain—or none will know
The conqueror at least; who, ere Time renders
   His last award, will have the long grass grow
Above his burnt-out brain, and sapless cinders.
   If I might augur, I should rate but low
Their chances;—they're too numerous, like the thirty
Mock tyrants, when Rome's annals wax'd but dirty.

62

This is the literary *lower* empire,
   Where the praetorian bands take up the matter;—

A "dreadful trade," like his who "gathers samphire,"
   The insolent soldiery to soothe and flatter,
With the same feelings as you'd coax a vampire.
   Now, were I once at home, and in good satire,
I'd try conclusions with those Janizaries,
And show them *what* an intellectual war is.

63

I think I know a trick or two, would turn
   Their flanks;—but it is hardly worth my while
With such small gear to give myself concern:
   Indeed I've not the necessary bile;
My natural temper's really aught but stern,
   And even my Muse's worst reproof's a smile;
And then she drops a brief and modern curtsy,
And glides away, assured she never hurts ye.

64

My Juan, whom I left in deadly peril
   Amongst live poets and *blue* ladies, pass'd
With some small profit through that field so sterile,
   Being tired in time, and neither least nor last,
Left it before he had been treated very ill;
   And henceforth found himself more gaily class'd
Amongst the higher spirits of the day,
The sun's true son, no vapour, but a ray.

65

His morns he pass'd in business—which dissected,
   Was like all business, a laborious nothing
That leads to lassitude, the most infected
   And Centaur Nessus garb of mortal clothing,
And on our sofas makes us lie dejected,
   And talk in tender horrors of our loathing
All kinds of toil, save for our country's good—
Which grows no better, though 'tis time it should.

66

His afternoons he pass'd in visits, luncheons,
   Lounging, and boxing; and the twilight hour
In riding round those vegetable puncheons
   Call'd "Parks," where there is neither fruit nor flower
Enough to gratify a bee's slight munchings;
   But after all it is the only "bower"
(In Moore's phrase) where the fashionable fair
Can form a slight acquaintance with fresh air.

67

Then dress, then dinner, then awakes the world!
   Then glare the lamps, then whirl the wheels, then roar
Through street and square fast flashing chariots hurl'd
   Like harness'd meteors; then along the floor
Chalk mimics painting; then festoons are twirl'd;
   Then roll the brazen thunders of the door,
Which opens to the thousand happy few
An earthly Paradise of *Or Molu*.

68

There stands the noble hostess, nor shall sink
   With the three-thousandth curtsy; there the waltz,
The only dance which teaches girls to think,
   Makes one in love even with its very faults.
Saloon, room, hall, o'erflow beyond their brink,
   And long the latest of arrivals halts,
'Midst royal dukes and dames condemn'd to climb,
And gain an inch of staircase at a time.

69

Thrice happy he who, after a survey
   Of the good company, can win a corner,
A door that's *in* or boudoir *out* of the way,
   Where he may fix himself like small "Jack Horner,"
And let the Babel round run as it may,

And look on as a mourner, or a scorner,
Or an approver, or a mere spectator,
Yawning a little as the night grows later.

70

But this won't do, save by and by; and he
    Who, like Don Juan, takes an active share,
Must steer with care through all that glittering sea
    Of gems and plumes and pearls and silks, to where
He deems it is his proper place to be;
    Dissolving in the waltz to some soft air,
Or proudlier prancing with mercurial skill,
Where Science marshals forth her own quadrille.

71

Or, if he dance not, but hath higher views
    Upon an heiress or his neighbour's bride,
Let him take care that that which he pursues
    Is not at once too palpably descried.
Full many an eager gentleman oft rues
    His haste; impatience is a blundering guide,
Amongst a people famous for reflection,
Who like to play the fool with circumspection.

72

But, if you can contrive, get next at supper;
    Or if forestall'd, get opposite and ogle:—
Oh, ye ambrosial moments! always upper
    In mind, a sort of sentimental bogle,
Which sits for ever upon memory's crupper,
    The ghost of vanish'd pleasures once in vogue! Ill
Can tender souls relate the rise and fall
Of hopes and fears which shake a single ball.

73

But these precautionary hints can touch
    Only the common run, who must pursue,

And watch, and ward; whose plans a word too much
   Or little overturns; and not the few
Or many (for the number's sometimes such)
   Whom a good mien, especially if new,
Or fame, or name, for wit, war, sense, or nonsense,
Permits whate'er they please, or *did* not long since.

74

Our hero, as a hero, young and handsome,
   Noble, rich, celebrated, and a stranger,
Like other slaves of course must pay his ransom,
   Before he can escape from so much danger
As will environ a conspicuous man. Some
   Talk about poetry, and "rack and manger,"
And ugliness, disease, as toil and trouble;—
I wish they knew the life of a young noble.

75

They are young, but know not youth—it is anticipated;
   Handsome but wasted, rich without a sou;
Their vigour in a thousand arms is dissipated;
   Their cash comes *from*, their wealth goes *to* a Jew:
Both senates see their nightly votes participated
   Between the tyrant's and the tribunes' crew;
And having voted, dined, drank, gamed, and whored,
The family vault receives another lord.

76

"Where is the world?" cries Young, at *eighty*—"Where
   The world in which a man was born?" Alas!
Where is the world of *eight* years past? *'Twas there*—
   I look for it—'tis gone, a globe of glass!
Crack'd, shiver'd, vanish'd, scarcely gazed on, ere
   A silent change dissolves the glittering mass.
Statesmen, chiefs, orators, queens, patriots, kings,
And dandies, all are gone on the wind's wings.

77

Where is Napoleon the Grand? God knows:
  Where little Castlereagh? The devil can tell:
Where Grattan, Curran, Sheridan, all those
  Who bound the bar or senate in their spell?
Where is the unhappy Queen, with all her woes?
  And where the Daughter, whom the Isles loved well?
Where are those martyr'd saints the Five per Cents?
And where—oh, where the devil are the Rents?

78

Where's Brummel? Dish'd. Where's Long Pole Wellesley? Diddled.
  Where's Whitbread? Romilly? Where's George the Third?
Where is his will? (That's not so soon unriddled.)
  And where is "Fum" the Fourth, our "royal bird"?
Gone down, it seems, to Scotland to be fiddled
  Unto by Sawney's violin, we have heard:
"Caw me, caw thee"—for six months hath been hatching
This scene of royal itch and loyal scratching.

79

Where is Lord This? And where my Lady That?
  The Honourable Mistresses and Misses?
Some laid aside like an old Opera hat,
  Married, unmarried, and remarried (this is
An evolution oft performed of late).
  Where are the Dublin shouts—and London hisses?
Where are the Grenvilles? Turn'd as usual. Where
My friends the Whigs? Exactly where they were.

80

Where are the Lady Carolines and Franceses?
  Divorced or doing thereanent. Ye annals
So brilliant, where the list of routs and dances is,—
  Thou Morning Post, sole record of the panels
Broken in carriages, and all the phantasies

Of fashion,—say what streams now fill those channels?
Some die, some fly, some languish on the Continent,
Because the times have hardly left them *one* tenant.

81

Some who once set their caps at cautious dukes,
  Have taken up at length with younger brothers:
Some heiresses have bit at sharpers' hooks:
  Some maids have been made wives, some merely mothers:
Others have lost their fresh and fairy looks:
  In short, the list of alterations bothers.
There's little strange in this, but something strange is
The unusual quickness of these common changes.

82

Talk not of seventy years as age; in seven
  I have seen more changes, down from monarchs to
The humblest individual under heaven,
  Than might suffice a moderate century through.
I knew that nought was lasting, but now even
  Change grows too changeable, without being new:
Nought's permanent among the human race,
Except the Whigs *not* getting into place.

83

I have seen Napoleon, who seem'd quite a Jupiter,
  Shrink to a Saturn. I have seen a Duke
(No matter which) turn politician stupider,
  If that can well be, than his wooden look;
But it is time that I should hoist my "blue Peter,"
  And sail for a new theme:—I have seen—and shook
To see it—the king hiss'd, and then caressed;
But don't pretend to settle which was best.

84

I have seen the Landholders without a rap—
  I have seen Joanna Southcote—I have seen

The House of Commons turn'd to a taxtrap—
    I have seen that sad affair of the late Queen—
I have seen crowns worn instead of a fool's cap—
    I have seen a Congress doing all that's mean—
I have seen some nations, like o'erloaded asses,
Kick off their burthens—meaning the high classes.

85

I have seen small poets, and great prosers, and
    Interminable—*not eternal*—speakers—
I have seen the funds at war with house and land—
    I have seen the country gentlemen turn squeakers—
I have seen the people ridden o'er like sand
    By slaves on horseback—I have seen malt liquors
Exchanged for "thin potations" by John Bull—
I have seen John half detect himself a fool.—

86

But "*carpe diem*," Juan, "*carpe, carpe!*"
    To-morrow sees another race as gay
And transient, and devour'd by the same harpy.
    "Life's a poor player,"—then "play out the play,
Ye villains!" and above all keep a sharp eye
    Much less on what you do than what you say:
Be hypocritical, be cautious, be
Not what you *seem*, but always what you *see*.

87

But how shall I relate in other cantos
    Of what befell our hero in the land,
Which 'tis the common cry and lie to vaunt as
    A moral country? But I hold my hand—
For I disdain to write an Atalantis;
    But 'tis as well at once to understand
You are *not* a moral people, and you know it
Without the aid of too sincere a poet.

88

What Juan saw and underwent shall be
　My topic, with of course the due restriction
Which is required by proper courtesy;
　And recollect the work is only fiction,
And that I sing of neither mine nor me,
　Though every scribe, in some slight turn of diction,
Will hint allusions never *meant*. Ne'er doubt
This—when I speak, I *don't hint*, but *speak out*.

89

Whether he married with the third or fourth
　Offspring of some sage husband-hunting countess,
Or whether with some virgin of more worth
　(I mean in Fortune's matrimonial bounties),
He took to regularly peopling Earth,
　Of which your lawful, awful wedlock fount is,—
Or whether he was taken in for damages,
For being too excursive in his homages,—

90

Is yet within the unread events of time.
　Thus far, go forth, thou lay, which I will back
Against the same given quantity of rhyme,
　For being as much the subject of attack
As ever yet was any work sublime,
　By those who love to say that white is black.
So much the better!—I may stand alone,
But would not change my free thoughts for a throne.

1822　　　　　　　　　　　　1823

CANTO THE FOURTEENTH

. . . . .

8

You know, or don't know, that great Bacon saith,
  "Fling up a straw, 'twill show the way the wind blows;"
And such a straw, borne on by human breath,
  Is poesy, according as the mind glows;
A paper kite which flies 'twixt life and death,
  A shadow which the onward soul behind throws:
And mine's a bubble, not blown up for praise,
But just to play with, as an infant plays.

9

The world is all before me—or behind;
  For I have seen a portion of that same,
And quite enough for me to keep in mind;—
  Of passions, too, I have proved enough to blame,
To the great pleasure of our friends, mankind,
  Who like to mix some slight alloy with fame;
For I was rather famous in my time,
Until I fairly knock'd it up with rhyme.

10

I have brought this world about my ears, and eke
  The other; that's to say, the clergy—who
Upon my head have bid their thunders break
  In pious libels by no means a few.
And yet I can't help scribbling once a week,
  Tiring old readers, nor discovering new.
In youth I wrote because my mind was full,
And *now* because I feel it growing dull.

11

But "why then publish?"—There are no rewards,
  Of fame or profit when the world grows weary.

I ask in turn,—Why do you play at cards?
   Why drink? Why read?—To make some hour less dreary.
It occupies me to turn back regards
   On what I've seen or ponder'd, sad or cheery;
And what I write I cast upon the stream,
To swim or sink—I have had at least my dream.

12

I think that were I *certain* of success,
   I hardly could compose another line:
So long I've battled either more or less,
   That no defeat can drive me from the Nine.
This feeling 'tis not easy to express,
   And yet 'tis not affected, I opine.
In play, there are two pleasures for your choosing—
The one is winning, and the other losing.

13

Besides, my Muse by no means deals in fiction:
   She gathers a repertory of facts,
Of course with some reserve and slight restriction,
   But mostly sings of human things and acts—
And that's one cause she meets with contradiction;
   For too much truth, at first sight, ne'er attracts;
And were her object only what's call'd glory,
With more ease too she'd tell a different story.

14

Love, war, a tempest—surely there's variety:
   Also a seasoning slight of lucubration;
A bird's-eye-view, too, of that wild, Society;
   A slight glance thrown on men of every station.
If you have nought else, here's at least satiety,
   Both in performance and in preparation;
And though these lines should only line portmanteaus,
Trade will be all the better for these Cantos.

15

The portion of this world which I at present
  Have taken up to fill the following sermon,
Is one of which there's no description recent:
  The reason why, is easy to determine:
Although it seems both prominent and pleasant,
  There is a sameness in its gems and ermine,
A dull and family likeness through all ages,
Of no great promise for poetic pages.

16

With much to excite there's little to exalt;
  Nothing that speaks to all men and all times;
A sort of varnish over every fault;
  A kind of common-place, even in their crimes;
Factitious passions, wit without much salt,
  A want of that true nature which sublimes
Whate'er it shows with truth; a smooth monotony
Of character, in those at least who have got any.

17

Sometimes, indeed, like soldiers off parade,
  They break their ranks and gladly leave the drill;
But then the roll-call draws them back afraid,
  And they must be or seem what they were: still
Doubtless it is a brilliant masquerade:
  But when of the first sight you have had your fill,
It palls—at least it did so upon me,
This paradise of pleasure and *ennui*.

18

When we have made our love, and gamed our gaming,
  Drest, voted, shone, and, may be, something more;
With dandies dined; heard senators declaiming;
  Seen beauties brought to market by the score,
Sad rakes to sadder husbands chastely taming;

There's little left but to be bored or bore.
Witness those *ci-devant jeunes hommes* who stem
The stream, nor leave the world which leaveth them.

19

'Tis said—indeed a general complaint—
  That no one has succeeded in describing
The *monde*, exactly as they ought to paint:
  Some say, that authors only snatch, by bribing
The porter, some slight scandals strange and quaint,
  To furnish matter for their moral gibing;
And that their books have but one style in common—
My lady's prattle, filter'd through her woman.

20

But this can't well be true, just now; for writers
  Are grown of the *beau monde* a part potential:
I've seen them balance even the scale with fighters,
  Especially when young, for that's essential.
Why do their sketches fail them as inditers
  Of what they deem themselves most consequential,
The *real* portrait of the highest tribe?
'Tis that, in fact, there's little to describe.

. . . . .

1823   1823

[The setting of Cantos XIII to XVI (and the fragment of Canto
XVII) is a house party given at Norman Abbey (Newstead
Abbey) by Lord Henry and Lady Adeline Amundeville, the
"Queen Bee" of English society, with whom Byron implies Juan
eventually will become dangerously involved. But at the moment
Lady Adeline is trying to marry Juan off to some one of the
house guests of whom she approves. The following excerpt in-
troduces Aurora Raby, Byron's most sympathetic portrait of an
English woman.]

CANTO THE FIFTEENTH

. . . . .

40

But Adeline determined Juan's wedding
  In her own mind, and that's enough for woman;
But then, with whom? There was the sage Miss Reading,
  Miss Raw, Miss Flaw, Miss Showman, and Miss Knowman,
And the two fair co-heiresses Giltbedding.
  She deem'd his merits something more than common:
All these were unobjectionable matches,
And might go on, if well wound up, like watches.

41

There was Miss Millpond, smooth as summer's sea,
  That usual paragon, an only daughter,
Who seem'd the cream of equanimity,
  Till skimm'd—and then there was some milk and water,
With a slight shade of blue too, it might be
  Beneath the surface; but what did it matter?
Love's riotous, but marriage should have quiet,
And being consumptive, live on a milk diet.

42

And then there was the Miss Audacia Shoestring,
  A dashing *demoiselle* of good estate,
Whose heart was fix'd upon a star or blue string;
  But whether English dukes grew rare of late,
Or that she had not harp'd upon the true string,
  By which such sirens can attract our great,
She took up with some foreign younger brother,
A Russ or Turk—the one's as good as t'other.

43

And then there was—but why should I go on,
  Unless the ladies should go off?—there was

Indeed a certain fair and fairy one,
    Of the best class, and better than her class,—
Aurora Raby, a young star who shone
    O'er life, too sweet an image for such glass,
A lovely being, scarcely form'd or moulded,
A rose with all its sweetest leaves yet folded;

44

Rich, noble, but an orphan; left an only
    Child to the care of guardians good and kind;
But still her aspect had an air so lonely!
    Blood is not water; and where shall we find
Feelings of youth like those which over-thrown lie
    By death, when we are left, alas! behind,
To feel, in friendless palaces, a home
Is wanting, and our best ties in the tomb?

45

Early in years, and yet more infantine
    In figure, she had something of sublime
In eyes which sadly shone, as seraphs' shine.
    All youth—but with an aspect beyond time;
Radiant and grave—as pitying man's decline;
    Mournful—but mournful of another's crime,
She look'd as if she sat by Eden's door,
And grieved for those who could return no more.

46

She was a Catholic, too, sincere, austere,
    As far as her own gentle heart allow'd,
And deem'd that fallen worship far more dear
    Perhaps because 'twas fallen: her sires were proud
Of deeds and days when they had fill'd the ear
    Of nations, and had never bent or bow'd
To novel power; and as she was the last,
She held their old faith and old feelings fast.

47

She gazed upon a world she scarcely knew,
 As seeking not to know it; silent, lone,
As grows a flower, thus quietly she grew,
 And kept her heart serene within its zone.
There was awe in the homage which she drew;
 Her spirit seem'd as seated on a throne
Apart from the surrounding world, and strong
In its own strength—most strange in one so young!

48

Now it so happen'd, in the catalogue
 Of Adeline, Aurora was omitted,
Although her birth and wealth had given her vogue,
 Beyond the charmers we have already cited;
Her beauty also seem'd to form no clog
 Against her being mention'd as well fitted,
By many virtues, to be worth the trouble
Of single gentlemen who would be double.

49

And this omission, like that of the bust
 Of Brutus at the pageant of Tiberius,
Made Juan wonder, as no doubt he must.
 This he express'd half smiling and half serious;
When Adeline replied with some disgust,
 And with an air, to say the least, imperious,
She marvell'd "what he saw in such a baby
As that prim, silent, cold Aurora Raby?"

50

Juan rejoin'd—"She was a Catholic,
 And therefore fittest, as of his persuasion;
Since he was sure his mother would fall sick,
 And the Pope thunder excommunication,
If——" But here Adeline, who seem'd to pique

Herself extremely on the inoculation
Of others with her own opinions, stated—
As usual—the same reason which she late did.

51

And wherefore not? A reasonable reason,
   If good, is none the worse for repetition;
If bad, the best way's certainly to tease on,
   And amplify: you lose much by concision,
Whereas insisting in or out of season
   Convinces all men, even a politician;
Or—what is just the same—it wearies out.
So the end's gain'd, what signifies the route?

52

Why Adeline had this slight prejudice—
   For prejudice it was—against a creature
As pure as sanctity itself from vice,
   With all the added charm of form and feature,
For me appears a question far too nice,
   Since Adeline was liberal by nature;
But nature's nature, and has more caprices
Than I have time, or will, to take to pieces.

53

Perhaps she did not like the quiet way
   With which Aurora on those baubles look'd,
Which charm most people in their earlier day:
   For there are few things by mankind less brook'd,
And womankind too, if we so may say,
   Than finding thus their genius stand rebuked,
Like "Antony's by Caesar," by the few
Who look upon them as they ought to do.

54

It was not envy—Adeline had none;
   Her place was far beyond it, and her mind.

It was not scorn—which could not light on one
  Whose greatest *fault* was leaving few to find.
It was not jealousy, I think: but shun
  Following the *ignes fatui* of mankind.
It was not——but 'tis easier far, alas!
To say what it was *not* than what it was.

55

Little Aurora deem'd she was the theme
  Of such discussion. She was there a guest;
A beauteous ripple of the brilliant stream
  Of rank and youth, though purer than the rest,
Which flow'd on for a moment in the beam
  Time sheds a moment o'er each sparkling crest.
Had she known this, she would have calmly smiled—
She had so much, or little, of the child.

56

The dashing and proud air of Adeline
  Imposed not upon her: she saw her blaze
Much as she would have seen a glow-worm shine,
  Then turn'd unto the stars for loftier rays.
Juan was something she could not divine,
  Being no sibyl in the new world's ways;
Yet she was nothing dazzled by the meteor,
Because she did not pin her faith on feature.

57

His fame too,—for he had that kind of fame
  Which sometimes plays the deuce with womankind,
A heterogeneous mass of glorious blame,
  Half virtues and whole vices being combined;
Faults which attract because they are not tame;
  Follies trick'd out so brightly that they blind:—
These seals upon her wax made no impression,
Such was her coldness or her self-possession.

58

Juan knew nought of such a character—
  High, yet resembling not his lost Haidée;
Yet each was radiant in her proper sphere:
  The island girl, bred up by the lone sea,
More warm, as lovely, and not less sincere,
  Was Nature's all: Aurora could not be,
Nor would be thus:—the difference in them
Was such as lies between a flower and gem.

             . . . .

1823   1823

LETTERS

To Thomas Moore
                    Newstead Abbey, Sept. 20, 1814.

> Here's to her who long
>   Hath waked the poet's sigh!
> The girl who gave to song
>   What gold could never buy.

My dear Moore,

I am going to be married—that is, I am accepted, and one usually hopes the rest will follow. My mother of the Gracchi (that *are* to be), *you* think too strait-laced for me, although the paragon of only children, and invested with 'golden opinions of all sorts of men,' and full of 'most blest conditions' as Desdemona herself. Miss Milbanke is the lady, and I have her father's invitation to proceed there in my elect capacity,—which however, I cannot do till I have settled some business in London, and got a blue coat.

She is said to be an heiress, but of that I really know nothing certainly, and shall not enquire. But I do know, that she has talents and excellent qualities; and you will not deny her judgment, after having refused six suitors and taken me.

Now, if you have any thing to say against this, pray do; my mind's made up, positively fixed, determined, and therefore I will listen to reason, because now it can do no harm. Things may occur to break it off, but I will hope not. In the mean time, I tell you (a *secret*, by the by,—at least, till I know she wishes it to be public) that I have proposed and am accepted. You need not be in a hurry to wish me joy, for one mayn't be married for months. I am going to town to-morrow: but expect to be here, on my way there, within a fortnight.

If this had not happened, I should have gone to Italy. In my way down, perhaps, you will meet me at Nottingham, and come over with me here. I need not say that nothing will give

411

me greater pleasure. I must, of course, reform thoroughly; and, seriously, if I can contribute to her happiness, I shall secure my own. She is so good a person, that—that—in short, I wish I was a better.

Ever, etc.

To Lady Byron

Mivart's Hotel [Easter]Sunday April [14] 1816.

"More last words"—not many—and such as you will attend to —answer I do not expect—nor does it import—but you will hear me.——I have just parted from Augusta—almost the last being you had left me to part with—and the only unshattered tie of my existence—wherever I may go—and I am going far—you and I can never meet again in this world—nor in the next—Let this content or atone.—If any accident occurs to me—be kind to *her*,—if she is then nothing—to her children;—Some time ago—I informed you that with the knowledge that any child of ours was already provided for by other and better means—I had made my will in favor of her and her children—as prior to my marriage:— this was not done in prejudice to you for we had not then differed —and even this is useless during your life by the settlements—I say therefore—be kind to her and hers—for never has she acted or spoken otherwise towards you—she has ever been your friend— this may seem valueless to one who has now so many:——be kind to her—however—and recollect that though it may be advantage to you to have lost your husband—it is sorrow to her to have the water now—or the earth hereafter—between her and her brother.—

She is gone—I need hardly add that of this request she knows nothing—your late compliances have not been so extensive—as to render this an encroachment:—I repeat it—(for deep resentments have but *half* recollections) that you once did promise me thus much—do not forget it—nor deem it cancelled it was not a vow.——

Mr. Wharton has sent me a letter with one question and two

pieces of intelligence—to the question I answer that the carriage
is yours—and as it has only carried us to Halnaby—and London
—and you to Kirkby—I hope it will take you many a more pro-
pitious journey.—

The receipts can remain—unless troublesome, if so—they can
be sent to Augusta—and through her I would also hear of my little
daughter—my address will be left for Mrs. Leigh.—The ring is of
no lapidary value—but it contains the hair of a king and an an-
cestor—which I should wish to preserve to Miss Byron.—

. . . . .

TO THOMAS MOORE

Venice, February 28, 1817.

You will, perhaps, complain as much of the frequency of my
letters now, as you were wont to do of their rarity. I think this is
the fourth within as many moons. I feel anxious to hear from
you, even more than usual, because your last indicated that you
were unwell. At present, I am on the invalid regimen myself.
The Carnival—that is, the latter part of it, and sitting up late o'
nights, had knocked me up a little. But it is over—and it is now
Lent, with all its abstinence and sacred music.

The mumming closed with a masked ball at the Fenice, where
I went, as also to most of the ridottos, etc., etc.; and, though I did
not dissipate much upon the whole, yet I find "the sword wearing out the scabbard", though I have but just turned the corner
of twenty-nine.

> So we'll go no more a roving
>   So late into the night,
> Though the heart be still as loving,
>   And the moon be still as bright.
>
> For the sword outwears its sheath,
>   And the soul wears out the breast,
> And the heart must pause to breathe,
>   And Love itself have rest.

Though the night was made for loving,
    And the day returns too soon,
Yet we'll go no more a roving
    By the light of the moon.

.   .   .   .   .

If I live ten years longer, you will see, however, that it is not over with me—I don't mean in literature, for that is nothing; and it may seem odd enough to say, I do not think it my vocation. But you will see that I shall do something or other—the times and fortune permitting—that, "like the cosmogony, or creation of the world, will puzzle the philosophers of all ages." But I doubt whether my constitution will hold out. I have, at intervals, exorcised it most devilishly.

.   .   .   .   .

To JOHN MURRAY

Venice, April 9, 1817.

DEAR SIR,

Your letters of the 18th and 20th are arrived. In my own I have given you the rise, progress, decline, and fall of my recent malady. It is *gone* to the Devil: I won't pay him so bad a compliment as to say it *came* from him;—*he* is too much of a Gentleman. It was nothing but a slow fever, which quickened its pace towards the end of its journey. I had been bored with it some weeks— with nocturnal burnings and morning perspirations; but I am quite well again, which I attribute to having had neither medicine nor Doctor thereof.

In a few days I set off for Rome: such is my purpose. I shall change it very often before Monday next, but do you continue to direct and address to *Venice*, as heretofore. If I go, letters will be forwarded: I say "*if*," because I never know what I shall do till it is done; and as I mean most firmly to set out for Rome, it is not unlikely I may find myself at St. Petersburg.

You tell me 'take care of myself';—faith, and I will. I won't be posthumous yet, if I can help it. Notwithstanding, only think what a "Life and Adventures," while I am in full scandal, would be worth, together with the *membra* of my writing-desk, the six-teen beginnings of poems never to be finished! Do you think I would not have shot myself last year, had I not luckily recollected that Mrs. Clermont, and Lady Noel, and all the old women in England would have been delighted;—besides the agreeable "Lu-nacy," of the "Crowner's Quest," and the regrets of two or three or half a dozen? Be assured that I *would live* for two reasons, or more;—there are one or two people whom I have to put out of the world, and as many into it, before I can "depart in peace"; if I do so before, I have not fulfilled my mission. Besides, when I turn thirty, I will turn devout; I feel a great vocation that way in Catholic churches, and when I hear the organ.

. . . . ;

To John Murray

Venice, May 30, 1817.

. . . . .

The day before I left Rome I saw three robbers guillotined. The ceremony—including the *masqued* priests; the half-naked ex-ecutioners; the bandaged criminals; the black Christ and his banner; the scaffold; the soldiery; the slow procession, and the quick rattle and heavy fall of the axe; the splash of the blood, and the ghastliness of the exposed heads—is altogether more impres-sive than the vulgar and ungentlemanly dirty "new drop," and dog-like agony of infliction upon the sufferers of the English sen-tence. Two of these men behaved calmly enough, but the first of the three died with great terror and reluctance, which was very horrible. He would not lie down; then his neck was too large for the aperture, and the priest was obliged to drown his exclama-tions by still louder exhortations. The head was off before the eye could trace the blow; but from an attempt to draw back the head, notwithstanding it was held forward by the hair, the first head was cut off close to the ears: the other two were taken off more cleanly. It is better than the oriental way, and (I should think) than the axe of our ancestors. The pain seems little; and yet the effect to the spectator, and the preparation to the criminal, are very striking and chilling. The first turned me quite hot and thirsty, and made me shake so that I could hardly hold the opera-glass (I was close, but determined to see, as one should see every thing, once, with attention); the second and third (which shows how dreadfully soon things grow indifferent), I am ashamed to say, had no effect on me as a horror, though I would have saved them if I could.

· · · · ·

To John Murray

Venice, April 6, 1819.

DEAR SIR,

The Second Canto of *Don Juan* was sent, on Saturday last, by post, in 4 packets, two of 4, and two of three sheets each, containing in all two hundred and seventeen stanzas, octave measure. But I will permit no curtailments, except those mentioned about Castlereagh and the two *Bobs* in the Introduction. You sha'n't make *Canticles* of my Cantos. The poem will please, if it is lively; if it is stupid, it will fail; but I will have none of your damned cutting and slashing. If you please, you may publish *anonymously;* it will perhaps be better; but I will battle my way against them all, like a Porcupine.

So you and Mr. Foscolo, etc., want me to undertake what you call a "great Work"? an Epic poem, I suppose, or some such pyramid. I'll try no such thing; I hate tasks. And then "seven or eight years!" God send us all well this day three months, let alone years. If one's years can't be better employed than in sweating poesy, a man had better be a ditcher. And works, too!—is *Childe Harold* nothing? You have so many "*divine*" poems, is it nothing to have written a *Human* one? without any of your wornout machinery. Why, man, I could have spun the thoughts of the four cantos of that poem into twenty, had I wanted to book-make, and its passion into as many modern tragedies. Since you want *length*, you shall have enough of *Juan*, for I'll make 50 cantos.

And Foscolo, too! Why does *he* not do something more than the *Letters of Ortis*, and a tragedy, and pamphlets? He has good fifteen years more at his command than I have: what has he done all that time?—proved his Genius, doubtless, but not fixed its fame, nor done his utmost.

Besides, I mean to write my best work in *Italian*, and it will take me nine years more thoroughly to master the language; and then if my fancy exist, and I exist too, I will try what I *can* do *really*. As to the Estimation of the English which you talk of, let them calculate what it is worth, before they insult me with their insolent condescension.

I have not written for their pleasure. If they are pleased, it is that they chose to be so; I have never flattered their opinions, nor their pride; nor will I. Neither will I make "Ladies books" *al dilettar le femine e la plebe*. I have written from the fullness of my mind, from passion, from impulse, from many motives, but not for their "sweet voices".

I know the precise worth of popular applause, for few Scribblers have had more of it; and if I chose to swerve into their paths, I could retain it, or resume it, or increase it. But I neither love ye, nor fear ye; and though I buy with ye and sell with ye, and talk with ye, I will neither eat with ye, drink with ye, nor pray with ye. They made me, without my search, a species of popular Idol; they, without reason or judgement, beyond the caprice of their good pleasure, threw down the Image from its pedestal; it was not broken with the fall, and they would, it seems, again replace it—but they shall not.

You ask about my health: about the beginning of the year I was in a state of great exhaustion, attended by such debility of Stomach that nothing remained upon it; and I was obliged to reform my "way of life," which was conducting me from the "yellow leaf" to the Ground, with all deliberate speed. I am better in health and morals, and very much yours ever,

B.

To the Countess Guiccioli

Bologna, August 25, 1819.

My Dear Teresa,

I have read this book in your garden;—my love, you were absent, or else I could not have read it. It is a favourite book of yours, and the writer was a friend of mine. You will not understand these English words, and *others* will not understand them—which is the reason I have not scrawled them in Italian. But you will recognize the handwriting of him who passionately loved you, and you will divine that, over a book which was yours, he could only think of love. In that word, beautiful in all languages, but most so in yours—*Amor mio*—is comprised my existence here and hereafter. I feel I exist here, and I fear that I shall exist hereafter,—to *what* purpose you will decide; my destiny rests with you, and you are a woman, eighteen years of age, and two out of a convent. I wish that you had stayed there, with all my heart,—or, at least, that I had never met you in your married state.

But all this is too late. I love you, and you love me,—at least, you *say so*, and *act* as if you *did* so, which last is a great consolation in all events. But *I* more than love you, and cannot cease to love you.

Think of me, sometimes, when the Alps and the ocean divide us,—but they never will, unless you *wish* it.

Byron

To Percy Bysshe Shelley

Ravenna, April 26, 1821

. . . . .

I am very sorry to hear what you say of Keats—is it *actually* true? I did not think criticism had been so killing. Though I differ from you essentially in your estimate of his performances, I so much abhor all unnecessary pain, that I would rather he had been seated on the highest peak of Parnassus than have perished in such a manner. Poor fellow! though with such inordinate self-love he would probably have not been very happy. I read the review of *Endymion* in the *Quarterly*. It was severe,—but surely not so severe as many reviews in that and other journals upon others.

I recollect the effect on me of the *Edinburgh* on my first poem; it was rage, and resistance, and redress—but not despondency nor despair. I grant that those are not amiable feelings; but, in this world of bustle and broil, and especially in the career of writing, a man should calculate upon his powers of *resistance* before he goes into the arena.

> "Expect not life from pain nor danger free,
>   Nor deem the doom of man reversed for thee."

You know my opinion of *that second-hand* school of poetry. You also know my high opinion of your own poetry,—because it is of *no* school. I read *Cenci*—but, besides that I think the *subject* essentially *un*dramatic, I am not an admirer of our old dramatists *as models*. I deny that the English have hitherto had a drama at all. Your *Cenci*, however, was a work of power and poetry. As to *my* drama, pray revenge yourself upon it, by being as free as I have been with yours.

I have not yet got your *Prometheus*, which I long to see. I have heard nothing of mine, and do not know that it is yet published. I have published a pamphlet on the Pope controversy, which you will not like. Had I known that Keats was dead—or that he was alive and so sensitive—I should have omitted some remarks upon his poetry, to which I was provoked by his *attack* upon *Pope*, and my disapprobation of *his own* style of writing.

You want me to undertake a great poem—I have not the inclination nor the power. As I grow older, the indifference—*not* to life, for we love it by instinct—but to the stimuli of life, increases. Besides, this late failure of the Italians has latterly disappointed me for many reasons,—some public, some personal. My respects to Mrs. S.

Yours ever,

B.

P.S.—Could not you and I contrive to meet this summer? Could not you take a run here *alone*?

To John Murray

R[avenna] July 30th, 1821

. . . . .

Are you aware that Shelley has written an elegy on Keats, and accuses the *Quarterly* of killing him?

> "Who killed John Keats?"
>   "I," says the Quarterly,
>   So savage and Tartarly;
> " 'Twas one of my feats."
>
> "Who shot the arrow?"
>   "The poet-priest Milman
>   (So ready to kill man),
> Or Southey or Barrow."

You know very well that I did not approve of Keats's poetry, or principles of poetry, or of his abuse of Pope; but, as he is dead, omit *all* that is said *about him* in any *MSS*. of mine, or publication. His *Hyperion* is a fine monument, and will keep his name. I do not envy the man who wrote the article: your review people have no more right to kill than any other foot pads. However, he who would die of an article in a review would probably have died of something else equally trivial. The same thing nearly happened to Kirke White, who afterwards died of a consumption.

To Thomas Moore

Pisa, August 27, 1822

. . . . .

The other day, at Viareggio, I thought proper to swim off to my schooner (the Bolivar) in the offing, and thence to shore again—about three miles, or better, in all. As it was at midday, under a broiling sun, the consequence has been a feverish attack, and my whole skin's coming off, after going through the process of one large continuous blister, raised by the sun and sea together. I have suffered much pain; not being able to lie on my back, or even side; for my shoulders and arms were equally St. Bartholomewed. But it is over,—and I have got a new skin, and am as glossy as a snake in its new suit.

We have been burning the bodies of Shelley and Williams on the sea-shore, to render them fit for removal and regular interment. You can have no idea what an extraordinary effect such a funeral pile has, on a desolate shore, with mountains in the background and the sea before, and the singular appearance the salt and frank-incense gave to the flame. All of Shelley was consumed, except his *heart*, which would not take the flame, and is now preserved in spirits of wine.

. . . . .

I have nearly (*quite three*) four new cantos of *Don Juan* ready. I obtained permission from the female Censor Morum of *my* morals to continue it, provided it were immaculate; so I have been as decent as need be. There is a deal of war—a siege, and all that, in the style, graphical and technical, of the shipwreck in Canto Second, which "took," as they say in the Row.

Yours, etc.

P.S.—That . . . Galignani has about ten lies in one paragraph. It was not a Bible that was found in Shelley's pocket, but John Keats's poems. However, it would not have been strange, for he was a great admirer of Scripture as a composition. *I* did not send my bust to the academy of New York; but I sat for my picture to young West, an American artist, at the request of some members of that Academy to *him* that he would take my portrait,—for the Academy, I believe.

I had, and still have, thoughts of South America, but am fluctuating between it and Greece. I should have gone, long ago, to one of them, but for my liaison with the Countess G.; for love, in these days, is little compatible with glory. *She* would be delighted to go too; but I do not choose to expose her to a long voyage, and a residence in an unsettled country, where I shall probably take a part of some sort.

To [MARY SHELLEY]

[December, 1822]

. . . . .

I presume that you, at least, know enough of me to be sure that I could have no intention to insult Hunt's poverty. On the contrary, I honour him for it; for I know what it is, having been as much embarrassed as ever he was, without perceiving aught in it to diminish an honourable man's self-respect. If you mean to say that, had he been a wealthy man, I would have joined in this Journal, I answer in the negative. . . . I engaged in the Journal from good-will towards him, added to respect for his character, literary and personal; and no less for his political courage, as well as regret for his present circumstances: I did this in the hope that he might, with the same aid from literary friends of literary contributions (which is requisite for all journals of a mixed nature), render himself independent.

. . . . .

I have always treated him, in our personal intercourse, with such scrupulous delicacy, that I have forborne intruding advice which I thought might be disagreeable, lest he should impute it to what is called "taking advantage of a man's situation."

As to friendship, it is a propensity in which my genius is very limited. I do not know the *male* human being, except Lord Clare, the friend of my infancy, for whom I feel any thing that deserves the name. All my others are men-of-the-world friendships. I did not even feel it for Shelley, however much I admired and esteemed him; so that you see not even vanity could bribe me into it, for, of all men, Shelley thought highest of my talents,—and, perhaps, of my disposition.

I will do my duty by my intimates, upon the principle of doing as you would be done by. I have done so, I trust, in most instances. I may be pleased with their conservation—rejoice in their success—be glad to do them service, or to receive their counsel and assistance in return. But as for friends and friendship, I have (as I already said) named the only remaining male for whom I feel any thing of the kind, excepting, perhaps, Thomas Moore. I have had, and may have still, a thousand friends, as they are called, in *life*, who are like one's partners in the waltz of this world—not much remembered when the ball is over, though very pleasant for the time. Habit, business, and companionship in pleasure or in pain, are links of a similar kind, and the same faith in politics is another. . . .

To Thomas Moore

Cephalonia, December 27, 1823.

I received a letter from you some time ago. I have been too much employed latterly to write as I could wish, and even now must write in haste.

I embark for Missolonghi to join Mavrocordato in four-and-twenty hours. The state of parties (but it were a long story) has kept me here till *now;* but now that Mavrocordato (their Washington, or their Kosciusko) is employed again, I can act with a *safe conscience.* I carry money to pay the squadron, etc., and I have influence with the Suliotes, *supposed* sufficient to keep them in harmony with some of the dissentients;—for there are plenty of differences, but trifling.

It is imagined that we shall attempt either Patras or the castles on the Straits; and it seems, by most accounts, that the Greeks, at any rate the Suliotes, who are in affinity with me of "bread and salt,"—expect that I should march with them, and—be it even so! If any thing in the way of fever, fatigue, famine, or otherwise, should cut short the middle age of a brother warbler,—like Garcilasso de la Vega, Kleist, Körner, Joukoffsky (a Russian nightingale—see Bowring's *Anthology*), or Thersander, or,—or somebody else—but never mind—I pray you to remember me in your "smiles and wine".

I have hopes that the cause will triumph; but whether it does or no, still "honour must be minded as strictly as milk diet." I trust to observe both.

Ever, etc.

To the Hon. Augusta Leigh

Missolonghi, [Monday] February 23, 1824.

My Dearest Augusta,

I received a few days ago yours and Lady B.'s report of Ada's health, with other letters from England for which I ought to be and am (I hope) sufficiently thankful, as they were of great comfort and I wanted some, having been recently unwell, but am now much better. So that you need not be alarmed.

You will have heard of our journeys and escapes, and so forth, perhaps with some exaggeration; but it is all very well now, and I have been for some time in Greece, which is in as good a state as could be expected considering circumstances. But I will not plague you with politics, wars, or *earthquakes,* though we had another very smart one three nights ago, which produced a scene ridiculous enough, as no damage was done except to those who stuck fast in the scuffle to get first out of the doors or windows, amongst whom some recent importations, fresh from England, who had been used to quieter elements, were rather squeezed in the press for precedence.

I have been obtaining the release of about nine and twenty Turkish prisoners—men, women, and children—and have sent them at my own expense home to their friends, but one, a pretty little girl of nine years of age named Hato or Hatagèe, has expressed a strong wish to remain with me, or under my care, and I have nearly determined to adopt her. If I thought that Lady B. would let her come to England as a Companion to Ada—(they are about the same age), we could easily provide for her; if not, I can send her to Italy for education. She is very lively and quick, and with great black oriental eyes, and Asiatic features. All her brothers were killed in the Revolution; her mother wishes to return to her husband who is at Prevesa, but says that she would rather entrust the child to me in the present state of the Country. Her extreme youth and sex have hitherto saved her life, but there is no saying what might occur in the course of the *war* (and of *such* a war), and I shall probably commit her to the charge of some English lady in the islands for the present. The Child herself has the same wish, and seems to have a decided character for her age. You can mention this matter if you think it worth while. I merely wish her to be respectably educated and treated, and, if my years and all things be considered, I presume, it would be difficult to conceive me to have any other views.

With regard to Ada's health, I am glad to hear that it is so much better. But I think it right that Lady B. should be informed, and guard against it accordingly, that her description of much of her indisposition and tendencies very nearly resemble my *own* at a similar age, except that I was much more impetuous. Her preference of *prose* (strange as it may seem) *was* and indeed *is* mine (for I hate *reading* verse, and always did), and I never invented anything but '*boats—ships*' and generally relating to the Ocean. I showed the report to Col. Stanhope, who was struck with the resemblance of *parts* of it to the *paternal* line even now. But it is also fit, though unpleasant, that I should mention that my recent attack, and a very severe one, had a strong appearance of *epilepsy*. *Why*—I know not, for it is late in life—its first appearance at thirty-six—and, as far as I *know*, it is not *hereditary*, and it is that it may not *become* so, that you should tell Lady B. to take some precautions in the case of Ada. My attack has not yet returned, and I am fighting it off with abstinence and exercise, and thus far with success; if merely casual, it is all very well.

ON THIS DAY
I COMPLETE MY
THIRTY-SIXTH YEAR

'Tis time this heart should be unmoved,
   Since others it hath ceased to move:
Yes, though I cannot be beloved,
      Still let me love!

My days are in the yellow leaf;
   The flowers and fruits of love are gone;
The worm, the canker, and the grief
      Are mine alone!

The fire that on my bosom preys
   Is lone as some volcanic isle;
No torch is kindled at its blaze—
      A funeral pile.

The hope, the fear, the jealous care,
   The exalted portion of the pain
And power of love, I cannot share,
      But wear the chain.

But 'tis not *thus*—and 'tis not *here*—
   Such thoughts should shake my soul, nor *now*,
Where glory decks the hero's bier,
      Or binds his brow.

The sword, the banner, and the field,
   Glory and Greece, around me see!

The Spartan, borne upon his shield,
     Was not more free.

Awake! (not Greece—she *is* awake!)
   Awake, my spirit! Think through *whom*
Thy life-blood tracks its parent lake,
     And then strike home!

Tread those reviving passions down,
   Unworthy manhood!—unto thee
Indifferent should the smile or frown
     Of beauty be.

If thou regrett'st thy youth, *why live?*
   The land of honourable death
Is here:—up to the field, and give
     Away thy breath!

Seek out—less often sought than found—
   A soldier's grave, for thee the best;
Then look around, and choose thy ground,
     And take thy rest.

                Missolonghi, Jan. 22, 1824.

NOTES ON POETRY

LINES INSCRIBED UPON A CUP FORMED FROM A SKULL

When a skull was found in the garden of Newstead Abbey, "a strange fancy seized me," Byron told Medwin, "of having it mounted as a drinking cup. I accordingly sent it to town, and it returned with a very high polish and of a mottled colour like tortoise-shell."

INSCRIPTION ON THE MONUMENT OF A NEWFOUNDLAND DOG

When Byron's dog "Boatswain" died he was buried in a vault in the garden at Newstead Abbey and a monument with these verses inscribed was erected. The verse was preceded by a prose inscription which reads in part:

> Near this spot
> Are deposited the remains of one
> Who possessed Beauty without Vanity
> Strength without Insolence
> Courage without Ferocity
> And all the Virtues of Man without his Vices

WRITTEN AFTER SWIMMING FROM SESTOS TO ABYDOS

Byron and a friend Ekenhead swam the Hellespont from the European to Asian side on May 3, 1810. The legendary Leander swam nightly from Abydos to Sestos to see Hero and had to swim back at daybreak.

MAID OF ATHENS, ERE WE PART

Supposedly addressed to Theresa Macri, daughter of Byron's landlady. The Greek motto means "My life, I love you."

REMEMBER THEE! REMEMBER THEE!

After Byron had broken with Lady Caroline Lamb in the latter part of 1812, she had visited his apartment during his absence and written in his copy of *Vathek* the words "Remember me!" According to Medwin, "Byron immediately wrote under the ominous warning these two stanzas."

STANZAS FOR MUSIC (I SPEAK NOT)

Probably addressed to Augusta Leigh.

SHE WALKS IN BEAUTY

Written after meeting his cousin Mrs. Wilmot at a party. She was in mourning and wore a black dress with spangles.

THE DESTRUCTION OF SENNACHERIB

The poem is based on the biblical account in II Kings 19. Sennacherib was king of the Assyrians.

ENGLISH BARDS AND SCOTCH REVIEWERS

115. William Congreve (1670–1729), most brilliant of the Restoration comic dramatists, and Thomas Otway (1652–1685), whose tragedies (particularly *Venice Preserved*) were often ranked next to Shakespeare's by neoclassic critics.

128. *Little's lyrics:* Little was the name under which Thomas Moore published his early poems.

hot-press'd twelves: Printed sheets were passed between hot-rollers to give them smoothness. "Twelves" (duodecimo) refers to the size of the volume.

129. *the Preacher:* Eccles. 1:9.

130. *cow-pox:* vaccination for small pox.

tractors: metal rods for curing "Red Noses, Gouty Toes, Windy Bowels, Broken Legs, Hump backs."

galvanism: use of electric currents for curative purposes.

gas: laughing gas. Byron looks upon all of these as fake panaceas of the age and signs of degeneration, like the poetry.

142. *Stott:* A newspaper poet who wrote under the pseudonym "Hafiz." "This personage is at present the most profound explorer of the bathos," says Byron's note.

153. *Lays of Minstrels:* Scott's *Lay of the Last Minstrel* (1805) grew out of a suggestion that he write a ballad on the border legend of Gilpin Horner (157).

173. *Murray with his Miller:* Scott's publisher, Constable, paid him £1,000 for *Marmion.* One half of the copyright was divided between two London publishers, Miller and John Murray. Murray later became Byron's publisher.

190. *Maro:* Virgil.

203. *Camoëns:* famous Portuguese poet (1524–1580) author of the epic, *The Lusiads*.

Tasso: Italian Poet (1544–1595) author of the epic, *Jerusalem Delivered*.

205. Southey's *Joan of Arc* was published in 1796; *Thalaba the Destroyer* (211) in 1801; *Madoc* (221) in 1805.

222. *Cacique:* West Indian Prince.

231. *Berkley ballads:* Southey wrote a ballad called *The Old Woman of Berkeley* in which an old woman is carried off by Beelzebub "on a high trotting horse."

239. See Wordsworth's *The Tables Turned*, stanza 1.

242. In the *Preface to the Lyrical Ballads*, Wordsworth had argued that there "neither is, nor can be, any essential difference between the language of prose and metrical composition."

247. See Wordsworth's poem *The Idiot Boy*.

259. Byron refers to two of Coleridge's poems: *Songs of the Pixies* and *To a Young Ass*.

POEMS OF THE SEPARATION

FARE THEE WELL

Addressed to Lady Byron and printed by Byron for private circulation, these lines achieved wide notoriety when published on April 14, 1816, in John Scott's *Champion*.

EPISTLE TO AUGUSTA

St. 2. *no rest at sea*: Byron's grandfather, Admiral John Byron, was called "Foul Weather Jack" because of the legend that whenever he put to sea, he met with a storm.

St. 8. *a lake*: Lake Geneva (Leman) contrasted with the Lake at Newstead Abbey.

THE DREAM

23. What follows is an idealized account of his love for Mary Chaworth in 1803–1805. The scene of stanzas 2 and 3 is Annesley Hall, Mary Chaworth's home.

106. Byron's travels in Asia Minor in 1810.

127. Mary Chaworth married John Musters in 1805. Her married life was very miserable and ended in separation in 1814. Soon afterward she became a half-mad invalid (stanza 7).

145. Byron's marriage to Annabelle Milbanke in 1815.

191. *Pontic monarch:* Mithridates, King of Pontus (120–63 B.C.), is said to have protected himself against poisoning so effectively through the use of antidotes that when as an old man he tried to poison himself he could not do so.

LINES ON HEARING THAT LADY BYRON WAS ILL

13ff. See *Childe Harold* IV, stanzas 132–138 and note to stanza 132.
53. *Janus-spirits:* See note to *Childe Harold* IV, stanza 136.

THE PRISONER OF CHILLON

Poem is based on the experience of François Bonnivard (1493–1570) who was imprisoned in Chillon between 1530–1535 for his activity against the Duke of Savoy in behalf of the independence of Geneva. The castle of Chillon was on Lake Geneva.

CHILDE HAROLD

Canto the Third

St. 1. *my fair child:* Ada was only five weeks old when Lady Byron left Byron in 1816. He never saw his daughter again.

the waters heave around me: Byron sailed from Dover on April 25, 1816, for Ostend, Holland.

St. 3. *my youth's summer:* he began Childe Harold in 1809 when he was 21 years old.

St. 17. *an Empire's dust:* Battle of Waterloo, June 18, 1815.

St. 18. *"pride of place."* a falconry term meaning highest point of flight.

St. 19. *reviving Thraldom:* one result of the Congress of Vienna was to restore the conditions which had led to the French Revolution. For example, a Bourbon king was restored to the throne in France. Byron refers to the monarchs who formed the Holy Alliance as the *Wolf* in relation to Napoleon, the *Lion*, in the following lines.

St. 20. *Harmodius:* Athenian who became a symbol of the martyr-patriot because of his attempt to kill the tyrant Hippias in 514 B.C.

St. 21. *sound of revelry:* famous ball given by the Duchess of Richmond in Brussels on the eve of Waterloo.

St. 23. *Brunswick's fated chieftain:* Frederick William, Duke of Brunswick in Germany. His father had been killed in battle in 1806.

St. 26. *"Cameron's gathering":* war song of the Clan Cameron. *Evan*

NOTES 433

had fought against Cromwell and *Donald* had fought on behalf of the Young Pretender and had been wounded in the battle of Culloden in 1746. *Albyn* is a poetic name for Scotland.

St. 29. *one I would select:* Frederick Howard, son of the Earl of Carlisle whom Byron had viciously satirized in *English Bards and Scotch Reviewers.*

St. 36. *the greatest:* Napoleon.

St. 41. *Philip's son:* Alexander the Great.

St. 49. *Love, which lent a blazon:* the usual device on the shields was a bleeding heart.

St. 53. *one fond breast:* his half-sister Augusta to whom the following lyric is addressed.

St. 55. *Drachenfels:* the ruins of a castle on the right bank of the Rhine near Bonn.

St. 56. *Marceau:* French general killed in 1796.

St. 58. *Ehrenbreitstein:* fortress on the Rhine, captured by the French after a prolonged siege in 1799 and dismantled and blown up upon the French evacuation in 1801.

St. 63. *Morat:* in 1476 the Swiss defeated an invading Burgundian army. An estimated 20,000 Burgundians were killed and left unburied. A small pyramid of bones still remained in 1816 and Byron carried off as souvenir "as much as may have made a quarter of a hero."

St. 64. *Cannae:* bloody battle in which Hannibal defeated the Romans in 216 B.C.

St. 65. *Adventicum:* the Roman capital of Switzerland, long since destroyed.

St. 66. *Julia:* an inscription, afterward proved to be forged, led Byron to believe that Julia Alpinula had died here after a vain effort to save her father, executed in A.D. 69 for leading a rebellion against Roman rule.

St. 79. *Julie:* heroine of Rousseau's novel, *La Nouvelle Héloïse.* The reference in the following lines is to Rousseau's account of his unrequited love for Madame D'Houdetot, *Confessions,* Bk. 9.

St. 81. *Pythian's mystic cave:* Apollo's oracle at Delphi. Rousseau has sometimes been called the father of the French Revolution.

St. 99. *Clarens:* a village on Lake Geneva, scene of *La Nouvelle Héloïse.*

St. 105. *Lausanne:* Edward Gibbon finished his *Decline and Fall of the Roman Empire* at Lausanne in 1788 and lived there until his death. *Ferney:* Voltaire's residence from 1758–1778.

St. 106. *the one:* Voltaire.

St. 107. *The other:* Gibbon. Both Voltaire and Gibbon were hostile to Christianity and highly critical of the social and political evils of their age.

St. 110. *Carthaginian:* Hannibal.

Canto the Fourth

St. 1. *winged Lion:* emblem of the republic of Venice: it stood on a column near the Doge's palace.

St. 2. *Cybele:* mother of the gods in Greek mythology who was generally represented in art as wearing a turreted crown.

St. 3. *Tasso's echoes:* until the latter part of the eighteenth century, gondoliers were accustomed to sing to each other alternate stanzas of Tasso's *Jerusalem.*

St. 4. *dogeless city:* Venice had been an independent state until 1798 when she was conquered by Napoleon. By 1817 she had become an Austrian possession.

Rialto: site of the original city which became the financial and commercial center of Venice. Byron uses the word symbolically for the former greatness of Venice as the center of Mediterranean trade.

the Moor: Othello.

Pierre: a character in Otway's *Venice Preserved.*

St. 10. *Spartan's epitaph:* answer of the mother of Brasidas, Spartan general killed in battle in 422 B.C., when he was praised by strangers as a hero.

St. 79. *Niobe of nations:* in Greek mythology, the queen whose twelve children were killed before her eyes and who became the symbol of eternal sorrow.

Scipio's tomb: discovered and rifled in 1780.

St. 82. *trebly hundred triumphs:* the 320 triumphs, honoring successful generals, which were supposed to have taken place from the founding of Rome to its decline.

Tully: Cicero.

St. 126. *upas:* a Javanese tree that yields an intensely poisonous milky juice used as an arrow poison. There was a widespread legend in the late eighteenth century that the tree destroyed all animal life within a radius of 15 miles.

St. 132. *Nemesis:* Greek goddess representing fortune and specifically the Avenger of crimes. Orestes had killed his mother, Clytemnestra, to avenge his father, Agamemnon, and in punishment had been hounded by the Furies. Byron's meaning is that, unlike Orestes, he will not take vengeance for his disgrace upon himself but will leave the retribution to Nemesis.

St. 136. *Janus:* a Roman god with two faces, one seeing the past, the other the future. Byron uses the word here in the sense of "two-faced." He is accusing his wife and her supporters of duplicity.

St. 139. *listed spot:* the field of the list or tournament, such as the arena of the Coliseum.

St. 140. *Gladiator:* Byron's description is suggested by the famous statue usually called the *Dying Gaul.*

St. 141. *Dacian:* the Roman Emperor Trajan conquered Dacia in A.D. 101, and brought 10,000 Dacians back to Rome as gladiators.

Arise! ye Goths: the Goths under Alaric sacked Rome in A.D. 410.

St. 144. *bald first Caesar's head:* "Suetonius," says Byron, "informs us that Julius Caesar was particularly gratified by that decree of the senate which enabled him to wear a wreath of laurel on all occasions. He was anxious not to show that he was conqueror of the world, but to hide that he was bald."

St. 145. *"While stands the Coliseum":* quoted by Gibbon in *Decline and Fall of the Roman Empire* from the Venerable Bede and ascribed to Anglo-Saxon pilgrims of the eighth century.

St. 153. *the dome:* Church of St. Peter's.

Diana's marvel: Temple of Diana at Ephesus, sixth wonder of the ancient world.

Sophia's bright roofs: Church of St. Sophia in Constantinople.

St. 161. *Lord of the unerring bow:* the Apollo Belvedere.

St. 177. *one fair Spirit:* probably Byron's sister Augusta.

St. 181. *Trafalgar:* most of the French ships captured by Nelson at Trafalgar in 1805 were destroyed in a storm immediately following the battle.

St. 186. *sandal-shoon:* sandals indicated travel by land; *scallop-shells,* travel by sea.

MANFRED

"There are more things . . . philosophy." Hamlet, I, v, 166–167.

Scene of the drama: Byron, commenting upon Goethe's remark that he had taken "my *Faustus* to himself," wrote Murray on June 7, 1820: "It was the *Staubach* [*sic*] and the *Jungfrau,* and something else, much more than *Faustus,* that made me write *Manfred.* The first scene, however, and that of *Faustus* are very similar." The Staubback is a waterfall, the Jungfrau a mountain in the Swiss Alps. The "something else" is probably an oblique reference to his relations with Augusta.

I, ii, 98. *Mount Rosenberg:* a mountain in Switzerland from which a landslide in 1806 destroyed several villages and killed over 450 people.

II, ii, 91. *Magi:* philosopher-priests of ancient Persia.

92. *He: Jamblicus,* a Neo-Platonic philosopher of the fourth century. While bathing in the hot baths of Gadara in Syria he called up the two gods of love from the springs which bore their names.

181. *buried Prophet:* Samuel who was raised from the dead by the Witch of Endor. See I Sam. 28.

182. *Spartan Monarch:* Pausanias (d. 470 B.C.) who had demanded Cleonice for his mistress. When she entered his room in the dark, he had mistaken her for an assassin and killed her. Overcome by

remorse, he asked the priests of Phigalia to summon up her spirit so that he could ask her pardon. She replied that he would soon be delivered from his troubles. The prophecy was fulfilled by his death.

187. *Phyxian Jove:* protector of exiles.

II, iv: *Arimanes:* Ahriman, the name of the principle of evil in the Persian religion of Zoroaster. Equivalent of Satan.

83. *Astarte:* the name of Manfred's sister is the same as that of the ancient Syrian goddess of love.

III, i, 13. *"Kalon":* the beautiful, the highest good of human existence.

88. *Rome's sixth emperor:* Nero.

III, ii, 5. See Gen. 6:2–4.

III, iv, 132. Compare Satan's speech in Milton's *Paradise Lost*, I, 254–255.

VISION OF JUDGMENT

St. 1. *Gallic era "eighty-eight":* the French Revolution began in 1789.

St. 6. *both generals:* Napoleon and Wellington.

St. 7. *Saint John's foretold beast:* See Rev. 13.

St. 8. *freedom's second dawn:* Byron is referring to the revolutionary activity in Italy in which he was involved.

St. 18. *the last we saw here:* Louis XVI who was guillotined in 1793.

St. 20. *St. Bartholomew:* one of the twelve apostles who was flayed alive and then decapitated, according to tradition.

St. 27. *Captain Parry:* in 1819, while searching for a northwest passage, Parry and his crew spent the winter in Melville Bay, an inlet of northwest Greenland.

St. 28. *Johanna Southcote:* A religious fanatic who prophesied that she would give birth to a second messiah in October, 1814, at the age of 64. When the time came, she fell into a trance and died soon afterward.

St. 46. *Apicius:* a famous epicure of the time of Augustus and Tiberius (first century).

St. 48. *Five millions:* the Roman Catholics who were refused political rights by George III.

St. 49. *Guelph:* the great German family from which George III traced his descent.

St. 54. *gilt key:* a gold key is an ensignia of the office of Lord Chamberlain.

St. 65. *Jack Wilkes* (1727–1797) had been one of the most successful of George III's opponents both as member of Parliament and Lord Mayor of London.

St. 71. *Bute and Grafton:* ministers of George III.

St. 73. *Fox's lard:* Charles James Fox (1749–1806), famous Whig statesman, was very fat.

gagg'd: a reference to the Treason and Sedition bills of 1795 through which Pitt as Prime Minister severely restricted freedom of press and speech.

St. 74. *Junius:* pseudonym of the author of a series of public letters written between 1769 and 1772 attacking George III and his ministry. His identity is still uncertain.

St. 84. *"Nominis Umbra":* shadow of a name, part of the motto on the title page of the letters.

John Horne Tooke: an English radical leader (1736–1812) who supported the American and French Revolutions.

St. 86. *Skiddaw:* mountain near Southey's home in the Lake District.

St. 91. *Non Di, non homines:* "Neither gods, nor men, nor booksellers will permit mediocre poetry," Horace, *Ars Poetica*, 372.

St. 92. *Pye:* Henry Pye, a very bad poet, was Southey's predecessor as poet laureate.

St. 94. *felony "de se":* felony upon himself, that is, suicide.

St. 97. *pantisocracy:* name of the system for a utopian community which Southey and Coleridge planned to set up in the United States in 1794.

anti-jacobin: anti-revolutionary; anti-republican.

St. 101. *King Alfonso:* King of Spain (1252–1284) who said that if he had been consulted at the creation of the world, he would have spared the Maker some absurdities.

St. 104. *Phaeton:* son of the sun who was killed and hurled into a river.

St. 105. *Welborn:* a character in Philip Massinger's play, *A New Way to Pay Old Debts.*

DON JUAN

Dedication

St. 1. *Lakers:* Wordsworth, Coleridge, Southey were called the Lake Poets because they lived in the Lake district.

St. 4. *"Excursion":* Wordsworth's long philosophical poem which appeared in 1814.

St. 6. *Excise:* Wordsworth had been made Distributor of Stamps for Westmoreland County in 1813. In a note to this passage Byron calls him a "poetical charlatan and political parasite."

St. 11. *heartless daughters:* Milton's two elder daughters are said to have robbed and cheated him.

Castlereagh: chief Tory statesman between 1812 and 1822; as Foreign Secretary he was responsible for the coalition that brought about Napoleon's defeat and settled the peace terms at the Congress of Vienna. In his youth he was responsible for suppressing the Irish Rebellion of 1798 (stanza 12). He was identified with all the repressive legislation following the Napoleonic Wars.

St. 13. *Ixion:* figure in Greek myth who was bound in hell to an ever-turning wheel.

St. 15. *Eutropius:* Eunuch who was minister of the Roman emperor Arcadius (378–408).

St. 17. *"buff and blue":* colors of the Whigs.

   ultra-Julian: Roman emperor, Julian (331–363), called the Apostate because he renounced the Christian religion in which he had been reared and attempted to restore pagan polytheism as the state religion. Southey had renounced his youthful republican principles and turned Tory.

Canto the First

St. 2. *Vernon . . . Howe:* English generals and admirals of the eighteenth century, famous for particular battles.

   Wellesley: Duke of Wellington.

   Banquo's monarchs: See *Macbeth,* IV, i, 65.

   Dumourier: French Revolutionary general.

St. 3. *Barnave . . . La Fayette:* famous French philosophers and politicians, most of them active in the French Revolution. Several (Barnave, Brissot, Condorcet, Clootz, Danton) were executed in the Reign of Terror.

   Joubert . . . Moreau: French generals under Napoleon.

St. 4. *Duncan . . . Jervis:* English admirals during the Napoleonic Wars.

St. 10. Byron's wife is satirized in the character of Juan's mother.

St. 11. *Calderon:* Spanish dramatist (1600–1681). *Lope de Vega:* Spanish poet and dramatist (1562–1635).

   Feinagle: inventor of a system for training the memory.

St. 15. *Romilly:* a lawyer who, at first retained by Byron, became an advisor to Lady Byron at the time of the separation. He committed suicide upon the death of his wife.

St. 16. *Edgeworth:* Maria Edgeworth (1767–1849) author of *Castle Rackrent.*

   Trimmer: Sarah Trimmer (1741–1810) who wrote edifying stories for children and pamphlets on the necessity of moral education.

   "Coelebs' Wife": Hannah More (1745–1833) was the author of many books of moral instruction, including *Coelebs in Search of a Wife.*

St. 17. *Harrison:* John Harrison, a famous watchmaker.

   Macassar: hair oil.

St. 27. Lady Byron had consulted physicians about the sanity of Byron.

St. 30. *"malus animus":* malice aforethought.

St. 35. *Numa:* second legendary king of Rome, noted for his wisdom and piety and for his long, peaceful reign.

St. 36. *Doctors' Commons:* divorce court.

St. 37. *messuages:* dwelling houses with adjacent buildings and lands.

St. 42. *Formosum Pastor:* Beautiful Shepherd Corydon, 2d Eclogue.

St. 47. *Jerome and to Chrysostom:* two church fathers of the fourth century. Jerome published the Latin version of the Bible known as the Vulgate.

St. 53. "*Verbum sat*": a word to the wise is sufficient.

St. 56. *Boabdil:* last Moorish king of Granada who was forced to surrender the city to the Spaniards in 1492.

St. 62. "*mi vien in mente*": it occurs to me.

St. 71. *Armida:* sorceress in Tasso's *Jerusalem Delivered*.

St. 75. *Tarquin:* the ravisher in Shakespeare's *Rape of Lucrece*.

St. 88. *The bard:* Thomas Campbell in *Gertrude of Wyoming*.

St. 95. *Boscan* (1500–1544) and *Garcilasso* (1503–1536) Spanish poets, known for their sonnets in the Italian manner.

St. 104. *Anacreon Moore:* Thomas Moore who translated the Odes of the Greek poet, Anacreon.

St. 122. *Adria:* the Adriatic Sea. Here Venice.

St. 129. *Congreve's rockets:* an explosive shell invented by Sir William Congreve.

St. 130. *galvanism:* experiments had been conducted in 1803 in sending electric currents through the body of a corpse.

St. 132. *lantern:* Sir Humphry Davy invented the miners' safety lamp in 1815.

St. 148. *Cortejo:* lover.

O'Reilly: Spanish general of Irish extraction was in reality defeated in an expedition against Algiers in 1775.

St. 159. *Achates:* the faithful friend of Aeneas in Virgil's *Aeneid*.

St. 166. *Clarence:* See Shakespeare's *Richard* III, I, xiv.

St. 189. *Gurney:* famous shorthand specialist who had reported the proceedings of many celebrated English trials in the early nineteenth century.

St. 206. *Sotheby:* William Sotheby (1757–1833) a minor poet and patron of writers.

Blues: Bluestockings, women who cultivated an interest in literature and politics. Byron is referring to his wife.

St. 212. "*Non ego hoc . . . Planco*": I should not have endured this in the heat of youth when Plancus was consul. Horace, *Odes*, III, xiv, 27.

St. 217. *Friar Bacon's brazen head:* See Robert Greene's *Friar Bacon and Friar Bungay*.

chymic: counterfeit.

Canto the Second

St. 7. *Fazzioli:* little veils.

St. 23. *breathes a vein:* lets blood.

St. 26. Many of the details of the shipwreck were taken from Dalzell's *Shipwrecks and Disasters at Sea* (1812). Byron wrote Murray, "There was not a *single circumstance* of it *not* taken from *fact.*"

St. 83. *Ugolino:* See Dante's *Inferno*, XXXIII, 76–78.

St. 123. *Achilles order'd dinner:* when Ajax, Ulysses and Phoenix came to Achilles' tent to persuade him to return to the battle against Troy, he prepared a great feast for them. (*Iliad*, IX).

St. 130. "νοῦς": mind or intelligence.

St. 131. *St. Paul says:* Heb. 10:34.

St. 133. *pelisse:* a kind of long outer garment.

St. 137. *grand-dad's "Narrative":* *A Narrative of the Honorable John Byron.* Relates hardships encountered in a trip around the world.

St. 155. *Minotaur:* mythical monster, half-man, half-bull, son of Pasiphaë, queen of Crete.

St. 161. *Romaic:* name given to vernacular Greek.

St. 165. *Barrow* (1630–1677); *South* (1633–1716); and *Tillotsen* (1630–1674) were all theological writers.

Blair: Hugh Blair (1718–1800) wrote *Lectures on Rhetoric*, an influential textbook.

St. 174. *Io:* according to Greek myth she was carried off by Phoenician traders.

St. 201. *write a novel:* Lady Caroline Lamb wrote a novel, *Glenarvon* (1816), in which she gave an account of her affair with Byron. See *Remember Thee!*

St. 206. *Belisarius:* famous Roman general (c. 505–565).

St. 207. *Aristippus:* Greek Hedonist philosopher (d. 356 B.C.).

Sardanapulus: last king of Assyria (d. 880 B.C.).

Canto the Third

St. 70. *jelicks:* sleeveless jackets.

St. 78. *a poet:* satiric portrait of Southey.

St. 85. "Ça ira": "It will succeed." Popular song of the French Revolution.

St. 86. *De Staël:* Madame De Staël had said that Goethe represented the entire literature of Germany.

Song: "Isles of Greece."

St. I. *Delos:* an island in the Cyclades off the coast of Greece where Apollo was born.

St. II. *Scian and the Teian muse:* Homer and Anacreon.

St. IV. *king:* Xerxes, King of Persians, who watched the defeat of his fleet by the Greeks in the battle off Salamis in 480 B.C.

St. IX. *Turkish:* Greece was still subject to Turkey at this time.

St. X. *Pyrrhic dance:* war dance.

Pyrrhic phalanx: formation devised by Pyrrhus, famous general of the third century, B. C.

Cadmus: brought the Phoenician alphabet to Greece, according to legend.

St. XII. *Miltiades:* hero of Marathon.

St. XIII. *Heracleidan:* of Hercules, that is, blood of ancient Greece.

St. XVI. *Sunium:* ancient name for a promontory in southwestern Attica.

St. 90. *Hoyle:* author of rules for card games.

St. 92. *Titus' youth:* The Roman Emperor Titus, Julius Caesar, and Robert Burns were all notorious for dissipation in youth. As a boy, Oliver Cromwell got into trouble through robbing orchards.

St. 93. *milliners of Bath:* Coleridge and Southey married two of the Fricker sisters in 1795.

St. 94. *Botany Bay:* in Australia where convicts and political prisoners were sent.

St. 96. *Ariosto:* famous Italian poet (1474–1533).

St. 97. *"longueurs":* tedious passages.
   epopée: epic.

St. 98. *"Waggoners":* reference to Wordsworth's poem *The Waggoner*, published in 1819.
   "a little boat": reference is to *Peter Bell*, stanza 1.

St. 99. *Charles's Wain:* constellation called the Dipper.

St. 100. *Jack Cade:* Led a rebellion in the fifteenth century; his name became synonymous with ignorant rebelliousness.
   him who drew "Achitophel!": Dryden.

St. 105. *Boccaccio's lore . . . Dryden's lay:* Dryden's *Theodore and Honoria*, a tale of a specter huntsman of Ravenna, alluded to in the last four lines of the next stanza, was adapted from Boccaccio's *Decameron*, 5:8.

St. 110. *Cantabs:* Students of Cambridge University.

St. 111. Ποιητικῆς : Aristotle's *Poetics.*

Canto the Fourth

St. 4. *Thetis:* mother of Achilles.
   Lethe: river of forgetfulness.

St. 6. *Pulci:* Italian poet (1432–1487) who wrote a seriocomic epic, *Morgante Maggiore*, in *ottava rima* which greatly influenced the style and meter of *Don Juan*.

St. 50. *galliot:* small galley.

St. 52. *Bohea:* an inferior black tea.

St. 53. *qualified:* mixed with brandy.
   Phlegethontic rill: river of fire in Hades.
   rack: means both punch and a hangover.

St. 61. *fair Venus:* The Venus of Medici.

Canto the Eighth

St. 6. The names and details which follow were drawn from an account in the Marquis de Castlenau's *Histoire de la Nouvelle Russie* of the actual seige which took place in 1790.

Canto the Tenth

St. 71. *"Hundsfot"; "Verflucter":* German oaths.

St. 73. *Black Edward:* Edward the Black Prince (1330–1376).

Becket's bloody stone: Thomas à Becket, Archbishop of Canterbury, was murdered in the Cathedral in 1170.

St. 74. *Cressy:* Crécy, a village in northern France at which the English won a great victory in 1346.

St. 78. *Surgit amari aliquid:* something bitter wells up.

St. 80. *Shooter's Hill:* on the southeast approach to London.

Canto the Eleventh

St. 1. *Bishop Berkeley:* Irish philosopher (1685–1753).

St. 16. *max:* gin.

St. 17. *kiddy:* a petty thief.

full flash: knew his way around.

St. 19. *spellken:* play-house or theater.

high toby-spice: robbery on horseback.

flash the muzzle: show his face openly.

blowing: his moll.

nutty: both lovable and loving. All these terms are part of the underworld slang of the time.

St. 45. *west or worst end:* the west end was the fashionable section of London.

St. 48. *ceruse:* a cosmetic. Here he means an older woman.

St. 49. *"Drapery Misses":* fashionable young women, furnished with a wardrobe upon credit, to be paid for by the husband after marriage.

St. 51. *Drawcansir:* a braggart: empty boaster; from the play *The Rehearsal* by George Villiers.

St. 54. *Banquo's glass:* glass in which Macbeth saw Banquo and his descendants as kings of Scotland. *Macbeth,* IV, i.

St. 56. *Moscow, Leipsic, Mont Saint Jean:* battles in which Napoleon was defeated. *Marino Faliero* and *Cain:* Byron's dramas were severely attacked by critics.

La Belle Alliance: the beautiful alliance, a reference probably to the Lake poets.

Lowe: Sir Hudson Lowe, Napoleon's governor at St. Helena.

St. 57. *Reverend Rowley Powley:* Reverend George Croly (1780–1860) a mediocre and prolific poet and dramatist.

Ancient Pistol: See Shakespeare's *Henry IV*, II, iv, 197.

St. 58. *dull Dorus:* Henry Hart Melman (1791–1868) who, Byron believed, was author of the attack on *Endymion* in the *Quarterly Review* for April, 1818, which Byron mistakenly thought killed Keats.

The reference in the last two lines is to the "superiority" of Croly's (Cambyses') dramas on classical themes to Milman's on biblical themes.

    Sporus: name under which Pope satirized Lord John Hervey in the *Epistle to Dr. Arbuthnot.*

    St. 59. *Euphues:* Byron Waller Procter (Barry Cornwall) (1787–1874) a popular imitative poet who was compared favorably with Byron.

    Boeotian: dull and heavy.

    St. 61. *thirty mock tyrants:* the thirty pretenders to the throne in the reign of Gallienus in the third century.

    St. 62. *praetorian bands:* special guard of the Roman emperors who in the decline of the Empire frequently controlled the selection of emperor.

    Janizaries: private guard of the Turkish sultan.

    St. 65. *Centaur Nessus garb:* poisoned robe. The reference is to the manner of Hercules' death.

    St. 67. *Or Molu:* gilded brass.

    St. 72. *bogle:* goblin.

    St. 74. *"rack and manger":* waste and disorder.

    St. 76. *Young:* Edward Young who wrote a poem on this theme when he was over eighty.

    St. 77. *Gratton, Curran, Sheridan:* Famous orators and wits who had recently died. Sheridan was the dramatist.

    unhappy queen: Queen Caroline, wife of George IV, had died in August, 1821.

    Daughter: Princess Charlotte had died in childbirth in November, 1817.

    St. 78. *Brummel:* the famous "beau" (1778–1840) who had by this time fallen out of fashion and was hopelessly in debt.

    Wellesley: Nephew of the Duke of Wellington. He was going bankrupt at the time.

    St. *Whitbread, Romilly:* both had committed suicide.

    his will: the scandal was that "Fum" (George IV) had destroyed his father's will.

    St. 79. *Whigs:* they were out of power.

    St. 80. *Lady Carolines and Franceses:* Lady Caroline Lamb and Lady Frances Webster, two of the women in Byron's life between 1812 and 1814.

    St. 83. *a Duke:* Duke of Wellington.

    St. 84. *Congress:* Congress of Verona held in 1822.

    St. 86. *"carpe diem":* Seize the day; enjoy the present.

    St. 87. *Atalantis:* a famous book "full of court and party scandal" written in 1709.

Canto the Fourteenth

    St. 18. *ci-devant jeunes hommes:* once young men.

NOTES ON LETTERS

JOHN MURRAY, APRIL 9, 1817

Mrs. Clermont: housekeeper for Lady Noel, Byron's mother-in-law.

JOHN MURRAY, APRIL 6, 1819

Foscolo: an Italian poet who was living in England at the time.

PERCY BYSSHE SHELLEY, APRIL 26, 1821

attack upon Pope: in *Sleep and Poetry* (193–206).
late failure of the Italians: reference to the failure of the insurrection
of the Italian revolutionary party at Ravenna.

MARY SHELLEY, DECEMBER, 1822

Hunt's poverty: Byron had supported Leigh Hunt and his family
from the time of their arrival in Italy in June, 1822. He had also helped
Hunt establish a journal, *The Liberal*, to which he had contributed among
other things *The Vision of Judgment*.

THOMAS MOORE, DECEMBER 27, 1823

Of the poets mentioned at the end of this letter, all except Joukoffsky
(Zhukovsky) died of wounds received in battle.

AUGUSTA LEIGH, FEBRUARY 23, 1824

This letter was found unfinished on Byron's desk after his death.
  Hato: Compare with Don Juan's experience, Canto the Eighth,
stanza 91*ff.* An example of the way in which art and life overlapped for
Byron.

Rinehart Editions

Addison and Steele, SEL. FROM THE TATLER & THE SPECTATOR 87

AMERICAN THOUGHT: CIVIL WAR TO WORLD WAR I 70

ANTHOLOGY OF ENGLISH DRAMA BEFORE SHAKESPEARE 45

ANTHOLOGY OF GREEK DRAMA: FIRST SERIES 29

ANTHOLOGY OF GREEK DRAMA: SECOND SERIES 68

ANTHOLOGY OF ROMAN DRAMA 101

Arnold, SELECTED POETRY AND PROSE 62

Austen, PRIDE AND PREJUDICE 22

Balzac, PÈRE GORIOT 18

Benét, S. V., SELECTED POETRY & PROSE 100

THE BIBLE: SEL. FROM OLD & NEW TESTAMENTS 56

Brontë, Charlotte, JANE EYRE 24

Brontë, Emily, WUTHERING HEIGHTS 23

Browning Robert, SELECTED POETRY 71

Bunyan, THE PILGRIM'S PROGRESS 27

Burke, REFLECTIONS ON THE REVOLUTION IN FRANCE 84

Butler, THE WAY OF ALL FLESH 7

Byron, SELECTED POETRY AND LETTERS 54

Chaucer, THE CANTERBURY TALES 65

Coleridge, SELECTED POETRY AND PROSE 55

COLONIAL AMERICAN WRITING 43

Conrad, LORD JIM 85

Conrad, NOSTROMO 111

Cooper, THE PIONEERS 99

Cooper, THE PRAIRIE 26

Crane, RED BADGE OF COURAGE, SEL'D PROSE & POETRY 47

Dante, THE DIVINE COMEDY 72

Defoe, MOLL FLANDERS 25

De Forest, MISS RAVENEL'S CONVERSION 74

Dickens, GREAT EXPECTATIONS 20

Dickens, HARD TIMES 95

Dreiser, SISTER CARRIE 86

Dryden, SELECTED WORKS 60

Eliot, ADAM BEDE 32

ELIZABETHAN FICTION 64

Emerson, SELECTED PROSE AND POETRY 30

ENGLISH PROSE AND POETRY 1660–1800: A SELECTION 110

Fielding, JOSEPH ANDREWS 15

FIFTEEN MODERN AMERICAN POETS 79

Flaubert, MADAM BOVARY 2

FOUR MODERN PLAYS: FIRST SERIES, Ibsen, Shaw, O'Neill, Miller 90

FOUR MODERN PLAYS: SECOND SERIES, Ibsen, Wilde, Rostand, Gorky 109

Franklin, AUTOBIOGRAPHY AND SELECTED WRITINGS 12

Frederic, THE DAMNATION OF THERON WARE 108

Garland, MAIN-TRAVELLED ROADS 66

Godwin, CALEB WILLIAMS 103

Goethe, FAUST: PART I 75

Goethe, SORROWS OF YOUNG WERTHER, NEW MELUSINA, NOVELLE 13

Gogol, DEAD SOULS 5

GREAT ENGLISH AND AMERICAN ESSAYS 34

Hardy, FAR FROM THE MADDING CROWD 98

Hardy, THE MAYOR OF CASTERBRIDGE 9

Hardy, THE RETURN OF THE NATIVE 39

Hauptmann, THREE PLAYS: The Weavers, Hannele, The Beaver Coat 52

Hawthorne, THE HOUSE OF THE SEVEN GABLES 89

Hawthorne, THE SCARLET LETTER 1

Hawthorne, SELECTED TALES AND SKETCHES 33

Howells, THE RISE OF SILAS LAPHAM 19

Ibsen, THREE PLAYS: Ghosts, Enemy of the People, Wild Duck 4

Irving, SELECTED PROSE 41

James, Henry, THE AMBASSADORS 104

James, Henry, THE AMERICAN 16

James, Henry, SELECTED SHORT STORIES 31

Johnson, RASSELAS, POEMS, & SELECTED PROSE 57

Keats, SELECTED POETRY AND LETTERS 50

Lincoln, SELECTED SPEECHES, MESSAGES, AND LETTERS 82

LITERATURE OF THE EARLY REPUBLIC 44

London, MARTIN EDEN 80

MASTERPIECES OF THE SPANISH GOLDEN AGE 93

Melville, MOBY DICK 6

Melville, SEL'D TALES AND POEMS 36

Milton, PARADISE LOST AND SELECTED POETRY AND PROSE 35

MODERN AMERICAN LITERATURE 53

Newman, THE IDEA OF A UNIVERSITY 102

Norris, Frank, MC TEAGUE 40

Parkman, THE DISCOVERY OF THE GREAT WEST: LA SALLE 77

PLUTARCH—EIGHT GREAT LIVES 105

Poe, SELECTED PROSE AND POETRY, REV. 42

POETRY OF THE NEW ENGLAND RENAISSANCE, 1790–1890 38

Pope, SELECTED POETRY AND PROSE 46

RINEHART BOOK OF SHORT STORIES 59

RINEHART BOOK OF VERSE 58

Robinson, E. A., SEL. EARLY POEMS AND LETTERS 107

Roosevelt, F. D., SPEECHES, MESSAGES, PRESS CONFERENCES, & LETTERS 83

Scott, THE HEART OF MIDLOTHIAN 14

SELECTED AMERICAN PROSE, 1841–1900 94

SELECTIONS FROM GREEK AND ROMAN HISTORIANS 88

Shakespeare, FIVE PLAYS: Hamlet; King Lear; Henry IV, Part I; Much Ado about Nothing; The Tempes 51

Shakespeare, AS YOU LIKE IT, JULIU CAESAR, MACBETH 91

Shakespeare, TWELFTH NIGHT, OTHEL LO 92

Shaw, SELECTED PLAYS AND OTHE WRITINGS 81

Shelley, SELECTED POETRY AND PROS 49

SIR GAWAIN AND THE GREEN KNIGHT 9'

Smollett, HUMPHRY CLINKER 48

SOUTHERN STORIES 106

Spenser, SELECTED POETRY 73

Sterne, TRISTRAM SHANDY 37

Stevenson, MASTER OF BALLANTRAE 6

Swift, GULLIVER'S TRAVELS 10

Swift, SELECTED PROSE AND POETRY 7

Tennyson, SELECTED POETRY 69

Thackeray, VANITY FAIR 76

Thoreau, WALDEN, ON THE DUTY O CIVIL DISOBEDIENCE 8

Trollope, BARCHESTER TOWERS 21

Turgenev, FATHERS AND CHILDREN 1'

Twain, THE ADVENTURES OF HUCKLE BERRY FINN 11

Twain, ROUGHING IT 61

Vergil, THE AENEID 63

VICTORIAN POETRY: Clough to Kipling 96

Whitman, LEAVES OF GRASS AN SELECTED PROSE 28

Wordsworth, THE PRELUDE, SEL'D SON NETS & MINOR POEMS, Rev. & Enl.